Wissenschaftliche Untersuchungen zum Neuen Testament

Begründet von Joachim Jeremias und Otto Michel
Herausgegeben von
Martin Hengel und Otfried Hofius

60

Studies
in the Jewish Background
of Christianity

by

Daniel R. Schwartz

J.C.B. Mohr (Paul Siebeck) Tübingen

Die Deutsche Bibliothek − *CIP-Einheitsaufnahme*

Schwartz, Daniel R.:
Studies in the Jewish background of christianity / by Daniel R. Schwartz. −
Tübingen : Mohr, 1992
  (Wissenschaftliche Untersuchungen zum Neuen Testament ; 60)
  ISBN 3-16-145798-6
NE: GT

© 1992 J.C.B. Mohr (Paul Siebeck), P.O. Box 2040, D-7400 Tübingen.

The book was typeset by Computersatz Staiger in Ammerbuch-Pfäffingen using Times typeface, printed by Gulde-Druck in Tübingen on acid-free paper from Papierfabrik Buhl in Ettlingen and bound by Heinr. Koch in Tübingen.

ISSN 0512-1604

To my Friends and Students
in Jerusalem

Preface

The studies in this volume have, in general, three foci. The first focus is upon the development of Judaism during the Second Temple period, and especially during its final, Roman, century: the passage, due to internal developments and external influences and pressures, from a religion oriented around Temple and priesthood — i.e., a religion bound up with a state, and which therefore competed with Rome — to one which could separate sanctity from birth and place.

The second focus is upon Josephus, and the history of Provincia Judaea, for which he is the major source in this period. On the one hand, Josephus' historiography and apologetics illustrate well the problematics of the relationship of religion and state. On the other hand, examination of his use of sources and the arrangement of his work, frequently using chronological problems as the analytical scalpel, can help us overcome various chronological problems and misunderstandings and also gain a greater appreciation of Jewish historiography, including lost historiography, in this crucial century. At times, furthermore, as in connection with the appointment and the suspension of Pontius Pilate, the study of such Josephan and chronological problems which have to do with Roman rule in Judaea lead us to a better understanding of the religion-state issues as well.

The third focus, finally, is upon modern historiography. In several of these studies, we argue that various consensuses of assertion or denial have to do more with the religious or national needs of modern Jews or Christians than with the evidence from antiquity. In several others, the scholarly misconceptions seem rather to have stemmed from processes more internal to the academic world. Repeatedly, we find unwillingness to deal with new data or theories and also its opposite, head-over-heels acceptance of them, as well as uncritical dependence upon past authorities and its opposite, the baby and bathwater syndrome — rejection of a good theory because someone incorporated it into a bad one. Understanding these processes in the life of historical study can be interesting and is certainly humbling.

At the conclusion of the introduction to the first volume of his collected studies, *Hellenismus und Urchristentum* (1990), H. D. Betz notes (p. 9) that due to his *Lebensweg* some of the essays were originally published in German and some in English; similarly, due to my *Lebensweg*, some of my studies have been published in Hebrew and some in English. It is unfortunate, however, that I cannot echo Betz when he next notes that there is no need to translate the former since "die heutige neutestamentliche Wissenschaft ist international und bewegt sich in verschiedenen Sprachgebieten." For lamentable reasons, and with lamentable consequences, Hebrew sources and publications remain off-limits to too many New Testament scholars, for whom the requisite *Sprachgebiete* do not include the one sacred to Jesus and the apostles. Therefore, I have taken advantage of Professor Martin Hengel's gracious invitation to publish a volume of studies, and have provided here, along with five new pieces, translations of ten essays which have already appeared in Hebrew, and of one which soon will. The need to translate these pieces gave me an opportunity to revise, correct and coordinate them, to some extent, and also to bring them somewhat up to date. I should emphasize, however, that I have not been able to respond to more than a fraction of all which has appeared, since the original publications (over the past decade), in all the fields addressed. My thanks to the Israeli publishers, listed on pp. 283–284, for the permission to publish these English versions here.

Much of the work of completing this volume was done during a six-month visit at the University of Basel. I would like to express my thanks to the librarians of Basel's Universitätsbibliothek, especially the inter-library loan librarians, who couldn't have been nicer or more efficient.

These studies are dedicated to my friends and students in Jerusalem, who have been the sounding-boards and critics of much of its contents. May God bring us all peace.

Basel, February 1991   D. R. S.

Table of Contents

Abbreviations

Agrippa I	D. R. Schwartz, *Agrippa I: The Last King of Judaea* (1990)
Ann.	Tacitus, *Annales*
ANRW	*Aufstieg und Niedergang der römischen Welt*
Ant.	Josephus, *Antiquitates Judaicae* (Jewish *Antiquities*)
BJ	Josephus, *Bellum Judaicum* (*Jewish War*)
BT	Babylonian Talmud
C. Ap.	Josephus, *Contra Apionem*
CBQ	*Catholic Biblical Quarterly*
CD	Cassius Dio, *Roman History*
Feldman	*Josephus,* IX (LCL; ed. and trans. L. H. Feldman: 1965)
GLA	M. Stern, *Greek and Latin Authors on Jews and Judaism*, I–III (1974–1984)
Haenchen	E. Haenchen, *The Acts of the Apostles: A Commentary* (based on 14th German edition [1965]; 1971)
Hist.	Tacitus, *Historiae*
Hist. eccl.	Eusebius, *Historia ecclesiastica* (*Church History*)
HTR	*Harvard Theological Review*
HUCA	*Hebrew Union College Annual*
IEJ	*Israel Exploration Journal*
INJ	*Israel Numismatic Journal*
JBL	*Journal of Biblical Literature*
JJS	*Journal of Jewish Studies*
JQR	*Jewish Quarterly Review*
JTS	*Journal of Theological Studies*
Leg.	Philo, *Legatio ad Gaium*
LCL	Loeb Classical Library
LSJ	*A Greek-English Lexicon* (edd. H.G. Liddell, R. Scott and H. St. Jones; 1940^9)
m.	Mishnah
MGWJ	*Monatsschrift für Geschichte und Wissenschaft des Judentums*
NTS	*New Testament Studies*
OGIS	*Orientis Graeci Inscriptiones Selectae*, I–II (ed. W. Dittenberger; 1903–1905)
PT	Palestinian Talmud
PWRE	*Paulys Realencyclopädie der classischen Altertumswissenschaft* (edd. G. Wissowa et al.; 1893–), cited by series and half-volume
RB	*Revue biblique*
RSV	Revised Standard Version

Smallwood,   E. M. Smallwood, *The Jews Under Roman Rule, From Pompey to*
  Jews   *Diocletian: A Study in Political Relations* (corrected ed.; 1981)
SVM   E. Schürer, *The History of the Jewish People in the Age of Jesus Christ*,
                  I–III (new English ed. by G. Vermes, F. Millar et al.; 1973–1987)
Tos.   Tosephta
ZNW   *Zeitschrift für die neutestamentliche Wissenschaft*

Introduction
On the Jewish Background of Christianity*

Christianity appeared in the first century C.E., centered around three major figures, all of whom were Jewish. John the Baptist summoned his countrymen to repentance; Jesus of Nazareth was among those who answered John's call, but his own circle of disciples and followers soon grew as well; and Paul, after the execution of John and Jesus, formulated a new religion which, due to his own efforts and those of his colleagues and disciples, and even to those of his competitors, spread widely throughout the Graeco-Roman world.

Of these three figures, it is most difficult, for the historian, to speak of Jesus. The evidence is simply too treacherous. Jesus left no writings of his own; Christian traditions about him, in the Gospels and elsewhere, are notoriously so divergent and infused with later concerns that it is often quite impossible to claim any reasonable degree of certainty regarding him; and the only potentially usable early account of him and his movement by an outside observer (Josephus' "Testimonium Flavianum" − Ant. 18.63−64) is either totally a Christian interpolation or so edited by Christian copyists as to be hardly retrievable.[1]

John the Baptist and Paul are much more accessible, on one or more of the above counts. Namely while Paul, as Jesus, was very central to the early Church, several of his epistles remain to show us, firsthand, what his thoughts and beliefs were, and Luke's Acts of the Apostles give us an account of his career. Whatever the difficulties of interpreting these works, and whatever

---

* An unpublished lecture first presented at the New York Theological Seminary in the winter of 1985/86. Given its popular nature, no attempt has been made to document it fully, although now and then I have added references to sources and literature. In particular, I have added cross-references to more detailed discussions in the present volume of some of the points broached, so that this essay may also serve as something of an introduction for the volume, especially its first half. For the understanding and perspectives, such as they are, I should especially thank the priests who participated in the courses on the Jewish Background of Christianity which I gave at the Pontifical Biblical Institute, Jerusalem, 1981−1988.

[1] Although there are perennial attempts either to reconstruct it or to demonstrate its basic authenticity. See below, p. 187, n. 23.

the difficulties in distinguishing between Paul's history and Luke's *Heilsgeschichte*, here, at least, the historian finds himself on familiar ground, with materials he can hope to manage with the aid of the usual tools of philology and historical criticism. As for John the Baptist, while he left no writings, he was not of central interest to the New Testament writers, the materials concerning him are, in comparison to the Jesus traditions, relatively unretouched, and the polemic concerns which guided the Christian editors are sufficiently clear as to allow, generally speaking, for their neutralization.[2] Moreover, as opposed to the *Testimonium Flavianum*, Josephus' account of John (*Ant.* 18.116−119) seems basically to be authentic.[3]

Thus, while "the quest for the historical Jesus" seems as doubtful as it ever was, the quest for what in fact constitutes his major significance for the historian − that to which he responded, on the one hand, and that version of his import which, on the other, in a short while came to claim the allegiance of the Western world − is much more promising.[4]

We must emphasize at the outset, however, that any historical study of religion has its bounds: there are data, at times very important ones for a religion, which historians must leave untouched. Christianity is based upon one such datum: the perceived resurrection of Jesus, without which the movement would certainly have disappeared along with the movements following other charismatic figures in first-century Judaism. But resurrection is not susceptible to historical verification, analysis or explanation. Similarly, calls from heaven, such as that to Paul on the way to Damascus, are not susceptible to historical verification, analysis or explanation. Resurrection, calls from heaven and the like can figure in historical studies only as perceptions which, as such, functioned and entered into chains of causation.

---

[2] For this standpoint concerning the Baptist, see, inter alia, O. Böcher, in *Rechtfertigung, Realismus, Universalismus in biblischer Sicht: Festschrift für Adolf Köberle zum 80. Geburtstag* (ed. G. Müller; 1978), pp. 45−68, and, most recently, J. Murphy O'Connor, *NTS* 36 (1990), pp. 359−374. See also my essay cited below, n. 5.

[3] See below, p. 191, n. 39.

[4] This contrast between scholarship on John and that on Jesus was pointed out by W. Wink, *John the Baptist in the Gospel Tradition* (1968), pp. pp. ix−x, who himself preferred to study another, equally legitimate, topic: John's function in the New Testament. The latter is also the major focus of the most recent (?) compendium: J. Ernst, *Johannes der Täufer: Interpretation − Geschichte − Wirkungsgeschichte* (1989). Nevertheless, it affords detailed information about John's history. For the record, note that D. Flusser's *Johannes der Täufer*, which Wink (p. ix: "1964") and Ernst (p. 394: "1963") both cite, has not yet appeared. When it does, it will, presumably, be oriented more toward the historical John and his Qumran background. In the meantime, see his study of Johannine and Qumran baptism in *Essays on the Dead Sea Scrolls in Memory of E. L. Sukenik* (edd. C. Rabin and Y. Yadin; 1961), pp. 209−238 (in Hebrew), along with his *Judaism and the Origins of Christianity* (1988), p. 713 (Index, s.v. John the Baptist); on p. xix, he characterizes his 1961 essay as showing that "John the Baptist was surely a non-orthodox Essene."

The sincerity of these perceptions needs no more proof than the numerous martyrdoms which literally testified to them.

In other words, the historian of the Jewish background of Christianity can hope to explain only how the Jewish world in which Christianity arose allowed for or encouraged that to occur. He cannot attempt to explain the most significant specific events which, according to Christian belief, set the new religion on its way, and he cannot, given the sources, hope to say anything very specific about Jesus. Even regarding John and Paul, moreover, we will not try to deal with them as individuals, although that can fruitfully be done to some extent. Rather, we will attempt only to suggest that the Jewish world at the time was ripe for the appearance of a movement such as the one which formed around this triumvirate, and to analyze the options they chose in light of those taken by their Jewish predecessors and contemporaries.

Finally, we should stress that this is only a sketch, of some of the main lines as they appear to me after a few years of study.

I. On John the Baptist and Paul

It is quite fascinating, for a student of ancient Judaism, to see figures from extremely disparate parts of the Jewish world participating in the formation of one and the same religion. Whether or not John spent any time at Qumran, it is clear that this ascetic community by the Dead Sea shows us the setting according to which he is to be understood.[5] Note, among other points, the fact that they shared the same desert (Luke 1:80; Mark 1:4−5 parr.) and a special interest in Isaiah 40:3 in connection with it; ascetism and a concern for ritual purity and immersion ("baptism"); priestly background (Luke 1:5); a call for sharing of property (Luke 3:11); and a special sensitivity to incest (Mark 6:17−18 parr.).[6] As for Paul, whatever one makes of his alleged Pharisaism and studies with Rabban Gamaliel in Jerusalem (Philippians 3:5; Acts 22:3; 23:6; 26:5), it is clear that his primary background is in the Hellenistic Jewish Diaspora — as is indicated by his birth in Tarsus, his dependence upon the

---

[5] The classic statement is that by W. Brownlee, in *The Scrolls and the New Testament* (ed. K. Stendahl; 1957), pp. 33−353, 252−256. My own contribution to the topic is in *Mémorial Jean Carmignac* (*Revue de Qumran* 13, edd. F. García Martínez and E. Puech; 1988), pp. 635−646; further literature is listed ibid., p. 644, n. 30. For Flusser, see above, n. 4.

[6] For the preceding, it is enough to cite some parallels from the Qumran *Manual of Discipline*: 8:13−14, 9:19−20 (Isaiah 40:3); 3:4−5 (purity and immersion); 5:1−3, 21−22; 8:1;9:7; etc. (priestly authority − cf. below, n. 46); 3:2, 5:2, 6:19−22 (common property). As for incest, note that all three cardinal sins denounced in the *Damascus Document* 4:17−18 and explained thereafter turn out to be of a sexual nature (bigamy, improper separation from impure women, and incest).

Septuagint, and the quality of his Greek; Philo of Alexandria is the best-documented non-Christian analogue.[7]

These two Jewish settings are quite disparate. It is difficult to imagine that there would be much in common between monks of the desert and cosmopolitan Jews of the Hellenistic metropolis. If Philo were to meet a contemporary Qumranite, or if Paul would have met John the Baptist, they probably would have thought each other's clothes and habits quaint, or reprehensible, and it may be doubted that either would be able to say more than a few words in the other's habitual language.[8]

One might be tempted, therefore, to suspect that their cooperation in the foundation of Christianity is a fluke, or, perhaps, only a *post factum* rewriting of history by the winners, who, faced with the ineluctable fact of John having baptized Jesus, remade John in the image of later Christianity. However, while there was some rewriting along those lines, it seems mostly to have regarded the specific issues of the personal relationship between John and Jesus: the evangelists were concerned to make John recognize Jesus as his superior, as the one whose coming he had preached, as the one even whose shoelace John considered himself unworthy to tie, etc.[9] With regard to the main points of John's message, in contrast, there is less reason to assume Christianizing rewriting.[10]

Turning, then, to the comparison of the Baptist and Paul, we note, to begin with, that both agree on the lack of importance of Jewish descent: John claims (Luke 3:8; Matthew 3:9) that God can make even stones into sons of Abraham (the obvious reflection of Hebrew wordplay [*avanim/banim*] argues strongly for authenticity), and Paul, in Romans 4 and Galatians 3, argues that anyone, through faith, can become a true son of Abraham. Second, Paul explicitly undercut and made irrelevant the Temple of Jerusalem, teaching that the home of the Holy Spirit, hence the true Temple, is rather the Christian individual or community (I Corinthians 3:16–17; 6:19; II Corinthians 6:16; cf. Ephesians 2:18), and that Christian life is the true "sacrifice" (Romans 12:1).

---

[7] On Paul and Philo, see below, p. 41, n. 33. Note that the most notable modern defense of the thesis that Jerusalem, not Tarsus, was "the city of Paul's youth," that by W. C. van Unnik (*Sparsa Collecta*, I [1973], pp. 259–327), does not deny the basically Hellenistic nature of Paul's teachings; he merely denies that that came directly out of a childhood in Tarsus. Rather, he suspects Paul picked it up during his travels in Syria and Asia Minor after his conversion (see p. 305). Similarly, depending upon one's notion of Hellenism in first-century Jerusalem, he could have picked it up there; cf. below, p. 40, n. 31.

[8] On Philo's minimal knowledge of Hebrew, see D. Rokeah, *JTS* n.s. 19 (1968), pp. 70–82. As for the much-debated question of the extent of the knowledge of Greek in ancient Palestine, see below, p. 40, n. 31. John the Baptist would seem to be one of those least at home in the cosmopolitan circles where such knowledge was most likely found.

[9] See above, n. 4.

[10] On John's preaching, see Ernst's summary (above, n. 4), pp. 300–319.

A similar subrogation of the Temple is implied by John's teaching of repentance and purification in the wilderness, of all places, to which people came out from the cities (Mark 1:5 parr.); traditionally, repentance was supposed to be completed, and purity achieved, in the Temple and via its sacrificial and purificatory rites, while the desert was rather a godless and frightening place.[11] Finally, on the positive side, John and Paul focused upon sin and atonement. John views the problem in an eschatological context (repent before its too late), and Paul views it existentially (the human condition and salvation from it), but both make it the central point of their messages.

II. Who is a Jew?

John and Paul, in other words, espoused — whatever their differences — similar positions vis à vis Jewish descent, the Temple, and sin. More generally, given the fact that the Temple was considered the holiest place in the Holy Land, and that sin is violation of the law, we may say that they espoused similar positions vis à vis people, land and law. These three factors just happen to be the ones at issue whenever the notorious "Who is a Jew?" question arises.

The postulates linking Jews to Abraham, to the land of Israel, and to the beliefs and especially the practices mandated by Jewish law (religion), always coexist in Jewish literature. Nevertheless, in some periods and circumstances, as in the thought of various individuals, one or the other criterion is at times more prominent.[12] A review of a few successive periods of ancient Jewish history will demonstrate this, and pave the way for an approach which, "in the fulness of time," would leave all three aside.

In the period of the Monarchy,[13] it appears that the territorial principle was

---

[11] See S. Talmon in *Biblical Motifs: Origins and Transformations* (ed. A. Altmann; 1966), pp. 31–63.

[12] Today, given the large Diaspora and the large non-Jewish population in the state of Israel, it is not surprising that one hardly hears of territory as a determining factor. The "Who is a Jew?" disputes which perennially threaten to bring down Israeli governments and split American Jewry have to do with the coordination of descent and law: problems concerning apostates (descent without law) and proselytes (law without descent). Cf. e.g. S. Z. Abramov, *Perpetual Dilemma: Jewish Religion in the Jewish State* (1976), pp. 270–320, also the symposium on patrilineal descent in *Judaism* 34 (1985), pp. 3–135.

[13] The term "First Temple Period" is inappropriate (formed in the image of "Second Temple Period") precisely because not the Temple, but rather the Monarchy, constituted the central institution. See M. Weinfeld, *Zion* 49 (1984), pp. 126–127 (in Hebrew). For a good example of the difference between an earlier focus on the Monarchy and a Second Temple period focus on the Temple and its cult, compare the accounts of Abiah in I Kings 15:1–8 and

most salient.[14] David, according to I Samuel 26:19, complained that Saul, by forcing him to flee Judaea, had caused him to sever his ties to "God's inheritance," as if to say "Go worship other gods;" in the next verse, correspondingly, David expresses the fear that he would die away from the presence of the Lord. That is, the in-group, Israel, is defined – as always – as party to a covenant with the God of Israel, but the latter is conceived of as a territorial sovereign. Just as one who is forced from one country into another must follow the laws of the host country although he yearns to be back in his homeland, so too, according to this conception, an exile from Judaea is no longer subject to the laws of the Sovereign of Israel. On the other hand, this same conception makes for the rule that all, whether native-born Israelites or immigrants, must follow the same law (Exodus 12:49; Numbers 15:16); the law is the law of the land. Similarly, this is the period when a Syrian general, after being cured by the waters of the Jordan River, is said to have concluded that "there is no God in the whole world apart from Israel" (II Kings 5:15), and when foreigners settled in Samaria quickly learned that they must worship "the Lord of the land" if they did not wish to feel His wrath (II Kings 17). Correspondingly, the ten tribes exiled from Israel lost their original identity – just as the children or grandchildren of emigrés usually lose their ties with the old homeland. On the other hand, the fact that the Assyrian army which conquered the north failed, miraculously (it seemed), to take Jerusalem (II Kings 19) certainly enhanced confidence in the belief that "This is the Temple of the Lord, the Temple of the Lord, the Temple of the Lord" (Jeremiah 7:4) and, therefore, the impregnable capital of His land.

One need not suppose that all the traditions which assume a transcendent God who could reveal Himself to the patriarchs in Mesopotamia or to Moses in Egypt and in the desert were totally unknown. We must, however, realize that a theologoumenon like that, even if documented by ancient traditions, was of only theoretical importance. In an age with Israelite territorial sovereignty and without a diaspora, it made sense to identify "us" as the people of the land, so "our" covenant with God made Him lord of the land. Thus, while some Israelites in this period may well have admitted that God could be active or worshipped elsewhere, most could live their lives without having to give that notion much attention.

II Chronicles 13; the cultic focus of II Chronicles (vv. 8–12) is entirely absent from I Kings. While Chronicles' material *may* reflect some earlier source – see v. 7 and v. 22, respectively – the fact remains that what Kings ignored Chronicles considered important enough to transmit at length.

[14] For our present purposes, the dates at which the biblical passages cited below were composed or edited matter little. Whether or not contemporary, they show an understanding of the Monarchy period quite different from that of the Second Temple period, and thus serve to highlight the latter – which is all we need here.

In the end, however, Jeremiah was right, the "temple of the Lord, temple of the Lord" believers were wrong, and the south followed the north into exile. The earliest evidence we have concerning responses to that simply shows the logical conclusion from the territorial conception of Israel, the same conclusion drawn (consciously or only practically) by the Ten Tribes: when the Temple singers, in Babylonian captivity, were asked to sing "the songs of Zion," they responded with a plaintive "How can we sing God's songs in a foreign land?" (Ps. 137). This includes some measure of "We don't feel like it," but also "It doesn't make sense." It would be like raising a foreign flag. Indeed, the very substitution of "God's songs" for "songs of Zion" makes the same point: God, and His songs, are limited to Zion. Similarly, when Babylon was overthrown and Cyrus allowed his Jewish subjects to return to Judaea and rebuild the Temple, the canonical memory of his decree was phrased according to the territorial conception: Cyrus allowed the Jews to rebuild the Temple "of that God who is in Jerusalem" (Ezra 1:3).

Nevertheless, things could not stay the same, for neither condition of the territorial conception obtained. In contrast to the Monarchy period, when there was territorial sovereignty and there was no diaspora, now there was no territorial sovereignty, and there was a diaspora. Jews in great numbers had discovered that they could sing God's songs in a foreign land, and found it meaningful to do so. Some, indeed, such as those represented by the best-known among the exiles, even proclaimed the fighting words that "Heaven is my stool and the earth is My footstool, what house would you build for Me and what is the place of My rest?!" (Isaiah 66:1). And probably many more, without engaging in such polemics against the territorial conception, came to prefer – even in such "Zionist" contexts as Cyrus' proclamation (Ezra 1:2) and Nehemiah's lament over Jerusalem's rundown situation (Nehemiah 1:4, 5) – to think of God as "the God of heaven," a characterization which virtually first appears in the Persian period, and then very frequently.[15]

---

[15] In the Bible, this term for God is found in Daniel (twelve times, in Aramaic), Ezra 1:2, Nehemiah 1:4–5, 2:4, 20, II Chronicles 36:23, Psalm 136:26, Jonah 1:9 and Genesis 24:3, 7. Even without entering into the dating of the last three items, it is clear that the weight of the evidence is for the Persian period. (On the term in Genesis, note that it appears here along with "and of earth" [in 24:7 only in Septuagint], which changes the nuance.) Other clear evidence for the Persian period is supplied by the Elephantine papyri, where the epithet occurs frequently (as in Cowley nrs. 30–32, 38); and a Persian dating for the Book of Judith, where it appears in 5:8, 6:19 and 11:17, has often been suggested (but remains controversial). On this term and its implications, cf. A. Vincent, *La religion des Judéo-Araméens d'Éléphantine* (1937), ch. 3, esp. pp. 100–105, and D. K. Andrews, in *The Seed of Wisdom: Essays in Honour of T. J. Meek* (ed. W. S. McCullough; 1964), pp. 45–57. Andrews, who realized that the term is suited to an international *Sitz im Leben*, suggests that it is especially to be located in diplomacy; it seems, however, that that is only one aspect of the Diaspora situation which fostered the term.

What, then, if not territory, could define such a collective? The answer is
clear: descent. To begin with, in the Persian period, descent was simply an
index of territory: those who descended from Judaeans were Jews. This stage
of development is clearly indicated by the list purporting to name those who
returned following Cyrus' decrees (Ezra 2 = Nehemiah 7), for many of those
who returned are identified simply by the Judaean town to which they traced
their family. Moreover, even later in the period the understanding of "Jew" as
"from Judaea" continues to function, such as in Esther 2:5–6, where the
identification of Mordechai as a "Jew" requires the author to explain how he
happened to be in Persia, and in Clearchus of Soli's report that Aristotle
explained that *Ioudaios* is the term used for Judaeans.[16] However, all the
Diaspora communities needed was to define those who were members of the
group by birth, and, in time, the territorial import could be forgotten.[17] Thus,
the list of returning exiles already includes groups defined by family instead of
by Judaean origin, and, indeed, the whole list is organized according to
genealogical categories (priests, Levites, etc.); it concludes, correspondingly,
with those who could not demonstrate their identity as priests because they
could not prove their pedigrees (Ezra 2:61–63//Nehemiah 7:63–65). Again,
when the Book of Ezra introduces its central character, it does so by list-
ing fifteen generations of his ancestors (Ezra 7:1–5), something quite
unparalleled in biblical narrative (as opposed to genealogical excurses), and
the list of those who returned with Ezra (ch. 8), more than a century after the
exile, has, in contrast to the list in ch. 2, only familial identifications. Again,
the book climaxes with a movement of repentance occasioned by the fact that
"the people of Israel and the priests and the Levites" (9:1) – (not just
"the Jews" – differing pedigrees are important!) had intermarried with
"Canaanites and Hittites and Perizzites and Jebusites and Amonites and
Moabites and Egyptians and Emorites" (not just "Gentiles" – ditto), a
phenomenon which brought about pollution of "the holy seed" (9:2). The
solution to this problem was the only one possible, given a racial definition of
Jews. There could be no thought of conversion, for seed cannot be converted.
Rather, the book ends with a list of those who expelled their non-Jewish wives
and children, and this list too is divided up among priests (10:18–22), Levites
(vv. 23–24) and Israel (vv. 25–43). The same problem was dealt with
similarly in the days of Nehemiah as well (Nehemiah 9–10), just as the
conception of the Jews as a group defined by its "seed" is the predominant one
of the Book of Esther (6:13; 9:28, 31; 10:3) and also supported by the Book of

---

[16] See below, p. 125, n. 41.
[17] Compare the *Landsmannschaften* of Jewish immigrants in New York, organized
according to the eastern European city or town from which the members came; within a
generation or two they largely disappeared, and all one remembers, or cares about, is which
families are Jewish.

Chronicles (I 16:13; II 20:7); Malachi too, yet another witness of the Persian period, considers the Jews to be "God's seed" (2:15).

Hand in hand with the Diaspora and the lack of sovereignty, another factor made for the ascent of descent in the Persian period: the rise of the priesthood. The return to Judaea under Cyrus was led by scions of the Davidic and Aaronite lines, but the former (Zerubbabel), who became the focus for hopes of the restoration of an independent monarchy (Haggai 2:20 ff.; Zechariah 4), soon disappeared. However that happened, it is in the nature of things that in a vassal Temple-state, in which the civil administration was in the hands of a Persian satrap, the most important Jewish figure would be the head of the Temple – the high priest.[18] But the latter was defined by his descent: he was an Aaronite, a member of the clan of Zadok.[19] Next to him, in importance, were the other priests; but they too were defined by their descent from Aaron. Non-Aaronite members of the same tribe formed the next echelon, the Levites. But high-priests and priests were the most important people in Israel in this period. This was, for example, the period when a prophet would claim that the priest is God's "angel" (*malach*) and God's Torah is in his mouth (Malachi 2:6–7), and when, indeed, the same prophet would omit all reference to a messiah in his vision of the coming day of the Lord (chs. 3–4); by the end of the period, a Gentile observer would come away with the impression, presumably given by some Jewish informant, that the Jews never had kings, but rather invested all authority in the priests and the high-priest, who was held to be God's *aggelos*.[20] Much more evidence for the centrality of the priests and high priests in this period may be assembled. But if the most important individual and classes of Jewish society were defined by their descent, it follows that descent is highly signficant – and should also, therefore, be the basis of the next distinction, that between Jews and non-Jews. Thus, the primacy of the priesthood was at once a result of the political circumstances of the Persian period and a reinforcement of the racial definition of Jews which they engendered.

Before moving on we must note, however, that the territorial conception did not disappear. Given the existence of the Temple, God's house, there was no way it could. *The central problem of the Second Temple period was the contradiction between the existence of the Temple in Jerusalem, which seemed*

---

[18] For Judaea in the Persian period as a Temple state, see Weinfeld (above, n. 13) and J. W. Doeve, in *La littérature juive entre Tenach et Mischna: Quelques problèmes* (ed. W. C. van Unnik; 1974), esp. pp. 118–127.

[19] It is clear that this was assumed to be so; the question of the historical truth of these assumptions (J. R. Bartlett, *JTS* n.s. 19 [1968], pp. 1–18) is of only antiquarian interest.

[20] On Hecataeus of Abdera, apud Diodorus Siculus 40.3.4–5 (*GLA* I, nr. 11), see F. R. Walton, *HTR* 48 (1955), pp. 255–257, and D. Mendels, *Zeitschrift für die alttestamentliche Wissenschaft* 95 (1983), pp. 96–110.

to be the palace of a sovereign in the capital of his state, and the fact of foreign sovereignty. This was a problem which could be resolved only by overcoming foreign sovereignty (which happened during the Hasmonean period, when, accordingly, high priests were to run the state), or by destroying the Temple (which would happen at the end of the period), or, apart from either extreme, either by making small compromises to avoid the problem (as would happen throughout the early Roman period) or by spiritualizing the notion of God's sovereignty so as to make it "not of this world" and therefore avoid conflict.[21] In the Persian period, however, as far as our meager sources go it seems that the fact of foreign rule was not very salient, and many Judaeans may have gone through most of their lives under the impression that they really lived in or near "Jerusalem Under the High Priests."[22] Rather than causing difficulties with the foreign overlords, therefore, the territorial conception in this period worked hand in hand with the racial one so as to reinforce priestly hegemony: after all, what made the priests so important was their monopoloy on access to the most holy place. The flip-side of this conjunction of holy race and holy place was the schism with the Samaritans, which has its roots in this period. Jewish complaints about the Samaritans, namely, had to do not with dogmas or practice, but rather with the Jewish claims that the Samaritans were of foreign descent (II Kings 17) and localized the divinity at the wrong mountain.

With the advent of Alexander the Great and the introduction of the Jews into the orbit of Hellenistic culture, things would again change. Jews of the Diaspora would soon find themselves in surroundings where Greek language and Hellenistic culture were regnant and encompassing, while the Jews of Judaea would find themselves ruled by governments whose presence – be it administrative or military – was felt much more than had previously been the case. New responses were forthcoming.

First and most profoundly, the impact of Hellenism must be underlined. What was most important about Hellenism was its last three letters: it is an *ism*. While it is derived from the same root which supplied "Hellas" and "Hellene," the term "Hellenism" means that one can truly be a Greek without any connection to Greece or Greek blood, if only he adopts their characteristic

---

[21] Cf. below, pp. 40–43, also, on the fiction which allowed peace-seeking Jews to sacrifice for Rome in Jerusalem, pp. 102–116.
[22] To borrow a classic title (E. R. Bevan, *Jerusalem Under the High-Priests* [1904]). See also Doeve (above, n. 18), pp. 122–123, who portrays Jerusalem of the Persian and early Hellenistic period more or less as an autonomous vassal state ruled by the high priest. We do hear of some Persian governors, however, so this is going too far; also, it seems that the Josephan notion of high-priestly *prostasia* corresponds more to the realities of Diaspora Judaism of his own day than to anything formal in Jerusalem of the Second Temple period; see *Scripta Classica Israelica* 7 (1983/84), esp. pp. 43–52. In general, however, "under the high priests" seems best to fit the evidence.

language and culture. And while all due respect must be given to the lapidary truism that the Greeks conquered the East to get rich, not because of any cultural mission,[23] it is nevertheless the case that they brought their culture with them, and in time established norms and institutions which allowed, gradually, for the transformation of barbarians into Greeks. The Jews of the Diaspora, as might perhaps be expected from minorities with little invested in the wounded national pride of the conquered lands in which they dwelt, were especially susceptible to the new culture, and profoundly influenced by it.

It is difficult to trace and measure the extent and rate of this influence. Some scholars would view it as slow and spotty, others prefer to extrapolate more confidently from the extant data. However, this discrepancy is of critical importance only with regard to the pre-Hasmonean period, that is, until the mid-second century.[24] All would agree that the succeeding centuries, the ones of most importance for the emergence of Christianity, saw widespread Hellenization.

In particular, with regard to the three criteria of Jewish identity, we should note that by the time II Maccabees was composed, some time in the wake of the Hasmonean rebellion, the term "Judaism" (*Ioudaismos*), which parallels and contrasts with "Hellenism" (*Hellenismos*) and even "foreignism" (*allophylismos*), was considered, at least by the Diasporan author of that book, an acceptable way of defining the Jews, just as it was later to be used by Paul and by the Diasporan author of IV Maccabees.[25] That is, Jews who came up against "Hellenists" defined by their culture rather than − or more than − by their descent or place of origin (and certainly not by their residence) responded in kind by defining themselves as "Judaists," adherents of "Judaism."

The other *novum* of the Hellenistic period, apart from Hellenistic culture, was the salience of foreign rule. As opposed to the Persian period, in which, as far as we can see, the foreign overlords were content to receive their taxes, which may well have been collected through the agency of the high priesthood,[26] in the Hellenistic period we read of the constant flow of foreign

---

[23] W. W. Tarn (with G. T. Griffith), *Hellenistic Civilization* (1952³), p. 201: "The Greeks came to Egypt to grow rich."

[24] Thus, for example, all would agree that the Letter of Aristeas demonstrates deep Hellenistic influence, but whether it should be dated to the third or second century B.C.E. is still debated. Cf. below, p. 40, n. 31.

[25] See II Maccabees 2:21, 4:13, 15; 8:1; 14:38. Nothing indicates that Jason of Cyrene (or the epitomator) coined any of these terms; contrast, for example, Josephus' self-conscious introduction of "theocracy" in *C. Ap.* 2.165. On "Judaism", which is also used in Galatians 1:13−14, IV Maccabees 4:26, and some later inscriptions, see M. Hengel, *ZNW* 57 (1966), pp. 178−181, and Y. Amir, *Studien zum Antiken Judentum* (1985), pp. 101−113.

[26] The few allusions to more assertive and even oppressive government in the Persian period, such as those in Nehemiah 5:15 and *C. Ap.* 1.191−193 (quoting Hecataeus [of

armies back and forth through Palestine and of the foundation of numerous cities, which incorporated the claims to territorial sovereignty.[27] Especially after the Seleucid takeover, the fact of being under foreign rule could hardly be ignored.[28] Whatever the specific causes of the eruption under Antiochus IV Epiphanes, it certainly was a Jewish response to the foreigner's assertion of sovereignty in what the rebels considered to be the very heart of God's kingdom's, His capital — the Temple. But when the rebellion was won, we find that Hellenization had been so profound that the Hasmonean victors, after first turning to forceful conversion as a way of dealing with the problem of Gentile subjects, quickly, already under Aristobulus I Philhellenos (! — *Ant.* 13.318), turned to a Hellenistic solution. Namely, accepting the definition of Judaism à la Hellenism as an *ism*, they added the royal crown to their high-priestly miter and called upon the Gentile subjects to render obedience to them not as religious figures but rather only as temporal overlords. That is, they separated religion from state — just as the Greeks, who created "Hellenism," had separated Greek from Greece.

Apart from the management of the Hasmonean state, other major Judaea evidence for the "-ization" of Jewish identity in this period comes from the phenomenon of the sects, which date at least to the mid-second century B.C.E. (*Ant.* 13.171−173). Not only with respect to some of the specific topics over which they argued (such as free will vs. determinism or the question of life after death) did they recall Greek analogues (as Josephus proudly noted −

Abdera?; *GLA* I, nr. 12]), are isolated and may be no more than mere *topoi*. Moreover, the doubts pertaining to the authenticity of the latter source remain (see SVM III, pp. 672−673; R. Doran in *The Old Testament Pseudepigrapha*, II [ed. J. H. Charlesworth; 1985], pp. 914−916; and esp. C. R. Holladay, *Fragments from Hellenistic Jewish Authors, I: Historians* [1983], pp. 279−290); even those who tend to defend its basic authenticity often admit that its allusion to persecutions in the Persian period may be an insertion reflecting the Maccabean period; and the attempt − *GLA* I, p. 42, following H. Lewy, *ZNW* 31 (1932), pp. 124−126 − to flesh the latter out out by reference to cancelled persecutions in Persia (Esther) or to a fine following a Jerusalem murder (*Ant.* 11.297−301) only points up the difficulty.

[27] On cities founded in the Palestinian region see V. Tcherikover, *Hellenistic Civilization and the Jews* (1959), pp. 90−116. As for the flow of foreign armies: an overview of the military history of the region in the Hellenistic-Roman period remains a desideratum. I. Abrahams, *Campaigns in Palestine from Alexander the Great* (1927), is merely a brief essay on a few episodes. B. Bar-Kokhva's *Judas Maccabaeus* (1989), although it focuses on a single decade, gives access to a great deal of relevant and up-to-date information. In general, cf. the literature cited below, p. 40, n. 31.

[28] It is noteworthy that both Josephus (*Ant.* 12.138−146) and epigraphy agree in locating visible and far-reaching expressions of government at the very beginning of the Seleucid period. For the Hefzibah inscription, see Y.H. Landau, *IEJ* 16 (1966), pp. 54−70 (also J. M. Bertrand, *Zeitschrift für Papyrologie und Epigraphik* 46 [1982], pp. 167−176, with references to other literature.)

Ant. 18.22; *Vita* 12; *BJ* 2.155–156); more importantly, their very assumption that it was important to argue about questions of belief and practice was a Hellenistic assumption. As long as "being Jewish" was basically a matter of place or race, there was no reason to assume that all should agree about belief or practice, any more than all French or all women do. But if being Jewish is a matter of adherence to a cultural agenda, then it must be defined, and the lack of agreement will be taken very seriously, and will crystallize into schools or "sects." Similarly, the widespread proselytism and "sympathizing" with Judaism ("God-fearers") are predicated on the notion that being Jewish is an *ism* available to all.[29]

The Roman annexation of Judaea, first as a client "ethnarchy," then as a vassal kingdom and finally as a province ruled directly from Rome, finalized this separation of religion and state, or, at least, should have. Coming in a few decades after Aristobulus had created the potentiality of splitting the personal union of temporal and religious rule, and after *Queen* Salome Alexandra had actualized it, the Romans could simply hope to carry on, taking for themselves or their agents only the temporal rule and leaving religion, the high priesthood, to the Jews. True, at first the Romans allowed for a personal union of the two spheres, under Hyrcanus I. But within a decade A. Gabinius (the Roman governor of Syria) denied Hyrcanus his temporal authority and left him high-priest alone, and, thereafter, Antipater (Herod's father) was granted various (if not entirely clear) positions of civil authority at Hyrcanus' expense.[30] And beginning with Herod, who could not be high-priest, the two spheres were totally split. Although Herod at first asserted the crown's control over the institutions of the Jewish religion, via patronage of the Temple but also by innovating the appointment and firing of high-priests (the office had previously been inherited and lifelong) and by keeping their vestments under lock and key as a means of keeping them under his thumb, the Romans, in the period of direct rule, by and large took pains to keep an arm's length away from them. Thus, they gave up the right to appoint and fire high-priests, and also returned the high-priestly vestments to the priests' own custody; they demonstratively punished those, even Roman soldiers, who desecrated the Temple, and allowed the Jews to punish those who wrongly trespassed into its courts; they kept their usual military *signa*, which the Jews considered idolatrous, out of Jerusalem; and they exempted the Jewish temple tax (*shekalim*) from the usual restrictions on the transfer of money from one province to another, prosecuting those – even high officials – who interfered

---

[29] For literature on these latter phenomena, see below, p. 195, n. 57.

[30] See esp. *Ant.* 14.90–91, 127, 139 (Strabo),143; E. Bammel, *Judaica: Kleine Schriften*, I (1986), pp. 17–20 (=*JJS* 12 [1961], pp. 159–162); SVM I, pp. 268–272; and Smallwood, *Jews*, pp. 31–39.

with it. Finally, by maintaining Caesarea as a separate provincial capital, they kept the potential for conflicts in the holy city as low as possible.[31]

However, Roman governors of Judaea were not always of the best caliber, and there were, now and then, nasty incidents which bruised Jewish religious sensitivities. Moreover, even without them, the fact is that the best governors and all the gestures in the world could not have erased the basic fact that the coexistence of the Temple and Roman rule in Judaea was intolerable, given the ancient understanding of the Temple as house of God. Here is the aforementioned central problem of the period in all its biting clarity: Roman rule in the Holy Land, even by the most sensitive governor imaginable, means God does not rule there – but the Temple meant He was there, and how could He be there and not rule? So His subjects, the faithful adherents to His covenant, were daily called upon to stand up for what was rightly His. Moreover, God being God, He, and His protegés, could scarcely fail to emerge victorious. On such presumptions, clash and catastrophe were inevitable. Gaius Caligula's attempt to Romanize the Temple in 39/40 C.E., which encountered massive Jewish resistance, was something of a dress rehearsal for the final clash, which avoided catastrophe only because the emperor was murdered *Deus ex machina*. A quarter century later, a demonstrative Jewish attempt to assert the Temple's non-Roman nature[32] resulted in the final conflict, and this time God did not intervene despite the death of even four emperors. Afterwards, life was again simple for the Jews and Rome (if dismal for the former), for without the Temple there was nothing to indicate that God was more in Judaea than anywhere else in the Roman world.[33] From now on, His kingdom could be only in the past, in the future, universal or not of this world; any attempt, such as Bar-Kokhba's to establish it in Judaea would be a rebellion against a clear present, not an attempt to assert one element of an ambiguous one.

Looking back, then, we see that in the latter half of the Second Temple period Hellenism, which led Jews to view themselves too as adherents of an *ism* (and so fostered sectarianism, proselytism and "sympathizers") and

---

[31] For the preceding paragraph see, inter alia: *Ant.* 15.40–41 (on Herod's innovative control of the high priesthood), and below, pp. 199–200 (on Rome's relinquishment of it); *Ant.* 18.95, 20.6–14 and below, p. 206 (on the high-priestly vestments); *BJ* 1.225, 231, 246// *Ant.* 18.108, 117, 136 (on Roman punishment of desecrating soldiers); below, p. 108, n. 19 (on Jewish capital jurisdiction over trespassers on the Temple Mount); *Ant.* 18.55–56, 121–122 on *signa* kept out of Jerusalem; and ibid. 16.160–173 (with SVM III, pp. 118–119), Philo, *Leg.* 311–316, and Cicero, *Pro Flacco* 26:67 (*GLA* I, nr. 68, pp. 196–201) on protection of *shekalim*.

[32] See below, pp. 111–116.

[33] For Josephus' assimilation of this new situation, and the difficulties he encountered when applying it to the description of pre-Destruction rebels, see below, pp. 29–34.

political circumstances, including the Hasmoneans' conquest of non-Jewish peoples and then non-Jewish (Roman) conquest of the Hasmoneans' state, led to a severe depreciation of the physical parameters of being Jewish. "Judaism," as opposed to Jewish territory or Jewish blood, became the only way of defining "Jews" which was well-founded in the logic and facts of Jewish existence in the first century. Those who chose to hang on to territory would be forced to fight it out with Rome, and the side with the more legions won that war.

In our opening observations about John the Baptist and Paul, we noted that neither had much use for the Temple (the linchpin of Jewish territorialism) or for Jewish descent, but they were very concerned with religion − sin and atonement. That is, Christianity, as bespoken by those two poles, very much reflects the state of affairs we have described. It now behooves us to pursue separately the religious developments in the Hellenistic Diaspora and in Qumran, the two specific settings which are most important for the emergence of these two figures. Religion is composed of a normative and spiritual elements − what one does, and what one thinks and feels, due to God. As we shall see, what is most significant for our present purposes is the fact that, in both settings, the weight of religion often came to rest upon the latter pillar alone.

III. Undermining the Law, I: In the Hellenistic Diaspora

Jews in the Hellenistic Diaspora were quite obvious candidates for undergoing the Hellenization of Judaism. Their ambience and language were Greek, and their lack of clear political self-definition − Alexandrian Jews were neither Judaeans nor quite Alexandrians − made it simpler for them to accept the political claims of the new Hellenistic regimes. Moreover, their distance from the holy land would lead them to deflate the religious significance of territory and emphasize in its stead God's transcendence; and their constant mixing with Gentiles would encourage them to proselytize, whether altruistically or as a defensive response to charges of aloof "misanthropy."[34] As we have noted, both the term "Judaism" and the phenomenon of widespread proselytism quite naturally arose in the Diaspora.

---

[34] For this standard charge see *GLA* III, p. 136, s.v., also I. Heinemann, *PWRE* Supplementband 5 (1931), cols. 19−20. Cf. J. N. Sevenster, *The Roots of Pagan Anti-Semitism in the Ancient World* (1975), pp. 89−144 (on "strangeness," including pp. 93−94 on the Philonic evidence), and J. L. Daniel, *JBL* 98 (1979), pp. 58−62 (on "exclusiveness"), along with the caveat by J. G. Gager, *The Origins of Anti-Semitism* (1983), p. 31. As for proselytism as an answer to such charges, it is enough to note that both modern Jewish handbooks on the subject were written and published when attacks upon Jews as being

Thus, Hellenism undercut territory and descent as criteria of "Who is a Jew?," instead placing the emphasis upon "Judaism," the practices and beliefs characteristic of the Jews. However, and most importantly in the current context, Hellenism also undercut the practical side of that religion itself. Why should spiritualization stop with territory and descent? Why should it not apply to all the manifold material elements of Jewish law as well? If something "essentially" Jewish could be distilled out of Judaea and out of the Jews, and established elsewhere and among non-Jews (proselytes), why couldn't something "essential" be distilled out of the matter of Judaism too? Quite characteristically, the writings of one of the earliest Jewish-Hellenistic sages, Aristobulus, show that he was concerned to explain away, as metaphors, biblical references to parts of God's body.[35] But if biblical references to parts of God's body are only metaphors, why should the biblical command to cut off a part of the body of male infants, or to wear phylacteries, or to abstain from eating certain flesh, or to slaughter other flesh as part of divine worship, etc., be any more literal? Why, indeed, should a spiritual God be concerned with any parts and aspects of the physical world, as if some were holier than others or could be endowed with holiness? Is it not indeed likely that He referred to them only to teach spiritual lessons?

This train of thought is already well in evidence in the Letter of Aristeas, which gives an account of the symbolic meaning of numerous laws. Philo does the same, at greater length and sometimes wearisome detail, a century or more later. But if the laws are here to teach spiritual lessons, need they also be observed in their literal sense? If, for example, the Torah prohibits the consumption of certain animals because they symbolize reprehensible traits (*Aristeas* 144–166), may we – who have learned that such traits should be avoided – now eat the animals? Aristeas and Philo answered in the negative, affirming the law's continued normative authority. But it must be said that the

---

racially separate were at their peak: B. J. Bamberger, *Proselytism in the Talmudic Period* (1939) and W. G. Braude, *Jewish Proselyting in the First Five Centuries of the Common Era* . . . (1940). Note also S. Zeitlin, *The Jews: Race, Nation, or Religion? A Study Based on the Literature of the Second Jewish Commonwealth* (1936). In fact, however, the ancient evidence indicates that Jewish willingness to allow Gentiles access to their God and covenant, via proselytism, does not seem often to have been appreciated by those who declined to take advantage of it. Philo assumes that proselytes instead became the "mortal enemies" of their former families (*De specialibus legibus* 4.178), and esp. Sevenster (above) collects further evidence for resentment of proselytism.

[35] See the fragments preserved by Eusebius in *Praeparatio evangelica* 8.10; for annotated translations see N. Walter in *Jüdische Schriften aus hellenistisch-römischer Zeit* III/2 (1975), pp. 270–273, and A. Y. Collins in Charlesworth (above, n. 26), II, pp. 837–839. On Aristobulus on anthropomorphisms, and for the line we are preparing to draw from Aristobulus to Philo, see also P. Borgen, *Philo, John and Paul: New Perspectives on Judaism and Early Christianity* (1987), pp. 13–14.

reasons Philo offered are hardly cogent. In the famous passage (*De migratione Abrahami* 89–93) in which he polemicizes against those who claim that only the symbolic import of the laws need be retained,[36] he argues that

1. To observe meaning without form is similar to attempting to maintain a bodiless soul.

2. Giving care for the body (the observance) will enhance the appreciation of its spiritual meaning.

3. Not to observe the laws, while still living in communities and not as hermits, would engender the disapproval of the *hoi polloi*.

4. If one were to abrogate the observances which he enumerated as examples, he should logically abrogate them all — "even the sanctity of the Temple and a thousand other things." This, evidently, Philo considered a reductio ad absurdum of his opponents' position.

However,

ad 1) Elsewhere, even in this same tract (§§ 9–11, 32–35) Philo himself posits the mystic ideal of living as a disembodied soul. He who would truly worship God, he teaches, must be able to leave his body.[37]

ad 2) As for the notion that the more one observes the law the better its meaning is inculcated, Philo's opponents here obviously thought they had practiced enough. Within a few decades, another Hellenistic Jew will compare the Torah to a pedagogue (Galatians 3:24), from whose tutelage one eventually graduates.

ad 3) While "when in Rome be like the Romans" is a common rule of human decency, it hardly covers what one does when one is not under public supervision. And Philo praises those who flee the cities and live in solitude.[38] If anything, this notion could encourage a Jewish teacher to dedicate his time to educating the masses so that they too, eventually, will give up their atavistic cleaving to material religion.

---

[36] This passage is treated several times by Borgen (above, n. 35), esp. pp. 65–68, 220–225, 234–239 and 258–261. However, his interest is limited to questions related to circumcision and conversion.

[37] See also *De specialibus legibus* 3.1–6, where Philo recalls the good old days before he was dragged into the affairs of this world, also *De ebrietate* 101, *Legum allegoriae* 3.39–48 and *Quis rerum* 69–74; the latter two are cited alongside *De migr. Abr.* 9–11 and 32–35 in H. Lewy, *Philo: Selections* (1946), pp. 71–74 (reprinted in A. Altmann, ed., *Three Jewish Philosophers* [1982]); cf. the passages collected ibid., pp. 36–37, and, on the ideal of living not "on the earth" (in contrast to the giants of Genesis 6:4), see *De gigantibus* 58–67, commented upon by D. Winston and J. Dillon (with V. Nikiprowetzky) in *Two Treatises of Philo of Alexandria: A Commentary on De Gigantibus and Quod Deus Sit Immutabilis* (1983), pp. 21–23, 267–273.

[38] See *De vita contemplativa* 19–20, 76. Note also his recurrent use of Exodus 9:29 ("when I leave the city") as an image for leaving the body, in passages cited in our preceding note (*Leg. All.* 3.43–44; *Ebr.* 101–103). And in the passage from *De gigantibus* (§ 61) it is held best not even to be "cosmopolitan," a citizen of the world city.

ad 4) Indeed, within a few decades Paul will consistently claim that the Temple cult has been replaced by spiritual substitutes and the whole Torah has been abrogated.

That is, a few decades before the birth of Christianity Hellenistic Judaism had already produced a spiritualized but lawless brand of Judaism against which the foremost spokesman of tradition was incapable of bringing cogent argument.

Perhaps the most striking point in Philo's polemic is the argument which he did not bring. He does not simply argue from authority: Who is man to stop observing what God commanded? Indeed, he instead characterizes the laws as "customs (*ethē*)[39] fixed by divinely empowered men greater than those of our time." Here too, Hellenism had prepared the way: given the fact that many nations had their individual codes and customs, it was natural to attribute them each to the given people's legislators, who were, of course, human — although they frequently claimed divine inspiration. As Diodorus Siculus explained, such claims — of Lycurgus, Moses and others — were made either sincerely or as well-meaning ploys to ensure obedience, but they need not be accepted as true.[40] Thus, Aristobulus, Ps.-Aristeas and Philo regularly refer to the law as written by Moses, and, although for them this is no reason to devalue it, the time would soon come when a view of the law as only "the customs of Moses" (instead of "the laws of God") would make it a foregone conclusion that it need not be imposed where it would be burdensome.[41]

Finally, Hellenism contributed in one further way to the undermining of Jewish law. By stressing the non-Hebraic distinction between body and soul, it encouraged man to yearn for a situation in which the soul could be freed of the body — a yearning we noted above, in Philo. But inasmuch as observance of the law is entrusted to the body, a yearning to be free of the body amounts to a yearning to be free of the law. And as such yearning reflects one's discontent with his present state, it is equal to a yearning for perfection. That is, it becomes very simple to align the body with imperfection, and so with death,

---

[39] For the second-class nature of *ethos* as opposed to law, see C. Spicq, *Notes de lexicographie néo-testamentaire*, Supplément (1982), pp. 194–201.

[40] Diodorus Siculus 1.94 (*GLA* I, nr. 58). This passage was already cited in this context by E. Bickermann, *Der Gott der Makkabäer* (1937), p. 130. In that part of his well-known critique of Bickermann's thesis which deals with the claim that the Jerusalem Hellenizers were familiar with the results of Hellenistic *Religionswissenschaft* (*MGWJ* 82 [1938], pp. 156–159), I. Heinemann ignores this argument, and argues only with the notion that Jerusalem Hellenizers thought Jewish law was post-Mosaic.

[41] I refer, of course, to Acts 15 ("customs of Moses" in v. 1 [as in 6:14], contrast between God and Moses/law in vv. 19–21). On the logic of the decision described in this chapter, see *Biblica* 67 (1986), pp. 276–281. In general, on Moses as the author of the Torah, see Y. Amir, *Die hellenistische Gestalt des Judentums bei Philon von Alexandrien* (1983), pp. 77–106 and *passim*.

together with the law, and to oppose to them an alignment of spirit and perfection and eternal life − without the law. While these two alignments are fully presented by Paul, the connection of perfection and immortality in the Garden of Eden (Romans 5) is already well adumbrated in the Wisdom of Solomon (2:24 and 5:15), an Alexandrian Jewish book which, while not totally ignoring Jewish law, nevertheless usually characterizes good people in the universal terms of righteousness and wisdom.[42]

To summarize, we may note that Hellenism not only engendered a focus upon religion (as opposed to territory and descent) but also, by socializing, spiritualizing, relativizing and establishing an otherworldly ideal of perfection, encouraged the abandonment of the observance of Jewish law. We will now turn to Qumran and see that, even without direct Hellenistic influence, the same period saw the same concentration upon religion (as opposed to territory and descent) and then similar processes adumbrating the same undermining of the law.

IV. Undermining the Law, II: In Qumran

Territory and descent were both undermined by the polemic situation of the Qumran sect. For whatever its origins, any Jewish group which held God preferred their desert community to Jerusalem ("the desert of Jerusalem"),[43] and condemned those who shared their descent and even Aaronite descent, evidently held that neither consideration was very important. Of course, neither criterion was abandoned. While the community considered itself a substitute for the Temple, it did not exactly call itself one[44] and went on expressing the hope for the return to a purified Temple in Jerusalem; and the sect's constitution and regulations enthroned the priests as its rulers. Nevertheless, any sect which lives for a century or two outside of Jerusalem and with no Temple cult may be presumed to have adjusted well to the situation, and the prominent texts which preach that the main distinctions among mankind are those between the good and the bad ("Sons of Light" and "Sons of Darkness") hardly give any support to the notion that descent matters. Correspondingly, while Qumran texts do frequently express the hope for the advent of pedigreed saviors (Aaronite and Davidic messiahs) it is just

---

[42] See D. Winston, *The Wisdom of Solomon* (Anchor Bible; 1979), esp. pp. 33−46 (on Torah, wisdom, universalism and particularism) and 59−63 (on the similarities between *Wisdom* and Philo).

[43] See below, p. 37.

[44] See below, p. 38, n. 25.

as or more significant that they also preserve great interest in such universal figures as Enoch and the hope for the advent of Melchizedek.[45]

Thus, while some Qumran texts portray a community reminiscent of the Persian period, run by the priests and looking forward to returning to Jerusalem, others ignore the cult and impart teachings which contradict the notion that one's birth as priest or Israelite is of any significance, for the true categories of good and evil cut across "all the sons of man" (*Manual of Discipline* 3:13; the very outset of the catechism on the sons of light and darkness). It stands to reason that the former ("right-wing") types of views represent the earlier life of the sect and the latter ("left-wing") developed later, as it became evident that there would be no return to Jerusalem and that the multitudes of wicked priests and Israelites would not repent. But for our purposes it is enough if we note that there were two such conflicting trends within the sect.[46] Whether or not they expressed themselves in any social or formal subdivision, we do not know. But we can see that any sectarian reading the texts carefully must have been torn between the two options. Suppose, for example, a young sectarian reading the *Manual of Discipline*. If a priest came up and gave him an order when he was reading cols. 5 or 9, he might jump up and fulfill it, for those texts make it clear that he was bound to follow the priests' authority. If, on the other hand, he was reading columns 3–4 or 11, he might wonder why being a son of Aaron meant anything; what counts is whether one is a son of light, and, anyway, all "born of woman" (11:21)[47] are equally vile, apart from God's special gracious election. In the latter event, he might angrily tell the priest not to rely on his being a son of Aaron, for God could make even stones into sons . . .

This devaluation of territory and descent leaves us with the third criterion

---

[45] On the hope for the two pedigreed messiahs, see J. Liver, *HTR* 52 (1959), pp. 149–185, and L. H. Schiffman, *The Eschatological Community of the Dead Sea Scrolls* (1989), pp. 6–8. As for the two sons of Adam, the main texts are collected in J. T. Milik (with M. Black), *The Books of Enoch: Aramaic Fragments of Qumrân Cave 4* (1976) and P. J. Kobelski, *Melchizedek and Melchireša'* (1981).

[46] This dualism is the point of departure for my study in *Archaeology and History in the Dead Sea Scrolls: The New York University Conference in Memory of Yigael Yadin* (ed. L. H. Schiffman; 1990), pp. 157–179, also of "Qumran Between Priestliness and Christianity," forthcoming in the proceedings of the 1987 Hebrew University symposium on "The Dead Sea Scrolls: Forty Years of Research" (in Hebrew). For a detailed, if somewhat dated, discussion of priests and priestliness in Qumran, see G. Klinzing, *Die Umdeutung des Kultus in der Qumrangemeinde und im Neuen Testament* (1971), pp. 22–41, 106–143, who, although naturally focusing upon the spiritualizing trend, nevertheless, in his concluding comments (p. 143), similarly emphasizes the dualism. With reference to Temple and sacrifices, this dualism is also the theme of H. Lichtenberger, in *Approaches to Ancient Judaism*, II (ed. W. S. Green; 1980), pp. 159–171.

[47] Also in *Hodayot* 13:14 and 18:13, 23–24, describing the lowness of the human condition; cf. below, n. 57.

of "being Jewish" – religion. But in Qumran, while some writings – most notably the *Temple Scroll* and the *Damascus Document*[48] – show firm commitment to Judaism's legal component, others do not. And when they do not, it is because of spiritualization, relativization and the yearning for perfection – just as we saw in the world of Hellenistic Judaism.

Spiritualization is the most obvious, for it figures in large letters in the transference of the Temple and its cult to the community: this is what allows for the characterization of the community as holy house which works atonement, wherein prayers are just as efficient as sacrifice, etc. Moreover, I would note that even the typical Qumran attitude toward law, which is realistic and not nominalistic (i.e., laws reflect reality and are not merely edicts), leads in the same direction.[49] Consider, for example, the Qumran willingness (*Damascus Document* 5:8–10) to generalize the biblical prohibition of marriage with aunts to include marriage with nieces as well, "for Moses said, 'You shall not approach your mother's sister, for she is your mother's near kinswoman' (Leviticus 18:13), and (although) the laws of incest are written with regard to men they are the same for women" (so a woman too is forbidden to her relative who precedes her by one generation and is removed by one lateral relationship). The prior assumption which allows for this generalization is that the relationship *is* bad, and that God has revealed one example of it, just as when one tells a child not to touch the exposed wire of a radio he should infer that it is dangerous and that he should not touch exposed wires of other appliances either. Had the presumption been that the statement had by fiat *created* the prohibition (and not pointed out a danger), there would be no basis for generalizing it. That is, even when it insists on the observance of law, the basic Qumran attitude seems to be that law must be observed because it reflects something – the same attitude which we saw in Aristeas and Philo (and especially among those Philo attacked in *De migr. Abr.*). When, as in the case of the Temple, that something (God's presence, atonement) can be had without reference to the law, then, it follows, the law is superfluous.

Next, *relativization*. In our sketch of developments in the Hellenistic world we saw a cosmopolitan relativism: so many claimants to divine authority couldn't all be right, so none is right. In Qumran, we find instead a diachronic relativism within Judaism: the law is ascribed to Moses (as in the

---

[48] Also the *Miqtzat Ma'ase haTorah* text which we are still awaiting; see, in the meantime, E. Qimron and J. Strugnell in *Biblical Archaeology Today* (1985), pp. 400–407. The legal content of the *Damascus Document* is growing considerably with the publication of the Qumran fragments; see, most recently, J. M. Baumgarten, *JJS* 41 (1990), pp. 153–165.

[49] On this basic attitude toward law and its priestly background (after all, priests are born priests), see my essay "Law and Truth: On Qumran-Sadducean and Rabbinic Views of Law," to appear in the proceedings of the 1988 Haifa University – Tel-Aviv University – Yad ben Zvi conference on "Forty Years of Research in the Dead Sea Scrolls."

above-mentioned passage on incest) not to make him one of a number of
legislators in the world, but rather to make him one of a series of prophets in
Israel. Correspondingly, Moses' promise that a prophet like him would arise
and should be obeyed was prominently enshrined in the sect's messianic
agenda (4Q *Testimonia*). In Qumran, it was held that revelation was not
closed; God could, and from time to time did, reveal Himself to members of
the sect, particularly the priests (who are charged with "seeking His will" —
Manual of Discipline 5:9). And the sect's future expectations included a
prophet who would appear alongside of the messiahs, at which time "the first
ordinances" would be replaced by something better (ibid. 9:9–11).[50] This,
however, implies that the current laws are not ideal.

This belief is simply part and parcel of the sect's general belief that the
present age is not ideal; far from it! The present age is the "epoch of Belial,"
and it was reasonable to hope that when the better future dawned, many
aspects of the present order would change. Why not law?

Consideration of this dissatisfaction with the present will also lead us to the
third factor which undermined the law: *perfectionism*. The legal process
involves two stages: law must be interpreted and law must be observed. One
must know what to do and one must do it. However, people are not inerrant;
they may fail with regard to both. The rabbis dealt with these problems by
assuming God took them into account when He entrusted the law to men who
were less than perfect: interpretation was entrusted to majority rule (so even
if the heavenly bodies or God screamed out that the court or the majority was
wrong, it was to be followed),[51] and repentance was provided to overcome the
effects of sin. In Qumran, however, the same problems were dealt with by
entrusting everything to God: acceptance of the legitimacy of continuing
revelation and assertion of the divine inspiration of the priests ensured that
there would be no errors of interpretation, and as for sin — whether or not a
man sinned was left to God, for no one can direct his own steps.

> But I have come to know that righteousness is not unto man,
>   neither unto the son of man the perfect way.
> Unto the most high God are all the deeds of righteousness;
>   and the way of man endureth not,
>   except through the spirit which God hath created for him,
>   to perfect a way unto the children of men . . .
> For thou atonest for sin and (purifiest man) from guilt
>   through thy righteousness . . .
> For thou, not for man . . . thou hast done,
>   for thou hast created both the righteous and the ungodly.
>
> (*Hodayot* 4:30–32, 37–38, trans. S. Holm-Nielsen)

---

[50] On this passage, see *Theologische Zeitschrift* 37 (1981), p. 262.
[51] See the famous stories in m.*Rosh HaShana* 2:8–9 and BT *Baba Metzia* 59 a–b.

In other words, the quest for perfection, so pronounced here (and else-where),[52] as is to be expected in a community of religious virtuosi, which was frustrated by the awareness of sinfulness (also so usual in such communities), led to the conclusion that man's own actions are meaningless; everything important is in God's hands. Failure to be completely perfect meant complete incapacity; note the passage from "For without you no way can be perfect" to "and without Your will nothing can be done" in *Hodayot* 11:17. But this makes the law, which is something God asked man to do, basically irrelevant. Thus, of the long scroll from which we just quoted, which is so intimately revealing of Qumran piety, it is no surprise that

. . . the innumerable themes based upon cult and references to the Temple and Temple worship [scil: in the biblical Psalms] do not come at all in the Hodayot . . . Moreover, it is worth noting how little use is made of the Pentateuch . . . Those parts of the Pentateuch which are made use of do not in any case have anything to do with the Law directly . . .[53]

This is just one step behind what we find in Paul, where the notion that anyone who does not fulfill all the Law is cursed (Galatians 3:10) leads not merely to a lack of interest in it, as in the *Hodayot*, but to a resentment and polemic against it.

As for the background of Qumran perfectionism, it could be that it has something to do with priestliness; a Temple *Sitz im Leben*, where pure people

---

[52] See especially the psalm concluding the *Manual of Discipline* (11:2, 11, 17).

[53] S. Holm-Nielsen, *Hodayot: Psalms from Qumran* (1960), pp. 309, 311–312. But Holm-Nielsen is not discerning enough, I believe, when he argues (p. 311) that, "when one realises the part that was played by the Law within the community," this lack of reference to the Law must mean only that the context of the *Hodayot* does not require attention to the details of laws. Similarly, J. Licht too is wrong, I think, to assume that the although the *Hodayot* do not pay attention to the details of law their yearning for "walking in the ways of God's heart" and for "righteousness" must be understood in terms of law (*IEJ* 6 [1956], p. 94); here, as in the introduction to his edition of the *Hodayot* (*The Thanksgiving Scroll* . . . [1957], pp. 48–49 [in Hebrew]), Licht's exposition is too dependent upon the *Manual of Discipline*. Rather, just as there was within the sect a tension between priestly tradition and universalist tendencies which undermined it (see above, n. 46), so too was there one between legal tradition and a perfectionist piety which undermined it. As Licht's long account shows, the piety of the *Hodayot* was of the latter variety. As Licht himself recognizes, "to be fully consistent, the teachers of the sect (scil. reflected in the *Hodayot*) would have to absolve man of all moral responsibility" (*IEJ*, p. 6); the fact that they were not fully consistent does not deny the tendency of their teaching, and that is one which leaves law pointless or worse. (Moreover, note that the *Hodayot* refer to the Law even less than Holm-Nielsen's translation might indicate, for in two passages [4:27; 14:14] where he refers to violation of "commandments" the text in fact speaks, as he notes at 4:27, of those who "violate [the words of] God's mouth;" it need not be that the reference is specifically to Jewish law, as opposed to divine decrees in general.)

and utensils and precise cult were the *minimum* standards,[54] probably encouraged such an attitude in priestly communities. And it could be that the Hellenistic factors which led to perfectionism elsewhere were somehow "in the air." But however that may be, the fact remains that at Qumran, as in the Hellenistic world, the contrast of the imperfection of man and the obligation to fulfill the law must have engendered, in sensitive souls, a pressure which could be relieved only by the death of the former or the abrogation of the latter.

V. Which Conflict Did Jesus Resolve?

The Jewish world into which Jesus was born was thus the scene of two major conflicts. The more obvious one was the national one discussed in Part II, the conflict of God *vs.* Rome: who is the sovereign of Judaea and the Jews? The other conflict, within sensitive individuals, discussed in Parts III–IV, was less obvious but just as pressing: continued observance of the Torah *vs.* its abrogation due to the undermining effects of spiritualization and relativization, and of a perfectionism which is ever frustrated by flesh and blood's attempts to fulfill the law. By themselves, the Jews could hardly hope to solve either problem. But if God were to step in, He, by definition, could easily solve both: He could throw out both the Romans and the law.

Now the story of Jesus is one which begins when John, whose Qumran background is clear, preaches that God is about to intervene and that man should repent before it is too late. While the precise political import of John's teachings is unclear, it is clear that Luke, our major source about him, had every reason to play it down, and that, in any event, John was executed by the sovereign of his region, Herod Antipas, who is said to have feared insurrection (Josephus, *Ant.* 18.116–119). That is, John expected the coming intervention would help deal with the first conflict, and, in standard prophetic fashion, called upon the Jews to repent before the Day of the Lord comes, lest they too be caught up in God's exercise of wrath. Jesus was among those who answered John's call and was baptized by him,[55] but later his own circle of disciples grew up around him too. Miracle-working and other expressions of charisma convinced numerous people that he was a Godsend, and, apparently, many or most of them thought that God had sent him to deal with the first conflict. That

---

[54] On priestly standards of purity shared by Qumran and the priestly "Sadducees" (as reported in rabbinic literature), see J. M. Baumgarten, *JJS* 31 (1980), pp. 157–170. Cf. below, p. 116, n. 43.

[55] For a reconstruction of Jesus' early Johannine discipleship as having been very considerable and extensive, see now Murphy-O'Connor (above, n. 2).

is, they thought he would redeem Israel from the Roman yoke.[56] Pilate heard of it and dealt with Jesus the way he and his colleagues dealt with such individuals — leaving his followers, such as those on the road to Emmaus, convinced that they had been mistaken ((Luke 24:17 [sad],21 [past tense hope]). For it is impossible that a true Godsend could be defeated.

However, Jesus' disciples somehow became convinced that he had risen from the dead, a miracle which meant they had not been fooled: Jesus was indeed a Godsend. But Roman rule remained unchanged, so all they could do, as the first several chapters of Acts show, is prophesy a second round: the Crucifixion was but the end of the first battle, but in the next God and His Messiah will be victorious. But such reliance on past miracles as guarantors of future salvation is nothing new in the Jewish world, and entailed no departures. Moreover, it wasn't really needed: if all the Resurrection meant was that God could intervene in history if He chose, what did it add to the Ten Plagues and the parting of the Red Sea? So Jesus' resurrection was still something of an answer looking for a problem.

This is where Paul fits in. He applied Jesus and his resurrection not to the nation's problem, but rather to the individual's. Man, yearning to be perfect, but bound to observe a law which, in his human frailty, he could never fully observe; man, bound by God to his body and to law, and thus to sin and to death; man, however, who has no authority to stop the treadmill himself — how can he ever be saved? For such a man, who admits that he is bound by the law, admits that he cannot fulfill it, and admits — as Philo's opponents in *De migr. Abr.* did not — that he himself lacks the authority to ignore it, it was ever so attractive to interpret the divine intervention as the final release. This was especially the case in that the final miracle of Jesus was specifically the imparting of new but spiritual *life,* which contrasts so well with the law which was entrusted to the body and led to sin and death. While Paul struggled to find an exegetical basis for the conclusion that Christ ended the law, the need for it is clear.[57]

---

[56] We sidestep here the question as to whether this popular Jewish and Roman understanding of Jesus was justified; cf. below, pp. 128–146.

[57] For Paul's understanding of Christ as a scapegoat whose death ends sin (which Paul identified with the Law), see *JBL* 102 (1983), pp. 259–268. Recently, R. G. Hamerton-Kelly (*NTS* 36 [1990], pp. 114–115) has accepted my suggestion that Galatians 3:13 and 4:4–6 are to be understood on the basis of the scapegoat notion, and that Romans 8:32 is to be understood on the background of II Samuel 21:1–14. However, he sees the relationship as one of "travesty," rather than analogy, primarily because God is not the recipient of either sacrifice. However, God is not the recipient of the scapegoat either; note the careful and repeated distinction between God and Azazel in Leviticus 16:8–10. Thus, this point supports the analogy. Moreover, I am not convinced that the "sending out" of Galatians 4:4–6 should be understood as a reference to the birth of Jesus, rather than his death. Both for the biblical scapegoat and for Paul on Jesus, death was the significant point; "born of a woman" seems to describe *who* was sent, not *how* (or whither) he was sent. Cf. above, n. 47.

Pauline Christianity, in other words, is a religion which responds to the universal condition of man, who yearns to be better than he is and feels that it is his body which holds him back from that. It holds up to him a model of dying to the flesh and being resurrected, "born again," into a spiritual life. Such a religion contrasts with classical Judaism, which hardly has the terminology to speak of souls without bodies, and which — its monotheism notwithstanding — is based around a specific covenant between God and one small part of humanity. So Pauline Christianity could arise out of Judaism only on the basis of developments which directed Jews not only away from territory and descent, but also toward perfectionism, and in contexts where the unrelativized and absolute obligation to fulfill the law had been at least called into question. Such developments, we have indicated, occurred in the contexts of Qumran and the Hellenistic Diaspora, the very contexts which, in the fulness of time, supplied John the Baptist and Paul.

Thus, while it would be foolhardy to attempt to fix John's precise relation with Qumran, or to discover Paul's curriculum in Tarsus (or Jerusalem) or what precisely happened to him on the way to Damascus, and while "the quest for the historical Jesus" is encumbered by obstacles which are perhaps insuperable, we may say that all their manifold differences notwithstanding, the Qumran and Hellenistic versions of first-century Judaism could indeed combine well in the foundation of a single movement. As so often happens, the extremes meet. Under the influence of such imponderable catalysts as a charismatic miracle-worker whose disciples met him after he died, something new emerged.

Politics and Sectarianism
in Second Temple Period Judaea

1. Temple and Desert:
On Religion and State in Second Temple Period Judaea[*]

This study's point of departure is a collection of obscure Josephan narratives, most in his *Antiquities* and one in the *Jewish War*, dealing with clashes between religious figures and Roman authorities in first-century Judaea. The obscurity results from Josephus' failure to explain the clashes. He merely reports what happens, without explaining why. While such obscurity is not entirely rare in Josephus, and may at times result merely from carelessness or the like, it seems that the obscurity in these cases has a meaningful origin.

In all of the cases we shall cite, Josephus reports religious figures who went out into the desert, whither they were followed by Roman soldiers and cavalry who attacked and stamped them out. Josephus always makes it clear that he approves of the Roman action and believes that the victims got their due. But he never clarifies what their crime was, he never clarifies why the Romans were justified in doing what they did. Thus, for our first example, we read of the following event in the mid-forties:

1. *Ant.* 20.97−99:[1]

During the period when Fadus was procurator of Judaea, a certain impostor named Theudas persuaded the majority of the masses to take up their possessions and to follow him to the Jordan River. He stated that he was a prophet and that at his command the river would be parted and would provide them an easy passage. With this talk he deceived many. Fadus, however, did not permit them to reap the fruit of their folly, but sent against them a squadron of cavalry. These fell upon them unexpectedly, slew many of them and took many prisoners. Theudas himself was captured, whereupon they cut off his head and brought it to Jerusalem.

As noted, it is clear that Josephus is on Fadus' side. Josephus' tone and diction makes his attitude clear. But what, in fact, motivated Fadus? Did he really believe that Theudas could split the Jordan? And even if Theudas had succeeded, what was threatening or illegal about him and his followers crossing to the other side of the river? How did Theudas threaten public order or any other legitimate concern of the Roman governor of Judaea?

---

[*] Hebrew original: *Priesthood and Monarchy* (Proceedings of the 1983 Convention of the Israel Historical Society; edd. I. Gafni and G. Motzkin; 1987), pp. 61−78.

[1] Here and below, the translations from *Ant.* 20 are Feldman's (LCL).

Of course, we could easily fill in the story. Fadus might have feared the growth of a movement of enthusiasts of a latter-day Joshua;[2] whether or not Theudas succeeded, such people might plan to pursue the conquest of the Holy Land,[3] and it was best to nip the movement in the bud. Had Josephus written something like that, all would have been clear. But he didn't.

Here are another four such passages:

2. *Ant.* 20.167−168:

With such pollution (scil. aforementioned murders in Jerusalem and the Temple) did the deeds of the brigands infect the city. Moreover, impostors and deceivers called upon the mob to follow them into the desert. For they said that they would show them unmistakable marvels and signs that would be wrought in harmony with God's design. Many were, in fact, persuaded and paid the penalty of their folly;[4] for they were brought before Felix and he punished them.

What is illegal or threatening about promising signs and wonders in the desert?

3. In *Ant.* 20.169−172, immediately after the preceding narrative, Josephus reports that an Egyptian "prophet" coaxed a multitude to follow him to the Mount of Olives, from which he would order the walls of Jerusalem to fall, thus allowing entrance into the city. Felix sent infantry and cavalry against this crowd, killing many and capturing hundreds of others. This story, with its reference to the city's defenses falling and an entrance into the city, at least explains what the governor might fear. But did Felix really think the walls would fall at this "prophet's" command?

4. *Ant.* 20.188, in Josephus' narrative about Festus (Felix's successor), after a report about the Sicarii and their murderous activities, is another enigmatically skeletal notice:

Festus also sent a force of cavalry and infantry against the dupes of a certain impostor[5] who had promised them salvation and rest from troubles, if they chose to follow him into the wilderness. The force which Festus dispatched destroyed both the deceiver himself and those who had followed them.

5. In *BJ* 7.437 ff., Josephus narrates the adventures of Jonathan the Weaver, in Cyrene. Jonathan, who seems to have been a Judaean rebel who wound up

---

[2] According to the other ancient source which mentions Theudas, Acts 5:36, Theudas thought himself to be "someone," listed in the same breath as Judas the Galilean and Jesus of Nazareth.

[3] We are not told in which direction Theudas hoped to cross the river. S. G. F. Brandon assumed that the crossing was eastward (*Jesus and the Zealots* [1967], pp. 100−101), but in light of the Roman fears, and of the Book of Joshua, westward seems more likely.

[4] *aphrosynē*, as in *Ant.* 20.98 (above).

[5] *anthrōpos goēs* − as *goēs anēr* in 20.97 and *goētes* in *Ant.* 20.167 (above). On its use of (false) prophets, see Feldman, pp. 440−441, n.b.

in Cyrene after the war, is said to have convinced not a few indigent Jews to follow him into the desert, where they would see "signs and visions." Most people, according to Josephus, realized that he was a fake, but the more respectable Jews of the region nevertheless informed the governor about Jonathan's "departure and preparations (*paraskeuē* – § 439)." Preparations for what? Josephus gives no information whatsoever about any crime or anti-Roman activity or plans for same, so the reader is left wondering – or imagining – why the army was sent out to squash him.

These narratives, and similar ones,[6] all leave the same question: Why did the Romans attack the Jews in question? And they all invite the same response: The Romans feared that those who went out into the desert would, whether or not the promised wonders occurred there, return and attack the Roman garrison and order. And this response is indeed a likely one; note, for example, the fact that in three of our five cases[7] the Romans killed some and captured some. This indicates that there was a battle, which in turn implies that the Jews were armed with more than mere hopes for miracles. Indeed, the account of the Egyptian prophet explicitly refers to such a "battle" (*Ant.* 20.172), and Acts 21:38, the only other ancient source to mention him, says his followers were Sicarii. Below, furthermore, we will bring decisive evidence for their warlike nature.[8] But if this expansion of Josephus' accounts is indeed the correct one, as seens apparent, then we must ask the historiographical question: Why does Josephus leave it to our imagination?

Moreover – and here is the decisive evidence promised above – the fact is that Josephus himself, in other versions of stories 2, 3 and 5 (the others are unparalleled in his writings), gives our explanation, identifying the governors' victims as dangerous rebels! Namely, *BJ* 2.259–260 specifies that the "signs and wonders" of *Ant.* 20.167–168 were "signs of freedom,"[9] and the promises encouraged "rebellion and revolution." Felix, accordingly, saw the exodus to the desert as "the onset of rebellion" – so his move to squash them is quite understandable. Again, *BJ* 2.261–263 has the Egyptian prophet planning not merely to *order* the walls of Jerusalem to fall (as in *Ant.*), but rather to enter Jerusalem with force and overcome the Roman garrison with the assistance of those who would attack together with him. Afterwards, he planned to rule the city as a tyrant. Felix, however, moved to forestall his "attack." (It is

---

[6] Such as the episode of the Samaritan prophet in the days of Pilate (*Ant.* 18.85–89) and two episodes which shall be discussed below: the death of John the Baptist (ibid. §§ 116–119) and the Essenes' suffering during the war of 66 (*BJ* 2.152–153).

[7] The exceptions are *Ant.* 20.167–168 and 20.185–187.

[8] Similarly, in the Samaritan episode mentioned in n. 6 Josephus specifically says that the prophet's followers were armed.

[9] For the political implications of *eleutheria*, see T. Rajak, *Josephus: The Historian and His Society* (1983), pp. 139–140.

important for our theme to add that *BJ* also gives an important detail missing
from the *Ant.* report: this prophet's followers came with him to the Mount of
Olives not simply from Jerusalem, but rather from the *desert*.) Finally, *Vita*
424—425 retells the story of Jonathan the Weaver, but plainly describes him as
one who "aroused rebellion" (*stasin exegeiras*) in Cyrene. Moreover, although
the *BJ* account had stressed that Jonathan and his followers had been unarmed
(*BJ* 7.440), the whole point of the *Vita* story is that Jonathan, after his capture,
had falsely accused Josephus of having supplied him arms and money. On the
other hand, *BJ* had stated that Jonathan promised "signs and visions" in the
desert, but nothing like this appears in the *Vita* account.

   If Josephus can tell these stories in a way which makes sense and which
conforms to our historical understanding, why did he abstain from doing so in
the versions we first cited?

   To answer this, it appears that we should give due weight to the fact that *BJ*
2, as most of *BJ*, was written well before *Ant.*, while *BJ* 7, or at least its
narrative on Cyrene and Jonathan the Weaver, was composed — as Seth
Schwartz has cogently shown — around the same time as *Vita* and *Ant.* The
bulk of *BJ* was written by Josephus no more than a decade after the Temple
was destroyed and after only a few years of life in Rome; *Ant.*, *Vita* and *BJ* 7
were composed in the nineties.[10] Now, in *BJ* 2, as we have seen, Josephus did
not try to hide the religious nature of the rebels he described. He condemned
them, of course, for he knew they had been false prophets and that people of
their ilk brought catastrophe upon the Jews, but he admitted that they
operated with religious claims and pretensions. In other words, in *BJ* 2
Josephus portrays religious people operating for religious reasons in the arena
of state, and it is therefore understandable that those responsible for the state
moved against them. In the *Antiquities* versions of the same stories, however,
as in those others cited above which are without parallel in *BJ*, Josephus splits
the two spheres. Those who move in the religious sphere have no connection
with the state (leaving us wondering why the state suppressed them). The case
of Jonathan the Weaver, of whom both narratives stem from the nineties, is
especially interesting: Josephus was willing to make him only an armed rebel
(as in *Vita*) or only an unarmed religious leader (as in *BJ* 7), but he is not

---

   [10] On the chronology of Josephus' works, see, inter alia, Rajak, ibid., pp. 195, 237—238; P.
Bilde, *Flavius Josephus between Jerusalem and Rome: His Life, his Works, and their
Importance* (1988), pp. 79 (*BJ*) and 103—104 (*Ant.*). All we know of the dating of *Vita* is that,
at least in its current form, it was completed after the *Antiquities* (see below, pp. 243—275).
As for *BJ* 7, see S. Schwartz, *HTR* 79 (1986), pp. 373—386, where it is shown that *BJ*
7.437—453 must have been added in the nineties, for the governor of Lybia, whose death is
described here so vividly, died no earlier than 93 C.E. (Indeed, Schwartz argues that this
episode was in fact added no earlier than under Trajan [see esp. p. 383]; this additional
precision is immaterial for us here.)

willing to allow him, as the villains of *BJ* 2, to operate in both spheres. Similarly, while *BJ* 2.264, right after the account of the Egyptian prophet, reports that the (religious) "impostors" and the "brigands" joined forces and incited to further revolt, the parallel in *Ant.* 20.172 has the "brigands" acting alone.

Josephus, in other words, in the nineties of the first century, is trying to convince his readers that the Jewish religion has no political implications. It is, therefore, no threat at all to the state, and should be tolerated, not persecuted.

It will readily be admitted that Josephus' approach is not totally consistent or unambguous. Apart from occasional "sloppiness" (to borrow one of S.J.D. Cohen's favorite terms), two special reasons may be adduced. First of all, although the best apologetic approach would have been simply to ignore these episodes, Josephus' conscience as an historian forced him to tell the stories (cf. below, p. 115). And, second, some of the more central rebels had undeniably religious platforms,[11] and they were so well-known that Josephus could not attempt to ignore them, as in the cases of these little-known desert prophets. Therefore, to the extent the former are mentioned in his later writings — luckily for Josephus, this was a small extent — he had to deal with them religiously. He does this by attacking them, as severely as possible. Nevertheless, the reader easily infers that there was a debate among various versions of Judaism, not a conflict between Judaism and rebels acting out of non- or anti-religious motives. In other words, Josephus was forced to admit that Judas the Galilean was the founder of a philosophy (*BJ* 2.118; *Ant.* 18.4–10, 23–25), however despicable that philosophy was. And this dispute was a matter of great consequence in Roman eyes, not merely obscure theological controversy about "words and names and your law" (Acts 18:15). Although Josephus would have rather avoided such matters, some rebels with religious platforms were so well known that they could not be swept under the carpet.

But, despite the inconsistencies, the fact remains that Josephus, in the nineties, attempted to portray the Jewish religion as unrelated to statehood. This attempt is reflected elsewhere in the *Antiquities* as well. A few other cases may be summarily mentioned: 1) his rewriting of I Maccabees in an attempt to make the Maccabees religious martyrs instead of rebels;[12] 2) his attempt to portray the Pharisees as religious figures divorced from involvement in the affairs of the state (see especially *Antiquities* 18.15);[13] and 3) his attempt, in

---

[11] The modern recognition of this is largely due to the influence of M. Hengel's *Die Zeloten* (1961; 1976²; English edition, 1989). Cf. below, pp. 134–135.

[12] See I. Gafni, in *Josephus, the Bible, and History* (edd. L. H. Feldman and G. Hata; 1989), pp. 116–131.

[13] On this not entirely successful attempt, see my study in *JSJ* 14 (1983), pp. 157–171. On the Pharisees in Josephus, see also below, p. 265, n. 60.

Antiquities and *Contra Apionem*, to portray the Jews as members of a religious community (*politeuma*), not as a people or a state, even in prior periods when they were one or the other.[14]

In *BJ*, in contrast, written in the seventies, Josephus has not yet made this attempt, although he does attempt to portray legitimate Jewish religion as opposed to rebellion against Rome.[15] Apparently, it took some time before Josephus grasped the full meaning of the destruction of the Temple. For it was the Temple, God's house, which embodied the notion of Jewish territorialism, statehood; it was the Temple which seemed to be a king's palace, making Jerusalem a capital and Judaea a Jewish state.[16] Only after the Temple was destroyed could Josephus begin thinking of "being Jewish" as matter of religion without state. And the fact that he himself was doing this rethinking in Rome, not in Judaea, made the conclusion all the more compelling.[17]

If we therefore suppose that Judaean rebels acted out of a religious motivation, a Holy Land ideology, a "zeal for the Temple" due to their view that it — not Rome or its branch office in Caesarea — constituted the seat of the Judaean sovereign, and that Josephus faithfully reflected this linkage of religion and state in his first book but apologetically tried to hide it in his later works, where he instead reflected the realities of post-Destruction Diaspora existence, then a new problem arises. Why, indeed, did the rebels he portrays, at a time when the Temple stood, seek the Sovereign's revelations in the desert of all places? By way of comparison, note that it is totally intelligible, if shocking, that many true believers gathered in the Temple courts on the very day they were burnt, due to the expectation, fostered by "false prophets," that "signs of salvation" would be given there (*BJ* 6.285). For the Temple was the most reasonable of all places for such revelations, and it was theologically reasonable (although in fact suicidal) to suppose that it "would be saved by

---

[14] See my study in *Scripta Classica Israelica* 7 (1983/84), pp. 30–52.

[15] On his attempt to camouflage the logic and motives of the rebellious priests who stopped the loyalty sacrifices for Rome and thereby touched off the rebellion of 66, and on his denial of their legitimacy, see below, below, pp. 108–116.

[16] One notes, for example, that the Temple was frequently the site of clashes with the Roman occupying force; see esp. *BJ* 1.58, also S. Safrai, *Die Wallfahrt im Zeitalter des Zweiten Tempels* (1981), pp. 204–206. On the national fervor awakened by mass pilgrimages, see also Philo, *De specialibus legibus* 1.69, and, in general, for the Temple as a focus of national sentiment, *BJ* 6.239 and 7.421. For invasions of Palestine being perceived as threats against the Temple, compare *Damascus Document* 1:3 with II Chronicles 36:16; see also Judith 4:2 and 9:8; I Maccabees 14:29, 31; II Maccabees 15:18; LXX Esther 4:17o (Rahlfs), etc. On "Zeal for the Temple," see also Hengel (above, n. 11 [1976]), pp. 188–229. Finally, on the incidents which almost touched off rebellion in 39/40 C.E. and did so in 66, see below, n. 38.

[17] This understanding of Josephus as a Diasporan Jew owes much to Abraham Schalit; see, for example, *Zur Josephus-Forschung* (ed. A. Schalit; 1973), p. viii. On his views and their development, see my essay in *Jewish History* 2/2 (Fall 1987), pp. 9–28.

Him who resides in it" (*BJ* 5.459). But what shall we say of prophets, and their believers, who sought revelations and signs in the desert?

Of course, a simple solution is that "one obvious advantage of disappearing into the desert was escaping the tax-collector."[18] Since the biblical days of Moses, David and Elijah, who were imitated by "Hasidim" (I Maccabees 2) and Qumranites in more recent times, the desert had always been a good place in which to flee undesired or feared governmental authority. Particularly apposite in the present context is the case reported in *BJ* 6.351: Simon ben Giora and John of Gischala, two of the leaders of the lost rebellion, asked Titus' permission to surrender and depart into the desert, "leaving him the city."

However, while the last paragraph might illustrate the obvious fact that anti-Romans might prefer the desert to the Roman city, it fails to explain the expectation of signs and wonders and revelations there. And as for Simon and John, why should they – attempting to avoid captivity, enslavement or worse – be compared to those we want to understand, who went into the desert of their own free will (not in order to escape punishment) and, it seems, planned to come back to the city thereafter? Rather, to understand such people, we ought to turn to the literature of the only documentable desert group of the period – the Qumran sect.

If we assume, as we do and as is usual, that the Qumran sect was Essene,[19] then it results that Josephus' account of the latter is especially notable due to its *failure* to note two important foci of the sect. Namely, Josephus' accounts

---

[18] Rajak (above, n. 9), p. 38, n. 77.

[19] There are, of course, continuing debates; see, among the more recent pieces, N. Golb and M. O. Wise in *Journal of Near Eastern Studies* 49 (1990), pp. 103–114 and 202–4, respectively. It seems clear, however, that the similarity is so great, and the lack of any other candidates for identification with the Qumran sect is so clear, that the Essene identification should be accepted until something stronger than hitherto be adduced against it or in favor of another identification. Most of the arguments stem from discrepancies between Josephus' account of the Essenes and what emerges from the Scrolls (so e.g., Wise, loc. cit.), but between what may reasonably be chalked up to change over time, to Josephus' ignorance or – as in the present case – to his apologetic needs, little remains. Thus, for example, Golb's major case is based on the contrast between the obvious fact that the Romans required military force to take the Qumran settlement, on the one hand, and Philo's claim (*Every Good Man is Free* § 78) that the Essenes were pacifists. However, Josephus does not say the Essenes were pacifists, and *BJ* 2.125 and 139 (as well as § 567 and 3.11–12) contradict that notion; see T. S. Beall, *Josephus' Description of the Essenes Illustrated by the Dead Sea Scrolls* (1988), pp. 67–68. Golb's claim is largely based on the *argumentum ex silentio* (p. 108) that Josephus "nowhere indicates that groups of Essenes militarily resisted the Romans" to which Golb immediately adds, in misplaced trust, that "judging from his careful descriptions of the parts played by zealots, *sicarii*, and others in the revolt, he would obviously have noted [such resistance], either in his recounting of the war or his lengthy description of the Essenes, were it true." The fact is that Josephus' accounts of the Essenes give them such a positive valence that he had every reason in the world to hide their military resistance, if he knew of it. In any

give us no more than an extremely faint hint of the extremely important role *priests* played in the sect,[20] and even less than that of its apocalyptic vision and tension. Given their prominence in the Qumran scrolls, it is difficult to imagine that Josephus (or his sources) did not know of these foci. Rather, it is far likelier that they were deliberately ignored due to apologetic considerations. For Josephus, a proud priest and descendant of the Hasmoneans, had no interest in revealing that his ancestors were bitterly criticized for usurping the Zadokite high priesthood and that there was a priestly opposition to his colleagues, "the last priests of Jerusalem."[21] Similarly, he had no interest in revealing that one of the three "legitimate" versions of Judaism − as opposed to that rebellious "Fourth Philosophy" (note the contexts of *BJ* 2.119 and *Ant.* 18.11!) − looked forward with gusto to the destruction of the Roman Empire (the "Kittim"), along with all other Sons of Darkness.[22] Such a revelation would have ruined the positive attitude toward this sect which his accounts all attempt to induce. Rather, Josephus has the Essenes swear always to obey constituted authority, for there is no authority not given by God (*BJ* 2.140).

Josephus' presentation of the Essenes forced him, however, into another case of his now-familiar predicament. For if the Essenes were such obedient subjects of constituted authority, why were so many of them tortured by the Romans at the time of the rebellion (*BJ* 2.152−153)? (And why, we may add, did the Romans destroy the Qumran settlement in 68 C.E.?) It is true that

---

case, finally, the fact that a religious settlement was taken in battle, in the course of a general rebellion, need not tell us anything significant about its usual population and its attitude toward war and the rebellion. Witness the case of Jerusalem's Old City in the 1948 war, in which the extremely Orthodox population, which was incapable of defending itself, and also somewhat constitutionally opposed to doing so, was taken over and defended − frequently against its own protests − by fighters sent in by groups of a radically different orientation. Similarly, Wise (p. 204) complains that Beall (p. 54), who cites evidence for Qumran use of a solar calendar as illustrating Josephus statement that the Essenes revere the sun (*BJ* 2.128), fails to cite other Qumran evidence, which indicates the use of a lunar calendar. For that evidence Wise refers to J. M. Baumgarten, *Revue de Qumran* 12 (1985−1987), pp. 399−407, and perhaps Beall should have too. But Wise fails to note Baumgarten's argument and evidence that that lunar calendar belonged to the early baggage of Qumran, which was later replaced − by Josephus' day − by the solar calendar.

[20] On priests in Qumran, cf. above, pp. 19−20. As for the Josephan non-evidence, cf. below, pp. 61−62, n. 17.

[21] On this topic see my essay in *Archaeology and History in the Dead Sea Scrolls: The New York University Conference in Memory of Yigael Yadin* (ed. L. H. Schiffman; 1990), esp. pp. 158−165, which, however, was unfortunately printed from uncorrected galleys. For Qumran criticism of the Jerusalem Temple and priesthood, see also G. Klinzing, *Die Umdeutung des Kultus in der Qumrangemeinde und im Neuen Testament* (1971), pp. 11−20, and J. M. Baumgarten, *Studies in Qumran Law* (1977), pp. 40−46.

[22] Apart from the War Scroll, see esp. *Pesher Nahum* and the *Manual of Discipline* 9:21−23, along with D. Flusser, *Zion* 48 (1982/83), esp. pp. 165−168 (in Hebrew).

Josephus does supply an explanation in this case: he claims that the Essenes were tortured "in order to induce them to blaspheme the(ir?) lawgiver or to eat some forbidden thing." However, we have no other evidence of religious persecution at the time of this rebellion. Rather, it is likely that Josephus simply did for the Essenes what he also did for the Hasmoneans (n. 12): he turned rebels into martyrs. The only hints he left of the real truth are the two references to John the Essene, one of the rebel generals (*BJ* 2.567; 3.11). Thus, what I Maccabees does for the Hasmoneans, and Josephus' own *BJ* account did for several of the desert prophets, the Scrolls do for the Essenes. Where would we be if we had to depend upon Josephus alone?

We turned to the Qumran sect to understand the desert prophets and have so far established that the sect shared their anti-Roman animus and was, therefore, treated somewhat similarly by Josephus. Returning, then, to our question about revelations in the desert, we will not be surprised to find that the Qumran literature is quite helpful. Namely, the sect not only condemned the current Temple and priesthood in Jerusalem; it also considered itself as their replacement. The sect's priests were the only legitimate priests, and the community replaced the Temple. As the Manual of Discipline, that central sectarian text, phrases it, the sect's membership is divided into two "houses," a holy house of Israel (laity) and a Holy of Holy house for Aaron (the priests); together, they fulfill that eminently Temple task of working atonement (see esp. *Manual of Discipline* 8:1–10 and 9:3–7). The Temple of Jerusalem, in contrast, is "desolate" (*4QFlorilegium* 1:5), and the sectarians awaited the day when they could return to "the desert (!) of Jerusalem" and restore the proper cult there (*War Scroll* 1:3; 2). Correspondingly, while until that day only the sect lived according to the correct calendar, in the end "all the times of desolation will come to an end" (*Hodayot* 12:16–17). In other words, the sectarians viewed Qumran as the Divine Presence's residence in exile, while the Temple in Jerusalem was itself an empty desert.[23]

On such a view, it is indeed reasonable to expect divine revelation more in the desert than in the polluted Temple. And, indeed, this seems to be reflected by the Qumran sect's repeated mobilization of Isaiah 40:3, "the voice calling in the wilderness" (so they construe the verse), in order to explain its own existence there (*Manual of Discipline* 8:13–16; 9:19–20). While the parallelism in the text leads *us* to divide "the voice" from "in the wilderness,"

---

[23] On the community as a functional replacement for the Temple in Qumran, see below, n. 25. As for my understanding of 4QFlorilegium, see *Revue de Qumran* 10 (1979–81), pp. 83–91. In general, on the notion of Qumran as a "Gegenstadt" in contrast to Jerusalem, cf. O. Betz's discussion apropos of *BJ* 5.73 (*antipolizontos*) in *Wort und Wirklichkeit: Studien zur Afrikanistik und Orientalistik*, I (*Festschrift E. L. Rapp*; ed. B. Benzing et al; 1976), pp. 104–106 (reprinted in Betz's *Jesus – Der Messias Israels: Aufsätze zur biblischen Theologie* [1987], pp. 33–35).

rather making the latter the beginning of a quotation, the sect rather inferred that the voice called in the wilderness. And it is interesting that John the Baptist apparently punctuated the verse the same way; as many scholars have agreed, John is probably to be understood on the background of Qumran. Indeed, from our point of view it is important to note that Josephus, in *Ant.* 18.116–119, leaves us in the familiar dark: he portrays John as a religious figure only, and thus leaves us no guessing why Herod Antipas feared him and had him killed. The Gospels, which report John's condemnation of the Herodian's incestuous relationship, fill out the picture.[24]

Qumran thus shows us religious Jews who expected and claimed revelation in the desert. These sectarians justified this by viewing their community as a functional substitute for the Temple.[25] Presumably something similar was the case for the rebels so incompletely reported by Josephus: although they did not form lasting communities, they obviously did feel that the locus of sanctity had been removed from Jerusalem to the desert. Perhaps, in other words, we should assume that they, or some of them, were like John the Baptist, people to be understood on the background of Qumran although not part of its sectarian framework. More likely, however, this willingness to divorce sanctity from the Temple and find it elsewhere was more general. As it seems, a few factors, traceable to the Hasmonean period, made such a development quite likely. In our opinion, three such factors are especially important, two negative and one positive:

1. If prior to the Hasmonean period Judaea was a small "Temple-state" (see above, p. 9, n. 18), the Hasmonean period saw it expand to include regions inhabited by non-Jews. This forced the Hasmonean high priests to explain by what right they ruled such Gentiles: What claim can a Jewish high priest make upon a Syrian, an Arab, or a descendant of Greeks or Macedonians? One approach was to convert the latter to Judaism under duress. But although this

---

[24] On John the Baptist and Qumran, see above, pp. 3, 24. On the text and authenticity of Josephus' account of John, see E. Nodet, *RB* 92 (1985), esp. pp. 322–331. On the discrepancy between Josephus' statement that Antipas feared John, and Josephus' own account of John as a "good man" who preached virtue, justice and piety, see J. Gnilka, in *Orientierung an Jesus: Zur Theologie der Syoptiker, Für Josef Schmid* (ed. P. Hoffmann et al.; 1973), p. 90.

[25] See Klinzing (above, n. 21), also B. Gärtner, *The Temple and the Community in Qumran and the New Testament* (1965), and H. Lichtenberger, in *Approaches to Ancient Judaism*, II (ed. W. S. Green; 1980), pp. 159–171. I refrain from saying more simply that the Qumran community considered itself a Temple because I know of no source which does so explicitly (see *Revue de Qumran* 10 [1979], pp. 83–91, 435–446), and the avoidance may have been important to them, just as Jews traditionally term their houses of worship "synagogues" and not "temples." Functionally, however, synagogues may well satisfy the same needs the Temple did, and the Qumran community did substitute for the Temple.

was tried in a few well-known cases,[26] it is not promising or tasteful. Rather, the more lasting solution was to turn the Jewish religious authority into a temporal authority, a king. This, then, is why the Hasmoneans, by the end of the second century, were forced to add the royal crown to the priestly diadem (*BJ* 1.70; *Ant.* 13.301). But it amounts to the separation of religion from state — a precedent which the Romans took over with open arms a few decades later. The end of the process would come in the Roman period, when Caesarea was constituted as a political capital of Judaea, leaving Jerusalem a religious capital alone in Roman eyes. But this process made it natural, especially for sectarian opponents of the Hasmoneans and the Romans, such as the Qumranites, to deny any link between sanctity and a given place; sanctity was where right religion was.

2. Parallel to the first development, we note, beginning with the early Hasmoneans or somewhat earlier, a good bit of criticism concerning the morality and the very legitimacy of the Jerusalem priesthood.[27] While the criticism at first related to the formal aspects of priestly legitimacy (Aaronite and Zadokite descent)[28] and formal complaints about the Temple service (such as the calendar controversy),[29] as time went by, and, especially, in the Roman period, we find more and more criticism of the ruling priesthood's morality.[30]

---

[26] For the most recent and most thorough examination of all the data, see A. Kasher, *Jews, Idumaeans, and Ancient Arabs . . .* (1988), ch. 3. However, I would agree with C. Hoffmann (*Historische Zeitschrift* 251 [1990], pp. 117−118) that Kasher's well-meaning attempt (in the wake of some predecessors) to deny the coercive nature of these conversions fails to convince. As for the motivation of these measures, I see no reason to complicate the matter by assuming that they resulted from a desire specifically *to purify* the Land (as assumed recently by E. Will and C. Orrieux, *Ioudaïsmos-Hellènismos: Essai sur le judaïsme judéen à l'époque hellénistique* [1986], pp. 191−193, 196, 211) rather than simply by a desire to establish jurisdiction.

[27] I have collected these sources in my dissertation, "Priesthood, Temple, Sacrifice: Opposition and Spiritualization in the Late Second Temple Period" (Hebrew University, 1979), pp. 14−25 (formal complaints), 26−35 (morality). Numerous references are also assembled by M.D. Herr in *Zion* 44 (1978/79 = *Yitzhak F. Baer Memorial Volume*; 1980), pp. 49−50 (in Hebrew).

[28] So among the Sadducees, the Essenes and the Oniads (of Leontopolis); see above, n. 21. In *JSJ* 14 (1983), pp. 161−162, I ventured the speculation that Josephus, in writing *Ant.* 13.171−173, eliminated his source's reference to such criticism.

[29] On the latter, see esp. S. Talmon, in *Aspects of the Dead Sea Scrolls* (Scripta Hierosolymitana 4, edd. C. Rabin and Y. Yadin; 1958), pp. 162−199 (somewhat revised in his *The World of Qumran from Within: Collected Studies* [1989], pp. 147−185). Cf. above, end of n. 19.

[30] See, inter alia, *Damascus Document* 4:6−8; Psalms of Solomon 8:17; *Testament of Levi* 14:3 and 17:1; *Pesher Habakkuk* 8:8−11; 9:4−6; 12:7−10; *Testament of Moses* 5−7; *Ant.* 20.181, 199−201; m.*Shekalim* 1:4; m.*Ketubbot* 1:2; Tos.*Menahot* 13:18−20; BT *Pesachim* 57a (on the "shrieks" recorded here, see *JQR* 72 [1981/82], pp. 262−268).

The first factor tended to deny the Temple's political function, but the latter tended to undermine its religious significance too. The third factor, the positive one, to which we shall now turn, opened the way to save the Temple, as it were, by moving it elsewhere.

3. Hellenism made more and more of an impact upon Judaea as time went by. True, such impact may be exaggerated, and it seems that the major attempt in our generation to assess Hellenism in Palestine put too much too early: it focused upon the pre-Hasmonean period. But the rebellion's success and the rise of the Hasmonean state brought Judaea into a new league, and it did not run away from it.[31]

Now from our point of view, what is especially interesting here is the fact that critiques of the Temple cult during the late Second Temple period frequently reveal Hellenistic influence. In earlier epochs one sometimes hears emphasis upon God's transcendence as part of a criticism or relativization of the Temple.[32] But it is only in the Second Temple period that we find something which is not a temple (world, community, sage or pious man) being called a temple — a transference of terminology made possible by the recognition of the presence of divinity within it. This seems to be predicated upon a Hellenistic analysis of being into matter and essence ("forms" or the like): if the Temple is the House of God, then it is where God is, so wherever God is is a Temple. And the Hellenistic background is proven by the fact that two Hellenistic Jews, Philo and Paul, were, along with Stephen "the Hellenist" (Acts 6–7) and the authors of the Gospel of John and of the Epistle

---

[31] The major attempt is, of course, M. Hengel's *Judentum und Hellenismus: Studien zu ihrer Begegnung unter besonderer Berücksichtigung Palästinas bis zur Mitte des 2. Jh. v. Chr.* (1969, 1988³; English version, 1974). Later, however, Hengel moved into later periods, where one can trace Hellenism much more securely; see his *Juden, Griechen und Barbaren: Aspekte der Hellenisierung des Judentums in vorchristlicher Zeit* (1976) and, most recently, his *The 'Hellenization' of Judaea in the First Century after Christ* (1989). For references to some critiques of *Judentum und Hellenismus*, which focused mostly on the propriety of inferences from the Jewish Diaspora, from non-Jewish Palestine and from later periods, see my review of Hengel's 1976 volume: *IEJ* 35 (1985), pp. 206–207; add A. Momigliano, *JTS* 21 (1970), pp. 149–153 (and *JTS* 27 [1976], pp. 168–169). On Hellenism in Palestine in the pre-Hasmonean period, see also M. Stern's essay in *Acculturation and Assimilation: Continuity and Change in the Cultures of Israel and the Nations* (edd. Y. Kaplan and M. Stern; 1989), pp. 41–60 (in Hebrew). The final chapter of Will-Orrieux (above, n. 26: pp. 177–224) is dedicated to the Hellenization of the Hasmonean state; so too a soon-to-be-published Hebrew paper presented by U. Rappaport at the 1989 Haifa/Tel-Aviv conference on "The Hasmonean State."

[32] So, for example, I Kings 8:27 and Isaiah 66:1. But divine transcendence need not lead to criticism of the Temple; on the natural passage in Psalm 24 from "the earth is the Lord's in all in its fulness," on the one hand, to "the mountain of the Lord" and "His holy place," on the other, see R.J.Z. Werblowsky's comments in *Das Land Israel in biblischer Zeit* (ed. G. Strecker; 1981), p. 1.

to the Hebrews, the prime exponents of such views.[33] But it must also be recognized that the Qumran community, which viewed its own essence as that of a Temple and Jerusalem's essence as that of a desert, derives from the same type of thought. Since we don't find Greeks or Greek literature in Qumran, such thought must have been in the air (although one need not subscribe to all which has been ascribed to it).[34] Some more evidence for this type of air may also be seen in the end of Acts 18, where an Alexandrian sage of scripture is said to have been a preacher of John the Baptist's movement.[35]

On the basis of these three factors, which all more or less began in the Hasmonean period and deepened as time went on, it appears that one may explain a fundamental development in the relations of religion and state in Second Temple period Judaea. Early in the period, they both had one capital: the Temple of Jerusalem. But the Hasmonean period saw the birth, in theory at least, of a split between the two. And if at first the same head wore both crowns, already Salome Alexandra demonstrated that this need not be so: she was temporal ruler, while one of her sons served as high-priest. The Romans accepted this situation, substituting vassal rulers or governors for the Hasmonean rulers but allowing the Jews to go on supplying high priests. Although it is usual to view the Sadducees, the party of the high priests, as

---

[33] For Philonic spiritualization of the Temple, see, inter alia, V. Nikiprowetzky, *Semitica* 17 (1967), pp. 97–116. As for Paul, out of the immense literature we may cite R. J. McKelvey, *The New Temple: The Church in the New Testament* (1968), pp. 92–124, and, especially, J. Coppens, in *Studia Evangelica* 6 (ed. E. A. Livingstone; 1973), pp. 53–66, who underlines the Hellenistic and Philonic (rather than Qumran) affinities. (In general, on Paul and Philo, see also H. Chadwick, *Bulletin of the John Rylands Library, Manchester* 48 [1965/66], pp. 286–307, and several of the studies in P. Borgen, *Philo, John and Paul: New Perspectives on Judaism and Early Christianity* [1987].) On spiritualization of the Temple in John and its specifically Hellenistic background, see O. Cullmann in *Jesus und Paulus: Festschrift für Werner Georg Kümmel zum 70. Geburtstag* (edd. E. E. Ellis and E. Grässer; 1975), pp. 44–56. Cullmann links the Johannine view to the anti-territorial view expressed by Stephen the "Hellenist," according to Acts 7; for that view, see also below, p. 120, n. 23. As for the Epistle to the Hebrews, see McKelvey, pp. 147–154. That epistle's Hellenistic background, specifically with regard to the heavenly temple, is examined ibid., pp. 205–206; see also H. W. Attridge, *JBL* 98 (1979), pp. 90–93 (esp. p. 90, n. 1), and idem, *The Epistle to the Hebrews* (ed. H. Koester; 1989), pp. 20–21. Ibid., p. 29, however, Attridge shows just how difficult it is to choose between a Qumran and a Hellenistic background for it. That is our point.

[34] On Hellenistic impact upon Qumran, see, inter alia, Hengel (above, n. 31 [1974], pp. 228–247); idem, in *Qumrân: Sa piété, sa théologie et son milieu* (ed. M. Delcor; 1978), pp. 333–372; D. Mendels, *HTR* 72 (1979), pp. 207–222; and Will-Orrieux (above, n. 26), pp. 203–206, where it is similarly traced to the fact that the sect "respirait l'air du monde." Hengel and Mendels cite additional bibliography.

[35] On this connection, see also my study in *Mémorial Jean Carmignac* (*Revue de Qumran* 13; edd. F. García Martínez and E. Puech; 1988), pp. 635–646.

quislings,[36] it must be noted that all they did was accept the implications of the first factor — which the Hasmoneans had introduced.

On the other hand, those — including Zealots in the Jerusalem priesthood — who continued to view the Temple as a political center, the capital of God's state, would have to go to war against Rome. And it was natural that the Temple itself was where they began the war, and where it ended. Both events which inaugurated the rebellion of 66 — the suspension of sacrifices for Rome in Jerusalem and the riots between Jews and Greeks in Caesarea — were, basically, expressions of the will to override the first factor. Namely, sacrifices for Rome constituted admission of the lack of Jerusalem's political significance,[37] and admission that Caesarea belonged to the Gentiles meant that it was part of a state defined by Rome, not by Jerusalem.[38]

As for those who, due to the second factor — criticism of the Temple and its priesthood — did not view the Temple of Jerusalem as a religious center, the third factor — Hellenism — opened a new option. Their belief that God had abandoned His home did not leave them in desperation, for they could find Him elsewhere. This approach too had two varieties: we must distinguish

---

[36] See for example, O. Cullmann, *The State in the New Testament* (1957), pp. 9–10: ". . . these Sadducee collaborationists had no genuinely religious, theological program, but only a political one . . ." In our understanding, on the contrary, the Sadducees settled for religion without state.

[37] See below, p. 114.

[38] Although Josephus states (*BJ* 2.266; *Ant.* 20.173) the Jewish claim that Caesarea was a Jewish city was based upon the fact that it had been built by a Jewish king, Herod, this is at best a legal fig-leaf suitable for use when arguing before Romans. Jews of the type willing to riot over such questions were not the type to view a vassal of Rome, descended from Idumaeans, as a Jewish king. (For doubts as to the Jewishness of the Herodians, see *Agrippa I*, pp. 124–125, 219–222.) Rather, the real logic of the Caesarean riots (ibid. §§ 173–178; *BJ* 2.266–270, 457 ff.) was the same as that of the Jewish destruction of an altar to Gaius in Jamnia in 39 C.E. (*Agrippa I*, p. 82): a Jewish demand that the coastal city be considered part of the Jewish state ("holy land" — Philo, *Leg.* 202), governed by the sovereign of Jerusalem, was countered by a Roman insistence that there was no such state, and that Jerusalem would be Romanized if Jews continued to demand that a Jewish Jerusalem have such a Jewish state around it. For detailed studies of the struggle in Caesarea, see A. Kasher, *The Jews in Hellenistic and Roman Egypt* (1985), pp. 289–297, and L. I. Levine, *JJS* 25 (1974), pp. 381–397. In the nature of things, the context of Kasher's study led him away from the specifically Palestinian nature of the struggle (p. 296: "the Jews of Caesarea were more importunate in their political demands than those of any other [!] city in the Diaspora"). See rather Levine, p. 392: "The assertion that the city was theirs . . . was another form of the claim concerning the ownership of Palestinian territory first made by Simon the Hasmonean centuries before" — referring to I Maccabees 15:33–34. (However, I doubt that one must infer, with Levine [p. 396], from the fact that the Jews of Caesarea pushed their case through the imperial courts, that they did not want to rebel against Rome. It would not have been the last time Palestinian rebels attempted to use the occupying power's legal system to their own advantage.) What happened with the destruction of the Temple was the assertion of Caesarea in Jerusalem as well; cf. Betz (above, n. 23).

between those who thought God's residence elsewhere was permanent, and those who thought it temporary, a fill-in until He could return to Jerusalem. The latter, our point of departure in this paper, searched for God in the unpolluted desert near Jerusalem and hoped to return from it in order to restore the Temple and a state around it. That is, they hoped to repeal the first factor, and therefore posed a real threat to Rome (and, therefore, a real problem for Josephus). But the former variety, who saw the other Temple as a permanent solution, did not need to stay near Jerusalem or to return to it: one can live anywhere if his Temple is heaven, the cosmos, the pure heart or the devout community or the like.

In summary, we shall offer a table summarizing – if only schematically and simplistically – the possibilities delineated:

	The Temple of Jerusalem is God's House	The Temple of Jerusalem is not God's House
The Temple should be a political center	"Zealots"	Essenes,[39] Josephus' desert prophets
The Temple should not be a political center	high priests	Hellenistic Jews[40]

The two side options, "should" and "should not," represent the rejection and the acceptance of the first factor. The two top options, "is" and "is not," represent the rejection and the acceptance of the second factor. Those listed in the right-hand column reflect, to a greater or lesser extent, the impact of the third factor, Hellenism.

---

[39] Especially of the right-wing variety; cf. above, pp. 19–20.

[40] To reiterate: this adjective applies to culture, not geography. Cf. above, n. 31.

2. On Pharisaic Opposition to the Hasmonean Monarchy[*]

Did the Pharisees oppose the Hasmoneans' kingship? That is, did the Pharisees, or some of them, oppose the constitutional innovation of the late second century B.C.E., apart from any complaints they may have had about the Hasmonean rulers' deeds and policies?

Until two or three generations ago this question was frequently discussed and usually answered in the affirmative. More recently, however, it has not received much attention, and those few who have addressed it have more frequently answered in the negative.[1] A few factors may explain this:

1. The baby and bathwater effect. The most ambitious study of this topic was V. Aptowitzer's 1927 *Parteipolitik*, which argued that rabbinic and other ancient Jewish literatures preserve numerous fragments of pro- and anti-Hasmonean propaganda.[2] But it was quickly agreed by most reviewers that imagination far outran reason in this acute and erudite monograph.[3] Therefore, as frequently happens, instead of proving his thesis Aptowitzer instead only succeeded in giving it a kiss of death.[4] Moreover, as we shall see,

---

* Originally presented at the Eighth World Congress of Jewish Studies (Jerusalem, 1981) and published in Hebrew in *Nation and History*, I (ed. M. Stern; 1983), pp. 39–50.

[1] This is part of a more general abandonment of earlier claims of Hassidic-Pharisaic opposition to the Hasmoneans. For criticism of the earlier theological approach to the Hasmoneans, which encouraged such claims, see J. Efron, *Studies on the Hasmonean Period* (1987), pp. 1–32, followed by B. Bar-Kochva, *Judas Maccabaeus: The Jewish Struggle Against the Seleucids* (1989), p. 59, n. 101. On our specific topic, see also, inter alia, C. Tchernowitz, *Toledoth Ha-Halakah: History of Hebrew Law . . .*, IV (1950), pp. 122–133 (in Hebrew); P. Churgin, *Studies in the Times of the Second Temple* (1949/50), pp. 63–82 (in Hebrew); G. Alon, *Jews, Judaism and the Classical World* (1977), pp. 1–47; V. Tcherikover, *Hellenistic Civilization and the Jews* (1959), pp. 256–257; and J. Liver, *The House of David . . .* (1959), pp. 114–116 (in Hebrew).

[2] V. Aptowitzer, *Parteipolitik der Hasmonäerzeit im rabbinischen und pseudo-epigraphischen Schrifttum* (1927). The fifth chapter is dedicated to our specific theme.

[3] See Tchernowitz, Churgin, Tcherikover and Liver (above, n. 1); J. Klausner, *Kiryat Sepher* 5 (1928/29), pp. 348–355 (in Hebrew); J. Hempel, *Theologische Literaturzeitung* 53 (1928), cols. 364–365; W. Staerk, *Orientalistische Literaturzeitung* 32 (1929), cols. 560–561; J. Bonsirven, *Recherches de science religieuse* 19 (1929), pp. 326–327; A. Marmorstein, *MGWJ* 73 (1929), pp. 244–250, 478–487 (cf. Aptowitzer, ibid., pp. 403–414); and J. Heinemann, *Aggadah and its Development* (1974), pp. 75–89 (in Hebrew).

[4] For similar cases in the same decade, see below, pp. 183 and 262.

it seems that also contemporary political circumstances encouraged the opposition to Aptowitzer.

2. Since the discovery of the Dead Sea Scrolls, which contain direct and explicit criticism of the Hasmoneans, most studies of the opposition to that dynasty have focused upon Qumran's.[5]

3. Moreover, since such Qumran opposition to the Hasmoneans focuses on them qua ("wicked") priests, not qua kings, there is little occasion to focus on our question, although some scholars argue that the Qumran hope for a priestly messiah alongside the royal one embodies a criticism of the Hasmonean linkage of the two roles.[6]

4. If formerly scholars agreed that *the* prime literary statement of opposition to Hasmonean kingship, in chapter 17 of the Psalms of Solomon, was of Pharisaic origin, today there is much more hesitance about viewing this book as Pharisaic. This is a result both of the general decline of pan-Pharisaism and of some specific similarities of this book to parts of the Qumran library.[7]

Nevertheless, it is clear that there were Jews who opposed the Hasmoneans' innovation. This is already indicated by I Maccabees, a pro-Hasmonean book which was most probably written before the constitutional innovation: the author praises the Romans for never having taken a crown (8:14),[8] and in the document in ch. 14 which ratifies the dynasty's rule, care is clearly taken to avoid calling Simeon a "king." While he is given clear titles ("high priest" and "*strategos*") to designate his religious and military functions, his ruling capacity is termed only by the participle *hēgoumenos* (vss. 41−42). The obvious term was "king," but it was avoided.[9] Again, according to Josephus

---

[5] See, inter alia, A. S. van der Woude, *Die messianischen Vorstellungen der Gemeinde von Qumrân* (1957), pp. 223−242; H. J. Schoeps, *Studien zur unbekannten Religions- und Geistesgeschichte* (1963), pp. 11−19, and − of the multitude of studies in the wake of the publication of the *Temple Scroll* and its "Law of the King" − J. H. Charlesworth, M. Hengel and D. Mendels, *JJS* 37 (1986), pp. 28−38, and E. Will and C. Orrieux, *Ioudaïsmos-Hellènismos: Essai sur le judaïsme judéen à l'époque hellénistique* (1986), pp. 205−210.

[6] For literature on that Qumran hope, see above, p. 20, n. 45. As for its being pointed against the Hasmonean linkage of priesthood and monarchy, see, inter alia, Will-Orrieux (above, n. 5), pp. 205 and 208.

[7] See J. O'Dell, *Revue de Qumran* 3 (1961/62), pp. 241−257; R. Wright, *Septuagint and Cognate Studies* 2 (ed. R. A Kraft; 1972), pp. 136−154. On the other hand, the book's Pharisaic authorship was still defended by J. Schüpphaus, *Die Psalmen Salomos* (1977), pp. 127−137, 158. For the demise of pan-Pharisaism, cf. below, p. 90, n. 7.

[8] For I Maccabees 8 as pro-Hasmonean propaganda which uses Rome to justify the Jewish dynasty, see M. Smith in *Donum Gentilicium: New Testament Studies in Honour of David Daube* (edd. E. Bammel, C. K. Barrett and W. D. Davies; 1978), pp. 1−7, also D. Flusser, *Zion* 48 (1982/83), esp. pp. 154−158 (in Hebrew). As for the date of I Maccabees, see the recent and detailed discussion in Bar-Kochva (above, n. 1), pp. 152−168; Bar-Kokhva, as many of his predecessors, assigns it to the early days of Johanan Hyrcanus I.

[9] Cf. H. Zucker, *Studien zur jüdischen Selbstverwaltung im Altertum* (1936), pp. 50−51. The title "ethnarch," which appears in 14:47 and 15:1, as also in *Ant.* 13.214, represents a

and Diodorus, when Pompey settled Judaean affairs in 63 B.C.E. he had to deal not only with Aristobulus II and Hyrcanus II, both of whom wanted to be king, but also with a third delegation which complained against the Hasmoneans for having introduced the royal title, in violation of the tradition which entrusted authority to high priests.[10] And in subsequent decades we find not only the Psalms of Solomon complaining that "instead of their excellence (= high priesthood) they put kingship" (17:6),[11] but also Philo postulating that "it is impossible for one person to fill both positions (priesthood and kingship)" (*De Virtutibus* 54); clearly the former, and probably the latter, denounce the Hasmonean experiment.[12]

Thus, this was a real issue for some, and it is, therefore, appropriate to ask about the position of one of the prominent groups known to have existed at the time — the Pharisees. Of course, it need not be that this group had a position on the question, or that it was shared by all Pharisees. Nevertheless, it is useful to show that at least some opposed the Hasmoneans' innovation. As we shall see, it seems that it points toward a fundamental difference between their brand of Judaism and that of their priestly opponents. The following sources are apposite.

1. Coins of Alexander Janneus, which bear the Hebrew inscription "Jonathan the High Priest," were overstruck over Hebrew and Greek inscriptions terming him "king."[13] It is reasonable to infer that Alexander gave up use of the latter title at some point, under the pressure of popular opposition.[14] As it appears clear from Josephus and from rabbinic literature

---

more elegant resolution of this problem. In passing, we may note that while there is no direct evidence for Hasmonean usage of the Hebrew title *nasi*, *hēgoumenos* is used for *nasi* a few times in the Septuagint (although it is usually rendered otherwise; see E. C. Dos Santos, *An Expanded Hebrew Index for the Hatch-Redpath Concordance to the Septuagint* [n.d.], p. 137). Perhaps this is the case in I Maccabees as well, and we have a title after all. But it wouldn't help much, for *nasi* is a second-rate term used demonstratively instead of "king;" see A. Rofé, *Textus* 14 (1988), pp. 169–174.

[10] See *Ant.* 14.41 and Diodorus Siculus 40.2 (*GLA* I, pp. 185–186).

[11] On the much-discussed interpretation of *anti hypsous autōn* see Schüpphaus (above, n. 7), p. 67, n. 300, also S. Holm-Nielsen in *Jüdische Schriften aus hellenistisch-römischer Zeit* IV/1–3 (1974–1983), p. 98, n. c. On any interpretation, the verse attacks the Hasmoneans for becoming kings. J. Begrich's acute suggestion (*ZNW* 38 [1939], pp. 141–142) that the verse, in its original form, denounced the Hasmoneans for substituting a royal crown for their priestly hat (*migba'at* — see Exodus 28:40 etc.), should not be dismissed too lightly.

[12] On Philo, cf. W. A. Meeks, *The Prophet-King: Moses Traditions and the Johannine Christology* (1967), p. 115.

[13] See Y. Meshorer, *Ancient Jewish Coinage*, I (1982), pp. 132–134.

[14] See SVM I, p. 604. Meshorer, who formerly accepted this inference, later expressed doubts (above, n. 13: pp. 77–78), due to the fact that not all of Jannaeus' coins were overstruck. However, as he himself notes, it may be that those coins which were already in circulation could not be recalled and overstruck. Hence, his doubt does not appear very decisive, and he suggests no alternative explanation for the overstriking.

that the Pharisees led that opposition,[15] it follows that among the issues was their opposition to the royal title.

2. According to *Testament of Moses* 6:1, *Ant.* 16.163 and a *baraita* preserved in BT *Rosh Hashana* 18b (bottom) and in the scholion to *Megillat Ta'anit*,[16] it was normal for a Hasmonean ruler to call himself "(high) priest of the most high God."[17] This title points clearly to Melchizedek (Genesis 14:18).[18] But adoption of Melchizedek as a legitimator is not at all to be taken for granted, for he was rather, in fact, an obvious proof-text for those who claimed that genealogy is irrelevant to religion (see Hebrews 7 and *11Q Melchizedek* [above, p. 20, n. 45]). This is the antithesis of the Hasmoneans' dynastic ideology, which, as is shown by their plaidoyer, depended on their descent from Aaron and Phineas (I Maccabees 2:26, 54) and upon God's special election of their family ("seed" − 5:62; see also 14:49). If the Hasmoneans nevertheless adopted Melchizedek as a legitimator, it must be because he was not only high priest but also king of (Jeru)salem (Genesis, ibid.), and his

---

[15] This despite the doubts of C. Rabin, *JJS* 7 (1956), pp. 3−11. Rabin wrote before the publication of the rest of *Pesher Nahum*, which made clear the identification of Alexander's enemies as Pharisees. See M. P. Horgan, *Pesharim: Qumran Interpretations of Biblical Books* (1979), pp. 161−162, also below, p. 101, n. 64. On the Pharisees and the revolt against Alexander, see SVM I, pp. 221−225; I. L. Levine, *Cathedra* 8 (July 1978), p. 115 (in Hebrew); idem, in *Jerusalem in the Second Temple Period: Abraham Schalit Memorial Volume* (edd. A. Oppenheimer, U. Rappaport and M. Stern; 1980), pp. 68−70 (in Hebrew); and J. Klausner and A. Schalit in *The Hellenistic Age* (World History of the Jewish People I/6, ed. A. Schalit; 1972), pp. 229−234 and 277−297.

[16] ed. Lichtenstein, *HUCA* 8−9 (1931/32), p. 337.

[17] "High" is added in the latter two sources. In *Test. Mos.*, the reading is "reges imperantes et in sacerdotes summi dei vocabuntur" (*Semitica* 19 [1970], p. 58), and there is no need to move the adjective from God to "priests;" for "priest" used of "high-priest," see H. Stegemann, *Die Entstehung der Qumrangemeinde* (1971), pp. 102 and A79−A82 (n. 328). "(Most) high God" also appears in *Test. Mos.* 10:7, as frequently elsewhere; cf. E. M. Laperrousaz's note in *Semitica*, loc. cit., p. 129.

[18] Flusser (above, n. 8: p. 153, n. 11) assumes that the Hebrew original of I Maccabees 14:41 termed Simon a *kohen le'olam*, which, given Psalm 110:4, would amount to another instance in which the Hasmoneans are set equivalent to Melchizedek. However, this would be surprising, in light of what we saw above about the way this very verse avoids calling Simon a king (although it is possible that the Hasmoneans first adopted the fancy title and only later, when they took the royal crown, exploited all of its potentialities). Moreover, Flusser's understanding of I Macc. 14:41 depends on two questionable assumptions: 1) *eis ton aiōna* applies only to Simon's priesthood, as opposed to his being *hēgoumenos*; and 2) the Hebrew original had only *kohen*, not *kohen gadol*.

example therefore showed that such a combination was legitimate.[19] Those who opposed the use of the title must have argued the opposite.[20]

For us, it is important to note that the *baraita* ascribes opposition to the use of the title to "the Sages of Israel."[21] True, it gives a quasi-technical explanation for the opposition: since promissory notes dated "in the year of NN High Priest of the Most High God" were discarded after the debt was repaid, use of such a date formula led to the profanation of God's name. But the *baraita* reports a holiday was fixed in memory of the abolition of the practice, and just as it is clear that this means there was opposition to the abolition, so too is it clear that those who supported the dating-formula did not do so because they wanted to profane the divine name. Rather, they must have been very interested in the propaganda value of the title. Here, then, was the real issue.

3. The famous *baraita* on the break between "King Jannai" and the Pharisees (BT *Kiddushin* 66a), which, as linguistic details and comparison with the Josephan parallel (*Ant.* 13.292–295) show, apparently derives from quite an ancient source,[22] reports that Judah ben Gedidiah, apparently a spokesman for the Pharisees, made the following demand: "King Jannai, the royal crown is enough for you! Leave the priestly crown to the seed of Aaron!" The phrasing of the demand is explained by rumors which claimed that the king's birth had not been untainted. True, "the matter was investigated and not substantiated," but such formal conclusions cannot stop rumors.

The formulation of Judah's demand is strange. Why mention the royal crown? If "King Jannai" had claimed priesthood alone, would not the same rumors have led to the same demand that he abdicate? It seems, rather, that Judah is also indicating another more basic complaint: the two crowns should not be joined in personal union. However, as he apparently could not point to any cogent biblical or traditional basis for this position, he had to seek some excuse which might force the king to give up one or the other title. (We posited a similar situation with regard to the sages' technical opposition to the use of

---

[19] So already R. Leszynsky, *Die Sadduzäer* (1912), p. 94, followed by B. Z. Lurie, *From Yannai to Herod* (1973/74), p. 106 (in Hebrew). However, there is no need to accept the notion that Psalm 110 was composed in the Maccabean period; see rather H.-J. Kraus, *Psalmen* II (1978³), pp. 929–930, and F. L. Horton, *The Melchizedek Tradition* (1976), pp. 29–33.

[20] Already Z. Frankel argued that opposition to the title must have reflected opposition to the Hasmonean monarchy: *Zeitschrift für die religiösen Interessen des Judenthums* 1 (1844), p. 110 (in the long footnote). However, he did not mention Melchizedek or deal with the special problem of attaching monarchy to priesthood.

[21] For "the Sages of Israel" as a rabbinic term for those Josephus termed "Pharisees," see J. Z. Lauterbach, *Rabbinic Essays* (1951), pp. 45–46, n. 21.

[22] See I. Lévi, *Revue des études juives* 35 (1897), pp. 218–223; M. J. Geller, *JJS* 30 (1979), pp. 210–211; and Levine (above, n. 15 [1980]), pp. 70–73. See also the next note.

Melchizedek's title.) Indeed, given the facts that some sixty or seventy years after the rebellion the claim "his mother had been taken captive in Modiin" was long out of date, and that the charge was indeed found to be unsubstantiable and was disavowed by the Pharisees (as Josephus agrees), the fact that Judah's complaint nevertheless led to a schism indicates that it was the more basic issue, and not the adventures of "King Jannai"'s mother, which led to the rupture. That is, if we do not assume that the more basic issue was at stake, we are forced to accept the *baraita*'s claim, echoed by Josephus, that the whole break was due to a misunderstanding and hostility fanned by one of the king's advisers.[23] That is good folk history and pro-Pharisaic apologetics. So too, for example, the rabbinic story about the outbreak of the rebellion of 66 C.E. (BT *Gittin* 55b–56a) argues it was due only to imperial misunderstanding fanned by an evil talebearer, just as the Gospels, for that matter, claim that Pilate found Jesus innocent and condemned and executed him due only to Jewish pressure. As history, all of these are as doubtful as they are useful as apologetics.

4. According to the end of another *baraita*, which deals with precedence:[24] "A sage takes precedence over a king (of) Israel (for) when a sage dies we have no replacement for him, but when a king dies all Israelites are fit for kingship" (BT *Horayot* 13a; Tos. ibid. 2:8; PT ibid. 3:9 [48b]; cf. *Midrash Tannaim*, ed. Hoffmann, p. 104). The statement that "all Israelites are fit for kingship" is typically cited as proof that the sages did not oppose the Hasmoneans simply because they took the royal title.[25] However, it seems that in fact the opposite conclusion is more likely.

---

[23] According to Josephus, who tells the story of Hyrcanus instead of Jannaeus, the adviser urged the king to have the Pharisees propose a punishment for the maligner, and when they suggested a lenient punishment the king was outraged – although, according to Josephus, they did so not because the sided with the maligner but rather because that was their usual penal policy. Apparently the same story lies behind the version in BT *Kiddushin*, but here the Pharisaic proposal has been lost, leaving the adviser's response ("Such is the proper punishment when a private person has been insulted, but you are a king . . .!") without a reference. On this point and its source-critical implications, see – apart from the literature cited above, n. 22 – J. Neusner in *Josephus, Judaism, and Christianity* (edd. L. H. Feldman and G. Hata; 1987), pp. 285–286.
[24] The primary application is with regard to the redemption of captives, but a general statement is being made.
[25] See Alon (above, n. 1), pp. 4–5, 23, followed, for example, by Will-Orrieux (above, n. 5), p. 207. C. Thoma went even one further, presenting this statement not only as one according to which one need not oppose the Hasmoneans, but, rather, as "politisch klug . . . damit unterstützten sie [the Pharisees] die Hasmonäerkönige gegen die akuten Naherwarter (Messianisten) . . . [die] nur ein Königtum aus dem Hause Davids gelten lassen" (*Bibel und Kirche* 4 [1980], pp. 119–120).

Why does the *baraita* refer specifically to "king (of) Israel" (*melech Yisrael*) and not just king?[26] Does it mean "Jewish king" or "king of the kingdom of Israel"? Hardly, for no one could even consider the possibility that the halacha would grant a pagan king precedence over a sage. So the addition of "(of) Israel" was not meant to exclude that possibility. Rather, the distinction implied is the usual one — it appeared in the BT just briefly prior to this tradition — between a king *who is a plain Israelite* and a Davidic king.[27] Thus, the *baraita*'s point is that when an Israelite king dies he may be replaced by any other Israelite; it could not say the same of Davidic kings, for whom the replacement pool is extremely limited.[28]

But if "Israel" here means non-Davidic, "Israel" is appearing in its frequent sense of "lay," of *only* Israelite but otherwise undistinguished birth. That is, it excludes priestly birth too.[29] Such usage is in evidence scores of times in the Mishnah alone,[30] and is especially to be expected in contexts such as the present one, where so much depends upon pedigree (e.g.: "a priest precedes a Levite, a Levite precedes an Israelite, an Israelite precedes a *mamzer* . . ." — m. *Horayot* 3:8). So, we conclude, this *baraita* does not consider the possibility that priests might reign as kings, although it does not polemicize against it.

Such a polemic is found, however, in another *baraita*, preserved in the Palestinian Talmud,[31] which we shall juxtapose with the preceding one because of its common focus upon the term "Israel."

Priests may not be anointed as kings. Rabbi Judan Anthondraya said: (This rule is) on the basis of "the scepter shall not depart from Judah" (Genesis 49:10). Rabbi Hiyya bar Adda said: (It is on the basis of) "So that his days over his kingdom shall be long, he and his sons in the midst of Israel" (Deuteronomy 17:20). What is written in the next verse

---

[26] Indeed, the Tosephta and PT versions of the *baraita* refer only to "king," without "Israel." The latter appears only in the BT version. However, the BT's clarification must be right, for if the opening reference were to any "king," including a Davidic king, the end of the *baraita*, which claims that any Jew could replace such a king, would be wrong.

[27] See, inter alia, BT *Horayot* 11b (on anointment), *Sanhedrin* 19a (on judging).

[28] It is surprising, however, that the question whether a Davidic king precedes a sage, or vice versa, is not raised. This shows how irrelevant the issue was by the rabbinic period; see the final section of this paper.

[29] We might phrase this conclusion as follows: when "Israelite" does not refer to the whole people, it refers to one of its three "estates:" monarchy, priesthood, people. This tripartite division of the people is well-reflected in ancient translations of Exodus 19:6; see below, pp. 58–59.

[30] See H. Danby, *The Mishnah* (1933), p. 826 (Index, s.v. "Israelites, ii: lay Israelites as distinct from priests"). Other cases are cited in *Agrippa I*, p. 222, n. 11.

[31] PT *Shekalim* 6:1 (49d), *Sotah* 8:3 (22c), and *Horayot* 3:2 (47c). For the assumption that this is a *baraita*, see Alon (above, n. 1), pp. 5,23–24 (n. 15), also B. Bokser in *ANRW* II/19.2 (1979), p. 175.

(18:1)? "There shall not be for the priests [and] the Levites[, the whole tribe of Levi, any portion or inheritance together with Israel . . .]."[32]

Although it has been suggested that this rule means merely that priests who are kings should not be anointed as such,[33] the two proof-texts clearly indicate that priests should not be kings at all. Indeed, some important medieval commentators who realized this accordingly condemned the Hasmoneans.[34] For our purposes, it is important to note the second proof-text, which is based upon the limited "lay" understanding of "Israel." This understanding is, in fact, quite reasonable in the present context, given the fact that, on the one hand, Deuteronomy 17:15 emphasizes that kings must be "from your brethren" and vs. 20 says they rule "in the midst of Israel," while, on the other hand, 18:1 and 18:3 clearly distinguish between the priests and "Israel"/"the people."[35]

5. Finally, one of the few chronological traditions in rabbinic literature seems to denounce the Hasmoneans for becoming kings. I refer to the tradition cited in the name of R. Jose, that "the wicked kingdom took over (*pash^eta 'al*) Israel 180 years before the Temple was destroyed."[36] It is clear that the Babylonian Talmud, which cites this tradition after a discussion of Jewish-Roman relations (*Avodah Zarah* 8b), assumed, as is usual, that "the wicked kingdom" is Rome. However, one may wonder if this is really the tradition's original sense. For, first of all, as M. D. Herr has pointed out,[37] the use of "the wicked kingdom" for Rome appears nowhere in tannaitic literature, and is also very rare in statements attributed to tannaim in amoraic literature. Moreover, there is no historical basis for dating Rome's takeover of Israel to 180 years before the destruction of the Second Temple, even if we

---

[32] I have added the continuation of 18:1 so as to exhibit the contrast between the references to "Israel" in these two successive verses. For the usual scribal practice of copying only the beginning of a verse although the continuation is also, or even primarily, intended, see J. L. Maimon, *Sinai Jubilee Volume* (1957/58), pp. 226–236 (in Hebrew) or, in brief, N. G. Cohen, *HTR* 69 (1976), p. 189, n. 6. It might be, however, that R. Hiyya's case rests merely on the juxtaposition of kingship "in the midst of Israel" (17:20) to the opening negation of 18:1: "There shall not be for the priests . . ." On either interpretation, the law is predicated upon the contrast between "Israel" and "priests."

[33] So, for example, Churgin (above, n. 1), p. 71, n. 11 and Liver (above, n. 1), pp. 115–116 ("perhaps").

[34] See Nahmanides' and Bahye's commentaries to Genesis 49:10, also *Abudraham HaShalem* (edd. S. A. Wertheimer – S. Creuzer, 1958/59), p. 201.

[35] For other halachic implications of this distinction between "the priests" and "the people," see *Responsa Maharatz Chayot* § 18 (in *Kol Sifrei Maharatz Chayot* [Collected Works of Z.H. Chajes], II [19557/58], pp. 664–665).

[36] BT *Abodah Zarah* 8b, *Shabbat* 15a, *Seder Olam Rabbah*, ch. 30, etc.

[37] "Roman Rule in Tannaitic Literature" (Dissertation, Hebrew University, 1970), pp. 132–133 (in Hebrew).

admit that the number might be rounded and schematic; Rome's takeover came in 63 B.C.E.[38] But R. Jose supplies other data which are strikingly accurate: he allots 180 years to the Greek monarchy, 103 years to the Hasmoneans and 103 to the Herodians prior to the Destruction.[39] Assuming one dates the first period from 332 B.C.E. (Alexander in Judaea), the second to 141/140 (abolition of Seleucid taxes, Simon's elevation – I Maccabees 13:41 and 14:27) and the third to 37 (Herod's conquest of Jerusalem),[40] these data are within a very few years of accuracy.[41] Why should R. Jose be so far off with regard to "the wicked kingdom?"

R. Jose's statement brings us to the last decade of the second century B.C.E. In our opinion, it is highly significant that this is the decade in which the Hasmoneans first took the royal title. Josephus quite decidedly attributes the innovation to Aristobulus I (*BJ* 1.70; *Ant.* 13.301), who reigned for a year in the middle of the decade; but even if out of deference to some other sources and scholars we allow the possibility that the first Hasmonean king was Johanan Hyrcanus I or Alexander Jannaeus,[42] the important point for us is that they too ruled in this same decade, just before and just after Aristobulus.[43] Thus, however surprising it may seem in light of the traditional application of "wicked kingdom" to Rome, it seems that the likelier

---

[38] The only possibility which might be suggested is the renewal of the treaty with Rome sometime late in Johanan Hyrcanus' rule (see SVM I, pp. 205–206, n. 7) – but that was for the Jews' benefit, had no practical results, and, in any case, was no innovation (see I Maccabees 8, 12 and 14).

[39] BT *Avodah Zarah* 9a (top).

[40] Cf. below, pp. 176–178.

[41] As has been noted by various scholars, despite some differences in the details of their reckonings. See, inter alia, I. Loeb, *Revue des études juives* 17 (1888), pp. 248–249; H. J. Bornstein, *HaTequfah* 9 (1920/21), p. 219 (in Hebrew); and J. Z. Lauterbach, *Proceedings of the American Academy of Jewish Research* 5 (1933/34), p. 80. The first datum in R. Jose's tradition, which allots 34 years to the Persian period, is, of course, off by ca. 170 years. The probable origin of this is the notion (based on an interpretation of Daniel 9:25–27) that the whole period from the destruction of the First Temple to the destruction of the Second is 490 years: if one subtracts out seventy years of exile and the other data on the Greek, Hasmonean and Herodian periods, for which the rabbis evidently had relatively solid data, only 34 years remain. On the chronology of the Persian period, cf. *JSJ* 21 (1990), pp. 175–199.

[42] For discussion of this question, see Aptowitzer (above, n. 2), pp. 13–17; Stern, *GLA* I, p. 307; and Schalit (above, n. 15), pp. 343–344, n. 65. Respectively, these scholars attribute the innovation to Hyrcanus, Aristobulus and Jannaeus.

[43] And it stands to reason that if (as we doubt) Hyrcanus was the first "king," he made the move toward the end of his long reign, as part of whatever lies behind the tradition in BT *Berachot* 29a which states that he was righteous throughout his long rule and only at its end became a heretic. Cf. D. Hoffmann, *Jahrbuch der Jüdisch-Literarischen Gesellschaft* 5 (1907), pp. 237–238.

interpretation, in this case, is one which applies it to the Hasmoneans and understands the term as one which condemns their kingship as wicked.[44]

Summary and Historiographical Remarks

The sources cited above indicate opposition to the Hasmoneans because they took the royal title. The opposition indicated was *not* out of opposition to kingship in general,[45] or because of the Davidic pedigree which the Hasmoneans lacked, but, rather, because of the Aaronite pedigree which they had. The critics whose expressions we have assembled held it was not legitimate to join priesthood and monarchy. While a specific exegetical basis for this claim has been noted (§ 4), it is apparent that the larger context in which this point is important is that of the relations of religion and state. As we have argued elsewhere, the Hasmonean innovation bespeaks a willingness to separate the two, occasioned by the state's conquest of territories inhabited by pagans.[46] However, the Hasmoneans maintained a personal union between the two positions. Opposition to this means an insistence that religion and state, territory, should rather have nothing to do one with another. While their linkage was a hallmark of priestly religion, and, therefore, the Hasmoneans hung on to it as best they could, their divorce was a hallmark of Pharisaic religion — which was, indeed, to survive the destruction of the Temple and, in its rabbinic development, exile as well. Indeed, in a broader sense we may

---

[44] The notion that this tradition refers to the Hasmoneans was also defended by J. Lehmann, *Revue des études juives* 37 (1898), p. 6; he referred the date, however, not to the innovation of monarchy but rather to Hyrcanus I's conquest of Samaria, taking *pash^eta al yisrael* to mean "spread out over all (the land of) Israel." However, it is difficult to understand why the tradition would condemn that, but condemnation is indicated by the usage of the term "evil kingdom." Here we should also note that the printed versions of BT *Avodah Zarah* 9a have R. Jose attribute 103 years to "the Hasmonean kingdom." If pressed, this, which indicates that "the Hasmonean kingdom" was thought of as beginning in the days of Simon, would militate against the assumption that R. Jose was aware of the constitutional innovation of a few decades later. However, it need not be pressed, any more than *Ant.* 17.162, where Josephus, who made much of the innovation (on the pomposity of *Ant.* 13.301, see A. Schalit, *König Herodes* [1969], p. 743), nevertheless speaks of 125 years of Hasmoneans *monarchy*. See also his undifferentiated reference in *Vita* 2. Moreover, note that the Munich manuscript of the BT, the highly thought-of MS Paris (Heb. 1337), and the Sephardic manuscript of BT *Avodah Zarah* published by S. Abramson (1957) all read "kingdom of the Hasmonean *house*," suggesting that R. Jose's tradition originally referred to the Hasmonean house (which could rightly begin with Simon, as we saw), "kingdom" being added in only due to assimilation to the surrounding references to the Persian, Greek and Herodian kingdoms.

[45] The general absence of such opposition is especially emphasized by M. A. Beek, in *The Sacral Kingship — La regalità sacra* (Studies in the History of Religions [Supplements to *Numen*] 4; 1959), pp. 349–355.

[46] See above, pp. 12 and 39.

note that such a divorce of religion from territory is only an aspect of the rabbinic tendency to separate religion from everything material, a tendency which we have termed "nominalism" in contrast to priestly "realism."[47]

At this point, two historiographical topics arise, and with them we shall conclude. The first concerns the use of rabbinic sources for the study of the Second Temple period, a highly risky business. So frequently, it may be shown that later interests or ignorance have outrun history, and, even more frequently, while the sources cannot be confuted, there is little to bridge the centuries between them and the events they claim to report, so their claim for credence must be based on faith alone. In the present case, however, it seems we may be more confident, for a few reasons:

a. It is clear that the Pharisees were among the leading opponents of Alexander Jannaeus, and that he, if not the first Hasmonean king, was the first to bear the title for any significant length of time (Aristobulus I reigned for only a year). Given the fact that kingship was an innovation about which some complained, it is hardly likely that Jannaeus' Pharisaic opponents, even if they were not upset about the innovation, would pass up the opportunity to add this to their arsenal. That is not the way of party politics.

b. Regarding the *baraita* in BT *Kiddushin* 66a (§ 3), as we noted (n. 22), specific philological arguments may be brought to indicate its antiquity.

c. In several cases, as we suggested, the rabbis seem to have misunderstood the polemics reflected by the traditions they reported. In §§ 2–3, the Talmud knows only of technical problems (deeds in garbage, captive mother); in the *Horayot* traditions cited in § 4, the special significance of "Israel" did not attract attention and the word itself was omitted in some versions;[48] and in the "wicked kingdom" tradition (§ 5) the Talmud apparently took the epithet to refer to Rome. But if the later rabbis did not fully understand these traditions, it follows that they are older.

d. The critical question is, of course, "how much older?" With the exception of § 3, to which already Josephus testifies, we do not know. We may only say that the question addressed was relevant in the Hasmonean period, but thereafter disappeared, and that in the rabbinic period it is difficult to find anyone, much less rabbis, who might have wanted to claim that priests may or should also be kings.[49] Indeed, even the question whether priests may be

---

[47] See above, p. 21, n. 49.

[48] Nor, accordingly, was the question raised as to whether a sage precedes Davidic kings.

[49] For other aspects of rabbinic competition with priests, see, in the present volume, pp. 56–80 and 99–101. In *Zion* 48 (1982/83), pp. 135–147 (in Hebrew), R. Kimelman collected as much evidence as he could for the preservation of a priestly oligarchy, or priestly oligarchic claims, in the talmudic period. He found very little, and most of the evidence does not point to rabbinic circles – such as those which transmitted the traditions we have considered. Moreover, his point of departure, the story in PT *Shabbat* 12:3 (13c) and PT

kings, not to mention the rule that they may not (§ 4), failed to find a place in the Babylonian Talmud. Such a lack of interest argues for the antiquity of what nevertheless was preserved.

Our other historiographical comment has to do with modern writers. At the outset of this study, we noted that Aptowitzer gave the thesis of Pharisaic opposition to the Hasmoneans a kiss of death. He did, however, have an important follower — Abraham Schalit.[50] The latter was attacked severely, just as he expected,[51] reviewers of his volume on Herod frequently condemning his positions as such which "no Jewish mind can tolerate" or which "take away the Jewish people's self-respect."[52] In Schalit's case, the main problem was that he justified Herod and Josephus for submitting to Rome; his claim that the Pharisees opposed the Hasmoneans was only ancillary.[53] For Aptowitzer, however, the discovery of attacks upon the Hasmoneans (and defense of them) in rabbinic literature was the main interest, but, to the extent that such a claim implied that opposition to Jewish statehood is a legitimate Jewish option, it aroused, in the generation which saw the struggle to found a new Jewish state, fervent opposition.[54] Note, for example, such polemic titles as "Did the Nation and its People Cause the Hasmoneans to be Forgotten?" and "Are there really Hasmonean and Anti-Hasmonean Aggadot?" (G. Alon and J. Heinemann — see nn. 1, 3). This was only natural, for Jewish historiography has always taken the Pharisees as positive models,[55] and the notion that even some of them were "anti-Zionists"

Horayot ch. 3 (end — 48c), wherein Rabbi Johanan quotes m.*Horayot* 3:8 ("a Torah sage who is a bastard takes precedence over a high priest who is an ignoramus"), shows only the notion that Torah scholars take precedence over ignoramuses, but not that there were priests claiming authority qua priests in third-century Sepphoris. Finally, since Kimelman wrote the notion of priestly significance in Sepphoris, especially in the first two centuries after the destruction of the Second Temple, has been seriously undermined. See S. S. Miller, *Studies in the History and Traditions of Sepphoris* (1984), Part II; D. Trifon, *Tarbiz* 59 (1989/90), pp. 77–93 (in Hebrew).

[50] For Schalit on Pharisaic opposition to the Hasmoneans, see above, n. 15. For the isolation of this follower of Aptowitzer, see Schalit's comments in *HaUmmah* 1 (1962/63), p. 591 (in Hebrew).

[51] See the preface to the 1960 Hebrew original of *König Herodes*, laundered in the German version.

[52] The quotations are, respectively, from B. Z. Lurie (above, n. 19), p. 283, and Y. Baer, *Zion* 36 (1970/71), p. 131, n. 14 (both in Hebrew). More of the same is collected in my essay on Schalit cited in the next note.

[53] See my essay in *Jewish History* 2/2 (Fall 1987), pp. 9–28.

[54] Here we should note that of the pieces cited in n. 1, above, several were originally published much earlier: Efron's in 1962/63; Churgin's in 1936/37; Alon's in 1937/38 and 1942/43; and Tcherikover's in 1930/31.

[55] See below, pp. 66–70.

was, for many, quite intolerable, just as intolerable as Schalit's rehabilitation of the Hasmoneans' nemesis was later to be.

In the meantime the atmosphere has changed, and it may be possible to return to a more balanced view. Opposition to the Hasmonean monarchy should be recognized, not as opposition to Jewish statehood in general, nor even as opposition to pre-messianic (non-Davidic) statehood, but, rather, as opposition to the linkage of religion and state, a linkage which, if preserved, would have brought the former down with the latter. A religion which was to survive by claiming that "since the Temple was destroyed God has in His world only four cubits of halachah," i.e., He has no fixed place, but is, rather, wherever people are occupied with Torah,[56] could well begin by preaching that also God's chief representative on earth, the high priest, should not be a territorial ruler as well.

---

[56] BT *Berakhot* 8a. Similar ideas are frequently expressed, as in m.*Avot* 3:2, PT Berakhot 1:1 (8d–9a), etc. On rabbinic approaches to the old notion of sacred space, and its spiritualization, see B. Bokser, *HTR* 78 (1985), esp. pp. 287–299.

3. "Kingdom of Priests" — a Pharisaic Slogan?[*]

The verse "You shall be unto Me a kingdom of priests and a holy people" (Exodus 19:6) awakened enormous interest and emotions in the history of Christianity, and much attention has been devoted not only to the verse's original meaning and its sense in the context of Exodus, but also to the history of its interpretation within the church.[1] In contrast, Jewish interpretation of the verse, apart from the ancient translations, has not attracted much interest. Here, no attempt will be made to cover the field. Rather, we will concern ourselves with two periods alone, in dealing with the following two questions: 1) Did the Pharisees and the sages attempt to achieve a "kingdom of priests" in the sense of a community in which all, and not only Aaronites, would be considered priests or priestly?, and 2) If not, as we shall argue, then what is it which brought so many modern scholars to claim that they did?

I. "Kingdom of Priests" in Ancient Jewish Literature

It seems that "kingdom of priests" has no parallel or echo in the Hebrew Bible itself, with perhaps one exception:[2] "But you shall be called the priests of the Lord, men shall speak of you as the ministers of our God; you shall eat the

---

[*] Hebrew original in *Zion* 45 (1979/80), pp. 96–117; built upon in "Kingdom of Priests" in *Contemporary Jewish Religious Thought* (edd. A. A. Cohen and P. Mendes-Flohr; 1987), pp. 527–534. The combination of ancient and German-Jewish interests reflected in this study stems from the fact that during 1977–1979, when it was written, I was working at the Research Foundation for Jewish Immigration in New York while completing a doctoral dissertation on "Priests, Temple, Sacrifices: Opposition and Spiritualization in the Late Second Temple Period" (Hebrew University, 1980).

[1] Beginning, in the New Testament, with I Peter 2:9; cf. ibid. 2:5 and Revelations 1:6 and 5:10. See C. E. Eastwood, *The Royal Priesthood of the Faithful: An Investigation of the Doctrine from Biblical Times to the Reformation* (1963) and idem, *The Priesthood of All Believers: An Examination of the Doctrine from the Reformation to the Present Day* (1962). For the linguistic and exegetical literature, see the bibliography cited by W. L. Moran in *The Bible in Current Catholic Thought* (ed. J. L. McKenzie; 1962), pp. 7–20, along with several of the studies cited below.

[2] M. Buber, *Königtum Gottes* (1932), p. 126, thought that Hosea 4:6 too refers to the priesthood of all Israel, but the context shows that it refers to the Temple priests, or, indeed,

wealth of the nations, and in their riches you shall glory" (Isaiah 61:6, RSV).
But note that the latter verse contrasts Jews and non-Jews, not different
classes within the Jewish people. Here, therefore, right at the outset, we must
differentiate between two possible applications of "kingdom of priests:" it can
serve as a slogan for setting the Jews above the Gentiles (or for the former's
"mission" vis à vis the latter), but it can also be used to militate against the
notion that, within the Jewish people, some (Aaronites) are more priestly than
others. Thus, even if Isaiah 61:6 reflects Exodus 19:6, it does not supply any
support for the inner-Jewish application of the verse — which is the one so
often ascribed to the Pharisees and the rabbis.[3]

The idea of a common priesthood of all Israelites is clearly stated in another
verse (although without echoing Exodus 19:6): "For the whole congregation is
holy and God is in their midst, so why do you [Moses and Aaron, Levite and
priest] hold yourselves above the community of God?" (Numbers 16:3). True,
there is no claim of common priesthood, but only of common holiness, but
from Moses' answer (v. 10) it becomes clear that there was also a demand for
priesthood; the same follows also from the end of the story (17:5).

But with all due respect to some scholars to be cited in Part II (§§ 3—4), the
Korah story could not possibly serve as a support for any Jew in the Second
Temple period who wished to demand that all Jews be considered priests,[4] for
the biblical story clearly and totally condemns the demand.

Moving on to the ancient translations of Exodus 19:6, we discover the
surprising fact that not one of them takes the phrase, despite its construct
state, to refer to a kingdom composed of priests.[5] The Aramaic, Syriac

---

to the high priest alone. See F. I. Andersen and D. N. Freedman, *Hosea* (Anchor Bible;
1980), pp. 342—354, esp. p. 353. It is interesting that although "a kingdom of priests" failed
to reverberate in the Hebrew Bible, "own possession" (*segulla* [Exodus 19:5]) and "holy
people" lived on; see W. Staerk, *Zeitschrift für die alttestamentliche Wissenschaft* 55 (1937),
pp. 8—11.

[3] This distinction was the main topic of my exchange with M. A. Meyer in the wake of the
Hebrew version of this article (*Zion* 46 [1980/81], pp. 57—60 (in Hebrew). Contrary to my
attempt to locate the popularity of "a kingdom of priests" within Reform Judaism, Meyer
pointed to its use by the Orthodox and others as well. In my response, I argued that such other
usage usually applied the verse to Jewish status vis à vis Gentiles, not to the inner-Jewish
question with which we are concerned here. Cf. below, n. 53.

[4] Even if we chose to overlook the fact that those demanding inclusion in the priesthood,
according to Numbers 16, were mainly *Levites* (see esp. vv. 5—8). According to J. Liver, it is
possible that the account of Korah's rebellion was linked in Numbers 16 to that of the non-
Levitical Dathan and Abiram due to the hostile desire "to present Korah not as one who
claims priestly rights for all the sons of Levi, but as one wanting to do away with the special
status of both Priests and Levites entirely" (*Studies in the Bible* [Scripta Hierosolymitana 8,
ed. Ch. Rabin; 1961] p. 198; cf. ibid., p. 215.) This would underline all the more how clear it
was, for the ancient editor, that no one could possibly approve of the latter demand.

[5] A fact already noted by various scholars, such as R.B.Y. Scott, *Oudtestamentische
Studiën* 8 (1950), pp. 213—214.

(Hexapla) and Peshitta translations, as also the echoes in Revelations 1:6 and 5:10, divide the phrase into two separate classes, either connected by a conjunction or juxtaposed with a pause: "kings (or: kingdom) and priests" (to which "holy people" is added, as a third class).[6] As for the Septuagint, while scholars do not agree as to the sense of its *basileion hierateuma*, it is clear that it does not mean that the people of the kingdom are priests.[7] We will not attempt to explain why these translations failed to render the phrase with what may seem most natural in our eyes. Rather, we shall merely note that — apart from the later Greek translations (Symmachus and Theodotion, and in the slavish version of Aquila) — the ancient translations do not reproduce the genitive relationship of "kingdom" and "priests," and hence afford no support for the interpretation we are seeking.

Three passages in apocryphal and pseudepigraphical literature have been adduced in support of the idea that all Jews are priests. In Jubilees 16:18, however, all that is said is that Isaac will be the father of a people which, in contrast to other peoples, will be God's possession and "a kingdom and priests and a holy nation"[8] — separating the elements, as in the ancient translations cited above. In Jubilees 33:20, in contrast, where the reflection of Exodus

---

[6] The translations are assembled by Scott, loc. cit., p. 214; by R. H. Charles, *The Book of Jubilees* [1902], p. 116; by G. Schrenk in the *Theological Dictionary of the New Testament*, III (1965), pp. 249–250; and by J. Le Moyne, *Les Sadducéens* (1972), p. 367. When O. Camponovo, after assembling the Aramaic renditions of our verse, comments that "so werden dem Volk drei Würdetitel zugesprochen" (*Königtum, Königsherrschaft und Reich Gottes in den frühjüdischen Schriften* [1984], p. 411), he seems to have missed the point.

[7] On *basileion hierateuma* see, in general, Camponovo, ibid., pp. 384–386. Suggestions by those mentioned in the preceding noted include "a hierarchy consisting of kings" (Charles) and "royal priesthood" (Schrenk and Scott). Philo (see below) apparently understood *basileion* as a noun rather than an adjective, and therefore inserted a conjunction: *basileion kai hierateuma*; some scholars think he was right. See L. Cerfaux, *Revue des sciences philosophiques et théologiques* 28 (1939), p. 10 (= *Recueil Lucien Cerfaux*, II [1954], pp. 287–288). For the sake of completeness, we should note that Exodus 19:5–6 are reproduced in the Septuagint version of Exodus 23:22. This is probably no more than a scribal error induced by the similarity of the passages. For similar cases, see Z. Frankel, *Über den Einfluß der palästinischen Exegese auf die alexandrinische Hermeneutik* (1851), pp. 103–104.

[8] Thus in the Ethiopic version, preferred by Charles (above, n. 6), p. 116. (O. S. Wintermute, in *The Old Testament Pseudepigrapha*, II [ed. J. H. Charlesworth; 1985], p. 88, gives "a kingdom of priests," but as Charles argues in his long note, ibid., the literal translation of the Ethiopic text, which corresponds to the Aramaic and Syriac versions and to the quote in Revelations 5:10, is to be accepted. Wintermute seems to have translated Jubilees according to the Masoretic text of the Exodus.) I do not see in Jubilees 16:18 any support for J. Blinzler's claim: "Jub scheint Ex 19.6 in dem Sinne zu verstehen, daß alle Israeliten Priester und Könige sind. Priester sind sie durch den Besitz und die Befolgung des Gesetzes, Könige dagegen nur in spe, durch die Aussicht auf eine künftige Herrscherstellung unter den Völkern" (in *Episcopus: Studien über das Bischofsamt seiner Eminenz Michael Kardinal von Faulhaber . . . dargebracht* [1949], p. 59).

19:5–6 is clear, the Jewish people is indeed termed a "priestly" one. However, as with Isaiah 61:6, here too we must note that there is no indication that the verse is applied to inner-Jewish relationships. Rather, Israel's priestly quality, just as its "holy" and "kingly" quality, is adduced as a reason for it to avoid incest, just as in Leviticus 18 Israel is warned to avoid such practices which characterized Egypt and Canaan (v. 3). Moreover, we must recall that Jubilees likely represents the views of a priest or a priestly circle,[9] and it is virtually unthinkable that such a circle would subscribe to a view which undercuts its own special status.

As for the third passage, it is in the festal letter quoted in II Maccabees 2:17, where the Jews of Judaea encourage their brethren in Egypt to celebrate the new holiday of Chanuka. In the epistle's high-sounding conclusion, they write that "God, after saving all His people, returned to all the inheritance, as well as the kingdom, the priesthood, and the holiness, as He promised in the Torah." This is a clear allusion to our verse.[10] But does this verse view the entire people as priests? Is that the implication of the repetition of "all?"[11]

As G. Alon noted, the answer is clearly "no:"[12]

[T]he verse has no bearing on our subject, for it does not speak of the relationship between "the people" and the priests, but comes to tell the Jews of Egypt, to whom the letter is addressed . . . that the national possessions, in their entirety, belong to the whole Jewish people, and do not appertain to the Jews of Eretz-Israel alone, that the kingship (the dominion to which the Hasmoneans attained) and the priesthood and the Temple (which had been desecrated by the Greeks and the Hellenists) and the land belong to the entire nation. Hence the Egyptian Jews too were involved in that miracle and have a duty to observe the precept of the festival.

This intepretation of "all His people" is required by the context, not only of the epistle, but of the whole book, which focuses on the return of independence ("the kingdom"), the true priesthood (as opposed to usurpers of the Jason-Menelaus-Lysimachus variety) and sanctity to the Temple (which had been polluted).[13] The "all" comes to include the Jews of Egypt along with

---

[9] See, inter alia, Le Moyne (above, n. 6), p. 76 ("son auteur était sans doute prêtre"); further literature is cited in *Agrippa I*, p. 119, n. 48.

[10] So, very insistently, Cerfaux (above, n. 7), p. 18 (295 f.).

[11] According to A. Geiger, this epistle was incorporated in II Maccabees by its Pharisaic author partly because of this verse's proclamation of universal priesthood (*Urschrift und Übersetzungen der Bibel in ihrer Abhängigkeit von der innern Entwickelung des Judenthums* [1857], pp. 223, 227).

[12] G. Alon, *Jews, Judaism and the Classical World* (1977), pp. 233–234, n. 113.

[13] For II Maccabees' focus on the Temple and priesthood, see especially R. Doran, *Temple Propaganda: The Purpose and Character of 2 Maccabees* (1981). As for 2:17, the basic idea is also correctly captured in J. Klausner's expanded translation (*The Messianic Idea in Israel from its Beginning to the Completion of the Mishnah* [1956], p. 263): "the heritage (the land of

the rest of the people, not the non-Aaronites along with the priests — which is what we are still seeking.

Moving next to Josephus, we find that in his rendition of Exodus 19 (*Ant.* 3.75 ff.) he skipped over our verse; similarly, it fails to function elsewhere in his writings. Not even in his account of Korah's rebellion does the claim that all should be priests appear; according to Josephus (*Ant.* 4.15, 23), all the rebels wanted was the right to participate in the choice of priests. But it is evident that Josephus had heard of the claim, for he imputes it to Jeroboam ben Nebat (*Ant.* 8.227−228). While the biblical account (I Kings 12:25−33) says only that this arch-villain appointed priests "from the extremes of the people, who were not Levites," Josephus has him emphasizing that he who built the Temple was only human, and that just as Aaron once built the Golden Calf and appointed priests ("as it is said"), so too he now allows anyone who wants to be a priest to come and offer sacrifices.

Thus, Josephus was familiar with the demand for breaking the Aaronite monopoly on the priesthood. This comes as no surprise; by the time Josephus wrote *Antiquities*, the idea had been popularized by Christians and Josephus had had opportunity to meet it in the world of Jewish Hellenism (see below). It is important to note, however, that if the Torah unequivocally condemns the notion by ascribing it to Korah, Josephus did no less by ascribing it to Jeroboam. We should expect no less from this proud Aaronite (see *BJ* 3.352; *Vita* 1−6; *Ant.* 16.187).

In the Dead Sea Scrolls published to date, there is, it seems, no reflection of our verse. One Cave 1 fragment bears the words ."..MLKWT KHWNT' RB' MN MLKWT . . .,"[14] but its meaning and context are anyone's guess. Liver suggested that this is a fragment of a text similar to Test. Judah 21:1−2, where, after it is said that priesthood has been given to Levi, "kingship" is assigned to Judah and his sons, and it is asserted that priesthood is greater than kingship.[15] If this reconstruction is correct,[16] then this fragment does not even reflect Exodus 19:6 at all. As for other evidence on Essenes, while *Ant.* 18.22 was at times claimed as evidence for a universal priesthood among them, this has long been rejected; the text does not say that the Essenes picked members to be priests, but, rather, that they assigned priests to certain special functions.[17]

Israel or even the land of the Gentiles), and the kingdom (the house of David), and the priesthood (the line of Aaron), and the sanctity (of the Temple)."

[14] See *Qumran Cave I* (Discoveries in the Judaean Desert, I, edd. D. Barthélemy and J. T. Milik; 1955), p. 88. Milik noted the similarity to Exodus 19:6 and suggested that the text is a fragment of Test. Levi 8:11 ff., which is similar to the passage suggested by Liver (see below).

[15] J. Liver, *HTR* 52 (1959), p. 171.

[16] For doubts, see A. Schalit, *König Herodes* (1969), pp. 310−311, n. 583.

[17] See E. Schürer, *Geschichte des jüdischen Volkes im Zeitalter Jesu Christi*, II (1907⁴), p. 666, n. 63 (also T. S. Beall, *Josephus' Description of the Essenes Illustrated by the Dead Sea*

Today, with the Scrolls showing just how important the Aaronite and even Zadokite priests were for the Qumran community,[18] and ignoring Exodus 19:6, such a claim must be totally abandoned. G. Klinzing, in his careful study of the Qumran antecedents of New Testament spiritualization of the cult, had to admit that the absence of the verse from the scrolls, in contrast to its prominence in the New Testament (I Peter 2:9; Revelations 1:6, 5:10, 20:6), casts doubt upon a takeover of this aspect of such spiritualization.[19]

Turning now to rabbinic literature, a few scholars have already noted that it hardly alludes to our verse.[20] In all the material on this verse assembled in M. M. Kasher's compendium, there is next to nothing which suggests that the Jewish people is priestly.[21] Those texts which do suggest this divide into two groups: 1) most assume (given the location of Exodus 19) that all Jews were priests before the Golden Calf affair, when that status was lost, some also assuming that such a status will return in the eschaton;[22] and 2) two stories *ascribe to Gentiles* the notion that Jews are priests: BT *Zebachim* 19a; *Avot de-Rabbi Natan*, A, 15.[23] But even here, in the latter case the Gentile emphasizes that the term is not to be taken literally.

Scrolls [1988], p. 60 [with bibliography]), for no apparent reason made more tentative in SVM II, p. 573, n. 68. On the theory of universal priesthood among the Essenes, see below, n. 26. As for the Qumran-Essene equation, see above, p. 35, n. 19.

[18] See above, pp. 20–21, 36.

[19] See his *Die Umdeutung des Kultus in der Qumrangemeinde und im Neuen Testament* (1971), pp. 217–218. For an earlier attempt to rescue a Qumran background for New Testament spiritualization and universalizing of the priesthood, see O. Betz, in *La secte de Qumrân et les origines du christianisme* (ed. J. van der Ploeg et al.; 1959), pp. 163–202. See esp. pp. 172–173: "La reprise des traditions sacerdotales dans la secte de Qumrân mène moins à un sacerdoce universel (comme on le recontre dans I Petr. II 9, basé sur Ex. XIX 6), qu'à l'exercise d'un ministère sacerdotal généralisé . . ." This distinction ("ministère sacerdotal" instead of "sacerdoce") basically confuses the issue, in order to reintroduce the same notion through a back door. All Betz really means, and shows, is that the Qumran community strove to be holy and pure, just as priests do. This is not the same as claiming to be priests. Below, we will have to make this same distinction with regard to rabbis.

[20] H. Wenschkewitz, *Die Spiritualisierung der Kultusbegriffe* . . . (1932), p. 43 (= *Angelos* 4 [1932], p. 107): "The concept of priesthood was virtually never ascribed to the whole people (in rabbinic literature). Exodus 19:6, which could have engendered such interpretations, hardly functions. In rabbinic exegesis (of this verse), the emphasis is totally upon royal rule." So too Schrenk (above, n. 6), p. 250, n. 7; Blinzler (above, n. 8), p. 59; and Klinzing (above, n. 19), p. 218, n. 38.

[21] See M. M. Kasher, *Torah Shelemah*, vol. 15 (1973), pp. 68–73 (in Hebrew). This collection includes numerous extracts from late sources, which may hardly be used as evidence for the Pharisees or even the Tannaim, but the point is immaterial here, for our findings are anyway negative

[22] See Kasher, ibid., §§ 90, 92, 94* and n. 92. For a text from the *Mechilta* linking the loss of Israelite priesthood to the Golden Calf, see below.

[23] Ed. Schechter, pp. 61–62. This is one of the famous stories about a Gentile who came to Hillel; the verse is not cited in its parallels ibid. B, 29 (p. 61) and BT *Shabbat* 31a.

To these passages we might, perhaps, add *Sifré Num.* § 119 (ed. Horovitz, p. 143):

Beloved are Israel, for when He gives them a(nother) name He only calls them (by the name of) priests, as it says (Isaiah 61:6) . . . Beloved are the priests, for when He gives them a(nother) name He only calls them (by the name of) ministering angels, as it says (Malachi 2:7) . . .

But this is only a literary exercise, and even it keeps the priests one step higher than "Israel."

This harvest is very unimpressive, and lacks the main object of our quest: with the sole exception of a statement attributed to "King Izgadar" in BT *Zebachim* 19a, we found no usage of Exodus 19:6 as a slogan requiring that non-Aaronite Jews act as or be considered priests.

Finally, we should note that although the *Mechilta of Rabbi Ishmael* on our verse (ed. Horovitz-Rabin, p. 209) views it as including a mandate to be *perushim* – the Hebrew form of "Pharisees" – it finds this mandate not in "kingdom of priests" but, rather, in "holy people:" "(you shall be) holy and sanctified, separated (*perushim*) from the nations of the world and their abominations." That is, it does not use the verse to level class distinctions within Israel and it does not associate "kingdom of priests" with Pharisees.[24] On the contrary: just prior to this comment, it (as some other passages alluded to above) uses "kingdom of priests" to show that "until they made the (Golden) Calf all Jews were entitled to partake of sacrifices, but after they made the Calf they were denied to them and given to the priests."

Before leaving rabbinic literature, however, we should address the claim made often by scholars to be cited later in this study, namely, that the Pharisees and the sages attempted to allow all Israel (or, at least: all members of their camp) to share in holiness. According to this claim, the Pharisees and the sages attempted to share as much as possible in the privileges and obligations of the priests. That is, even if a survey such as ours were to show – as it does – that our verse did not serve as a slogan from which such a policy could be deduced, we may induce – so it is claimed – from many Pharisaic or rabbinic laws that their authors did indeed aspire to priesthood, to a kingdom in which all are priests.

However, one must differentiate uncompromisingly between priesthood and holiness. In the absence of any textual evidence, why should we assume

---

[24] This midrash is cited by I. Elbogen, on p. 78 of his 1904 work cited in n. 38, and he makes it clear that the comment is on "holy people," not on "kingdom of priests." Baeck, in contrast, makes it appear that it is on the entire verse; see his work cited in n. 47, below, pp. 37–38 (6–7 in English). Even Baeck, however, does not attempt to incorporate this midrash into his basic thesis of the contrast between Pharisaic "Men of the Synagogue" and the Temple priests.

that the Pharisees and / or sages assumed that holiness was mediated by priesthood, so aspirants to holiness must aspire to priesthood? Why, for example, should we assume that a *ḥaber*, who insisted on eating his daily "profane" food (*ḥullin*) in the same state of purity in which a priest ate sacrificial food, thought that by doing so he was becoming (similar to) a priest? Indeed, in the polemic context normally assumed, would it not be a better strategy for non-priests to insist that all, priests and non-priests alike, have to answer to a common standard of holiness – that is, that God demanded the same of all Jews – than to admit that standards were set for the priests and non-priests were outsiders who could try to meet them? If the Pharisees and the sages admitted that God had established the Aaronites alone as priests, and condemned Korah and Jeroboam for attacking that monopoly, how could they possibly strive to be priests themselves? But holiness was a different matter entirely.

Thus, for example, we find the distinction in a late midrash (*Tanna Debe Eliyahu* 16 [ed. Ish-Shalom, p. 72]):

The (law of) hand-washing is derived from Moses, Aaron and his sons . . . But what is written of Israel? "And you shall make yourselves holy and be holy" (Leviticus 11:44; 20:7). On this basis Rabban Gamaliel used to say: Holiness was not given to the priests alone, but, rather, to priests, Levites and all Israel, as it says, "Say to all the children of Israel, You shall be holy . . ." (Lev. 19:1–2)

So too with regard to the other main Pharisaic practice which is at times viewed, along with holiness, as an aspect of an aspiration to share in priesthood: Torah-study. While it does seem to be the case that priests were early assumed to be the main repositories of Torah, there is nothing to indicate that Pharisaic or rabbinic claims to Torah authority were understood as claims to priesthood.[25] Rather, study of the Torah was an aspect of religion, of holiness, available to all. There is no reason to assume that this was viewed as something typically priestly. On the contrary, when *Sifré Deut.* § 48 (ed. Finkelstein, p. 112) urges Jews not to depend on religious virtuosi to learn in

---

[25] In the bitter exchange between Shemaiah and Abtalion, on the one hand, and a haughty high priest, on the other, in BT *Yoma* 71b, the "work of Aaron" is not Torah-study (as was assumed by J. Neusner, *The Rabbinic Traditions About the Pharisees Before 70*, I [1971], p. 149) but rather the pursuit of peace, according to a statement attributed to a successor of the two sages (m.*Avot* 1:12): "Hillel says: Be of the disciples of Aaron, loving peace and pursuing peace, loving people and bringing them near to the Torah." The story shows a contentious high priest whose behavior was not like Aaron's, and sages who, without claiming to be priests (descendents of Aaron), follow Aaron's example. As with Torah-study, so too with the seeking of peace, there is nothing inherently priestly about it. For the proper understanding of this passage see, inter alia, J. Z. Lauterbach, *Rabbinic Essays* [1951]), p. 155. For priests as teachers, see also below, p. 97, n. 45.

their stead, those others are "the sons of the elders, the sons of the rich, the sons of the prophets." The priests are not even mentioned.

The point of these examples is that it would be mistaken to assume that all claims that holiness or religious obligations devolve upon all Israel are predicated upon the notion that priesthood does.[26] Hence the need for specific evidence on that question, and the signficance of its absence.

This leads us to the final area to be surveyed. Scholars of antiquity who assume that claims to holiness imply claims of priesthood do so easily because Greek and Latin lead them to do so. In both languages, "priest" (*hiereus*, sacerdos) is derived from "holy" (*hieros*, sacer). This derivation makes it all the more natural and easy to identify the two categories. But in Hebrew and Aramaic, KHN has no associations at all. It is, therefore, very hard to generalize, and, as we have seen, it was not generalized.

But in Hellenistic Egypt, in the writings of Philo – who perhaps didn't even understand Hebrew[27] – the linkage between *hiereus* and *hieros* bore its natural fruit. As with Isaiah 61:6, however, we must note that in the two Philonic passages in which Exodus 19:6 is directly quoted[28] and elsewhere where the same concept is reflected,[29] "kingdom of priests" is used to describe Israel's relation to the world, not the relations among different castes of Israelites. Philo specifically compares non-Aaronite Israelites to priests only with regard to the unusual circumstances of the paschal sacrifice, where all participate in the slaughtering (Exodus 12:6), and in this connection he does not cite Exodus 19:6.[30] Indeed, there is hardly reason to expect Philo to reflect specifically Pharisaic ideas, especially such that might undercut the priesthood.[31]

---

[26] Already J. Wellhausen made this point in his critique of Geiger: *Die Pharisäer und die Sadducaäer* (1874), pp. 71 f., n. 2. This same error, in A. Ritschl's understanding of the Essenes, was pointed out by B. Beer, *Das Buch der Jubiläen und sein Verhältniss zu den Midraschim* (1856), p. 11, n. *. On Ritschl's school, which ascribed the idea of universal priesthood to the Essenes (either instead of the Pharisees or as part of the latter), see S. Wagner, *Die Essener in der wissenschaftlichen Diskussion vom 18. zum Beginn des 20. Jahrhunderts* (1960), pp. 88–90.

[27] See D. Rokeah, *JTS* n.s. 19 (1968), pp. 75–77, 82.

[28] *De sobrietate* 66; *De Abrahamo* 56.

[29] *De specialibus legibus* 1.243; 2.163–164; *De Vita Mosis* 1.149; *De Abrahamo* 98.

[30] See *De Vita Mosis* 2.224–225; *Quaestiones et solutiones in Exodum* 1.10 (on Exodus 12:6). For the extraordinary nature of non-priestly participation in the sacrificial slaughtering on the eve of Passover, see S. Safrai, *Die Wallfahrt im Zeitalter des Zweiten Tempels* (1981), pp. 286–287.

[31] For the possibility that Philo was a priest (as Jerome reported) and his commonalities with the Sadducees, see my essay in *Nourished in Peace: Studies in Hellenistic Judaism in Memory of Samuel Sandmel* (edd. F. E. Greenspahn, E. Hilgert and B. L. Mack; 1984), pp. 155–171.

In summary of our survey of the ancient sources, we may say that the promise or demand that the Jewish people be a "kingdom of priests" does not appear to have interested Palestinian Judaism of the Second Temple or rabbinic periods. At times, as in Isaiah 61:6, Jubilees 16:18 and Philo, the verse is applied to the relationship of Israel as a priest in comparison with the rest of the world. But the application of the verse, or the idea, which interests us here, namely, the claim that the whole people and not just the Aaronites are priests (or should be), appears only to be condemned (on the lips of Korah and Jeroboam) or as an opinion of Gentiles (who don't know any better) or with reference to the period before the Golden Calf and the eschaton (a few times in rabbinic literature). We did not find the verse being applied polemically in any anti-priestly contexts. The usual interpretation separates the verse's elements into three castes: kings, priests and the rest of the people; so in II Maccabees, Jubilees and the Aramaic and Syriac translations. Finally, we surmised that it was the linguistic isolation of KHN, as opposed to *hiereus* and sacerdos, which led to its failure to be generalized in Palestinian writings, as opposed to the Greek- and Latin-speaking world; holiness could be generalized, but not *kehunah*.

II. "Kingdom of Priests" in Historiography

Having established a negative response to our first question, we must now ask why so many scholars answered it in the affirmative. We may begin by noting that the affirmative answer is not typical of non-Jewish scholars (although a few copied it from Jewish writers to be mentioned below.)[32] Moreover, apparently only Christian scholars (n. 20) have pointed out that "a kingdom of priests" was not the object of much attention in rabbinic literature. Finally, although several Christian scholars followed Geiger in the claim that II Maccabees is to be seen as a Pharisaic work, in contrast to Geiger they did not

---

[32] Thus, for example, Wellhausen (above, n. 26: pp. 71−72) admitted that Geiger correctly attributed to the Pharisees the ideal of universal priesthood, although he downplayed its importance by denying Geiger's identification of the Sadducees with the priesthood. In contrast, the idea reappears in full bloom in L. Gaston, *No Stone on Another: Studies in the Significance of the Fall of Jerusalem in the Synoptic Gospels* (1970), pp. 131−132; his notes refer to Lauterbach and Baeck (see below, §§ 4, 7), as well as to J. Jeremias, who, in turn, was dependent upon Baeck (J. Jeremias, *ZNW* 42 [1949], p. 186, n. 19). More frequently, however, non-Jewish scholars − even those who positively evaluate the Pharisees − avoid viewing "a kingdom of priests" as their slogan; thus, for example, the idea does not appear in R. T. Herford's *The Pharisees* (1924), despite his dependence upon Lauterbach and Baeck (see pp. 7, 15−16).

include his "universal priesthood" interpretation of 2:17 among their arguments.[33]

The lack of support in the sources, and the limitation of the claim to Jewish writers, suggest that there was some special interest at work here. Let us, therefore, review the list of scholars who viewed our verse as a Pharisaic slogan.[34]

1. Abraham Geiger, one of the great German Reformers of the nineteenth century, was also among the first to link the Sadducees with the priests. In his opinion, the Pharisees opposed the Sadducees' monopoly on the priesthood, and it is their slogan, "a kingdom of priests," which is bespoken by II Maccabees 2:17.[35]

2. Kaufmann Kohler, a German-American Reformer and protegé of Geiger's, ultimately president of the Hebrew Union College in Cincinnati,[36] wrote the article on Pharisees in the *Jewish Encylopedia* (1905). At the outset, he emphasizes that the Pharisees demanded religious democracy, a demand expressed in II Maccabees 2:17 on the basis of Exodus 19:6. Within a few years, the verse in II Maccabees was to become, for Kohler, "the *leitmotif* for the Pharisaic school."[37]

3. Around the same time, in Germany, Ismar Elbogen — a professor at the liberal Hochschule für die Wissenschaft des Judentums which Geiger had founded — wrote an apologetic book on the Pharisees and a Hebrew survey article about them.[38] In the latter he claimed, inter alia, that the Pharisees "ascribed the sanctity of the priests to the entire congregation (LKL H‘DH

---

[33] See, for example, A. Bertholet, *Die jüdische Religion von der Zeit Esras bis zum Zeitalter Christi* (= B. Stade, *Biblische Theologie des Alten Testaments*, II; 1911), pp. 307–308; he found "Gesetzesfrömmigkeit" and other characteristics of Pharisaism in II Maccabees, but makes no reference to 2:17 in this context.

[34] Rather than encumber the following list with references to biographical literature on those who figure in it, we shall simply note that there are entries, at times substantial, on virtually all of them in the English *Encylopaedia Judaica* (1971) as well as in the more specialized sources on German Jewry: the incomplete German *Encylopaedia Judaica* (1928–1934), the *Jüdisches Lexikon* (1927–1930), S. Wininger, *Große Jüdische National-Biographie* (1925–1936), and J. Walk, *Kurzbiographien zur Geschichte der Juden, 1918–1945* (1988).

[35] See above, n. 11. In a separate booklet on the sects, Geiger again emphasized that the Pharisees were the people's spokesmen, and that their basic idea ("Grundgedanke") is expressed in all its fullness in II Maccabees 2:17: *Sadducäer und Pharisäer* (1863), p. 26 (= *Jüdische Zeitschrift für Wissenschaft und Leben* 2 [1863], p. 32). Cf. below, n. 87.

[36] See H. G. Enelow's biographical introduction to Kohler's posthumous *The Origins of the Synagogue and the Church* (1929); p. xiii on Kohler's links with Geiger.

[37] K. Kohler, *Jewish Encyclopedia* 9 (1905), p. 661; idem, *Jewish Theology* (1918), p. 346 (= *Grundriß einer systematischen Theologie des Judentums auf geschichtlicher Grundlage* [1910], p. 261.) See also p. 36 of his posthumous work cited in the preceding note.

[38] I. Elbogen, *Die Religionsanschauungen der Pharisäer* . . . (1904; cf. below, n. 46); idem, "Pharisees," in *'Otzar HaYahadut*, sample booklet (1906), pp. 85–94 (in Hebrew).

KWLH)."[39] It is remarkable that this laudatory article, written in Hebrew, could include such diction borrowed from Korah (Numbers 16:3).

4. Jacob Z. Lauterbach, who after completing his studies in Germany became a professor of rabbinic literature at Hebrew Union College, wrote several lengthy articles on the Pharisees. In one of them, which first appeared in the College's *Annual*, he suggested that as early as the third century B.C.E. the phrase and notion "kingdom of priests" had engendered doubts about the Aaronites' monopoly on the priesthood. So even if the terrible fate of Korah and his followers prevented open rebellion against the ruling priests, nevertheless, according to Lauterbach (as Elbogen, above), the Pharisaic sages of the time (and later) must have agreed in their hearts with Korah's insistence that all of the people is holy.[40]

5. Emil Hirsch – a prominent German-American Reform rabbi and alumnus of Geiger's Hochschule – published an apologetic book on the crucifixion of Jesus, and in the course of it gave a detailed presentation of what he viewed as the Pharisaic notion of Israel's priesthood. According to Hirsch, the Pharisees insisted on investing Israel with substitutes for the priestly appurtenances (prayer shawls to replace priestly vestments, phylacteries instead of the high-priest's *tzitz*, *mezuzot* for each house instead of the priestly guarding of the Temple's gates, the household table instead of the Temple's, etc.)[41] Even if one ignores the difficulty or impossibility of showing that these elements of Jewish practice were specifically Pharisaic and not biblical, here is a classic case of the argument we examined and dismissed above, which assumes that aspiration to holiness mean aspiration to priesthood. For Hirsch, the matter was simple: "The Pharisees represented the party of the people; they protested that every Jew by birth was a priest; that the priesthood of the people was as sacred as was the priesthood of the the temple."[42]

6. Rudolph Leszynsky, who was very active in liberal Jewish education in Berlin,[43] wrote two books on the Pharisees and Sadducees. In them, one does

---

[39] Ibid., p. 87; Elbogen did not identify the allusion. Note also his later statement, in a general essay on Judaism, that "the Pharisees set up an ideal based on the democratic belief in universal priesthood . . ." (*Encyclopaedia of the Social Sciences* 8 [1932], p. 431). In his 1904 German work on the Pharisees mentioned in the preceding note, in contrast, Elbogen was still wary of understanding the division between Pharisees and Sadducees as one between the people and the priesthood (p. 13). But a few pages later he basically follows Geiger in accepting the contrast of the Pharisees, followed by "das ganze Volk im Gegensatz zur Aristokratie," and in urging that one cannot enough emphasize "daß die Pharisäer Anhänger des Fortschritts waren" (p. 17).

[40] J. Z. Lauterbach, *HUCA* 6 (1929), p. 84 (= idem, above, n. 25: pp. 102–103).

[41] E. Hirsch, *The Crucifixion Viewed from a Jewish Standpoint* (1892), p. 26 (1908², p. 33). For Hirsch's explicit dependence upon Geiger, see ibid. p. 24 (1908², p. 26).

[42] Ibid., p. 26 (33).

[43] He was among the founders, and later the director, of the Freie jüdische Volkshochschule. On Leszynsky, see also below, n. 51.

not find the notion that the Pharisees demanded universal priesthood. But he too argued that Exodus 19:6 played an important role in sectarian debates, the Sadducees claiming that it justified their demand that only priests may be kings, while the Pharisees, who rejected the Sadducean claim, separated the elements of the verse (as we saw in the translations).[44] So Leszynsky too saw in II Maccabees 2:17 evidence that the book is Pharisaic. Thus, in his account of the sects he made use of all of the elements of Geiger's reconstruction: the Pharisees were on the side of the people, as opposed to the Sadducees who supported the priesthood; Exodus 19:6 played an important role in their debates (as above); II Maccabees 2:17 expresses a Pharisaic point of view. Moreover, at the conclusion of his chapter evaluating the Pharisees he emphasizes — in terms which show how alive this ancient conflict was for him — that the Pharisees "haben in einer schweren Zeit den Sieg des Fortschrittes erkämpft, die Macht der Priesterherrschaft gebrochen und der Volksfrömmigkeit freie Bahn gemacht;"[45] this formulation comes very close to attributing to the Pharisees a generalization of the priesthood. Thus, despite his peculiar use of Exodus 19:6, Leszynsky's approach is basically like that of the others in this list.

7. Leo Baeck — one of the central figures of liberal Judaism in the last generation of pre-Holocaust German Jewry, and professor at the Berlin Hochschule — already early in the century found an occasion to deprecate the priests and praise the Pharisees, in the course of his polemics with Harnack over "the essence of Judaism."[46] Later, in 1927, he summarized his understanding of the Pharisees in a separate monograph which appeared — as Elbogen's had in in 1904 — as a supplement to the Hochschule's annual report. Throughout this monograph, he presents the Pharisees as "the men of the

---

[44] See his *Pharisäer und Sadduzäer* (1912), pp. 18–19, also *Die Sadduzäer* (1912), pp. 95–96, 177–178. Basically the same understanding of Exodus 19:6 is offered by Schalit (above, n. 16), who saw it as underlying the view, held in Qumran and elsewhere, that the priestly messiah is superior to the Davidic ("Israelite") one.

[45] *Pharisäer und Sadduzäer*, p. 68.

[46] L. Baeck, *Das Wesen des Judentums* (1923³), p. 45 (first appeared in 1905; in English as *The Essence of Judaism* [revised ed.; 1948], p. 49). On the controversy between Jewish and Christian liberals, in which Adolf (von) Harnack was among the most prominent among the latter, see U. Tal, in *Juden im Wilhelminischen Deutschland 1890–1914* (edd. W. E. Mosse and A. Paucker; 1976), pp. 599–632, also idem, *Christians and Jews in German: Religion, Politics and Ideology in the Second Reich, 1870–1914* (1975), pp. 160–222, and I. Schorsch, *Jewish Reactions to Jewish Anti-Semitism, 1870–1914* (1972), pp. 169–170, 173. For Harnack's attack on the Pharisees, see his *Das Wesen des Christentums* (1900), p. 66 (quoted in part below, p. 101; this passage is cited at the very outset [p. iii] of Elbogen's 1904 monograph cited above, n. 38). With special reference to T. Mommsen, see also the chapter on "Das Dilemma des Liberalismus" in C. Hoffmann, *Juden und Judentum im Werk deutscher Althistoriker des 19. und 20. Jahrhunderts* (1988), pp. 87–132 (pp. 106–107 on the Pharisees). Cf. below, n. 67.

synagogue," which was a popular institution, as opposed to the Sadducean priests who were aristocratic "men of the Temple." In this context, he repeatedly cites Exodus 19:6, and its echo in II Maccabees 2:17, as the Pharisees' slogan; for the Pharisees, "every man was a priest."[47]

8. Hermann Vogelstein, a graduate of the Berlin Hochschule, was, as his father before him, a prominent figure in liberal Judaism in Germany, and participated, alongside Baeck, in the controversy with Harnack.[48] In a survey article on problems of ancient Jewish history, written the same year as Baeck's monograph, he gave special attention to the Pharisees, expressing the opinion that the "democratic principle," "the demand for a universal priesthood of all Israel," was a very significant part of their platform.[49]

9. In 1935, Ignaz Maybaum — yet another graduate of the Berlin Hochschule and one of the last community rabbis of the city — published a book of which the title says everything: *Parteibefreites Judentum: Lehrende Führung und priesterliche Gemeinschaft*. As historical precedent and justification for such a democratic orientation (the rabbi is not more holy, but rather only more learned — see esp. p. 17), he cites the ḥaberim-Pharisees. Correspondingly, he complains that rabbinic Judaism, which began from such democratic roots of Pharisaic opposition to the Temple priesthood, exchanged that orientation, in the Middle Ages, for an aristocratic one, turning itself into a "priesterlicher Stand" (pp. 14–15). The same approach reappears in Maybaum's post-war *The Jewish Mission* (1951), for which he coined the term "laypriest" in order to emphasize that ideal Judaism knows no such thing as "laymen" as opposed to clergy (pp. 9, 21); to exemplify such ideal Judaism he again adduces the Pharisees and their slogan, "kingdom of priests" (p. 15).

One could continue citing scholars who ascribed this slogan to the Pharisees, but they are not numerous and their dependence upon those cited is evident and often acknowledged.[50] It is clear that this historiographical tradition is one fostered and borne by prominent scholars and rabbis of German liberal Judaism and its insitutions in Berlin and Cincinnati.[51]

---

[47] L. Baeck, *Die Pharisäer* (*44. Bericht der Hochschule für die Wissenschaft des Judentums in Berlin*, 1927), esp. pp. 47, 52, 58 (in English in idem, *The Pharisees and Other Essays* [1947], pp. 21, 31, 41).

[48] See his lecture, *Die Anfänge des Talmuds und die Entstehung des Christentums* (1902).

[49] *Jewish Studies in Memory of Israel Abrahams* (ed. G. A. Kohut; 1927), pp. 424–425.

[50] See above, n. 32. For some more recent links in the chain, note that Alon (above, n. 12: pp. 233–234) repeats the idea, stating in his n. 113 that he found the "basic idea" in Geiger's writings (cited above, notes 11 and 35). Similarly, the theme appears frequently in the works of J. Neusner (including *From Politics to Piety: The Emergence of Pharisaic Judaism* [1973], pp. 83, 146, 154); in a letter, he stated that he got the idea from Alon.

[51] Although the Hochschule was not, formally, affiliated with any brand of Judaism, its liberal leaning is admitted by all, and is evident in the list of graduates and teachers cited above. Cf. A. Guttmann, *CCAR Journal* 19/4 (1972), p. 73: "Members of the Faculty were

III. "Kingdom of Priests"
in the Writings of the Reformers

In order to understand what led such scholars to this tradition, we must note that "kingdom of priests" was one of the best-loved slogans of the Reform movement itself,[52] due to several reasons: 1) the implied democracy allows for opposing the established rabbinate; 2) if every Jew is a "priest," then the old priesthood is superseded, thus contributing to Reform's rejection of hopes for a restored sacrificial cult; and 3) the phrase also played a role in supporting Jewish universalism, for it allows for turning Jewish claims of election from a liability to a concern for mankind: "Der Priesterberuf Israels."[53] Here we have

---

appointed solely on the basis of their scholarly qualification. They could be liberal, conservative, or orthodox — but they had to be first-rate scholars. In reality, however, most of them were liberal." Of all the scholars cited in the above list, only Leszynsky was neither alumnus nor teacher at one or the other liberal seminaries; in fact, he had studied at the Orthodox "Hildesheimer" Rabbinerseminar. But his liberal tendencies are clear, not only in his educational endeavors (above, n. 43) but also in his writings. Note, for example, his sarcastic attack on the traditional understanding of m.*Ḥagigah* 2:2 (*Die Sadduzäer*, pp. 117–118), his defense of the Sadducean understanding of Leviticus 16:12 (pp. 61–63, featuring the ironic assertion that the Pharisees presumed priests have three hands), and his acceptance of the critics' assertion of the Torah's relatively late origin (*Pharisäer und Sadduzäer*, p. 10). See the harsh criticism of *Die Sadduzäer* in the Orthodox *Der Israelit*, 14 August 1913, p. 11. (The review is signed "J.M.B.," which turn out to be the initials of Rabbi Jonas Marcus Bondi of Mainz — see my note in *Kiryat Sepher* 58 [1983], pp. 417–418 [in Hebrew]). – On "Hildesheimer" alumni who became liberal rabbis, cf. E. G. Lowenthal, *Emuna* 9 (1974), p. 105.

[52] And so it remains, as is shown, for example, by *Gates of Prayer: The New Union Prayerbook* (1975). Exodus 19:6 figures in two important parts of this Reform prayerbook: it closes the list of meditations with which the book begins (p. 15), and opens the list of verses cited in the chapter on the mission of Israel (p. 703). In the present study, however, we have confined ourselves to literature preceding the Second World War, the period in which we found the main tradition claiming "a kingdom of priests" as a Pharisaic slogan.

[53] This is the title of one of David Einhorn's sermons, published in 1872. On the notion of a Jewish mission to the nations, see M. Wiener, *YIVO Annual of Jewish Social Science* 2–3 (1947/48), pp. 9–24; J. Fleischmann, *The Problem of Christianity in Modern Jewish Thought, 1770–1929* (1963/64), pp. 68–105 (in Hebrew); and I. Schorsch (ed.), *Heinrich Graetz: The Structure of Jewish History and Other Essays* (1975), pp. 15–17. Several striking passages which use Exodus 19:6 in support of this theme, in the writings of M. Mendelssohn, S. R. Hirsch and N. Krochmal, were cited by M. A. Meyer in his response to the original Hebrew version of this study; cf. above, n. 3. This ideal of mission fits in well with Reform demands for abolishing Jewish laws which create barriers between Jews and Gentiles, such as the dietary laws. Correspondingly, in an article attacking a book calling for such reforms, a prominent spokesman of Orthodoxy admitted that the Jews are obliged to be a "kingdom of priests," but argued that it consists in observing the laws (D. Hoffmann, *Jüdische Presse*, 1895, p. 206). Interestingly, the pressure of anti-Semitism could bring liberal spokesmen to basically the same point of view. Thus, for a plainspoken example from one of those cited in Part II, above, note I. Maybaum, *Parteibefreites Judentum*, p. 79: "Durch das

no need to expand upon this last theme, for — as we noted already with regard to Isaiah 61:6 — it is to be distinguished from the phrase's inner-Jewish usage. Nevertheless, the mission-theme was very popular (Jost complained as early as 1852 about "unsre Schwätzer von Priestervolk und von besondern Missionen Israels und dergleichen")[54], and this helped ensure continued interest in our verse.

To illustrate the importance of our phrase for the Reformers, we shall return to our list of those who viewed it as a Pharisaic slogan:

1. Geiger, in a lecture published in the very same volume as his essay on the Pharisees, translated the verse with a "clarification:" "Ihr sollt mir allesammt sein ein Reich der Priester und ein heilig Volk."[55] As already Heynemann Vogelstein noted, "allesammt" has no basis in the Hebrew.[56] Geiger used it as part of his effort to show that the priesthood, and the sacrificial cult, are not integral to Judaism. As he argues, the prophets fought those institutions, as did also the Pharisees after them; history (the destruction of the Second Temple) showed them right,[57] as are also, therefore, those who demand Reform and the abrogation of the hope for the restoration of the Temple and the sacrificial cult.

2. Kohler too viewed "kingdom of priests" an elevated ideal of Judaism, for which the prophets and Pharisees fought the priests and Sadducees, and he uses the verse as part of his demand, from the Orthodox, to transfer the emphasis from the details of the Torah to its spirit.[58]

3. In an article on Judaism's attitude toward non-Jews, in the *Yearbook* of the [Reform] Central Conference of American Rabbis, Lauterbach used of the Jews, without explanation, the term "priest-people."[59] He did not explain, but he certainly meant the mission-idea; perhaps the idea of universal priesthood is also implied.

Diasporaschicksal ist dem Judentum ein Stück *Natur* (original emphasis) genommen . . . Die Umwelt hilft nicht nach, im Gegenteil, sie irritiert durch ihr Anders-sein. So aktualisiert die Diaspora die Idee des allgemeinen Priestertums: 'Ihr sollt mir sein ein Reich von Priestern' (Exod. 19, 6) . . . Die Diasporagemeinschaft ist gewaltloser Zusammenschluß . . . Priestertum ist Fremdlingschaft der natürlichen Ordnung gegenüber und Menschentum . . ." Here, for Maybaum, in Berlin in 1935, while the Diaspora still — as in the traditional liberal view — fulfills Exodus 19:6, this fulfillment, this priesthood, means not mission but rather the *separation* of Jews from the rest of mankind, via their divorce from nature.

[54] See his letter published by N. N. Glatzer in *In zwei Welten: Siegfried Moses zum fünfundsiebzigsten Geburtstag* (ed. H. Tramer; 1962), p. 404.

[55] *Jüdische Zeitschrift für Wissenschaft und Leben* 2 (1863), p. 210.

[56] See *Abraham Geiger: Leben und Lebenswerk* (ed. L. Geiger; 1910), p. 271, n. 1.

[57] For this argument, see his lecture cited above, n. 55, pp. 210–211.

[58] See his *Grundriß* (above, n. 37), pp. 259–260, 266 (in English: pp. 344–345, 352–353).

[59] *Central Conference of American Rabbis Yearbook* 31 (1921), p. 195.

4. Similarly, E. Hirsch's sermons use the phrase a few times of the relationship between the Jews and Gentiles.[60]

5. Baeck, already in his magnum opus on the essence of Judaism, returns again and again to "a kingdom of priests" as a description of a community all of whose members are priests[61] — i.e, in the sense he imputed to the Pharisees.

6. As for Ignaz Maybaum, enough was said in our entry in Part II, § 9 and n. 53.

Other prominent Reformers who harped on "a kingdom of priests" as an ideal of Judaism include:

7. Siegmund Maybaum (Ignaz's uncle) — historian, Reform rabbi in Berlin and professor at Geiger's Hochschule — wrote several times about the clash between prophets and Pharisees, on the one hand, and priests and Sadducees on the other.[62] Correspondingly, in a sermon on the Torah portion beginning "Speak to the priests" (Leviticus 21:1) he asserts that when the latter were finally defeated, with the destruction of the Second Temple, the priesthood was not destroyed, but rather transferred to all of Israel — which leads him to demand "priestly" behavior from his congregants.[63]

8. Hermann Cohen — the Kantian philosopher who dedicated his last years to Jewish philosophy and teaching at the Hochschule — emphasized in his *magnum opus* that Exodus 19:6 makes all Jews share in priesthood, so the Aaronite priests have no special advantage over the rest of the people.[64]

9. Joachim Prinz — one of the last Berlin rabbis and later one of the leading liberal rabbis in the U.S. — built a 1937 sermon upon the fact that the prophetic reading traditionally attached to the first chapters of Leviticus begins with Isaiah 43:21: "This people, which I created for Me, shall tell My praise." Prinz is emphatic: "Das Volk und nicht eine Kaste!" ("The people, not a caste!"), and concluded that the choice of this prophetic reading was meant to teach that the priests — who are so prominent in Leviticus — are not especially important but are, rather, only part of the people. Thereupon he concludes his sermon with Exodus 19:6 and another exclamation point.[65]

---

[60] E. G. Hirsch, *My Religion* (1925), p. 305; cf. pp. 292 f.

[61] See *Das Wesen* (above, n. 46), pp. 7, 40, 44, 47, 300 (in English: pp. 14, 44, 48, 51, 268).

[62] For example, see the passage cited below, at n. 82, also his *Predigten*, III (1907), pp. 81−82.

[63] Ibid., p. 128. For a similar sermon, see below, n. 74.

[64] H. Cohen, *Religion der Vernunft aus den Quellen des Judentums* (1929[2]), pp. 403 f.

[65] *Israelitisches Familienblatt*, 11 March 1937, p. 22. The sermon is signed "P," and Rabbi Prinz kindly confirmed, in a letter, that he is the author.

IV. The Reformers and the Pharisees

The upshot of the two preceding sections (II–III) is that the Reformers ascribed the slogan to the Pharisees because they were themselves interested in it and viewed the Pharisees as legitimizing precedent: What was good for them is good for us. However, such dependence upon the Pharisees as a legitimizing precedent is not to be taken for granted. As is well known, European languages, following the New Testament (esp. Matthew 23), use "Pharisee" and "Pharisaic" as pejorative terms. Moreover, the Christian Reformers built (and destroyed) worlds on the basis of "a kingdom of priests" and the notion of "universal priesthood" without needing to depend upon the Pharisees.[66] What, therefore, brought the Jewish Reformers to claim that they were the heirs of the Pharisees?

True, attacking the Pharisees was for many Christians a way of attacking Jews and Judaism; if one assumes that modern Judaism is the heir of Pharisaism, attacking the former, if at times in the guise of objective inquiry into an aspect of ancient history, can be a way of attacking the former. This forced modern Jewish Reformers to defend the Pharisees as a mode of defending themselves.[67] Indeed, students of modern historiography of the Pharisees, who quite properly begin their reviews with Geiger,[68] have already noted that it was this which gave rise to the widespread apologetic writing on the Pharisees in the nineteenth and twentieth century. However, if one

---

[66] See above, n. 1. For the pejorative usage of "Pharisee" and "Pharisaic" in European languages, see the dictionaries, also, inter alia, the 1983 German Bundestag debates cited in G. B. Ginzel, *Die Bergpredigt . . .* (1985), pp. 12–13.

[67] On the importance of the study of ancient Judaism in the struggle between detractors and defenders of Judaism, see the works mentioned above, n. 46, also the chapter on "Das traditionelle 'Spätjudentumsbild'" in K. Hoheisel, *Das antike Judentum in christlicher Sicht: Ein Beitrag zur neueren Forschungsgeschichte* (1978), pp. 7–60.

[68] See Le Moyne (above, n. 6), pp. 11–26, and Neusner, (above, n. 25), III (1971), pp. 320–368. Of course, everyone has forerunners. In Geiger's case, we should, perhaps, especially mention M. Creizenach, who devoted a good deal of positive attention to to the Pharisees in his *Dorsche Haddoroth, oder Entwickelungsgeschichte des mosaischen Ritualgesetzes . . .* (vol. IV of his *Schulchan Aruch*; 1840 [in German]), pp. 156–167, and also published a journal entitled *Geist der pharisäischen Lehre* (Mainz, 1823/24 – non vidi). Creizenach was a close collaborator of Geiger's in the latter's *Wissenschaftliche Zeitschrift für jüdische Theologie*, and in his discussion of the "Grundlehren des Israelitischen Glaubens," which appeared in its first volume (1835), he begins as follows (p. 327): "Das Ziel der israelitischen Religion ist Heiligkeit der Gesinnungen, der Gefühle und des Willens," followed immediately by the quotation of Exodus 19:6. However, in what I've seen, Creizenach does not apply this verse to the Pharisees, or to have presented them, or this verse, as democratic and anti-sacerdotal; right after our verse, he quotes Leviticus 19:2, where only holiness is mentioned, not priesthood. Thus, there is interest in the major ingredients of Geiger's position (Pharisees and Exodus 19:6), but not yet the thesis itself.

examines the period before Geiger, he will find that another option was also taken at times: some important liberal historians, whose names have so far been absent from our lists, solved the problem by turning their back upon the Pharisees and claiming that true modern Judaism is not their heir, or should not be.

I. Jost associated the Pharisees with the hair-splitting Polish rabbis he liked to denounce, copying and approving the New Testament's criticism of them.[69] Like contemporary rabbinism, Jost wrote, so too Pharisaism was characterized by "Werkheiligkeit" — the notion that one's works can make him holy.[70] Protestants since Luther (who apparently coined the term) had always attacked Catholics for subscribing to that low notion, and the Catholics threw the shibboleth at the Pharisees.[71] Now, just as the Christian Reformers had demanded the return of the New Testament to the position of authority which the Church had usurped, so too Jost demanded the return of the Bible instead of the new Pharisees — the rabbis. He adds that one cannot avoid the question if rabbinism is not a foreign growth which worked its way into Judaism,[72] and it is his affirmative answer which informs his account of the Pharisees.

Correspondingly, and making the contrast with Geiger all the starker, Jost even omitted Exodus 19:6 in an abbreviated youth Bible which he edited, despite his stated intention to retain the contents and spirit of the Bible.[73] We have already cited (n. 54) his complaint about those who prattle about "Priestervolk."

Samuel Holdheim, in contrast, another Berlin Reformer, frequently returned to our verse and emphasized its great significance as a slogan of "universal priesthood."[74] But that did not lead him to a positive view of the Pharisees — far from it! In a Hebrew volume which appeared in 1861 - the year after he died, and four after Geiger's *Urschrift* — Holdheim expressed severe

---

[69] See the passages assembled by Schorsch (above, n. 53), p. 7, n. 11, and cf. H. Graetz's criticism: *Geschichte der Juden*, XI (1870), p. 455.

[70] I. M. Jost, *Allgemeine Geschichte des Israelitischen Volkes*, II (1832), p. 65 (on Pharisees), 552 (on modern rabbinism).

[71] See the entries for werkheilig, Werkheilige, Werkheiligkeit in the *Deutsches Wörterbuch von Jacob Grimm und Wilhelm Grimm*, XIV, I/2 (1960), cols. 371–373: they all begin with references to Luther's writings, and most of the references are from Protestant literature, from the Reformation and later. For continued apologetics concerning "Werkheiligkeit," cf. J. J. Petuchowski, *Judaica* 46 (1990), pp. 17–18.

[72] Jost (above, n. 70), p. 541.

[73] See his *Neue Jugend-Bibel* (1823), p. iv; cf. p. 153, where our verse is skipped.

[74] See "Unser priesterlicher Beruf" in his *Neue Sammlung jüdischer Predigten*, I (1852), pp. 32ff, and cf. three sermons on the theme "The Decline of the Priesthood in Israel and its Transfer to the Whole People" in his *Predigten über die jüdische Religion*, III (1855), pp. 260–288. For the same theme, see above, Part III, § 7 (S. Maybaum).

criticism of the attempt to rehabilitate the Pharisees. He admits that Geiger's approach is new: "If we accept his approach, we must also accept that all the researchers and historians until now didn't know left from right and were as blind groping in the dark . . ."[75] But Holdheim did not accept Geiger's approach. In his opinion (as Jost's, if more moderately), the Pharisees, who were responsible for edicts and prohibitions, caused the people to depart from the way of the Bible, in contrast to the Sadducees, who did their best to preserve in purity the exclusive authority of the Torah. For a good example, we may note his account of the notorious story in BT *Yoma* 23a, according to which a priest was stabbed during the Temple service but since the knife was extracted before he died his father could rule that it was still pure – a ruling which elicited the lament that "they are concerned more with the purity of knives than with murder!" Under the influence of New Testament attacks on the Pharisees for paying attention to picayune details of purity and impurity, Holdheim assumes that the dying priest's father was a Pharisee:

Come and see how far the Pharisees' far-reaching edicts had gone, and their religious profit was certainly outweighed by their loss. We must be thankful to the Sadducees who arose against them to keep them from passing all bounds with their actions, and from abrogating the inner spirit by so overevaluating the externals of the Temple and the priestly cult.[76]

There were others who took this Jost-Holdheim approach, especially Moriz Friedländer,[77] but within a generation Geiger's approach became the dominant one.[78] As we have seen, an entire historiographical tradition grew up about it, despite the lack of any evidence for the specific claim concerning "kingdom of priests." Its success was due to the fact that it allowed the Reformers historical precedent for their approach: while Jost and Holdheim could give up on the Pharisees, they were forced to maintain that their Orthodox opponents were continuing historical Judaism. For their own part, they could only claim to be returning to biblical religion – which, on the one hand, is not particularly Jewish and which, on the other hand, laid them open

---

[75] S. Holdheim, *Maamar HaIshut 'al Techunat HaRabbanim vehaQaraim* (1860/61), p. 151; his critique of Geiger begins on p. 135.

[76] Ibid., p. 144.

[77] See his *Die religiösen Bewegungen innerhalb des Judentums im Zeitalter Jesu* (1905), pp. vi, xxi (criticism of Baeck?), xxii (on modern Pharisees), 13 (". . . mit Geiger und den ihm hierin blind nachbetenden Rabbinern den Pharisäismus als das 'Prinzip der fortschreitenden Entwicklung' erklären zu wollen, wäre gründlich verfehlt").

[78] I refer, of course, only to our particular part of Geiger's theory. For a partial list of reviewers and critics of Geiger, see pp. 49–51 of the appendix to the second edition of his *Urschrift* (1928). In general, on the differences between Holdheim and Geiger, see J. J. Petuchowski, *Leo Baeck Institute Year Book* 22 (1977), pp. 139–159.

to charges of Sadduceeism (and Karaism).[79] Indeed, as we saw, both Jost and Holdheim praised the Sadducees in comparison to the Pharisees.[80] But no founder or formulator of a new direction of Judaism could afford to associate it with Sadduceeism, which was long dead and condemned in Judaism's traditional sources. Geiger's approach solved the problem by turning the affiliations on their head: the Reformers could claim to be the true and admirable Pharisees, while the Orthodox turn out to be the letterbound Sadducees.[81] Thus, Reform Judaism was provided with a first-class lineage, one which was formulated by Siegmund Maybaum, only 23 years after the appearance of Geiger's *Urschrift*, as follows:

Twice, with the fall of the First Temple and of the Second Temple, history decided in favor of prophecy, but both times the priesthood reared its head again . . . This struggle still continues . . . It arose again, in another form, but with all its old force and decisiveness, in the debates between Pharisees and Sadducees and between rabbis and Karaites . . . We again encounter it in the struggle of later Jewish religious philosophers against a crass conception of God, and again in the opposition of modern religious development to the constricting limitations within which the Jewish decisors bound religious life. For struggle is just as ceaseless as development![82]

---

[79] Thus, for example, Hoffmann's review cited above (n. 53) bore the title "Die Überlieferung der Väter und der Neu-Sadducäismus." In this review, especially in its first and last installments (*Jüdische Presse* 1895, pp. 135–136; *Israelitische Monatsschrift* 1895, No. 11, p. 42), Hoffmann identifies the Reformers as Sadducees and Karaites. Indeed, as early as 1842 Geiger was forced to defend himself against the claim that he was a Sadducee or Karaite; he counterattacked by branding the Orthodox "rabbinic Karaites" enslaved to the letter of the Talmud and the halachic literature: *Abraham Geiger's Nachgelassene Schriften*, I (ed. L. Geiger; 1875), pp. 91–102.

[80] See above. Correspondingly, in a passage cited by Petuchowski (above, n. 78: p. 157), a Geiger disciple (I. M. Wise) accuses a Holdheim disciple (D. Einhorn) of Sadduceeism, for he held only to the Bible and wished to abandon historical tradition. I have not been able to locate the passage (Petuchowski's citation is inaccurate.)

[81] See Geiger (above, n. 79) and S. Maybaum, cited immediately below. By 1914, correspondingly, J. Wohlgemuth, a prominent Orthodox scholar and publicist of his day, complained that he could not find a suitable adjective to define his brand of Judentum: "gesetzestreues" played right into the hands of Reform critics who pictured Orthodoxy as sterile legalism, while "toratreues" is not sufficiently specific, for Geiger and the Reformers claimed that their religion was the true Torah, for the Torah's — as the Pharisees' — basic principle is that of progressive development. See his essay, which comes to no solution, in *Festschrift zum 70. Geburtstage David Hoffmann's* (edd. S. Eppenstein, M. Hildesheimer and J. Wohlgemuth; 1914), pp. 435–458.

[82] S. Maybaum, *Die Entwickelung des altisraelitischen Priesterthums* (1880), p. 126. Contrast Friedländer's version (above, n. 77: p. vii) of Judaism's true lineage, correcting m.*Avot* 1:1: from Moses to the prophets to the teachers of wisdom to the "leading spirits" of Judaism in the Greek-speaking Diaspora to Christianity, "completely circumventing the Jewish people, which deviated from universal Judaism ('Weltjudentum') and was introduced, by 'the Men of the Great Congregation,' into a narrow national bed."

To illustrate the turnabout worked by Geiger's theory, we need only note that the same writer, in a sermon cited above, quotes, as did Holdheim, the *baraita* in BT *Yoma* 23a about murder and the purity of knives. But while Holdheim used it as a whip to beat the Pharisees, Maybaum — who had learned from Geiger to identify priests as Sadducees — used it to illustrate Sadducean corruption denounced by the Pharisees.[83]

This reorientation of the Reform attitude toward the Pharisees entailed two new obligations:

1. On the internal front, comparison of Reform to Pharisaism required the demonstration that the Pharisees had changed, in accordance with their spirit and needs, the traditional laws of Judaism. This need was met by a long series of studies on the development of halachah,[84] and, of course, engendered just as long a series of polemic responses.[85]

2. On the external front, dependence upon the Pharisees as legitimators required apologetic literature defending them against Christian critics, as noted above.

The assumption that "a kingdom of priests" was a (or even *the*) Pharisaic slogan, in the sense that it claimed priesthood for all Jews, could be mobilized on both fronts. Internally, it supported the claim that the Pharisees were similar to the Reformers, for both opposed the established religious authorities of their times and preferred a spiritual cult to sacrifices.[86] Externally, correspondingly, it allowed for favorable comparison of Pharisaism with Protestantism — a surefire recommendation in the land of Luther.[87] Such double-bladed potency goes a long way toward explaining the

---

[83] Maybaum (above, n. 62), pp. 126–127. On the historical continuity of Geiger's program, as opposed to Holdheim's, see also M. A. Meyer, in *New Perspectives on Abraham Geiger: An HUC-JIR Symposium* (ed. J. J. Petuchowski; 1975), pp. 6–8. For Geiger's own formulation of this distinction, see his *Nachgelassene Schriften*, V (ed. L. Geiger; 1878), p. 246.

[84] Of those scholars we cited, such studies were especially characteristic of Geiger, Elbogen and Lauterbach.

[85] Note, for a characteristic example, J. Horovitz's essay in the Hoffmann Festschrift (above, n. 81): it opens (p. 139) with a citation of Geiger's account of the law's historical development, and is dedicated to disproving it. An expanded version of this essay later appeared as separate volume: *Untersuchungen zur rabbinischen Lehre von den falschen Zeugen* (1914); see p. 1.

[86] For an enthusiastic statement of this position, note Geiger's conclusion of his booklet on the sects (above, n. 35: p. 34 [40]): "Rabbinism, that is, Pharisaism as it developed, stands almost alone within Judaism. Now it wants again to move seriously according to its progressive principle. The establishment of full religious equality for the people, inner holiness instead of priestly externalism, the old Pharisaic slogan — let these be full and complete truths. All success to this young Pharisaism!"

[87] There were, of course, Jews who did not settle for defending Judaism and Pharisaism, but instead went on to attack Christianity. But even among them we find the claim that the

enigma addressed in this study — the popularity of a thesis virtually lacking evidential support.

V. Epilogue

In a 1929 article in the jubilee volume of the Breslau Seminary, Rabbi Ludwig Levy of Brünn (Brno, Czechoslovakia) proposed several new interpretations in the Book of Malachi.[88] Two are especially noteworthy. Both result from his basic premise that the book's rhetorical nature has not been properly understood, in that its statements are at times not the prophet's but rather those of his opponents, which he cites and denounces.

First, in 1:6, the prophet's attack on "you priests" is unintelligible, according to Levy, if it is really directed against the Temple priests. Is it their fault if worshippers bring them stolen animals for sacrifice (1:13)? Should they, could they be expected to investigate the ownership of every animal?! And what land did they own, which could fail to produce (2:2—3)? Rather, according to Levy, the prophet is in fact denouncing the people who bring such sacrifices, and the fact that he terms them "priests" indicates that they were used to take that honorific title for themselves on the basis of Exodus 19:6. Levy's conclusion is that Malachi, angered over the desecration of the Temple cult, used the title in bitter sarcasm.

Levy's second *novum* is linked to the first. If the sinful "priests" of ch. 1 are really non-Aaronite Israelites, then the prophet's call in 2:1—7 upon the

---

Reformation, in its attack upon the Catholic hierarchy, was fulfilling Jewish roots. See Fleischmann (above, n. 53), pp. 66, 75—76, 88—89, 117. Many emphasized the similarity of Protestant anti-sacerdotal democracy to that of Pharisaism or Judaism. So, for example, already Geiger (above, n. 35), p. 35 (= 41): "Die Reformation hat keine anderen als die oben angeführten Worte des zweiten Makkabäerbuches auf ihre Fahne geschrieben, daß Gott Allen das Priesterthum und die Heiligung gegeben. Der Protestantismus ist das volle Spiegelbild des Pharisäismus, wie der Katholicismus das des Sadducäismus . . ." It is particularly interesting to find this among the arguments advanced by liberal Jews in their struggle against rabbinic demands for more authority within their communities. See, for example, F. Makower's dependence upon the example of Luther, who emphasized the biblical ideal of universal priesthood, as a model for Jews as well: *Allgemeine Zeitung des Judenthums*, 10 December 1897, pp. 592—593. Elsewhere, similarly, he expressed the fear that rabbinic authority could lead to "Catholization" of Judaism, and hence to stagnation à la Spain (ibid., 21 October 1898, p. 502). For this struggle over community authority, which shows how well the liberal rabbis succeeded in inculcating the ideal of universal priesthood, see A. Altmann, *Leo Baeck Institute Year Book* 19 (1974), pp. 41—43. For insistence that Judaism and the Pharisees out-Protestanted the Protestants in this respect, see also a 1929 letter in Fr. Rosenzweig, *Briefe und Tagebücher*, II (edd. R. Rosenzweig et al.; 1979), pp. 1204—1205; cf. Baeck (above, n. 46), pp. 47—48 (in English: p. 51).

[88] *Festschrift zum 75jährigen Bestehen des jüdisch-theologischen Seminars Fraenckelscher Stiftung*, II (1929), pp. 273—284. According to documents in the archives of the RFJI (above, n. *), Levy emigrated to France in 1939 and died there in 1946.

"priests" to preserve their covenant must also be meant for the whole people. To this call, which is followed by castigation of the people for failure to observe the covenant of Levi (2:8–9), *the people responds* – so Levy – "Do we not all have one father?" (2:10). That is, the prophet's call for preservation of national separatism and purity encountered opposition from Jews who consider themselves all priests and argue for universalism instead of separatism.

It is not our purpose, here, to evaluate Levy's interpretation of Malachi.[89] Its importance in the present context is as illustration of the pervasiveness of the themes we have considered in this study. For Levy's account of Malachi's opponents, whether or not it corresponds to the realities of Judaea in the Persian period, definitely corresponds to the realities of the world of German-speaking Judaism at the time he wrote:[90] Malachi's opponents, who combined – according to Levy – the democratic claim of universal priesthood within the Jewish people and a universalist attitude toward the Gentiles, would fit right into the Berlin Hochschule and Temples where we found our material.[91] According to Levy, the prophet's point is that too much of such laudable ideals could endanger the people.

---

[89] For a broader discussion of this interpretive approach to the Bible, see R. Gordis, *HUCA* 22 (1949), pp. 157–219 (reprinted in idem, *Poets, Prophets, and Sages* [1971], pp. 104–159; see too its index, p. 434, s.v. Levy, Ludwig.)

[90] As Levy was well aware. See pp. 276–277, where he claims that Malachi, in attacking those who tend to universalism and belittle ritual, was warning against dangers which always recur "bis in unsere Zeit."

[91] Indeed, the ideal priest of Malachi 2 is frequently cited as a model for all Jews in sermons by Reform rabbis, such as Holdheim's "Unser priesterlicher Beruf" (above, n. 74), p. 34 and D. Leimdörfer's "Das Priestertum Israels," *Zwei Reden* (1883), pp. 13–21. So too with regard to "Do we not all have one father?" – the verse was so firmly established as a *legitimate* expression of Jewish universalism that M. Freudenthal saw in its ascription to Malachi's enemies sufficient reason to predict Levy's article would encounter "sehr starke Ablehnung" (*MGWJ* 73 [1929], p. 494). Indeed, such criticism may have convinced Levy: in his "official" translation of Malachi, a few years later, he (if not an editor) dropped the quotation marks around "Priester" (1:6; 2:1), and the corresponding parenthetical explanations in 2:10 ("so you say") and 2:4 ("and not a people composed totally of priests"), which he had inserted into the translation appended to the 1929 article. See *Die Heilige Schrift neu ins Deutsche übertragen*, III (ed. H. Torczyner; 1936), pp. 494–498.

4. "The Contemners of Judges and Men" (11Q Temple 64:12)*

(22) And if a man has committed a crime punishable by death and he is put to death, and you hang him on a tree, (23) his body shall not remain all night upon the tree, but you shall bury him the same day, for a hanged man is accursed by God (KY QLLT 'LHYM TLWY); you shall not defile your land which the Lord your God gives you for an inheritance. (Deut. 21:22–23 RSV)

A number of problems are raised by these verses, among them:

i. Are all criminals sentenced to death to be hung on a tree, or only some particular offenders?

ii. Does our text refer to post-mortem exhibition of the corpse (as the order of the clauses suggests) or to a mode of execution (with the general statement "put to death" later made more precise by reference to the mode – "hang him on a tree")?

iii. How is the criminal to be hung (by neck, arms, etc., or crucified, impaled, etc.)?

iv. What is the meaning of KY QLLT 'LHYM TLWY? And, particularly, is the construct state to be viewed as an objective genitive, meaning that he who is hung cursed or is cursing God? Or is it rather a subjective genitive, meaning that God cursed or is cursing him who is hung?

As is well-known, the usual tannaitic view was that (ad i) the verse mandates a punishment to be applied to only some criminals, namely, those who, as the blasphemer, deny a central dogma;[1] such a criminal is (ad ii) hung *after* his execution by (ad iii) tying his hands to a tree; and (ad iv) the words QLLT 'LHYM are in the objective genitive, namely, they both specify the crimes involved (above: i) and also explain that the corpse must be removed soon

---

* Hebrew original: *Leshonenu* 47 (1982/83), pp. 18–24, where, unfortunately, the English summary was somewhat botched.

[1] According to R. Eliezer's view (sources in the next note), the case of the blasphemer was only an example, so the same punishment was also to be inflicted upon other criminals whose execution, as the blasphemer's, was by stoning.

because the exposure of the human body (made "in the image of God") leads to continued disrespect for God.[2]

An entirely different approach appears in the Acts of the Apostles and in Galatians.[3] No answer is offered for question i. But questions ii and iii are clearly answered by both New Testament books, which apply our verse to the crucifixion of Jesus (Acts 5:30; 10:39; Gal. 3:13), thus indicating that we are dealing with that particular mode of execution. And Paul, at least, in the wake of the Septuagint, clearly assumes (ad iv) that QLLT 'LHYM is a subjective genitive, for he argues that by being crucified Jesus became cursed (and therefore could redeem others from the curse under which they labored).[4]

Various aspects of these New Testament answers to our questions may be found in ancient Jewish exegetical literature.[5] Thus, for example, the Peshitta agrees with regard to ii,[6] and the Septuagint and Targum Neofiti agree with regard to iv.[7] But in 1971 Y. Yadin published a section of the Temple Scroll from Qumran (64:6−13),[8] which apparently agrees with all three New Testament answers (questions ii−iv).[9] To wit: (ad ii) it twice reverses the order of the clauses in v. 22 so as to make hanging precede dying (although it once has the masoretic order); (ad iii) comparison of it with another Qumran text led Yadin, at least, to argue that it took our verse to refer to crucifixion;[10]

---

[2] See *Sifré Deut.* § 221 (ed. Finkelstein, pp. 253−255); *Midrash Tannaim* to Deut. 21:22−23 (ed. Hoffmann, pp. 131−132); m.*Sanhedrin* 6:4; Tos. ibid. 9:6−7; etc.

[3] On the use of Deut. 21:22−23 in the New Testament see especially M. Wilcox, *JBL* 96 (1977), pp. 85−99, as well as some of the studies cited below.

[4] For the scapegoat notion underlying Gal. 3:10−14 and 4:4−5, cf. above, p. 25, n. 57.

[5] For a full review of ancient interpretations of KY QLLT 'LHYM TLWY, see M. J. Bernstein, *JQR* 74 (1983), pp. 21−45 (which was published after the Hebrew original of this paper).

[6] See Wilcox (above, n. 3), p. 90; Y. Yadin, *The Temple Scroll*, I (1983), p. 375; Y. Maori, "The Peshitta Version of the Pentateuch in its Relation to the Sources of Jewish Exegesis" (Diss. Hebrew University, 1975), pp. 171−173 (in Hebrew).

[7] And both, as Paul, have an additional "all" in v. 23 (yielding "*any* who is hung"), which apparently clarifies the understanding of the genitive as subjective. It may be assumed that Paul was simply following the Septuagint; so Wilcox (above, n. 3), pp. 86−87, also J. A. Fitzmyer, *CBQ* 40 (1978), p. 512, n. 68.

[8] First published in *IEJ* 21 (1971), p. 6, now available in the complete edition of the scroll (above, n. 6). For a German version of Yadin's article, see *Qumran* (ed. K. E. Grözinger et al.; 1981), pp. 167−184.

[9] As has been emphasized by many, including Wilcox (above, n. 3), pp. 89−90; Fitzmyer (above, n. 7), pp. 511−512; O. Betz, *Jesus: Der Messias Israels − Aufsätze zur biblischen Theologie* (1987), pp. 71−74 (first published in Hebrew translation in *Jerusalem in the Second Temple Period: Abraham Schalit Memorial Volume* [edd. A. Oppenheimer, U. Rappaport and M. Stern; 1980], pp. 95−97); and J. M. Ford, *Expository Times* 87 (1975/76), pp. 275−278. Concerning question iv, which will especially interest us here, see also H.-W. Kuhn, *Zeitschrift für Theologie und Kirche* 72 (1975), pp. 33−34.

[10] See *Pesher Nahum* frgs. 3−4, col. 1, lines 7−8. For an account of the first several years

and (ad iv) it reads MQWLLY, with a *vav*, and it is generally taken for granted that this is the passive participle (vocalized *m^{e}qull^{e}lé*): "those who are cursed." In other words, this passage has been taken to be a Hebrew representative of the same interpretation found otherwise only in Greek (Septuagint and Paul) and Aramaic (Neofiti).[11] Now, while points ii and especially iii have been the object of vigorous debate,[12] which I will not enter, iv has not.

Translators and commentators agree that MQWLLY is to be vocalized as a *pu'al* participle: *mequll^{e}lé*, "are cursed." My opinion is different, as shall be seen. Investigation of the matter may be useful, it seems, not only with regard to question iv, but also for the proper understanding of the passage as a whole.

The text reads as follows (my translation):

6   If
7   there is a man who is RKYL B'MW and betrays his nation to a
     foreign people and does evil to his nation,
8   you shall hang him on a tree and he shall die. On the
     testimony of two witnesses or three witnesses
9   he shall be executed, and they shall hang him [on] the tree.
     If a man shall be guilty of a capital crime and he flees to
10   among the peoples and curses his people and[13] the Children of
     Israel, you shall hang him too upon the tree

---

of the debate, see M. P. Horgan, *Pesharim: Qumran Interpretations of Biblical Books* (1979), pp. 176–179 (and text, p. 47).

[11] Among those who see here a subjective genitive, the precise sense is not always clear. Some follow the word-order ("cursed . . . hung") and imply, apparently, that the man is to be hung because he was cursed, while others, at times reversing the word-order, seem to impute to the Scroll the same interpretation as Paul: because the man was hung, he is cursed. (For the same alternatives in ancient exegesis, see Bernstein [above, n.5], p. 42). The following seem to belong to the first group: F. García, *Estudios Bíblicos* 36 (1977), p. 290; J. Maier, *Die Tempelrolle vom Toten Meer* (1978), p. 64 (but in *The Temple Scroll* [1985], pp. 55, 134, it sounds more Pauline); and M. Bernstein, *Gesher* 7 (1979), p. 154. For the second interpretation, see Wilcox (above, n. 3), p. 89; Fitzmyer (above, n. 7), p. 503; and A. Caquot, *Etudes théologiques et religieuses* 53 (1978), p. 498.

[12] See J. M. Baumgarten, *JBL* 91 (1972), pp. 472–481 (and in his *Studies in Qumran Law* [1977], pp. 172–182) and idem, *Eretz-Israel* 16 (Harry M. Orlinsky Volume, 1982), pp. 7* –16* (in English). In this Yadin-Baumgarten debate, it is characteristic that the Israeli had no qualms about publishing – years before the rest of the scroll! – a text and argument which could support New Testament claims of Jewish initiative for the crucifixion of Jesus, while it was the American rabbi – who introduced me to the Scrolls – who immediately set out to rebut. For further literature, see Fitzmyer (above, n. 7), pp. 498–499, n. 24; Horgan (above, n. 10); and D. J. Halperin, *JJS* 32 (1981), pp. 32–46.

[13] The conjunction (*vav*) was added in after the text was first written (copied). Without it, the text is smoother.

11   and he shall die. And you must not leave his corpse on the
      tree overnight; rather, you must surely bury him on that day, for
12   MQWLLY 'LHYM W'DM are hung on the tree, and you should not
      defile the land which I[14]
13   give you for an inheritance.

Returning to our four questions, it is apparent, first of all, that the author of
this text, as the rabbis, did not assume that hanging applies to all capital
crimes.[15] Moreover, it seems clear that he, again as the rabbis, viewed the
words QLLT 'LHYM as the clue to be followed in narrowing the application
of this law. The rabbis (above, n. 2) followed this hint to Leviticus 24:13–23,
where the punishment of him who curses God (MQLL 'LHYW) is stated to be
death by stoning. This led them to the conclusion that he who blasphemes God
(or commits a similar "denial of the main principle"), or — according to a
minority view — he whose punishment, as the blasphemer's, is death by
stoning, is to be hung thereafter.

It is clear, however, that the Temple Scroll does not use Leviticus 24 to
specify the scope of our law, for: a) the Scroll does not relate to the execution
by stoning mandated there; b) Leviticus 24 refers only to the blasphemer,
whereas the Scroll (also — ? [see on]) applies this punishment to sins against
the nation; and c) there is no reason which would have led the exegete of
Deuteronomy 21[16] from Leviticus 24 to Leviticus 19:16, L' TLK RKYL
B'MYK, which is obviously used in the first line of our passage.

It appears, therefore, that our commentator, looking for a way to specify
the capital crimes to which Deuteronomy 21:22–23 apply, turned to the only
other pentateuchal passage, apart from Leviticus 24, which contains QLL
together with 'LHYM: 'LHYM L' TQLL WNSY' B'MK L' T'R (Exodus
22:27).[17] This assumption evades all three difficulties listed in the preceding
paragraph with regard to Leviticus 24. Namely, a) Exodus 22:27 specifies no
penalty for the crimes it prohibits, so there is no problem with linking it to the
punishment of Deuteronomy 21:22–23; b) it refers to at least one crime

---

[14] This pronoun corresponds to the Scroll's usual point of view: God is the speaker.

[15] In fact, he could not have done so, for he considered hanging the mode of execution, and
not (contra the rabbis) a post-mortem exposure. As the Bible prescribes other specific modes
of execution for various capital offenses, it followed that hanging could not apply to all such
offenses.

[16] And it is clear that our text is a commentary on this pericope, just as the passages
preceding and following it deal with the adjacent pericopae in Deuteronomy.

[17] A few scholars have already suspected that this verse plays a role in the Scroll here:
Yadin (above, n. 6), II, p. 290, in his note to line 10; Fitzmyer (above, n. 7), pp. 511–512;
Bernstein (above, n. 11), p. 153. However, none drew what appear to be the ensuing
conclusions.

against the nation, namely, cursing its prince; and c) it may easily be associated with Leviticus 19:16, both because both verses refers to crimes consisting of speech against the people, and because the use of B'MK/B'MYK gives a further exegetical peg which invites their association.

The flow of the exegete's argument may, therefore, be analyzed as follows. First, he linked Deuteronomy 21:22−23, a punishment for unspecified crimes, to Exodus 22:27, crimes with an unspecified punishment. The justification for this linkage was the common use of QLL together with 'LHYM. But the latter verse dragged along Leviticus 19:16, as it were, due to their common topic (evil speech) and B'MK/B'MYK. (It may also be that the exegete felt he needed more than one verse, for otherwise it would be strange that the Torah did not simply specify the punishment of hanging along with the prohibition in Exodus.) Therefore, finally, the exegete inferred that hanging was the punishment for the crime of Leviticus 19:16 too.[18] In writing his paraphrase, therefore, he first specified that crime (lines 6−8), taking "going RKYL in your people" not as simple talebearing in the midst of the people but rather as revealing national secrets, treason.[19] Next, *we would assume* (see below), in lines 9b−10 he further specified the crimes of Exodus 22:27. Finally, in summarizing, in line 12, he expanded Deuteronomy's QLLT 'LHYM into MQWLLY 'LHYM *W'DM* to account for the fact that the law in fact applies not only to those who curse 'LHYM (as in Exodus 22:27 and the text of Deuteronomy) but also to those who curse men, viz., the nation.

There are, however, two obvious difficulties. First of all, the description of the second crime, in lines 9b−10, does not seem to refer to the cursing of God,[20] so how can we assume it reflects Exodus 22:27? The answer is that a widespread Jewish tradition assumes that 'LHYM in Exodus 22:27 does not

---

[18] This analysis of the argument is intended only to expose the elements of the exegete's thought, not to reconstruct its genesis. It might be, for example, that he first associated the prohibitions in Exodus and Leviticus, and then linked them to the punishment in Deuteronomy, or it might be that he grasped the whole subject organically.

[19] For the preposition *bet* of speaking *against* someone or something, see for example Numbers 12:1, 8; 21:5, 7; Psalm 58:19; so too Bernstein (above, n. 11), pp. 147−148. As for "going RKYL," it seems to appear in this sense, although without the *bet*, in *Hodayot* 5:25.

[20] Note that this difficulty pertains not only to our interpretation; it encumbers all those which assume 'LHYM here is God. To get around it, Betz (above, n. 9: p. 69 [in Hebrew: 92]) asserted that "Das Suffix der 3. Person Singularis im mehrfach erwähnten Wort *'ammo* (Z. 7.10) ist nicht etwa auf das Subjekt der Sätze, d.h. den verräterischen und fluchenden Mann, zu beziehen, sondern umschreibt wie so oft in der jüdischen Literatur den Namen Gottes; Sein Volk ist gemeint. Wer Israel preisgibt, tastet Gottes Eigentum an . . ." But this acute suggestion appears to be overly artificial, and, moreover, according to the Scroll's usual point of view (see n. 14) would require 'MY ("My people"). Yadin (above, n. 6: vol. II, p. 290, n. to line 10) indeed suggested that the proper reading is 'MY, the copyist having erred due to the style of the preceding lines. But this suggestion, which is meant to preserve the identification of 'LHYM as God, seems to be a product of circular reasoning alone.

refer to God, but rather to some lesser beings. In the wake of the Septuagint (*theous*), Josephus and Philo thought the verse prohibited cursing pagan "gods."[21] But it is unlikely that our Scoll's author shared their apologetic stance; in general, his attitude toward Gentiles is a negative one.[22] Rather, it is likely that his view was the one typical of rabbinic literature,[23] according to which 'LHYM here refers to judges — as it does, apparently, in a few verses in the immediate context as well (22:8, 9, 11), as various modern commentators and translators agree. That this is the case in our Scroll is made especially likely by the fact that lines 9b—10 require hanging for a man who, *after having committed a capital crime*, "flees" to the Gentiles. While some scholars have taken the Scroll to mean that his capital crime was going to the Gentiles and cursing his nation among them,[24] this ignores the order of the text and, moreover, cannot account for the word "flees."[25] Rather, the Scroll refers to a man who is a fugitive from justice; he is fleeing capital punishment for some other offense. Our text does not clarify whether the fugitive in question fled before, during or after trial and condemnation. But, however that may be, flight in such circumstances evinces scorn for the legal system ("contempt of court" or worse), QLLT 'LHYM, and hence the special punishment.[26]

The second difficulty is morphological. Assuming, as we have, that line 12 of our text is to be translated "those who curse *'elohim* and man [are] hung on a tree", MQWLLY should be active: "those who curse." But for active QLL we should expect the *pi'el* form, *meqall^elé*, without the *vav*. As we have it, the verb — as apparently all have assumed — seems to be the passive *pu'al* form, "those who are cursed." However, it seems that one of the following two explanations may suffice to overcome this difficulty: either a) the *vav* is simply to be ignored, as this *mater lectionis* is frequently to be ignored, or explained away as a figment of Qumran pronunciation, in this scroll as in others;[27] or

---

[21] Philo, *De spec. leg.* 1.5; *Vita Mosis* 2.203—208 (based on Lev. 24); Josephus, *Ant.* 4.207, *C. Ap.* 2.237.

[22] See 51:19, 57:7—11, 58:3 and 59:18—20.

[23] See Maori (above, n. 6), pp. 115—117; M. M. Kasher, *Torah Shelemah*, XVIII (1957/58), pp. 123—127 (in Hebrew). Cf. A. E. Draffkorn, *JBL* 76 (1957), p. 216.

[24] So Yadin (above, n. 6), I, pp. 373—374 and Bernstein (above, n. 11), p. 149.

[25] Yadin and Bernstein (see the preceding note) avoid this problem by speaking of flight to the *enemy*, out of fear of an impending war. But the Scroll speaks of Gentiles, not particularly of enemies, and as 58:3—4 shows, not all Gentiles were assumed to be combatant enemies. For a proper emphasis on the fact that the text speaks of Gentiles, not enemies, see Baumgarten's 1982 article (above, n. 12), pp. 11*—12*.

[26] For the basic meaning of MQLL as "make light of" or "show disrespect for," see H. Ch. Brichto, *The Problem of "Curse" in the Hebrew Bible* (1963), pp. 118—177, esp. 137—165; G. R. Driver, *Journal of Semitic Studies* 10 (1965), pp. 94—95.

[27] On apparently superfluous *vavs* in the Temple Scroll, of unknown origin and purpose, see E. Qimron, *Leshonenu* 42 (1977/78), p. 90 (in Hebrew). For *vav* instead of an expected

b) we should view MQWLLY as a case of QLL not in *pu'al*, but rather in *polel*, similar to MḤWLL, MGWLL, MḤWLL, M'WLL, etc.[28] Indeed, it seems that *4Q Pesher Psalmᵃ*, fragments 1–10, col. iii, lines 9–12, where MQWLLW (the pronominal suffix refers to God) is identified as a wicked and ruthless Jew, who could have chosen to join the congregation of the righteous (lines 4–5) but did not do so, gives another example of active QLL in *polel*.[29]

Summary

According to our understanding of this passage in the Temple Scroll, it does not contain Paul's understanding of Deuteronomy 21:22–23, according to which God curses the hanged man. God is not mentioned at all. Rather, the author attached this punishment to two biblical verses which prohibit

---

pataḥ in this scroll, as in our case, see 47:7 and 48:3. The latter case is especially interesting, in that the scribe first "forgot" the superfluous *vav* and later inserted it. Probably he had copied it from a text which used masoretic spelling and then corrected according to his own norms. Note also the repeated usage of ḤWQWT 'WLM (18:8; 19:8; 22:14; etc.) instead of the masoretic ḤWQT. H. Yalon viewed such extra *vav*s, in different morphologies, as products of Aramaic influence (*Studies in the Dead Sea Scrolls – Philological Essays (1949–1952)* [1967], pp. 59–60, 98 [in Hebrew, commenting on ḤWZYR instead of ḤZYR in the Isaiah Scroll); see also E. Y. Kutscher, *The Language and Linguistic Background of the Isaiah Scroll (I Q Isaᵃ)* (1974), p. 374. The late Meir Medan kindly referred me to the last-named studies. Finally, regarding MQWLLY instead of MQLLY we should note – as Prof. J. Blau reminded me – that in rabbinic Hebrew a *lamedh* may cause a preceding *pataḥ* to turn into a *vav*; see E. Y. Kutscher, *Archive of the New Dictionary of Rabbinical Literature*, I (ed. E. Y. Kutscher; 1972), pp. 38, 91 (in Hebrew). For other "extra" *vav*s in Qumran Hebrew, cf. M. Bar-Asher, *Leshonenu* 45 (1980/81), pp. 91–92 and *11Q Melchizedek*, line 10 (BQWRB instead of BQRB in Psalm 82:1).

[28] On *polel* in the Scrolls, see E. Qimron, "A Grammar of the Hebrew Language of the Dead Sea Scrolls" (Diss., Hebrew University, 1976), pp. 199, 207 (in Hebrew; these sections are among the many not reproduced in his English *The Hebrew of the Dead Sea Scrolls* [1986]). Bernstein (above, n. 5: p. 39, n. 36), states that a number of his colleagues subscribed to the thought that our MQWLLY should be read as *polel*, but I have not seen such in print. Bernstein admitted that the suggestion is attractive, and "both syntactically and contextually smooth," but tended to reject it because "Qumran Hebrew seems to use Polel forms of geminate verbs only in those instances where the Polel of the verb exists already in biblical Hebrew," while QLL is in evidence in Qumran only in *pi'el*. This, however, is only an argument from silence, and even that silence is not complete; see immediately below.

[29] For this text, see Horgan (above, n. 10), pp. 197 (translation), 217–218 (commentary and bibliography); texts, pp. 53–54. In the Hebrew version of this study, n. 26, I left open the possibility that the *pesher* assumes that the wicked are bad because God cursed them. That would leave the verb passive, as in the masoretic version of Psalm 37:22 (as Bernstein assumes – see our preceding note). However, to assume such a notion involves a good bit of textless interpretation here, so I now more confidently cite this pesher's orthography in support of our reading of the Temple Scroll.

slandering the people (Lev. 19:16) or its leaders (judges and princes — Exodus 22:27), and accordingly expanded the enigmatic phrase, QLLT 'LHYM, which he took to designate the sort of criminals to be hung, into one which included both categories: "those who contemn judges or men."[30]

---

[30] The usage of *vav* for "or" hardly requires comment. As for the failure to coordinate the numbers (plural MQWLLY, singular TLWY), it is either a mistake or the result of a tendency to preserve the biblical diction (TLWY) as much as possible. For another possibility, based on the usual assumption that the verb is to be vocalized as *pu'al*, see Baumgarten's *Studies* (above, n. 12), p. 173, n. 4 (not in the original *JBL* version).

5. "Scribes and Pharisees, Hypocrites:"
Who are the "Scribes" in the New Testament?[*]

The Synoptic Gospels and Acts frequently mention Jewish leaders called "scribes" (*grammateis*). Their functions seem to be varied: they appear as interpreters of the Bible and as teachers, and therefore argue with Jesus and his teachings, but they also appear among those who arrested Jesus and among his judges, as well, finally, as among those who mocked him when he was on the cross.[1] At times they appear alone, but more often they are paired with others: the high priests or the Pharisees.[2] In this study, we will attempt to identify these "scribes."

I. Scribes = Pharisees?

It is usual to identify the scribes as Pharisees, "rabbis."[3] Moreover, it appears that this is quite an ancient assumption: comparison of Matthew to Mark indicates that the former wrote "Pharisee" in some places where Mark, his

---

[*] Hebrew original: *Zion* 50 (1984/85 = *Zion Jubilee Volume L (1935−1985)*), pp. 121−132. Since then, much has been published, including D. Lührmann, "Die Pharisäer und die Schriftgelehrten im Markusevangelium," *ZNW* 78 (1987), pp. 169−185; A. J. Saldarini, *Pharisees, Scribes and Sadducees in Palestinian Society* (1988); and E. S. Malbon, "The Jewish Leaders in the Gospel of Mark: A Literary Study of Marcan Characterization," *JBL* 108 (1989), pp. 259−281.
[1] For surveys of the references, see H. Lesêtre, in *Dictionnaire de la Bible*, V (1912), cols. 1540−1542; G. Baumbach, in *Exegetisches Wörterbuch zum Neuen Testament*, I (edd. H. Balz and G. Schneider; 1980), cols. 624−627.
[2] In the Gospels and Acts, the *grammateis* appear 22 times alongside the Pharisees, 21 times alongside the high priests, and 22 times alone or in other contexts. (Outside of these five books, the *grammateis* are mentioned only once in the New Testament − in I Corinthians 1:20, a quote from Isaiah 33:18.) See *A Concordance to the Greek Testament* (edd. W. F. Moulton and A. S. Geden, revised by H. K. Moulton; 1963⁴), pp. 175−176.
[3] See, inter alia, E. Lohse, *The New Testament Environment* (1976), pp. 115−120; J. Jeremias, *Jerusalem in the Time of Jesus* (1969), pp. 233−245; idem, in *Theological Dictionary of the New Testament*, I (1964), pp. 740−742; SVM II, pp. 322−325, 388; M. J. Cook, *Mark's Treatment of the Jewish Leaders* (1978), pp. 85−97; E. Rivkin, *HUCA* 49

source, wrote "scribe."[4] Correspondingly, Matthew in general seems to have used the two terms as synonyms, as in the well-known series of "woe to you, scribes and Pharisees, hypocrites" in ch. 23.[5] Indeed, the New Testament twice mentions "scribes of the Pharisees."[6] And, for the final and fundamental consideration, it is — or has been thought, on the basis of such texts as *Ant.* 18.15−17 and m.*Avot* 1 — difficult to imagine non-Pharisaic Torah scholars in the first century; who else, in other words, could the scribes be?

However, recent decades have seen the collapse of pan-Pharisaism. We now know that other varieties of first-century Judaism must be taken very seriously, and that Josephan and rabbinic statements about Pharisaic hegemony must be taken with more than a grain of salt.[7] And as for the specific considerations mentioned in the preceding paragraph, they can cut both ways. First of all, if Matthew replaces his source's "scribe" with "Pharisee," this *might* mean that they are synonymous in his mind, but it also might mean that he no longer wished to polemicize against "scribes" and preferred to make the text attack Pharisees, with whom he was more familiar.[8] We may not simply assume that the Pharisees Matthew was familiar with (rabbis of the Jabneh generation) were identical with the Jewish leaders

---

(1978), pp. 135−142. Some of these scholars, as others, admit that there may have also been Sadducean scribes, but by and large they assume they were Pharisees. J. Neusner, who distinguished scribes from Pharisees and justifiably emphasized that Josephus does not identify the two, nevertheless identified scribes as rabbis. See his *Early Rabbinic Judaism* (1975), pp. 64−69 (= *History of Religions* 12 [1972/73], pp. 264−269).

[4] See Matthew 9:34; 12:24 (contrast Mark 3:22); Matthew 22:41 (contrast Mark 12:35). For bibliography, see below, n. 8.

[5] See vv. 2, 13, 15, 23, 25, 27, 29; also Matthew 5:20; 12:38, and J. P. Meier, *Law and History in Matthew's Gospel* (1976), pp. 111−113.

[6] Acts 23:9; Mark 2:16. On the latter, see B. M. Metzger, *A Textual Commentary on the Greek New Testament* (1971), p. 78; C. M. Martini, in *Text-Wort-Glaube: Studien . . . Kurt Aland gewidmet* (ed. M. Brecht; 1980), pp. 31−39.

[7] In 1956, within a decade of the first discoveries at Qumran, there appeared two seminal essays which pointed the way toward much of what would occur in the next three decades: M. Smith's essay on first-century Judaism in *Israel: Its Role in Civilization* (ed. M. Davis; 1956), pp. 67−81; and E. Stauffer's essay on "Priestertradition" in *Theologische Literaturzeitung* 81 (1956), cols. 135−150. A decade later, Neusner was already writing the epitaph for the notion of "normative Judaism;" see *Judaism* 15 (1966), pp. 230−240, reprinted in his *Early Rabbinic Judaism*, pp. 139−151. Cf. below, p. 141, n. 33. By the 1970's, the whole notion of there having been a Jewish orthodoxy in the first century was under fire: see the protracted dispute in *JSJ* (N.J. McEleney in vol. 4, D.E. Aune in vol. 7, L.L. Grabbe in vol. 8, and McEleney again in vol. 9). Concerning the self-serving motive which led to the omission of the priests from rabbinic chains of tradition, see M. D. Herr in *Zion* 44 (1978/79 = *Yitzhak F. Baer Memorial Volume* [1980]), pp. 44−51 (in Hebrew); B. Lewis, *History — Remembered, Recovered, Invented* (1975), pp. 18−20.

[8] See esp. P. Winter, *On the Trial of Jesus* (revised ed. by T. A. Burkill and G. Vermes; 1974), pp. 170−178, also M. Smith, *Jesus the Magician* (1978), pp. 153−154, and O. L. Cope, *Matthew: A Scribe Trained for the Kingdom of Heaven* (1976), pp. 126−127.

termed "scribes" in Jesus' day. Similarly, the very juxtaposition of the two terms in Matthew 23 could imply that they are not identical in the writer's mind (although both might be equally hypocritical), and the phrase "scribe of the Pharisees" may indicate that not all scribes are Pharisees;[9] indeed, it may even imply that most scribes, without additional description, are not Pharisees.

Furthermore, we must note that rabbinic literature provides no support for the notion that rabbinic sages of the first century called themselves "scribes." The term *sopher* was applied to people who wrote or copied for a living or to teachers of Bible, or, at times, to sages of an earlier generation ("the *Soph^{e}rim*").[10] Indeed, the one time the New Testament mentions a known Pharisaic leader, Gamaliel I, it does not term him "scribe," but rather "teacher of the Law" (Acts 5:34).[11] Finally, we must note that it is difficult, *a priori*, to assume that "scribe" and "Pharisee" are identical, for, in that case, why were two terms needed?

II. *Shot^{e}rim*

It appears that a helpful point of departure will be the fact that the New Testament's "scribes" at times function as secondary figures in the realm of law and law enforcement.[12] Thus, for example, in Jesus' prophecies that he will suffer at the hands of the Jews, the "scribes" are mentioned last, after the

---

[9] So, for example, D. Chwolson, *Das letzte Passmahl Christi und der Tag seines Todes* (1892), p. 113; for his conclusions, see below, n. 59. See also W. R. Telford's review of Cook (above, n. 3), in *JTS* n.s. 31 (1980), pp. 161–162, and Baumbach (above, n. 1), col. 625.

[10] See E. E. Urbach, *Tarbiz* 27 (1957/58), pp. 172–174 (in Hebrew); H. L. Strack and P. Billerbeck, *Kommentar zum Neuen Testament aus Talmud und Midrasch*, I (1922), pp. 79–82; S. Légasse, *RB* 68 (1961), pp. 497–498; B. Gerhardsson, *Memory and Manuscript* (1961), pp. 44-45. Similarly, recall that Josephus does not identify scribes and Pharisees; see above, n. 3.

[11] It has been suggested that the mysterious father of Gamaliel I is also mentioned in the New Testament (Luke 2:25–35): A. Cutler, *Journal of Bible and Religion* 34 (1966), pp. 29–35. This suggestion, presented with a large question mark, remains doubtful, and, in any case, this Simon is not termed a *grammateus*. Neither is Paul, although he is termed a Pharisee (Acts 23:6; Philippians 3:5).

[12] This aspect of their activity was especially emphasized by Winter (above, n. 8), p. 177, n. 25 and A. T. Olmstead, *Jesus in the Light of History* (1942), pp. 178–179, and both also drew the conclusion that these "scribes" were not necessarily Pharisees. In fact, Winter opines that the equation of scribes and Pharisees is one of the most frequent errors in New Testament studies, and Olmstead even asserts that *all* (!) the scribes mentioned in the New Testament were *Sadducees*. Cook (above, n. 3: p. 88, n. 27) admits that the administrative meaning (secretary, registrar) is usual for *grammateus* in classical Greek, the Septuagint and Josephus, but he tends to deny it to the ones mentioned in the New Testament.

elders and the high priests (Mark 8:31; 10:33; Matthew 16:21; 20:18; Luke 9:22). Again, in Mark 3:22 we read of the scribes who went from Jerusalem to the Galilee to argue with Jesus; a similar story appears in John 1:19 in connection with Jesus' predecessor, John the Baptist, but there it is explicitly said that the delegation *had been sent* to hold the inquiry.[13] Mark 14:53 reports that the scribes, the elders and the high priests assembled with the high priest to judge Jesus,[14] but after v. 54 reports that the servants (*hypēretai*)[15] sat outside v. 55 gives the story's continuation without mentioning the scribes. In other words, it sounds like v. 53's "scribes" are v. 54's "servants." Similarly, Acts 4:5−6 reports that the apostles were brought to judgement before the rulers, the elders, the scribes and all the high priests, but when Peter begins his speech, shortly thereafter (v. 8), he addresses the rulers and elders alone; when he is released, he reports only what the high priests and the elders told him (v. 23). Here, in other words, as in Jesus' trial, it seems that the "scribes" are connected to the legal process but are not among the judges. So too, finally, we should note that the only non-Jewish *grammateus* mentioned in the New Testament was a legal official (Acts 19:35).[16]

It will readily be admitted that these cases do not *prove* the scribes were only some sort of judicial officers but not members of the court. They do, however, open up that possibility. This opening will be greatly widened by the fact that the Septuagint uses *grammateus* not only for *sopher* but also, and consistently, for *shoter*.[17] This term − used for "policeman" in modern Hebrew − denotes some sort of minor official, usually in the realm of law and enforcement, who functions alongside of more senior officials.[18] Interestingly, Josephus says the Torah requires the appointment of *hypēretai* alongside of every local

---

[13] We shall return below to John's statement that the delegation was composed of priests and Levites.

[14] On "high priests" as opposed to "the high priest," see M. Stern, *The Jewish People in the First Century*, II (edd. S. Safrai and M. Stern; 1976), pp. 600−603; see also below, p. 223, n. 23.

[15] On these, see C. Spicq, *Notes de lexicographie néo-testamentaire*, II (1978), pp. 901−906; J. Blinzler, *Der Prozess Jesu* (1969⁴), pp. 126−128.

[16] See D. Magie, *Roman Rule in Asia Minor* (1950), I, pp. 60, 645; II, pp. 848−849, 1510, 1511. And see below, end of n. 17.

[17] Thus, for example, in all thirteen appearances of *grammateus* in the Septuagint version of the Hexateuch. Or, coming from the other side, of the twenty-five appearances of *shoter* in the Hebrew Bible, the LXX renders seventeen by *grammateus*, four by the cognate *grammatoeisagōgeus*, and once by the verb *grammateuein*; only four are rendered by unrelated words. On the Hellenistic background of this rendering, see D. Cohen, *Bijdragen en Mededeelingen van het Genootschap voor de Joodsche Wetenschap in Nederland* 5 (1933), pp. 101−113; F. Preisigke, *Wörterbuch der griechischen Papyrusurkunden*, III (1931), pp. 101−103.

[18] See M. Weinfeld, *Israel Oriental Studies* 7 (1977), pp. 83−86.

government (*Ant.* 4.214);[19] while he is obviously reflecting Deuteronomy 16:18, it is important to note that he uses the same term Mark 14:58 used, as we suspected, instead of *grammateis*. Our conclusion from all of this is that some allusions to *grammateis* in the New Testament (and elsewhere) refer not to "scribes," but rather to *shoterim*, "bailiffs."

III. Levites

Let us now return to our major question: Who were those "scribes" mentioned in the New Testament not as "bailiffs" but rather as teachers and spiritual leaders? Our identification of some other *grammateis* as bailiffs will help us, I believe, for it may be assumed that the same group supplied both types of *grammateis*; otherwise the confusion would be insufferable. Now it is well-known that traditional societies frequently link functions to certain families; this is well-documented in ancient Judaea.[20] From our point of view, therefore, it is very interesting that one important text of the Second Temple period, the biblical book of Chronicles, viewed the *shoterim* as a sub-group of the *Levites*, parallel to other better-known Levitical functionaries: gate-keepers and musicians.[21]

It is true that Chronicles claims a great deal for the Levites, in a variety of fields,[22] so that it is possible that its view of them as *shoterim* was no more than an unrealized claim. Even such a claim, however, would not be insignificant. Moreover, other sources offer similar testimony. The Testament of Levi (8:17) includes *grammateis* among Levi's progeny,[23] the War Scroll from Qumran (7:13, 15) explicitly identifies *shoterim* as Levites, the same seems to

---

[19] Below, we shall return to Josephus' notice that these *hypēretai* were Levites.

[20] See, inter alia, E. Stauffer, *Zeitschrift für Religions- und Zeitgeschichte* 4 (1952), pp. 194–197; E. E. Urbach, *Proceedings of the Israel Academy of Sciences and Humanities* 2, Nr. 4 (1966), pp. 5–7; Stern (above, n. 14), pp 561–618; and, on the Mishnaic and Talmudic periods, R. Yankelevitch, in *Nation and History*, I (ed. M. Stern; 1983), pp. 151–162 (in Hebrew). For the early medieval period, see A. Grossman in *Zion* 50 (above, n. *), pp. 189–220.

[21] I Chronicles 23:4, 26:29; II Chronicles 19:11; 34:13. There are also references to *sopherim* who were Levites, but no general claim in this regard.

[22] On Levites in Chronicles, see G. von Rad, *Das Geschichtsbild des chronistischen Werkes* (1930), pp. 80–119; A. C. Welch, *The Work of the Chronicler* (1939), pp. 55–80; R. H. Pfeiffer, *Introduction to the Old Testament* (1948), pp. 794–801; and M. Smith, in *The Greeks and the Persians from the Sixth to the Fourth Centuries* (1968), pp. 396–397. On unfulfilled demands by the Levites, see S. Japhet, *The Ideology of the Book of Chronicles and its Place in Biblical Thought* (1989), pp. 241–242, and M. Hengel, *Judaism and Hellenism* (1974), I, p. 49; II, pp. 38–39, notes 384–385.

[23] Cf. G. Alon, *Studies in Jewish History* . . ., II (1958), p. 161 (in Hebrew; originally in *Kiryat Sepher* 16 [1939/40], p. 167).

be indicated by the Qumran Community Rule (1QSa 1:23−25) as well,[24] and the identification is again unambiguous in the tannaitic midrash on Deuteronomy 1:15: "'And *shot̄erim*' −these are the Levites who whip with straps, as it is said: 'and the Levites are *shot̄erim* before you' (II Chronicles 19:11)."[25] Again, it may be assumed that the *grammateis tou hierou* in Jerusalem, which a famous Seleucid document mentions alongside of priests and elders and temple-singers (*Ant.* 12.142), were Levites.[26]

The Fourth Gospel is especially significant in the present context. For in contrast to the other gospels, which apart from the schematic parable of the Good Samaritan (Luke 10:32) never mention Levites but do mention *grammateis*, John never mentions *grammateis*[27] but does mention Levites: the above-mentioned delegation to John the Baptist was composed of priests *and* Levites (John 1:19). As we have noted, this delegation is similar to others reported in the Synoptic Gospels,[28] but they included *grammateis*. The suspicion arises, therefore, that this episode in John − an episode which

---

[24] This understanding of this verbose and somewhat obscure text − assumed, for example, by J. Licht, *The Rule Scroll* (1965), p. 260 (in Hebrew) and by Weinfeld (above, n. 18), p. 71 − rests on the parallelism between the opening reference to the Levites, followed by *'al pi*, and the closing reference to the "officers, judges and *shot̄erim*," again followed by *'al pi*, also on the parallelism between the opening *lamedh* clause (of the Levites' functions [*lehavi' ulehotzi'*]) and the *lamedh*s which introduce the terms denoting the officials. Recently, however, L. H. Schiffman (*The Eschatological Community of the Dead Sea Scrolls* [1989], pp. 28−29), while admitting this interpretation is possible, has argued for a different one. His claim, however, is based only on the argument that "Levitical judges and provosts are known among the officials of the sect, but a claim of exclusivity on their behalf is nowhere made." But whatever the strength of such an argument from silence might be, I see no reason not to read this text as the others to which Schiffman alludes, i.e., as one which refers to Levitical officials.

[25] *Sifré Deut.* § 15 (ed. Finkelstein, p. 25). Cf. BT *Yevamot* 86b: "Rabbi Hisda said: 'At first they would only appoint Levites to be *shot̄erim*, as it says "And the Levites were *shot̄erim* before you" (II Chronicles 19:11), but now we only appoint ("lay") Israelites as *shot̄erim*, as it says, "and the many are *shot̄erim* at your head."' " For conjectures as to the identity of the second proof-text, see S. Kaatz in *Festschrift zum siebzigsten Geburtstage David Hoffmann's* (edd. S. Eppenstein, M. Hildesheimer and J. Wohlgmuth; 1914), pp. 109−111, also A. M. Habermann, *Sinai* 32 (1952/53), p. 143 (in Hebrew).

[26] See A. Büchler, *Die Priester und der Cultus im letzten Jahrzehnt des jerusalemischen Tempels* (1895), pp. 119−120; M. Stern, *The Documents on the History of the Hasmonean Revolt* (1973²), p. 38 (in Hebrew); J. Liver, *Chapters in the History of the Priests and the Levites* (1968), p. 24 (in Hebrew).

[27] Apart from John 8:3; but it is generally agreed that John 7:53−8:11, which has its own peculiar style and is missing from this gospel's best witnesses, is inauthentic and stems from a tradition similar to that of the Synoptic Gospels. See Metzger (above, n. 6), pp. 219−22; U. Becker, *Jesus und die Ehebrecherin* (1963), pp. 50, 173.

[28] See Mark 3:22; 7:1; 11:27; 12:28.

several details show to be of good historical value for the period in question[29] − preserves early knowledge that *grammateis* were Levites.

Two more tenuous arguments may offer some support for the same conclusion, although they cannot prove it. First, we may note that Matthew's positive attitude toward the *grammateis*,[30] and his special approach to the use of the Hebrew Bible,[31] have already led various scholars to conclude that he was a "scribe," if not a Pharisee.[32] It is, therefore, interesting to note that the combination of Mark 2:14 and Luke 5:27, on the one hand, with Matthew 9:9 and 10:3, on the other, leads to the conclusion that Matthew was also known as Levi.[33] Hence, it may be supposed that this "scribe" was a Levite.[34] Second,

---

[29] See C. H. Dodd, *Historical Tradition in the Fourth Gospel* (1963), pp. 251−278. For the assumed source for this pericope, see D. M. Smith and J. L. Martyn, in *Jews, Greeks and Christians . . . Essays in Honor of William David Davies* (edd. R. Hamerton-Kelly and R. Scroggs; 1976), pp. 175−180, 197−219. It has been denied that a source underlies the report, and instead suggested that John invented the priests and Levites in order to make this delegation parallel the double delegation (two disciples) mentioned in Luke 7:18 (F. E. Williams, *JBL* 86 [1967], p. 318) but this appears quite arbitrary and unfounded. Neither is "priests and Levites" merely "a stock phrase readily coming to mind" (J. A. Bailey, *Gospel of Luke and John* [1963], p. 10). This duo appears nowhere else in the New Testament, and John never again mentions Levites or "the priests;" he refers only to "high priests."

[30] See especially M. D. Goulder, *Midrash and Lection in Matthew* (1974), pp. 13−15, who assembles the evidence for Matthew's rehabilitation of the scribes as opposed to Mark. See also J. Hoh, *Biblische Zeitschrift* 17 (1926), pp. 256−269, who focuses upon Matthew 13:52.

[31] K. Stendahl, *The School of St. Matthew and its Use of the Old Testament* (1954), p. 127; R. H. Gundry, *The Use of the Old Testament in St. Matthew's Gospel* (1967), pp. 172−174; R. S. McConnell, *Law and Prophecy in Matthew's Gospel* (1969), pp. 135−138.

[32] See especially Goulder (above, n. 30), pp. 5, 22. For further bibliography on this topic, see J. Schwark, *Theokratia* 2 (1970−1972; *Festgabe für K. H. Rengstorf*) (1973), pp. 138−140. Schwark, as others, assume that Matthew was a *Pharisaic* scribe, but this is only due to the usual view (above, n. 3) which basically identifies scribes and Pharisees. (Although O. L. Cope took the title of his *Matthew: A Scribe Trained for the Kingdom of Heaven* [1976] from Matthew 13:52 [see n. 30], he does not attempt to develope the specific claim that the gospel's author was a scribe.)

[33] There is another possibility, namely, that the author of the first Gospel preferred to *change* the publican's name from Levi to Matthew. Thus, for example, R. Pesch has suggested that the evangelist did this because he assumed that all of Jesus' disciples (including the publican) were also apostles, but the name "Levi" did not appear in his list of apostles (*ZNW* 59 [1968], pp. 40−56). But Pesch finds it difficult to explain (pp. 55−56) why "Matthew," and not the name of some other apostle, was substituted, according to his theory, for "Levi." It is much more usual and simple to assume that the same man bore both names; see the bibliography assembled by Pesch, p. 40.

[34] Assuming that "Levi" was a name typical of Levites, and that the apostle Matthew stands behind the gospel bearing that name. For the first assumption, see Stern (above, n. 14), p. 599 and Jeremias' *Jerusalem* (above, n. 3), p. 213, n. 209. For the conclusion that Matthew was a Levite, see Gundry (above, n. 31), p. 183, and the bibliography listed by Pesch (above, n. 33: p. 40, n. 3). As for the second assumption, see W. G. Kümmel, *Introduction to the New Testament* (1975[17]), pp. 120−121; D. Guthrie, *New Testament Introduction* (1970), pp. 33−44.

we may also note that the only Levite mentioned by name in the New Testament, Barnabas of Cyprus (Acts 4:36), is said to have been a gifted preacher and is the first among the "prophets and teachers" listed in Acts 13:1.[35] This might have been a result of his education as a Levite.[36]

Be all that as it may, the main reason for viewing the *grammateis* as Levites is the fact we cited at the outset of our study (n. 2): they are usually mentioned alongside of high priests or Pharisees. That is, they appear either as secondary figures in the realm of cult or law (remember that the New Testament makes the high priests responsible for the legal system!) or as spiritual/scriptural authorities. Such a combination of functions is in evidence only with regard to the Levites.

As second fiddles to the priests, the Levites' functions in the cult are well known.[37] Here, we should underline only two points which are particularly apposite to the New Testament *grammateis*. First, note that the Mishnah mentions *ḥazzanim*, who seem to have been Levites, who served the high priests.[38] This term is also used by the tannaim for officials who execute a court's decisions – and the tannaitic midrash cited above explicitly identifies these as Levites.[39] This brings us back to Josephus' reference to *hypēretai* (*Ant.* 4.214), *and we may now add that he says these were Levites.*[40] This completes the chain begun by Mark, who apparently identifies *hypēretai* as *grammateis*, as we have seen. Second, the Levites' tasks in the Temple

---

[35] Cf. ibid. 9:27; 11:22; 14:12; 15:2; and Galatians 2:9.

[36] As is suggested by Jeremias in *Jerusalem* (above, n. 3), p. 213. On the education of Levites, cf. below, n. 48.

[37] For surveys of the evidence, see S. Safrai in *The Herodian Period* (edd. M. Avi-Yonah and Z. Baras; 1975), pp. 293–294; Büchler (above, n. 26), pp. 118–159.

[38] See m. *Sotah* 7:7; m.*Yoma* 7:1; m.*Tamid* 5:3; m.*Makkot* 3:12. Cf. Büchler (above, n. 26), pp. 149–151 and S. Krauss, *Synagogale Altertümer* (1922), p. 122.

[39] Compare *Sifré Deut.* § 15 (ed. Finkelstein, p. 25) to m.*Makkot* 3:12. On *ḥazzanim* outside of the Temple, see also H. Mantel, *Studies in the History of the Sanhedrin* (1965), pp. 199–200, n. 181 and Weinfeld (above, n. 18), p. 85, who also cites literature on the linguistic background of the term.

[40] There is no reason to assume, with Büchler (above, n. 26: pp. 179–180), that these "Levites" were in fact priests. It should be noted that the midrash applied *meḥoqeq* of Genesis 49:10 to "the two *sophᵉrim* of the judges who stood before them (scil. the Sanhedrin)" (*Genesis Rabbah* § 98[99] ad loc., edd. Theodor-Albeck, p. 1259), and *4Q Patriarchal Blessings* similarly applied *sheveṭ* to the sectarian Interpreter of the Law (see *Theologische Zeitschrift* 37 [1981], pp. 263–266). In contrast, the *Damascus Document* (6:7) finds that figure in the *meḥoqeq* of that same verse. Be that as it may, G. Vermes, *Scripture and Tradition in Judaism* (1973²), pp. 49–55, points to the equivalence of *meḥoqeq* and *grammateus* in Ben Sira 10:4[5] and infers that the application of the terms of Genesis 49:10 to the Sanhedrin and its scribes must have been established by the Hasmonean period. The Interpreter of the Law apparently was, however, a priest and not a Levite (see D. Flusser, *IEJ* 9 [1959], pp. 104–107); for the Qumran preference for priests, see above, pp. 19–20, 37.

included one eminently "police" function: they guarded the gates.[41] True, some priests did too, but they did so only formally, in the Temple's inner precincts.[42] The Levites, in contrast, were charged with patrolling the public areas of the Temple and the Temple Mount, a very real function. Philo, indeed, seems to have considered it the Levites' main task.[43] Under these circumstances, it is understandable that those Levites whose main duties were police functions might come to be called by the specific term *shot^erim*, and not merely by the general term "Levites."[44]

The Levites' status as teachers is less clear. This might be simply a result of the circumstance that most of the surviving relevant literature from the New Testament and post-Destruction period preserves either priestly or rabbinic points of view, of which the former held that "the lips of the *priest* guard knowledge and the Torah should be sought from his mouth" (Malachi 2:7)[45] while the latter insisted that the Crown of the Torah is not contingent upon any particular pedigree.[46] Nevertheless, the cupboard is not entirely empty. We hear of Levites "who cause the people to understand" in the days of Ezra (Nehemiah 8:7−8; Ezra 8:18), and the Chronicler (II 17:7−9; 30:22; 35:3) attributes this to the Monarchy period as well, as usual; von Rad has found what he views as Levitical sermons in this book.[47] Again, it is interesting that of all the Testaments of the Twelve Patriarchs, only Levi's (13:1−2) requires his descendants − without distinguishing between priests and Levites − to

---

[41] See Büchler (above, n. 26), pp. 132−136; Jeremias' *Jerusalem* (above, n.3), pp. 209−211. Cf. *Ant*. 9.155 − an addition to the biblical account.

[42] See m.*Middot* 1:1. For a comparison of the priests' and Levites' guard duties, see Büchler (as in the preceding note).

[43] See *De specialibus legibus* 1.156. Already B. Ritter expressed surprise that Phio gave a relatively detailed account of the Levites' guard duties but completely omitted their responsibilities as Temple-singers: *Philo und die Halacha* (1879), p. 116, n. 3.

[44] The use of the more specific terms *shoter* and *hazzan* (*hypēretēs*), as well as *meshorer* (Temple-singer), instead of "Levite," probably arose out of a natural tendency to distinguish among officials whose spheres of activity were so different. But we should not expect any hard and fast rule governing when the professional terms were used, and when the genealogical.

[45] See also Ezekiel 44:23; Haggai 2:11−12; Zechariah 7:3; Ben Sira 45:30[17]; *Aristeas* 53, 310; Philo, *Hypothetica* apud Eusebius, *De praeparatio evangelica* 8.7.13; Josephus, *Ant*. 4.209; *C. Ap*. 2.184−187; etc. Cf. Herr (above, n. 7), pp. 45−46, and S. N. Mason, *JBL* 107 (1988), pp. 657−661.

[46] See *Sifré Numbers* § 119 (ed. Horovitz, p. 144); E. E. Urbach, *The Sages*, I (1975), pp. 637−639. Cf. above, pp. 64−65.

[47] See his *The Problem of the Hexateuch and other Essays* (1966), pp. 267−280. Criticizing von Rad, A. Cody argued that one may not speak of the Levites having taught the Law, but rather only of their having interpreted it (*A History of Old Testament Priesthood* [1969], pp. 187−190). I am not convinced that this distinction is a meaningful one. On the other hand, it has also been suggested that Jubilees was written by a Levite (E. Schwarz, *Identität durch Abgrenzung* [1982], pp. 127−129). Cf. ibid., pp. 69−70, 82−84, and 151 on Jubilees' links to the priesthood, which point in the same general direction.

learn to read and write, explaining that it is impossible to teach well without these skills.[48] In fact, it seems obvious that the canonical picture of the Levite Moses and the priest Aaron, the ideal pair, should have fostered the notion that the priests, responsible for the cult and the Torah, should be assisted by Levites in both spheres. In rabbinic literature, indeed, Moses is sometimes termed "the great *sopher*."[49]

Here, finally, we should assemble what is known and what is surmised about the Levites in Qumran. On the one hand, it seems that the *Maskil*, a highly respected community figure charged with teaching the sect's special doctrine (*Manual of Discipline* 3:13), was a Levite.[50] And, on the other hand, the community *Mebaqqer* ("supervisor"), a senior administrative official, also seems to have been a Levite.[51] (It may be that they were both, indeed, the same individual,[52] but that does not matter here.) Thus, even in Qumran, a bastion of priestliness,[53] Levites were entrusted with teaching and administrative fuctions, the functions of the "scribe" and the "*shoter*," i.e., the functions of the *grammateus*.

IV. Summary

New Testament scholars admonish us incessantly not to depend upon the Gospels' statements about Jewish leaders.[54] Their authors or editors, we are warned, were apparently unfamiliar with the different types of Jewish leaders and could not distinguish among them. Moreover, some bias was added to their ignorance. We have already noted, for example, Matthew's contemporizing approach to the Pharisees (n. 8) and his personal bias vis à vis

---

[48] See also the rest of ch. 13. On literacy among Levites and *shot^erim* in the biblical period, see also A. Demsky, "Literacy in Israel and among its Neighbors inthe Biblical Period" (Diss. Jerusalem, 1976), pp. 42–43 (in Hebrew), including the reference to LXX Joshua 21:29, where one of the Levitical cities is termed *Pēgēn grammatōn* ("well of writings?").

[49] BT *Sotah* 13b and *Targum Onqelos* to Deuteronomy 33:21. See Vermes (above, n. 40), pp. 51–52; S. Lieberman, *Hellenism in Jewish Palestine* (1950), p. 82, n. 274. On priestly responsibility for the Torah in the Second Temple period, see above, n. 45.

[50] See G. Vermes, *The Dead Sea Scrolls in English* (1975²), pp. 22–25. For Levites as *maskilim*, cf. II Chronicles 30:22.

[51] As is indicated by *Damascus Document* 13:2–7 and, perhaps, by some other texts as well. Cf. B. E. Thiering, *JBL* 100 (1981), pp. 59–69.

[52] So Vermes (above, n. 50), p. 25, and in his *The Dead Sea Scrolls: Qumran in Perspective* (1977), p. 91.

[53] See above, n. 40.

[54] See, inter alia, Cook (above, n. 3), pp. 15–28; Meier (above, n. 5); S. van Tilborg, *The Jewish Leaders in Matthew* (1972), pp. 1–6; J. P. Meier, *Matthew* (1980), pp. 177–178, 253 (cf. B.J. Hubbard, *JBL* 100 [1981], p. 122).

the scribes (nn. 30, 32). It has even been suggested that one Jewish group, "the Herodians," never existed; Mark, we are told, made them up in order to serve a literary-theological purpose.[55] Do not these problems eliminate the possiblity of identifying the people termed "the *grammateis*?"[56]

Our obviously negative reply is based upon a few considerations. First, the more certain we are that the Gospel writers did not know who "the scribes" were, the likelier it is that they existed, as a separate group. Otherwise, why make them up? Again, most of the above-mentioned doubts apply to Matthew's gospel, which we hardly touched here. Finally, we may underline the fact that most of our arguments were taken from other ancient Jewish evidence, which we used to illuminate the New Testament evidence. The latter, for the most part, supplied only the question, not the answer. Thus, we feel justified in suggesting that the New Testament's *grammateis* be viewed as Levites.

This conclusion may help illuminate a serious problem in the study of first-century Judaism.[57] Scholars have long noted that the priests are missing from the picture of religious leadership in the Gospels' picture of first-century Judaism. Priests serve as political leaders, but hardly as religious or theological authorities. Their absence is especially evident in the lists of Jewish leaders attacked by Jesus.

Scholars have responded to this situation in two basic ways. Most simply accepted the data and drew the natural conclusion: the priests did not function importantly in Judaean religious life in the first century, at least not in the horizons of Jesus and his disciples.[58] But that would be very surprising, in light of the very numerous references, in literature of the Second Temple period, to the priests' important role with regard to the Torah (n. 45), not only with regard to cult. Chwolson, therefore, followed by Büchler, offered a radical alternative approach: in those passages where the Pharisees are attacked, the text originally referred to priests.[59] However, this solution, which arose to a

---

[55] W. J. Bennett, Jr., *Novum Testamentum* 17 (1975), pp. 9–14.

[56] For such doubts especially with reference to the "scribes," see D. W. Riddle, *Jesus and the Pharisees* (1928), p. 102.

[57] It may also help with some other problems, such as the paucity of information concerning the Levites, the relationship of *ḥazzanim* and Levites in m.*Sotah* 9:15, and the puzzling translation of "prophet and prophet" by "priest and scribe," usual in *Targum "Jonathan"*; for a list of such passages, see Büchler (above, n. 26), p. 87, n. 2.

[58] See A. Epstein, *MGWJ* 40 (1896), p. 139 (review of Büchler [above, n. 26]); A. Bertholet, *Die jüdische Religion von der Zeit Esras bis zum Zeitalter Christi* (B. Stade's *Biblische Theologie des Alten Testament*, II; 1911), p. 324; R. Bultmann, *Gnomon* 26 (1954), p. 187

[59] So Chwolson (above, n. 9), pp. 113–114, who argues that copyists turned "scribes" (i.e., priests) into "Pharisees" or added the latter to attacks upon the scribes. Büchler (above, n. 26: pp. 80–88) suggests not only that "Pharisees" were at times simply substituted for

large extent out of apologetic considerations[60] — Jews would rather Jesus attacked the extinct Sadducees than the rabbis' forebears — is totally arbitrary and groundless.[61]

Our suggestion can help alleviate this mystery. The representatives of priestly law are indeed mentioned and attacked frequently in the Gospels, as one would expect: they are "the scribes."[62] As Matthew's Jesus says (23:2), both the scribes and the Pharisees sat on Moses' seat.[63] But they were neither identical nor partners. They were competitors, representatives of two opposing schools: the Pharisees claimed to inherit Moses' role due to their excellence as lawyers, while the scribes, who certainly claimed legal excellence, also argued that the fact that they shared Moses' Levitic pedigree made them the true heirs to his authority.

"scribes," but also the only somewhat more subtle suggestion that "Pharisees and scribes" represents the Aramaic *kehanaya [ve]saphraya* ("priests and scribes" — see above, n. 57).

[60] Cf. above, p. 69, n. 46.

[61] And reviewers usually refrained from arguing the point. See E. Schürer, *Theologische Literaturzeitung* 18 (1893), col. 183; XX (1895), col. 518; L. Blau, *Revue des études juives* 31 (1895), p. 153; Urbach (above, n. 10), p. 174, n. 29. Epstein (above, n. 58), pp. 139–140 adds some arguments against Büchler's thesis.

[62] Sadducean scribes would indeed seem to be mentioned in Luke 20:39–40: after some irritating questions were posed by "the *grammateis* and the high-priests" (vv. 19–26) and by "the Sadducees" (vv. 27–38), and Jesus managed to give suitable answers in both cases, vv. 39–40 go on to report that "some of the scribes responded "Well spoken, master," "for they did not dare to ask him anything anymore." According to the plain reading of this pericope, those who had asked now gave up; this identifies these "scribes" as Sadducees. Those who maintain the usual identification of scribes and Pharisees must chose one of two possibilities: either "they" in v. 40 refers not to the scribes of the preceding verse but rather back to the Sadducees (so T. Zahn, *Das Evangelium des Lucas*, II [1913¹⁻²], p. 646), which is highly artificial, or vv. 39–40 mean that the Pharisees didn't dare ask any questions after they saw how the others had fared (A. Loisy, *L'Évangile selon Luc* [1924], p. 487) — a solution which cannot deal very well with "anymore." Thus, if all we had to do were to read this pericope, it would be difficult to avoid the impression that it depicts Sadducean scribes. However, the parallel to this pericope in Mark 12 raises a problem, for its vv. 28, 32, 34, almost identical to the ones in Luke, form the framework of a conversation between Jesus and a scribe who asked him a question after the defeat of the Sadducees and because of it. That question appears in Luke not here, but rather at 10:25–28. Thus, we have here an aspect of the Synoptic Problem. Those who maintain Markan priority will argue that the juxtaposition of scribes and Sadducees in Luke 20 is only the mechanical result of the removal of the scribe's question, so it is improper to draw any historical conclusions of the type suggested at the outset of this note. Indeed, even T. Schramm, who argued that Luke used a non-Markan source for the debate with the Sadducees, admitted that vv. 39–40 are from Mark: *Der Markus-Stoff bei Lukas* (1971), pp 170–171. I have, therefore, relegated this passage and its potential implications to a footnote.

[63] Today, it is clear that "to sit on NN's seat" means to be his heir. See M. Ginsburger, *REJ* 90 (1931), p. 164; D. E. Garland, *The Intention of Matthew 23* (1979), pp. 42–43, n. 27; Y. Yadin, *IEJ* 7 (1957), p. 67 (on 4Q *Patriarchal Blessings*, line 2); and the *Temple Scroll* 59:14, 17.

It thus appears that the Gospels, just as the Nahum *pesher* from Qumran,[64] confirm Josephus' basic picture of Judaean Judaism being divided into two main strands: Sadducees (a priestly party) and Pharisees ("sages," proto-rabbis).[65] Members of smaller groups, such as the Qumran sect and Christians, found themselves facing two types of competitors, and reacted by calling, more or less nicely, for a plague upon both their houses. When Harnack, in *Das Wesen des Christentums*, passes from "Die Priester und die Pharisäer hielten das Volk in Banden und mordeten ihm die Seele" to Matthew 23, "Wehe euch, Schriftgelehrten und Pharisäern, ihr Heuchler . . .," he seems, indeed, apparently without realizing it, to have captured the "essence" of the matter.[66] For when the Gospels portray Jesus as attacking the Pharisees and the scribes, just as when Luke-Acts portrays the Pharisees as only relatively less negative than the Sadducees,[67] they are reflecting a self-consciousness of Christianity as a sect separate from *both* main trends within contemporary Judaism.

---

[64] See D. Flusser, in *Qumran* (edd. K. E. Grözinger et al.; 1981), pp. 121–166 (English summary in *Immanuel* 1 [Summer 1972], pp. 39–41), also M. Hengel, *Rabbinische Legende und frühpharisäische Geschichte* (1984), p. 55, n. 125.

[65] Josephus' basic picture of the Pharisees and the Sadducees as being the main sects emerges not only from his central accounts of the sects in *BJ* 2 and *Ant.* 18, wherein the Essenes are portrayed as exotic separatists, but also from such passages as *BJ* 2.411, where Josephus characterizes the mainstream leadership of the Jews as being composed of high priests, Pharisees and other respected people. As for the priestly nature of the Sadducees, see Stern (above, n. 14), pp. 609–612, also *Agrippa I*, p. 116, n. 35 (bibliography). It is interesting that Josephus, a priest who claimed to be a Pharisee (*Vita* 12), failed to note, explicitly, the typically priestly nature of the Sadducees. Discovery and development of that point – on the basis of other sources and of hints in Josephus – had to wait until the nineteenth century; see above, pp. 67, 74.

[66] A. von Harnack, *Das Wesen des Christentums* (1900), p. 66 (= *What is Christianity?* [1957], pp. 103–104). On the massive controversy engendered by Harnack's attack upon the Pharisees, see above, p. 69, n. 46.

[67] On the sects in Luke-Acts, see J. T. Sanders, *The Jews in Luke-Acts* (1987), esp. pp. 84–131, along with my review of R. L. Brawley, *Luke-Acts and the Jews: Conflict, Apology, and Conciliation* (1987), in *JQR* 80 (1989/90), pp. 427–429.

6. On Sacrifice by Gentiles in the Temple of Jerusalem[*]

The simplest, and historiographically most natural, way to begin a discussion of this topic is by responding to Emil Schürer's classic review of it.[1] In this excursus, which is the standard underpinning of scholarly statements on this topic,[2] Schürer reviews the evidence under three headings: sacrifices *by* Gentiles in the Jerusalem Temple, Jewish sacrifices *for* Gentiles (i.e., foreign rulers) there, and votive offerings by Gentiles to the Temple. It is the first topic, sacrifices by Gentiles, which especially concerns us here. But the other two are related to it — even more closely, it seems, than Schürer or his dependents and editors realized.

Schürer is totally affirmative regarding sacrifices by Gentiles in Jerusalem: the Hebrew Bible, the rabbis, and especially Josephus all show, he says, that such sacrifices were accepted in both theory and practice (pp. 309–311). After assembling similarly affirmative evidence under the other two headings (pp. 311–313), Schürer felt well justified in concluding, in the last sentence of this excursus, that "In a sense, therefore, even the exclusive Temple of Jerusalem became cosmopolitan; in common with the renowned sanctuaries of the Gentiles, it received the homage of the whole world" (p. 313).

Now while I have no doubts about the acceptance of votive offerings from gentiles, and difficulty with only some of the details of Schürer's account of Jewish sacrifices for foreign rulers, my reading of the evidence regarding sacrifices *by* Gentiles is quite different. Namely, while Schürer finds it posited by the Hebrew Bible, the rabbis, and especially by Josephus, I would say that

---

[*] This paper was first given in 1987 at the international congress at Hebrew University (Jerusalem) on "A Member of Another Religion in Religious Law."

[1] The appendix appeared in the *Geschichte* beginning with II (1886^2), pp. 243–248 (= pp. 299–305 in Second Division, vol. I, of the 1891 English edition); the standard version is II (1907^4), pp. 357–363. Here, I shall quote according to SVM II, pp. 309–313, which is basically identical with the latter.

[2] For dependence upon it see, inter alia, Smallwood, *Jews*, pp. 88–89, n. 99; S. Safrai, *Die Wallfahrt im Zeitalter des Zweiten Tempels* (1981), p. 110, n. 75; the commentaries to II Maccabees 3:35 in F.-M. Abel, *Les livres des Maccabées* (1949), p. 327, and J. A. Goldstein *II Maccabees* (1983), p. 215; and the notes on *Leg.* 297 in the translations by A. Pelletier (*Legatio ad Caium* [1972], p. 271, n. 5) and A. Kasher (in *Philo of Alexandria: Writings*, I [ed. S. Daniel-Nataf; 1986], p. 134, n. 434 [in Hebrew]).

it is not contemplated by the Hebrew Bible, that the rabbis posit it in a way much more restricted than Schürer would admit, and that Josephus' evidence is to be taken with several grains of salt in light of his apologetic tendency to present Judaism as a religion as universalist as he can.[3] References to Josephus account for almost all of Schürer's evidence for the Jerusalem Temple becoming cosmopolitan,[4] and while that is certainly the impression Josephus wished to give, it is doubtful that it can be squared with the facts. Let us review the evidence.

Although Schürer writes that "the Old Testament assumes that a sacrifice may be offered by an unconverted Gentile (*ben nekhar*)" (p. 309), neither of the two passages he cites supports this. I Kings 8:41−43 speaks of foreigners not as sacrificing, but only as praying in the Temple,[5] and, in fact, the diction strangely speaks not even of them praying "in" the Temple, but rather "to" it.[6] As for his other, and principal, biblical proof-text, Leviticus 22:25 speaks of Gentiles only as suppliers of animals for Jewish sacrifice.[7] This is made quite clear both by the beginning of the pericope, which defines it as one dealing with vows and votive offerings made by Israelites and "the *ger* who lives among you" (v. 18) − *ger* was taken in the Second Temple and rabbinic periods to refer to proselytes[8] − and by the end of the pericope (v. 25), which warns that if "you" (Jews or proselytes) sacrifice mutilated animals which you have taken from Gentiles (*ben nekhar*) they will not be accepted by God "for *you*." In context, vv. 24−25 mean only that animals should not be mutilated, and mutilated animals should not be sacrificed no matter who inflicted the mutilation, for the problem is in the animal itself, as v. 25b emphasizes (*bahem . . . bam*), not in the fact that an Israelite perpetrated it.

---

[3] See, for an apposite example, L. H. Feldman's comments on *Ant.* 8.117, in Josephus' version of Solomon's prayer (to which latter we shall next turn): *Aspects of Religious Propaganda in Judaism and Early Christianity* (ed. E. S. Fiorenza; 1976), pp. 78−79. In general, see Cohen's account, in an important article cited below (n. 9), of Josephus' pride concerning Gentile respect for Judaism.

[4] "The fact that sacrifice was offered by and for Gentiles is nowhere better attested than by Josephus . . ." (p. 310) − not the best recommendation when the topic is such a sensitive one!

[5] A point emphasized by L. Finkelstein, *New Light from the Prophets* (1969), p. 99.

[6] Equally emphasized by Finkelstein, ibid. (read "The author of the prayer evidently held that pagans could *not* enter the Temple precincts" ["not" was mistakenly omitted]), and by A.M. Rabello in his article on the entrance prohibition for Gentiles: *Christian News from Israel* 21 (1970/71), nr. 3, pp. 28−29.

[7] This understanding of these verses is especially emphasized by A. B. Ehrlich, *Mikrâ Ki-Pheshutô: Die Schrift nach ihrem Wortlaut*, I (1899), p. 236 (in Hebrew). A similar distinction with regard to rabbinic texts, in which R. Eliezer refers to Gentiles as suppliers and not as sacrificers, is made by E. E. Urbach in *Tarbiz* 49 (1979/80), p. 423, n. 3 (in Hebrew).

[8] For *ger*, "proselyte," as distinct from *ben nekhar*, "Gentile," cf. *4QFlorilegium* I,3−4, along with *Agrippa I*, p. 128.

Thus, there seems to be no biblical support for the notion that a non-Israelite or non-proselyte could sacrifice in the Temple of Jerusalem. Nor, I believe, was such support likely: while the "comprehensive piety of paganism" may have allowed and encouraged the participation in one cult by an adherent of another, I see no reason to expect that biblical monotheism would.[9]

Rabbinic literature, to which Schürer next turns, supplies much more relevant material, and the views to which it testifies are more varied and more complex. As Schürer indicates, the basic principle, for the rabbis, was that Gentiles may make voluntary offerings, such as gifts and sacrifices resultant from vows (see below, n. 12), but they may not offer obligatory sacrifices (m.*Shekalim* 1:5; *Sifra, Emor* 7:7, ed. Weiss, p. 99a). Similarly, although Schürer does not note this, the rabbis held that Gentiles may not even participate in funding the obligatory public cult; this is the meaning of the mishnaic rejection (ibid., also *Sifra* ibid.) of money offered by Gentiles as Temple tax (*shekalim*).[10] Finally, we should note that while tannaitic opinion apparently unanimously held that Gentiles' contributions to the upkeep of the Temple were considered to be as fully sanctified as those of Jews and violation of them was therefore subject to the same penalties, there was debate as to whether this was the case regarding their sacrifices. According to the undisputed anonymous view in m.*Zebachim* 4:5, three technical violations which disqualify sacrifices are unpunishable with regard to the sacrifices of gentiles, while regarding a fourth violation, slaughtering outside the sacred area, there was an argument: R. Simeon held that it too was unpunishable while R. Jose demanded punishment in this case.[11] The anonymous and authoritative view opening this mishnah is justified by the tannaitic midrash on Leviticus 22:2, which emphasizes that this verse enjoins upon the priests special care, and hence makes them liable for punishment, only with regard to "the sacrifices of the children of Israel" (*Sifra, Emor* 4:3, ed. Weiss, p. 96a)

---

[9] Indeed, even Schürer admitted, at the very outset of his excursus, that "Bei der schroffen Scheidewand, welche das Judentum in religiöser Hinsicht zwischen sich und dem Heidentum aufgerichtet hat, wird man nicht leicht auf die Vermutung kommen, daß auch Heiden am Kultus zu Jerusalem sich beteiligten;" he thought that the evidence he assembled nevertheless required this. The phrase "comprehensive piety . . ." is borrowed from E. M. Smallwood, *Philonis Alexandrini Legatio ad Gaium* (1961), p. 240; cf. SVM 311, "acts of courtesy or cosmopolitan piety." The latter two possibilities are also both left open by S.J.D. Cohen in *HTR* 80 (1987), pp. 414–415.

[10] For the *shekalim* as a substitute, introduced in the sovereign Hasmonean period, for the subsidies formerly provided by Persian and Hellenistic kings – i.e., for *shekalim* taking over where Gentiles left off – see J. Liver, *HTR* 56 (1963), pp. 186–198.

[11] For the exegetical basis of this argument, see *Sifré Deut.* on Deut. 12:13 (§ 70 in ed. Finkelstein, pp. 133–134, with Finkelstein's first note on p. 134). I am indebted to my friend, Dr. Peretz Segal, for this reference.

However, another tannaitic tradition (Tosephta, *Zebachim* 5:6 [ed. Zuckermandel, p. 487]; BT ibid. 45a and *Temura* 2b) indicates that R. Jose in fact disagreed with the anonymous opinion and held that, with regard to Gentiles' sacrifices, the first three violations too are punishable Moreover, this latter tradition adds yet another violation (*me'ilah* − misappropriation of sacred property) which R. Jose, but not R. Simeon, would punish with regard to Gentiles' sacrifices.

In other words, R. Simeon's view excluded the offerings of Gentiles from the protection of the laws of sacrificial sanctity, but R. Jose included them. This virtually means that R. Simeon did not consider the Gentiles' offerings to be sacrifices, while R. Jose did. While one might feel tempted to to explain R. Simeon's position on the basis of his well-known antipathy to gentiles in general and Romans in particular (see the discussion between him and R. Jose in BT *Shabbat* 33b!), it is nevertheless the case that his position is, as we have seen, the better defensible on the basis of biblical precedent and the logic of monotheism. Similarly, his position regarding the inapplicability of technical violations may be read directly out of Leviticus 22:2, as we have seen. What requires explanation is R. Jose's view, that sacrifices of Gentiles are as fully sanctified and protected as those of Jews.

This problem regarding R. Jose's view is, however, just the tip of the iceberg, because it points in the direction of a much greater problem: Given the biblical precedent, why did the rabbis allow Gentiles to sacrifice at all? The standard rabbinic answer, repeated in various texts, is that this is mandated by Leviticus 22:18. Since this text refers to sacrifices by *'ish 'ish mibet yisrael*, which means "any Israelite" but literally reads "a man, a man of the house of Israel," atomistic exegesis could view one of the occurrences of "a man" as superfluous and, therefore, as a reason "to include" someone not of the house of Israel − a Gentile.[12] However, this is clearly *post factum* exegesis, for it is not at all required by the biblical text or by rabbinic exegetical presumptions. Note, for example, that the very same tannaitic midrash which brings this interpretation of Lev. 22:18 ignored, earlier in the same chapter (v. 4), another occurrence of *'ish 'ish*. So it seems that the interpretation of v. 18 indicates rabbinic recognition that sacrifices had in fact been accepted by Gentiles, and their conclusion that the practice must therefore be justified, by hook or by crook.

This, however, only puts the problem off: instead of asking about the rabbis, we must ask about the priests who ran the Second Temple, who too were Jews who presumably wished to live in good conscience before God and according to His law. How could they allow a Gentile, perhaps a visitor who normally worshipped pagan deities, the use of the altar of the one God of the

---

[12] See *Sifra, Emor* 7:6, ed. Weiss, p. 98a; BT *Hullin* 13b; *Temura* 2b; *Menachot* 73b.

universe? While their desire to allow such sacrifices probably reflected political considerations (see below), it nevertheless needed to be squared with the divine law. How could this be done?

I would hypothesize that refuge was taken in a subterfuge, which allowed Gentiles to think they were sacrificing while allowing the priests to tell God and their own consciences that they did not. Such a subterfuge is indicated by the rabbinic evidence and also by Josephus.

In order to understand this subterfuge, we should remember, first of all, that the rabbinic sources allow the acceptance of gifts from Gentiles for the upkeep of the Temple.[13] That was, in fact, a practice with much well-known historical precedent.[14] Next, we should recall that the verse upon which the rabbis chose to pin their license for sacrifices by Gentiles, Lev. 22:18, comes in the biblical pericope dealing with freewill offerings, *nedarim* and *nedavot*. That this is so is not because they had no choice. Modern apologists, for example, are quick to point already to Lev. 1:2, which opens the entire book with a reference to "a man" who wishes to sacrifice, as evidence for biblical universalism and the acceptance of sacrifice from Gentiles.[15] But the ancient rabbis did not do so; they took "man" there to "include" proselytes alone

---

[13] See below, on *qodᵉshei bedeq habbayit*.

[14] See SVM II, 311–313, also below, n. 22; K. Galling, *ZDPV* 68 (1946–1951, entitled *Beiträge zur biblischen Landes- und Altertumskunde*), pp. 134–142; E. Bickerman, *Studies in Jewish and Christian History*, II (1980), pp. 53–56, 160–161.

[15] See, for two examples, S. R. Hirsch, *Der Pentateuch*, III (1873), p. 5 (in English as *The Pentateuch*, III/1 (1958), p. 5: "By *mikem* a *mumar*, one 'who has become changed,' has become 'un-Jewish,' is excluded. To the non-Jew, the Jewish Temple is open without exception, everyone who has the calling to be '*adam*' may bring his offering to the Altar . . ."), and J. H. Hertz, *The Pentateuch and Haftorahs* (1938), p. 410 ("Even a heathen may bring an offering, if he is moved to do so. A man's faith, not the accident of birth, is regarded by God. An apostate is therefore denied the privilege of bringing an offering at Israel's Sanctuary (Sifra). God would accept the offering of a heathen who turned to Him (I Kings VIII, 41 f), but not the sacrifice of a disloyal Israelite.") The latter, a commentary by the late Chief Rabbi of the British Empire, is a case of apologetic obfuscation which compares well with any offered by the Chief Jewish Historian of the Roman Empire. Hertz claims that not birth but only faith matters, so an apostate Jew may not sacrifice. The logical corollary is that a Gentile *who converts to Judaism* may sacrifice, and, indeed, the *Sifra* makes that stipulation. But Hertz quotes the *Sifra* only to exclude the apostate but not to exclude the unconverted Gentile, and avoids stipulating conversion while nevertheless not excluding it either ("if he is moved to do so . . . heathen who turned to Him"). In contrast to Hirsch's and Hertz's commentaries, it is an interesting, and not altogether positive, comment on the stance of parts of post-Holocaust Orthodoxy, which feel that they owe nothing to Gentiles, that the next commentary published by Soncino after Hertz's simply, and consistently, explains that the Torah says "*mikem*" "to exclude offerings brought by a heathen or scoffer" (*The Soncino Chumash* [ed. A. Cohen; 1947], p. 605), while the recent English abridgement of Hirsch omits this topic altogether from the commentary to Leviticus 1:2 (*T'rumath Tzvi: The Pentateuch* [ed. E. Oratz; 1986], p. 371).

(*Sifra, Vayiqra* 2:2 ad loc., ed. Weiss, p. 4b). Similarly, *Sifré Deut.* § 354 (on 33:19 — ed. Finkelstein, p. 416) stipulates that Gentiles who admire the Jews' sacrificial cult must convert if they wish to participate in it.[16] What, then, is indicated by the fact that when the rabbis do allow Gentiles to sacrifice, they do so within the context of Leviticus 22:17—25?

Now it is important to note that while Greek distinguishes between two types of items dedicated at temples by giving them two names, *anathemata* and *thysiai*, i.e., objects dedicated to a temple for its use or decoration and objects sacrificed upon an altar, rabbinic terminology knows only of a subdivision within the single category of "holy things," *qodashim*: *qod*e*shei mizbeaḥ* ("holy things for the altar"), i.e., sacrifices, and *qod*e*shei bedeq habbayit* ("holy things for the upkeep of the House"), corresponding to *anathemata*. The latter, which Gentiles may donate, are basically gifts brought to the Jewish authorities in the Temple for use as they see fit. The lesser sanctity of such gifts, in contrast to sacrifices, is explicit in the Torah in our pericope (Leviticus 22:23), and is also indicated by *Ant.* 18.19, where we read that although the Essenes, due to differences concerning purity, would not send sacrifices (*thysiai*), they did — according to Josephus — send it *anathemata*.[17] What does this have to do with the rabbinic understanding of permitted sacrifices by Gentiles as coming under the rubric of freewill sacrifices only?

There is no way in which one could consider an obligatory sacrifice to be a gift: the Law *requires* that it be *sacrificed*. But as for freewill offerings, animals which are brought to be sacrificed without the Law requiring it, there is more room for redefinition. One cannot imagine someone obligated to bring a sin- or purification-offering opting to donate the victim for sale with the proceeds going for the Temple's upkeep. But one can well imagine a donor bringing in an animal for a freewill sacrifice but deciding, instead, to donate it for use or sale by the Temple authorities; if the need existed, it might even be considered more pious on his part to do so. My suggestion is, therefore, that the rabbinic sources indicate license for sacrifices by Gentiles specifically with reference to Leviticus 22 because they assimilated them to *qod*e*shei bedeq habbayit*. Thus,

---

[16] The same results from *Or. Sib.* 3:624—627, where Gentiles are urged to convert and sacrifice. In a way reminiscent of Hertz (above, n. 15), however, the demand for conversion is not spelled out.

[17] For the permissibility of such donations to the Temple by Gentiles, see BT *Arakhin* 6a, where it is stipulated that a Gentile may donate to the Temple only if his donation will not be something specific recognizable as coming from him. A similar qualification is made, ibid. (and in Tos.*Megillah* 2[3]:16, ed. Lieberman, p. 352), requiring that a Gentile's contribution of building material for a synagogue is acceptable only if he gave it "according to the opinion of Jews" — i.e, that he intended to give it as a gift to the Jews, who will use it in the synagogue as they see fit. As for Leviticus 22:23, see the *baraita* in the *Sifra* ad loc. (ed. Weiss, *Emor* 7:7, p. 98d) and in BT *Temura* 7a—b, which clearly allows the donation to the Temple of animals unfit for sacrifice, as *qod*e*shei bedeq habbayit*. On the Essenes, see below, n. 28.

for example, if a Gentile brought a bull for sacrifice, it could be considered a gift to the Jews for use as they saw fit in their Temple; they could, for example, sell it and use the proceeds for repairs to the Temple buildings. If, however, the priests turned around and sacrificed it — as they did — they could consider it their own sacrifice.[18] In short, rabbinic license for Gentile sacrifices was predicated upon there formally being no such thing.

Let us confront this hypothesis with the evidence of our foremost witness, Josephus. We first note that, although he tries to be as universalist as possible, Josephus now and then lets through some relevant information of an entirely different color. First, he does note, more than once, that Gentiles were not allowed into the inner precincts of the Temple, not to mention anywhere near the altar.[19] Similarly, when in *Ant.* 11.87 he appeasingly adds to the exclusivist Ezra 4:3 (1 Esdras 5:67−68) the note that Gentiles could worship in the Temple, the best he can offer is a general *proskyneō* (so too *BJ* 4.262).[20] This is reminiscent of Solomon's reference to Gentiles praying in/to the Temple (I Kings 8:41−43): as there, so too here (as well as in Josephus' rendition of Solomon's prayer [*Ant.* 8.116]), nothing is said of sacrifice. But the most interesting case to cite here is *Ant.* 3.318−319, a passage wherein Josephus' point is the widespread and lasting veneration of Moses. To illustrate this point, he tells of a group of non-Jews who came from Mesopotamia to sacrifice in Jerusalem. They were not allowed to partake of the sacrifices, however, because Moses had forbidden that to foreigners. Therefore, although they had tolerated much danger and expense in their long voyage, these would-be

---

[18] This notion of sacrifice-laundering was succinctly phrased by a Karaite writer of the ninth/tenth century, Daniel b. Moses al-Qumisi, in his Hebrew commentary to Lev. 1:2 (in S. Schechter, *Saadyana* [1903], p. 145) and Lev. 22:25 (in L. Ginzberg, *Genizah Studies in Memory of Doctor Solomon Schechter*, II [1929], p. 482). In both of these, which are cited by I. Knohl in *Tarbiz* 48 (1978/79), pp. 343−344 (in Hebrew), al-Qumisi adduces Exodus 10:25 as further proof of the impossibility of Gentiles' sacrificing to God, and emphasizes that "Cyrus and the other Gentiles gave their gifts to Israel and Israel sacrificed them on its own behalf." If we now return to R. Jose, we can suggest that his view was that the sacrifices brought by Gentiles in fact fully become sacrifices of Jews, and are therefore protected by all the usual sanctions. R. Simeon and his followers, in contrast, held that whatever subterfuge had been used to allow the sacrifices, Lev. 22:2 still excludes them from the scope of the sanctions.

[19] In addition to his well-known evidence about the warning inscriptions, see, for example, *Ant.* 11.101, *Ant.* 12.145 and *BJ* 2.341; the wording of the latter ("prostrated to the sanctuary from where it was allowed") is quite similar to III Macc. 1:9 and *Leg.* 297, which also emphasize that Gentiles who wished to respect the Temple did only what was allowed. On the warning inscriptions, see SVM II, pp. 284−285; Rabello (above, n. 6), nr. 3, pp. 28−32, and nr. 4, pp. 28−32; and, most recently, P. Segal, *IEJ* 39 (1989), pp. 79−84.

[20] Just as this is all which is used of Gentiles in the Temple in John 12:20 and Acts 8:27. On the sense of this verb, see the lexica and S.J.D. Cohen, *AJS Review* 7−8 (1983/83), p. 52, n. 29.

sacrificers, out of respect for Moses, turned around and went home: "some without sacrificing at all, others leaving their sacrifices half completed, many of them unable so much as to gain entrance to the temple" (trans. Thackeray [LCL]). This quite plainly indicates that they were expelled as soon as their identity as Gentiles was discovered.[21] Had they been able to sacrifice in some legitimate way, Josephus would have preferred to leave the story with a happy ending reporting that fact.

Next, note that Josephus' examples of Gentiles sacrificing in Jerusalem are few and far between.[22] If we leave aside the general references in *BJ* 4.262 and 4.275 to Gentiles "prostrating" or "worshipping" in the Temple, and if we leave aside Josephus' statements in *BJ* 2.409 ff., to which we shall return in detail below, we are left with sacrifices by Alexander the Great (*Ant.* 11.336),[23] Ptolemy III (*C. Ap.* 2.48), Antiochus VII Sidetes (*Ant.* 13.242−243) and Marcus Vipsanius Agrippa (*Ant.* 16.14). To this we may add the notice that L. Vitellius, the governor of Syria in 37 C.E., intended to sacrifice in Jerusalem (*Ant.* 18.122); nothing is said of his having done so, although it may perhaps be assumed. Finally, to this evidence from Josephus we may add what seem to be the only other relevant data: III Maccabees 1:9 reports that Ptolemy IV Philopator sacrificed to God in Jerusalem after his victory at Raphia; II Macc 3:35 reports that Heliodorus offered sacrifice after

---

[21] One may wonder why the ones who had entered the sacred precincts were not executed, in line with the law of the inscriptions and complementary literary evidence (see above, n. 19). Indeed, S. Klein, who began his discussion of this episode by noting that "es hat den Anschein, als wollte J[osephus] etwas verschweigen," surmised that the Gentile worshippers were indeed executed, Josephus apologetically hiding the fact: *Jeschurun* 7 (1920), pp. 459−461. However, while his impression of Josephus' apologetic needs is correct, it appears extravagant to read so much into Josephus' plain words. Cf. *Agrippa I*, p. 212, on similar overinterpretation of the end of Acts 12:17. Rather, one should infer that the Temple authorities were not always in the position of imposing the death penalty for such violations − just as Paul's adventures show (Acts 21 ff.). In fact they were probably only rarely in such a position; cf. *Ant* 20.200−203 and E. Bammel, *Judaica: Kleine Schriften, I* (1986), pp. 59−72 (= *JJS* 25 [1974], pp. 35−49); J.-P. Lémonon, *Pilate et le gouvernement de la Judée* (1981), pp. 74−97.

[22] Cohen (above, n. 9: pp. 412−415) gave some brief attention to respect shown by Gentile kings and dignitaries to the Temple, and assembled much Josephan evidence. However, under the rubric "sacrifice and worship in the temple" (p. 413, n. 14), most of the passages he lists in fact refer not to that but, rather, to Gentiles subsidizing the cult or giving *anathemata* (the noun or verb is frequently used): so *Ant.* 11.31−32, 58(−63),78, 97−103, 123−130; 12.78−84 (so instead of "12.2.10 § 90"?); 13.55; and 14.488 (//*BJ* 1.357). As for *BJ* 2.341, it speaks only of Neapolitanus "prostrating to the sanctuary," and even emphasizes that he did it "from where it was allowed" (cf. Philo's careful wording in *Leg.* 297, cited below). The cases discussed in the next two sentences, already listed by Schürer, are thus the only ones that fit this rubric.

[23] "According to the instructions of the high priest" − on the phrase, see Cohen (above, n. 20), p. 48, n. 19.

his miraculous recovery after being stricken for violating the Temple; and
Suetonius reports that Augustus commended his grandson, Gaius Caesar,
because he "non suplicasset" in Jerusalem when he passed through in 1
B.C.E.[24] The implication is that he could have done so had he so preferred,
and it may perhaps be assumed that "suplicasset" covers sacrifices too.

Regarding this dossier, a few observations are in order. First, and most
importantly, we note that all of the above cases have to do with rulers: kings or
very senior members of their administrations. It is not difficult to imagine a
willingness to deviate from normal exclusiveness out of deference to such
august personalities, who could be dangerous if insulted (as is well illustrated
by the continuation of the III Maccabees, whatever its historical truth).

Second, note that in the cases of Alexander, Agrippa and Vitellius,[25] the
sacrifices come along with gestures honoring the people or are themselves
portrayed as such. This lends us confidence in our hypothesis that Jews could
construe Gentiles' sacrifices as gifts to them.

Third, note that the Gentile donor of the sacrifice was himself outside of the
sacred courts. This may be taken for granted (see above, n. 19), and, in the
cases under review, this is specifically stated with regard to Ptolemy IV and
Antiochus Sidetes; the case of Heliodorus, who forced his way in over
the Jews' protests, is an exception which proves the rule. Under such
circumstances, the sacrifice had to be brought in by Jews, making it all the
easier to tell oneself that the Gentile had given his sacrifice to Jews, who
thereafter decided to sacrifice it.

Fourth, finally, note that in some of the few cases which we assembled, the
historical facts themselves are in doubt. Most scholars deny that Alexander
the Great even visited Jerusalem, much less offered sacrifices there, and the
reliability of III Maccabees is similarly disputed.[26] But even if we view these
stories not as fact but rather as evidence for what was considered acceptable,
we should note that two of the events are recorded elsewhere without any
reference to sacrifices. Namely, the rabbinic stories of Alexander in
Jerusalem, of which one is otherwise quite similar to Josephus', have no
reference to sacrifices,[27] and Philo's account of M. Agrippa's visit to Jerusalem
(*Leg.* 296–297), while highly laudatory, likewise omits them. Indeed, Philo
seems studiously to avoid giving the impression that sacrifices were offered:

---

[24] *Divus Augustus* 93 = Stern, *GLA* II, nr. 304, pp. 110–111.

[25] For the latter, see also *Ant.* 18.90–95 and below, pp. 202–217.

[26] On the Alexander stories, see, *inter alia*, V. A. Tcherikover, *Hellenistic Civilization and
the Jews* (1959), pp.42–48; further literature is cited in *JSJ* 21 (1990), p. 185, nn. 25–26. As
for III Maccabees, see SVM III/1, pp. 537–540.

[27] See BT *Yoma* 69a and the scholion to *Megillat Ta'anit*, 21 Kislev, (ed. H. Lichtenstein,
HUCA 8–9 [1931/32], pp. 339–340); cf. also ibid., 25 Sivan (p. 330) and *Bereishit Rabbah*
61:7 (ed. Theodor-Albeck, pp. 668–669).

while he goes on and on about Agrippa's visits to the Temple courts, where he viewed the sacrificial ritual, nevertheless, Agrippa is only said to have left "after decking the temple with all the dedicatory gifts (*anathemata*) which the law made permissible and benefiting the inhabitants by granting every favour which he could without causing mischief" (§ 297, trans. Smallwood). While the careful qualifications are meant, in context, to edify Gaius Caligula, who had ordained the erection of a pagan idol in the Temple, nonetheless, together with the lack of reference to sacrifice, they are quite striking. Just as elsewhere Josephus notes that the Essenes send *anathemata* to the Temple but due to a dispute concerning purities they are excluded from the common precincts and sacrifice (*thysias epitelousin*) separately (*Ant.* 18.19),[28] so too M. Agrippa, as a gentile, seems, according to Philo, to have been allowed to offer only *anathemata*, not sacrifices.[29] If Agrippa, however, used to pagan cosmo-politanism, insisted (whether out of piety or courtesy or both) on offer-ing real sacrifices, as Josephus claimed, then, so I suspect, Jews could have accepted them and nevertheless salved their monotheistic consciences by considering the sacrifices, formally, as *anathemata* all the same.

This brings us to the main text on sacrifices by Gentiles: Josephus' account of the provocation which touched off the revolt in summer of 66 C.E. According to *BJ* 2.409:

Eleazar, son of Ananias the high-priest, a very daring youth, then holding the position of captain, persuaded those who officiated in the Temple services to accept no gift or sacrifice from a foreigner. This action laid the foundation of the war with the Romans, for the sacrifices offered on behalf of that nation and the emperor were in consequence rejected. (trans. Thackeray [LCL])

Since Josephus goes on to tell how the leading citizens, chief priests and most notable Pharisees opposed this decision (§§ 411 ff.) and even brought forth "priestly experts on the traditions, who declared that all their ancestors had accepted the sacrifices of aliens" (§ 417), Schürer (p. 310) felt confident in viewing Eleazar and his followers as revolutionaries and innovators. That, of course, is the impression Josephus worked hard to give.

However, it is very curious that although the practical issue was sacrifices for Rome, the virtually exclusive thrust of the response to the revolutionaries was, according to Josephus, the acceptability of *gifts* from Gentiles, not their

---

[28] On the text and sense of this problematic passage, see Feldman's detailed notes ad loc. (LCL) and J. Strugnell, *JBL* 77 (1958), pp. 113–115. T. S. Beall, *Josephus' Description of the Essenes Illustrated by the Dead Sea Scrolls* (1988), pp. 115–119, is more occupied by questions of its historical truth, which need not concern us here.

[29] So too, according to Philo, also Agrippa's imperial father-in-law (Augustus) is only said to have sent *anathemata* (*Leg.* 157) and to have *financed* daily sacrifices (on the latter, cf. below, n. 34).

sacrifices.[30] Thus, according to §§ 412−413, the principal citizens, chief priests and most notable Pharisees

proceeded to expose the absurdity of the alleged pretext. Their forefathers, they said, had adorned the sanctuary mainly at the expense of aliens and had always accepted the gifts of foreign nations; not only had they never taken the sacrilegious step of hindering anyone's sacrifices,[31] but they had set up around the Temple the dedicatory offerings which were still to be seen and had remained there for so long a time.

Here Josephus begins by referring to the subventions given by gentile kings, beginning with Cyrus, for the building and maintenance of the Temple, and he concludes, correspondingly, by pointing out the dedicated objects (*anathemata*) still visible around the Temple. There is only a single fleeting reference to sacrifices,[32] and even it is carefully worded, saying only that the Jews' forefathers never rejected sacrifices from Gentiles; it does not say that those sacrifices were offered. Similarly, the priestly experts cited in § 417 testify only that their ancestors had *accepted* sacrifices from Gentiles.

---

[30] This difficulty is especially pointed up in Simchoni's Hebrew translation of our passage (and in Safrai's summary of it [above, n. 2: p. 111]), according to which the decision adopted at Eleazar's urging forbade acceptance of sacrifices from Gentiles. This omits the prohibition of gifts, which in Josephus' text precedes that of sacrifices; the oversight probably occurred because it was clear to Simchoni that the important point was the prohibition of sacrifices. In my experience, similarly, many who read the passage come away with the impression that the decision was said to have been the prohibition of sacrifices for Rome, or, after they are pressed, recall only the general prohibition of sacrifices from Gentiles. The reference to gifts is the last thing recalled, because it is seemingly so irrelevant. But for Josephus, the gifts are the first point of the decision and the main topic of the debate. This discontinuity between the practical issue and the arguments brought in the debate is one of the two main pillars of M. Auerbach's remarkable argument that there were, in fact, no regular sacrifices on behalf of Rome or its emperor in the Temple of Jerusalem: *Sinai* 51 (1961/62), esp. pp. 35−36 (in Hebrew). The other main pillar was the fact that Philo has the Jews refer only to three special sacrifices on behalf of Gaius (*Leg.* 356), although a reference to daily sacrifices would have been even better apologetics, according to Auerbach (pp 34−35). That second argument may be dismissed by assuming that Philo thought a reference to extraordinary sacrifices specifically concering Gaius to be even more impressive than routine sacrifices concerning the empire and all emperors; so too Y. Baer, *Zion* 36 (1970/71), pp. 130−131, n. 13 (in Hebrew). As for the argument from discontinuity, it is the foundation of our own explanation of the debate offered below.

[31] The last three words are my own more exact translation of *ou diakekōlukenai thysias tinōn*, instead of Thackeray's "forbidding anyone to offer sacrifice." The rest of the excerpt is according to Thackeray's translation.

[32] To illustrate its fleeting nature, note that C. Roth, in an article on the debate, mentioned only the testimony about the precedents for accepting gifts from foreigners. This led him to remark, if only in passing, that such precedents did not prove that Gentiles had been permitted to sacrifice: *HTR* 53 (1960), p. 94. Similarly, Roth (ibid.) suspects that Josephus ("the Romanophile historian") did not report all the views expressed in the debate, and infers from Josephus' emphasis on the unusual nature of the sacrifices on behalf of Rome (*C. Ap.* 2.77) that in general such sacrifices were "to some extent irregular, and could hence have been considered as improper by rigorists . . ." However, Roth did not pursue these points.

This leads us directly to the central problem in understanding this episode: What is the relationship between the decision not to accept gifts or sacrifices *from* Gentiles and the decision not to continue sacrificing *for* Rome? Josephus, twice, portrays the latter as a corollary of the former: in § 409 (quoted above) he says the decision to stop accepting gifts or sacrifices from Gentiles caused the rebellion because those who adopted it consequently stopped the sacrifices for Rome and the emperor, and in § 412 he speaks of the rebels' decision as a pretext (*prophasis*)[33] for stopping the sacrifices for Rome. But why does the stoppage of sacrifices *from* Gentiles entail the stoppage of those *for* Rome? This is especially problematic in view of the fact that, according to Josephus, the *Jews* financed the daily sacrifices for Rome.[34]

Indeed, there was precedent enough, from the Persian and Hellenistic periods and down to the Roman period, for Jewish sacrifice on behalf of the ruling powers.[35] To cite it, however, was apparently not enough, because the rebels would have denounced it as just as illegitimate. But why should the moderates (or Josephus) have supposed the argument from Gentiles' gifts would be any more cogent?

The answer, it seems, has to do with the theory of sacrifice. To borrow terminology from the world of banking, sacrifices credit an account. Therefore, if one has sinned or otherwise "owes" God a sacrifice,[36] the proper sacrifice can wipe out the deficit, while if one has a balanced account a freewill offering can create a positive balance, which one can draw on, or hope to, in times of need. In the world of sacrifices, as in the world of banking, one usually deals only with his own account. However, as in banks, so too with sacrifices, while one may not withdraw from someone else's account, one may deposit into it. Thus, for example, the Talmud (BT *Temurah* 2b–3a) takes for granted the possibility that a gentile might offer a sacrifice for the purpose of atoning for the sins of a Jew; there is evidence from Josephus, the New Testament and the rabbis for the pious practice of paying for the atoning sacrifices required of Nazirites;[37] and the notion of the vicarious atonement worked by the death of scapegoats, and of Jesus, further testifies to the notion that the benefits of a sacrifice may be reassigned.[38]

---

[33] For the connotations of this term, see C. Spicq, *Notes de lexicographie néo-testamentaire*, II (1978), pp. 765–767: in the New Testament, "toujours en mauvaise part," and so too in the evidence from Josephus collected ibid., pp. 765–766, n. 3.

[34] So explicitly in *C. Ap.* 2.77, and implicitly in *BJ* 2.197. Philo, however, holds that Rome financed the sacrifices (*Leg.* 157, 317). See SVM II, p. 312; *Agrippa I*, pp. 201–202.

[35] See Ezra 6:10; I Esdras 7:31; I Macc. 7:33; II Macc 3:32; *Aristeas* 45; Philo, *Leg.* 232, 356.

[36] As my friend Dr. Victor (Avigdor) Hurowitz pointed out, to vow a sacrifice in return for a boon (e.g., Jonah 2:9[10]) is similar to buying on credit.

[37] See *Ant.* 19.294; Acts 21:23–24; m.*Nazir* 2:5–6, etc.; *Agrippa I*, p. 68, n. 4.

[38] On this theme, see *JBL* 102 (1983), pp. 260–263.

If one applies this line of thought to sacrifices on behalf of Rome, it follows that the Jews could understand these sacrifices as Jewish sacrifices with the benefits assigned to Rome: Jewish deposits into Rome's account with God. This means, however, that the Jerusalem altar was being used for the benefit of pagans (and, in this case, pagans who competed with God for the rule of His land and His people!). Now, just as usually a person deposits into his own account, so too, the more usual way such a benefit might be had was by allowing the Gentiles to sacrifice. But that, as we have seen, was not contemplated by the Bible, apparently violates the principles of monotheism, and even the rabbis allowed it, apparently, only via a fiction which considered the sacrifices to be those of Jews.

That is, while all agreed that a gentile could not make "deposits" at the Temple by sacrificing, the fiction allowed for Gentiles to have "accounts" there into which Jews could sacrifice. So when Eleazar ben Hananiah decided to attack the sacrifices on behalf of Rome, something which he probably did out of an ideology which precluded Roman rule in the Holy Land,[39] and had to come up with a rationalization showing that the practice of such sacrifices was illegitimate, the best approach was to claim that the prohibition of sacrifices by Gentiles — which even his moderate opponents in theory admitted — was itself only a corollary of the basic principle that God's altar was not to be used on behalf of pagans. Gentiles could not have an "account" there. Given the fact that it is usually the owner of the account who makes deposits into it, this explains the framing of the rebels' decision, as stated by Josephus. But if the root principle is that Gentiles may not have an "account" at the Temple of Jerusalem, then it follows that even Jewish sacrifices on behalf of pagans were forbidden. (Children and mentally unfit people may have accounts at a bank, used on their behalf by guardians; the rebels held that pagans, however, were totally outside of the system.) Moderates bent upon preserving the peace attempted, according to Josephus, to avoid the question of basic principle and concentrate on precedent. So their response was to claim that since Eleazar's

---

[39] Similar to that of the zealots in Jabneh who destroyed the altar to Gaius Caligula in 39 C.E. because they saw it as a pollution of the Holy Land, as Philo states in *Leg.* 202. See *Agrippa I*, pp. 81–82. M. Hengel proposed an alternative motivation: the rebels did not want to sacrifice to God for the emperor because the latter considered himself a god and was worshipped as such by Gentiles (*Die Zeloten* [1976[2]], p. 111, n. 2 = *The Zealots* [1989], p. 107, n. 162). However, the logic here is less compelling: why should Jews avoid praying to their God on behalf of someone others wrongly consider to be a god? Nevertheless, both explanations have in common the notion that the emperor competes with God and that Jews should not recognize his claims. On the other hand, Y. Baer's claim (above, n. 30: p. 133), that the sacrifices were suspended because "the Jews rebelled and arose against the cult of a flesh and blood ruler, just as they did in the days of Antiochus Epiphanes," is hardly justified. In no way may the loyalty sacrifices, whoever financed them (see above, n. 34), be likened to a pagan cult introduced forcibly into the Jewish Temple.

argument precluded the acceptance of sacrifices from Gentiles, and the latter were traditionally viewed as *anathemata*, Eleazar's argument really meant that it was forbidden to accept *anathemata* from Gentiles – a straw man against which the moderates could easily argue on the basis of precedent. (Eleazar's answer, obviously, would be the rejection of the fictional assimilation of Gentiles' sacrifices to their gifts.)

Josephus, in other words, or those whose arguments he claims to report, stood Eleazar's argument on its head in order to refute it. What Eleazar and his followers really wanted was to stop the sacrifices on behalf of Rome; that was the only real issue, and the focus of the debate (§§ 409, 416). We know of no Gentiles waiting on line to sacrifice or give gifts to the Temple. Eleazar was probably motivated by the Holy Land notion. But in order to introduce a change in the cult one must offer a formal argument, and Eleazar found it by appealing to a principle which could reasonably be posited as the source of the rule which even his moderate opponents accepted – that Gentiles could not sacrifice in Jerusalem. That is, Eleazar's argument went from the top down: from God, to "accounts" with Him, to sacrifices, which are the deposits in such accounts. Josephus, and/or the moderates of 66, could respond to Eleazar's argument only via the traditional subterfuge, which went from the bottom up: since Gentiles' gifts are allowed, as many precedents show, their sacrifices are too (since among ourselves we view them too as mere gifts). But Josephus could not make this response clear, because to do so would require the explanation of the subterfuge, and that would run completely counter to his apologetic needs. So, as often elsewhere, Josephus, torn between the historian's desire to report what happened and the apologists' desire not to arouse hostility to his people and religion, left us with an account which doesn't hang together well.[40] In this case, we are fortunate to have the rabbinic evidence, which, by clarifying the categories used of sacrifices offered by Gentiles, allowed us a reasonable understanding of what Josephus was hiding.

Before concluding, we should note that there is another obvious argument which could have been made to justify sacrifices for Rome, and the fact that Josephus does not cite it is quite significant. The other argument is, that sacrificing for Rome is in fact sacrificing for the Jews, because the peace and prosperity of the empire entail the same for Jews as well. Indeed, the best-known Jewish statements of the obligation to *pray* for the ruling power, Jeremiah 29:7 and m. *Avot* 3:2, both emphasize this very dependence.[41]

---

[40] For other examples, see the episodes treated above, pp. 29–34, wherein Josephus hides Judaism's involvement in politics, and the episode reported in *Ant.*19.332–334, where Josephus blurs the fact that some Jews denied proselytes were fully Jews (see *Agrippa I*, pp. 124–130)

[41] See also Baruch 1:10–11, the context of Ezra 6:10, and the argument, "Could it possibly be that you [Alexander] would be misled by pagans/Gentiles to destroy the house in which we

However, as far as we can see this argument was not adduced, but, instead, the dispute proceeded along the technical lines outlined above. This reinforces the distinction upon which we insisted a few times in this paper, beginning with Schürer's allusion to Solomon's prayer, between prayers and sacrifices. Prayer is very private and it would be absurd to think that anyone can forbid it. But Jewish sacrifice was very public and centralized, and took place in the midst of an institution where descent held sway.[42] So it is not surprising that it was only with the greatest reserve and difficulties that Gentiles were allowed the use of its altar, and to the extent that happened it should not be viewed as evidence that the Temple "became cosmopolitan." Rather, the compromises made reflected the realities of life as a small province amidst great and potentiallly malevolent empires.

Finally, I would note only that when some late midrashim express opposition to the acceptance of sacrifices from gentiles, it seems extravagant to link that, as some have done, to similar Karaite opinion and wonder whether they preserve, via some underground or otherwise unknown conduit, sectarian opinion of the Second Temple period, and that Eleazar ben Hananiah was a spokesman for such sectarian views.[43] Rather, it seems that Eleazar, as so many other hotheaded youths, was simply demanding that his elders stop playing compromising games and rather live up, in practice, to the monotheistic principles which they admitted in theory. The elders' defense of the fiction which avoided confrontation, based as it was only upon the grim realities of life in the Roman Empire rather than upon ideals, was too weak to carry the day, so the youths won and the Jews lost.

---

pray that you and your kingdom not be destroyed?!" – cited in the first two sources listed above, n. 27. On ancient Jewish prayers for the government, of which little is known, see E. Bammel, in *Jesus and the Politics of his Day* (edd. E. Bammel and C.F.D. Moule; 1984), pp. 372–373. On the origin of the prayers in the now-traditional liturgy, see B. Schwartz, *HUCA* 57 (1986), pp. 113–120.

[42] See especially Ezra 6:10, where there is a loud contrast between sacrificing to God and praying for the king and his sons (less so in I Esdras 6:31, but again accented in *Ant.* 11.102).

[43] See I. Knohl, *Tarbiz* 48 (1978/79), pp. 341–345 (in Hebrew) (also D. Gilat's notes thereto, ibid. 49 [1979/80], pp. 422–423 and E. E. Urbach's well-founded rejoinder on p. 423). According to a 1986 lecture by Prof. E. Qimron, the soon(?)-to-be-published *Miqtzat Ma'asé haTorah* text from Qumran (see above, p. 21, n. 48) raises the topic of sacrifices by Gentiles but, in the document's fragmentary state, its opinion of them is lost. However, Qimron supposes, on the basis of the rest of the document, that its sectarian author would have opposed such a practice. Presumably, such an author adhered to the strict ideals of priestly Judaism and would have condemned compromises with political realities – which is why he found himself in exile. (On the stringent and priestly nature of the halacha in *MMT*, see now Y. Sussmann, *Tarbiz* 59 [1989/90], pp. 11–76 [in Hebrew]; on our issue – p. 33, n. 97.)

7. Residents and Exiles, Jerusalemites and Judaeans
(Acts 7:4; 2:5, 14):
On Stephen, Pentecost and the Structure of Acts

It seems that commentators have been so occupied with the first part of Acts 7:4, and the contradiction which it (along with vv. 2−3) poses to the apparent order of events in Genesis 11−12,[1] that the latter part of the verse has escaped detailed scrutiny. Nevertheless, examination of two problems there may lead not only to a better understanding of this verse, but also to a better appreciation of a major point of the speech as a whole. In addition, our investigation will, I believe, help clarify the nature of the "Hellenists" (Acts 6:1; 9:29) and of the crowd which is said to have witnessed the Pentecost miracle (Acts 2). Furthermore, our investigation may also contribute to a better understanding of the composition of the Pentecost narrative and, given its prominent placement in Acts, of the structure of the book as a whole.

I. Acts 7:4 (*metōkisen . . . katoikeite*)

Thereupon he left the land of the Chaldaeans and settled in Harran. From there, after his father's death, God led him to migrate (*metōkisen*) to this land where you now live (*nun katoikeite*). (New English Bible)

The first problem regards the translation of *metōkisen*. The verb *metoikizō* appears only twice in the New Testament, both in this chapter of Acts (vv. 4, 43).[2] The latter case is part of a quote from Amos 5:27, wherein God threatens to *banish* the Israelites − and so it is usually rendered in translations of Amos.[3]

---

[1] This is all that is discussed, for example, in the commentaries on this verse in H. Conzelmann, *Acts of the Apostles* (1987), p. 52 (= *Die Apostelgeschichte* [1972²], pp. 51−52) and G. Schille, *Die Apostelgeschichte des Lukas* (1983), p. 180. Cf. below, n. 25.

[2] There seems to be no room for doubt about the text in either case. On v. 4, see T. Zahn, *Die Apostelgeschichte des Lucas*, I (1922³), p. 249. On the form of the verb in v. 43, see F. Blass - A. Debrunner, *Grammatik des neutestamentlichen Griechisch* (ed. F. Rehkopf; 1976¹⁴), pp. 58−59 (§ 74, 1, with n. 4).

[3] E.g., "take you into exile" (RSV), "drive you into exile" (New English Bible),

It is noteworthy, however, that in translations of Acts 7:43 we at times find a watered-down verb, such as "remove" (RSV), "umsiedeln" or "verpflanzen."[4] The reason, it seems, is a desire for consistency, based upon the reasonable assumption that the two juxtaposed appearances of such a rare verb should be taken together:[5] since in v. 4 translators are naturally unwilling to have Stephen speak of God as having banished Abraham into Canaan, and they therefore seek more neutral renderings (such as "led to migrate" in the New English Bible, cited above), they do the same in v. 43 as well.[6]

As a matter of fact, however, such a watered-down translation of *metoikizō* does not appear to be justified. First of all, its use in v. 43 with regard to a punitive measure points in the same direction for v. 4, as we have noted. Next, we note that the Septuagint (a good guide for Luke's usage in biblical contexts)[7] uses the verb only of exile;[8] so too Ps.-Aristeas (§§ 4, 12) and Josephus.[9] As for non-Jewish usage, while several lexicographers refer to the Pergamene Chronicle (*OGIS* I, nr. 264, l. 7) as evidence for merely "transport," "transfer," "lead settlers to another abode," and the like, it in fact refers there to "la deportation en masse, [un] procédé tout à fait conforme aux traditions du despotisme oriental."[10] Apart from this inscription and Acts

---

"déporterai" (*La Bible de Jérusalem* [= *La sainte Bible*, 1973] and *Traduction oecuménique de la Bible*).

[4] For the German translations, see G. Stählin, *Die Apostelgeschichte* (1962), p. 105; H. Balz - G. Schneider, *Exegetisches Wörterbuch zum Neuen Testament*, II (1981), col. 1034, s.v.

[5] Cf. E. Richard, *Acts 6:1–8:4: The Author's Method of Composition* (1978), pp. 44–45: "The verb *metoikizō* is particularly interesting in this context [scil. 7:4]. It appears twice in the entire NT . . . Since the verb is never employed in relation to Abraham, and in light of the author's tendency to repeat key terms for a given effect, I see a close connection between the two [scil. appearances of *metoikizō*]." However, Richard does not develop this interest and connection.

[6] Thus, the RSV and the scholars cited in n. 4, above, give the same translations in both verses in Acts 7 (although this requires the RSV to deviate from its own translation of Amos). In contrast, the two French translations cited in n. 3, above, leave "déporterai" in Acts 7:43 as in Amos 5:27, although they reduce the verb in Acts 7:4 to the tepid "le fit passer."

[7] For the Septuagintal background of the speeches in Acts, see E. Plümacher, *Lukas als hellenistischer Schriftsteller: Studien zur Apostelgeschichte* (1972), pp. 38–50; E. Richard, *CBQ* 42 (1980), pp. 330–341 (especially on ch. 7).

[8] According to E. Hatch and H. A. Redpath, *A Concordance to the Septuagint . . .* II (1897), p. 918, *metoikizō* appears eleven times in the LXX: eight times for forms of GLH, once for GRSh (*pi'el*), and twice where no Hebrew parallel is extant. Of the latter, I Esdras 5:7 refers to the Babylonian exile, and Judith 11:14 is an error (see *Iudith* [Göttingen Septuaginta 8/4, ed. R. Hanhart; 1979], p. 119).

[9] See *Ant.* 1.51 (cf. Gen. 3:24); 2.190; 9.278 (cf. II Kings 17:6); 9.288 (cf. ibid. vs. 24); 11.91 (on Babylonian exile); *C. Ap.* 1.132. According to *A Complete Concordance to Flavius Josephus*, III (ed. K. H. Rengstorf; 1979), pp. 99–100, these are all the cases of active *metoikizō* in Josephus.

[10] So Th. Reinach, *Revue historique* 32 (1886), p. 83; for the text, see ibid. pp. 76, 472. (On the oriental despotic tradition, see B. Oded, *Mass Deportations and Deportees in the Neo-*

7:4, LSJ also cites Ps.-Aristotle, *Oeconomica* 1352ᵃ 33, Plutarch, *Romulus* 17, and Melanthius Tragicus 1[11] in support of "lead settlers to another abode." However, Ps.-Aristotle refers to one of those "déplacements forcés, qui répugnent à nos idées sur la liberté,"[12] Plutarch too speaks of the exile of a conquered population,[13] and Melanthius is referring metaphorically to the way the temper forcibly banishes the mind, as Plutarch's paraphrase of the passage quite clearly shows (*De cohibenda ira* 2 [453E−F]). Therefore, while a neutral translation in Acts 7:4 cannot be ruled out entirely,[14] the evidence of v. 43 and usage in the Septuagint and elsewhere indicates, however surprisingly, that Stephen is supposed to have said that God exiled Abraham into Canaan.[15]

An attempt to deal with this paradox leads us to the other problem regarding Acts 7:4b: why does Stephen term Judaea "this land in which *you* now live"? Haenchen found this "striking: Stephen himself lives there too."[16] However, it seems that this is precisely the point: Stephen does not live in Judaea. He happens to be there, perhaps even for an extended period of time, but he does not view himself as a resident of Judaea. He is portrayed as a

---

Assyrian Empire [1979].) Note the parallelism of the verbs: *ekratēsen . . . kai metōikisen . . .* This inscription − on which see esp. M. Fränkel, *Altertümer von Pergamon*, VIII/2 (1895), pp. 378−381 − is cited by J. H. Moulton and G. Milligan, *The Vocabulary of the Greek Testament* (1930), pp. 405−406, in support of "transport," "transfer;" by W. Bauer, *Griechisch-deutsches Wörterbuch zu den Schriften des Neuen Testaments . . .* (edd. K. and B. Aland; 1988⁶), col. 1041 in support of "einen andern Wohnsitz anweisen, umsiedeln, wegführen," and by LSJ, p. 1121, in support of "lead settlers to another abode." Moulton and Milligan also cite another inscription, but there the verb is intransitive (as LSJ notes), which is probably why Bauer omitted reference to it.

[11] *Tragicorum Graecorum Fragmenta* (ed. A. Nauck; reprinted 1964), pp. 760−761.

[12] B. A. van Groningen, *Aristote: Le second livre de l'Économique* (1933), p. 187; the verb reappears, in the same sense, in 1352ᵇ 3−4.

[13] See also *Phil.* 16.4 (365E), *Sol.* 20.5 (89E) and *Amat.* 6 (752B). In two other cases, however, Plutarch uses the active verb in a more neutral sense: *Sollert. Anim.* 18 (972E); *Commun. Notit.* 12 (1064D). See D. Wyttenbach, *Lexicon Plutarcheum et Vitas et Opera Moralia Complectens*, II (1843), p. 553, s.v.

[14] Doubts linger due not only to the strangeness of the thought, given biblical notions, and to the Plutarchian exceptions (see the preceding note), but also because Philo, in his only two instances of active *metoikizō*, uses it without negative connotations (*Opific.* 1.171 and *Alleg. Int.* 3.19; see G. Mayer, *Index Philoneus* [1974], p. 186), and various writers use the *middle* voice simply of migration or moving about (for examples, see the Mayer [ibid.] and the concordances listed above, nn. 9 and 13).

[15] Of the commentaries and studies I've seen, Zahn's (above, n. 2) comes the closest to such an understanding: "eine nicht freiwillige Ansiedlung eines *metoikos . . .* nicht als ein Bürger und Grundbesitzer sondern nur als ein Fremdling . . ." This is correct, and explains 7:5, but does not go far enough.

[16] Haenchen, p. 278 (p. 270 in 1977 edition of his *Die Apostelgeschichte*). Haenchen does not attempt to resolve this enigma.

Diasporan Jew in Jerusalem: while he shares the Judaeans' ancestors ("our fathers:" vv. 2, 11, 15, 19[?],39, 44, 45),[17] he does not share their land.[18]

This distinction is borne out by the use of *katoikeite*: Stephen's hearers *reside* in Jerusalem. That this verb indicates an intimate and permanent relation to a place, residence, is shown sufficiently by Luke's usage elsewhere, beginning with Acts 7:2, 4a, where it is used of Abraham's residence in Haran (cf. Gen. 11:31), and on to Acts 7:48, where — as also in 17:24 — it is God's *residence* in the Temple, not His presence in it, which is denied,[19] and all over Acts, where the verb is used of local communities of Jews and Christians (1:19, 20; 4:16; 9:22, 32, 35; 1129; 13:27; 19:10, 17; 22:12).[20] Finally, note that in those passages in Acts where this verb corresponds to one in the Hebrew Bible, the latter uses *yashav* (Acts 1:20 = Ps. 69:25[26]; Acts 7:2, 4 = Gen. 11:31).[21] Thus, Stephen's audience was composed of *residents* of Judaea, while he was only visiting.

Now these two juxtaposed points, regarding *metoikizō* and *katoikeō*, go hand in hand, and have their implications for the interpretation of the speech and for the nature of the "Hellenists," of whom Stephen is one.[22] For it is apparent, first of all, that terming Abraham's move to Canaan an "exile" goes well with the anti-territorial thrust of Stephen's speech, which has often been noted.[23] But it is also apparent that such an anti-territorial thesis is most to be expected from a Diasporan Jew. In response to those Judaeans who claimed that the Temple and the Holy Land *contain* God's holiness,[24] and therefore

---

[17] In contrast, "your fathers" in vv. 51–52 reflects the Christian standpoint of the speaker, which only now becomes explicit, either as a rhetorical self-distancing or as a trace of Christian editing of a non-Christian Jewish text. On the prehistory of Stephen's speech, see below, n. 28.

[18] "Er selbst ist zwar Volksgenosse, aber nicht Landsmann der Angeredeten" (Stählin, *Apostelgeschichte*, p. 106).

[19] See M. Simon, *Journal of Ecclesiastical History* 2 (1951), pp. 128–137. On the affinity of Stephen's speech and Acts 17:24–25 (although the latter attacks sacrifices as well as the Temple), and the point that it is "rigid localisation" of God which is condemned, see B. Gärtner, *The Areopagus Speech and Natural Revelation* (1955), pp. 206–209.

[20] On Acts 2:5, 14, see below, Part II.

[21] On the permanence of *yashav*, as opposed to transient *shachan*, see Simon (above, n. 19), pp. 132–133.

[22] As is usually assumed, although not explicit in the text of Acts 6. On the Hellenistic names of all those mentioned in 6:5, see G. Schneider, *Die Apostelgeschichte*, I (1980), pp. 427–428. Luke's failure to make it clear that these "deacons" were "Hellenists" might stem from a desire to obscure, as much as possible, disunity in the Church; cf. Conzelmann (above, n. 1), pp. 44, 45, 61 (pp. 49, 50, 59 in German), on Acts 6:1–6, 6:5–6, and 8:1.

[23] See esp. vv. 2, 9, 33, 44–50; B. Reicke, *Glaube und Leben der Urgemeinde* (1957), pp. 129–161; W. D. Davies, *The Gospel and the Land: Early Christianity and Jewish Territorial Doctrine* (1974), pp. 267–273; Richard (above, n. 5), pp. 325–327.

[24] For a classic Palestinian formulation of the view that God's presence in the Temple's inner sanctum is the source of all holiness, and that this holiness spreads from there, with

look askance or with supercilious condescension upon Diasporan Jews, Stephen, according to Acts 7, not only explicitly attacked the Temple's part in this containment theory, at the end of his speech (vv. 44−50), but also artfully adumbrated this theme at the very outset of his speech, by using the grating term *metoikizō* with reference to residence in the Holy Land.[25]

Now it is quite widely held, lately, that the "Hellenists" of Acts are to be understood as Greek-speaking Jews (as opposed to "Hebrews"), of whom some became Christians and some − such as those mentioned in Acts 9:29 − did not.[26] But within this consensus one must still inquire whether these Hellenists were residents or visitors in Jerusalem. The answer depends to a large extent upon one's notion of the extent of native Greek culture in Jerusalem in the first century, an oft-debated subject which I do not intend to broach here.[27] I would only note that our attention to some details in Acts 7:4 indicates that Stephen, however long he had stayed in Jerusalem (and

---

dwindling intensity the farther it goes, until it ends at the borders of the Holy Land, see m.*Kelim* 1:6-9. Davies (above, n. 23: pp. 58−60) gives an English translation but an overly-legalistic interpretation; cf. J. Z. Smith, *Map is not Territory* (1978), pp. 112−115.

[25] Whether the speech's emphatic opening statement, according to which God told Abraham to leave Ur for Haran (not Haran for Canaan) is traditional or rather deliberately contradicted an accepted understanding of Genesis 11−12, it is another early announcement of the same theme. So is the use of "now" in 7:4, which undercuts the notion that there is anything more permanent, or providentially guaranteed, about life in the land of Israel as compared to the Diaspora. Diasporan resentment against being considered second-rate Jews due to distance from the holy is suspected by Simon (above, n. 19), p. 132. For a modern analogue, a resentful Diasporan Jew triumphantly emphasizing, in the wake of the Yom Kippur War, that his brethren in Israel live in a situation just as exilic as his own, cf. J. Neusner, "Now We're All Jews − Again," *Response* 20 (Winter 1973/74), pp. 151−155. See also his essay − in the wake of the Pollard affair − on America as the Promised Land for the Jews, which appeared in the *Washington Post* on 8 March 1987 and in another ca. 450 publications as well. There were many who would have stoned Neusner for either article, had they and he, as Stephen, lived in the first century. (For Neusner's account of the responses to his 1987 article, see the *WP*, 4 October 1987.)

[26] See M. Hengel, *Zeitschrift für Theologie und Kirche* 72 (1975), esp. pp. 161−172 (= *Between Jesus and Paul: Studies in the Earliest History of Christianity* [1983], pp. 6−11), followed, basically, by R. Pesch (with E. Gerhart and F. Schilling) in *Biblische Zeitschrift* 23 (1979), pp. 87−90; G. Schneider, in *Les Actes des Apôtres: Traditions, rédaction, théologie* (ed. J. Kremer; 1979), p. 218 (reprinted, with original pagination indicated, in his *Lukas, Theologe der Heilsgeschichte: Aufsätze zur lukanischen Doppelwerk* [1985], pp. 227 ff.); N. Walter, *NTS* 29 (1983), pp. 370−393; etc. (Walter, p. 370, speaks of a broad consensus which developed in the preceding decade; his own contribution is based upon the somewhat daring corollary that the dispute reported in Acts 6:1 was not limited to the Christian community alone.)

[27] On this topic see T. Rajak, *Josephus: The Historian and His Society* (1983), pp. 46−64 (with bibliography), and, most recently, M. Hengel, *The 'Hellenization' of Judaea in the First Century after Christ* (1989). Cf. above, p. 40, n. 31.

certainly Acts 6:1–6 envisions provision for more than transient tourists!), is portrayed as a non-Judaean.[28]

II. Acts 2:5, 14 (*katoikountes*)

The only apparent exceptions in Acts to the use of *katoikeō* for permanent residence are in 2:5, 14, where the witnesses of the Pentecost miracle, said to include many who reside (v. 9: *katoikountes*) abroad of whom the Romans are even explicitly termed "visitors" (v. 10) in Jerusalem,[29] are nevertheless said to be *katoikountes* in Jerusalem. This problem, however, which has led some to water down their translations of the latter or even to emend the text,[30] is linked to another more notorious one: Who are the *Ioudaioi* mentioned in these same verses? Namely, v. 5 begins its description of the crowd with "Now there were living in Jerusalem *Ioudaioi*, devout people from all nations . . .,"

---

[28] This conclusion reminds us how well the speech fits into its narrative framework, just prior to the beginning of the mission outside of Jerusalem (ch. 8); see Richard [above, n. 5], pp. 229–242, and *Agrippa I*, pp. 213–216. This, of course, may lead to conclusions of historicity or non-historicity; see Schneider (above, n. 26), pp. 234, 237, vs. Hengel (above, n. 26), pp. 186–187 (in German = p. 19 in English). For bibliography and discussion concerning Luke's possible source(s) for Stephen's speech, see Schneider, pp. 224–237 and Hengel, p. 186, n. 126 (p. 149, n. 126 in English).

[29] The same term, *epidēmountes*, is similarly used in Acts 17:21, in sharp contrast (*xenoi*) to the "locals." It is obvious, some scattered commentaries notwithstanding, that 2:10 refers to Romans in Jerusalem, not to visitors or residents in Rome. G. D. Kilpatrick's suggestion that the author of Acts 2 used a list in which these words meant "Romans resident in Rome" (*JJS* 26 [1975], pp. 48–49) is limited to the Vorlage and does not apply to its use in Acts. For much comparative material differentiating between Romans and "locals," see E. Kornemann, *De civibus romanis in provinciis imperii consistentibus* (1892), esp. the appendix, pp. 97–114; add *OGIS* II, nr. 532, ll. 6–8, where, in 3 B.C.E., the "locals" are the *katoikountes*, among whom (*par' autois)* the Romans do business. I see no reason to ignore this distinction and translate as if the Romans were "dwelling" or "ansässig" in Paphlagonia (so N. Lewis and M. Reinhold, *Roman Civilization, II: The Empire* [1955], p. 35; P. Herrmann, *Der römische Kaisereid: Untersuchungen zu seine Herkunft und Entwicklung* [1968], pp. 19, 96). While such businessmen may have been there for an extended period of time, as Stephen probably was in Jerusalem as well, they are still viewed as foreign visitors.

[30] For watering down, see, e.g., the *New International New Testament*: "were staying" in v. 5 and "you who are in Jerusalem" in v. 14. Similarly, already Ed. Leigh (*Annotations upon all the New Testament, Philogicall and Theologicall* [1650], p. 186), claimed that "Hellenistic" Greek used *katoikeō* indifferently for sojourning as well as dwelling. Leigh refers to Genesis 27:44 and I Kings 17:20; one would be hard put to adduce more. As for emending *katoikountes* out of v. 5, see K. Lake in *The Beginnings of Christianity, I: The Acts of the Apostles*, V (edd. K. Lake and H.J. Cadbury; 1933), p. 113. Alternatively, one could take *katoikountes* in v. 9 as plusquamperfectum (so A. Harnack, *Die Apostelgeschichte* [1908], p. 65), although only if one is willing to admit that Luke's identification of the spectators according to their former residences is "ungeschickt" (ibid.)

and v. 14 has Peter open his speech by addressing the crowd as "*Ioudaioi* and all residents (*katoikountes*) of Jerusalem." If, as is usual, one renders *Ioudaioi* simply as "Jews," which contrasts with "non-Jews,"[31] then all sorts of problems arise, as B. M. Metzger's comments illustrate:

Why should Luke think it necessary to mention that Jews were dwelling in Jerusalem? Likewise, why should it be said that they were devout men; would not this be taken for granted from the fact that they were Jews? Most amazing of all is the statement that these Jews were persons from every nation under heaven. Out of all *lands* under heaven could be understood — but since the Jews were already an *ethnos*, to say that these were from another *ethnos* is tantamount to a contradiction of terms.[32]

These problems may be solved in a few ways. One may use them as an argument for eliminating *Ioudaioi*,[33] or for inserting a *kai* between *Ioudaioi*

---

[31] So, for example, J. Weiss: "die Adresse 2, 14 sich richtet an Juden *und hoi katoikountes Ierousalēm pantes*, also an in Jerusalem ansässige Nichtjuden . . ." (*Über die Absicht und den literarischen Charakter der Apostel-Geschichte* [1897], p. 6; original emphasis). Schneider (above, n. 26: p. 219, with n. 24) would rather harmonize: "Jews and all the residents of Jerusalem" (2:14) means "Jews and proselytes," who together comprise "all the house of Israel" (2:36). This would go well with translating 2:5 "fromme Juden aus allen Völkern unter dem Himmel" (ibid.) but renders *andres* superfluous and entails the practical elimination of "Cretans and Arabs" (see below, n. 35).

[32] B.M. Metzger, *A Textual Commentary on the Greek New Testament* (1971), p. 290 (original emphasis). This paragraph is almost a literal translation from F. Blass, *Neue kirchliche Zeitschrift* 3 (1892), pp. 826–827, to which Metzger refers; the same arguments are also repeated by E. Güting, *ZNW* 66 (1975), pp. 164–165. Of Blass' enigmas apart from "Jews dwelling in Jerusalem," the first ("devout men") is not very cogent, for in two of its other three appearances in Luke-Acts (Luke 2:25; Acts 22:12), and probably in the third as well (Acts 8:2), *eulabēs* in fact describes Jews. (Blass claims that the addition "according to the Law" in Acts 22:12 indicates that the adjective need not refer to Jews, which is true but does not prove the opposite. The addition in 22:12 is probably there because of the context. Cf. Weiss [above, n. 31], pp. 41–42.) But Blass' final query seems well taken. Weiss (above, n. 31: p. 6, n. *) cites Josephus, *C. Ap.* 2.38–39 as evidence that Jews might be called "Cretans" and the like, but Josephus' (and other similar) references have to do with cities and have a technical sense, namely, citizenship (whether of the those cities or of the Jewish *politeumata* in them); cf. A. Kasher, *The Jews in Hellenistic and Roman Egypt: The Struggle for Equal Rights* (1985), pp. 274–278, 297–309 (and cf. 192–207, on "Alexandrians" in the papyri). Similarly, although V. Fusco (in *Gerusalemme: Atti della XXVI settimana biblica in onore di Carlo Maria Martini* [1982], p. 204, n. 13) points to Acts 4:36, 6:9 and 11:20 as evidence that Jews could be called "Cypriots" and "Alexandrians" and the like, the context in each case clarifies that Jews are meant; indeed, 4:36 makes clear that Barnabas is a Cypriot only with regard to his place of birth, after first defining him ethnically. Cf. also *OGIS* II, nr. 437, lines 66, 69–70, which distinguishes between "Ephesians" and "Sardians," on the one hand, and those who are *katoikountes* in those cities, on the other. For another attempt to defend taking "people from all nations" as a reference to *Jews* from all *lands*, see J. Kremer, *Pfingstbericht und Pfingstgeschehen: Eine exegetische Untersuchung zu Apg 2, 1–13* (1973), pp. 127–131. In my opinion, all Kremer shows is that *if* vv. 5a and 11 ("Jews and proselytes") forced us to then we could live with this interpretation of v. 5b, but that if 5b is taken by itself, or with vv. 9–11, no one would ever have thought of it.

[33] As Metzger notes (above, n. 32: pp. 290–291), this has been suggested by some modern

and *andres eulabeis*, thus making the verse refer both to Jews and to devout Gentiles;[34] the latter are familiar in Acts. Either solution allows the audience to include Gentiles, a position supportable also on the basis of 2:11, where "Jews and proselytes" appear as part of the long list of spectators, not in a summary position at its beginning or end.[35] However, 2:22 ("Men of Israel") and 2:29, 37 ("Brothers") seem plainly to indicate that the spectators are envisaged as Jews only, and, indeed, it seems plain that prior to chapters 10–11, or at least prior to ch. 8, there can be (according to Luke) no talk of evangelizing Gentiles.[36]

Three observations point to a solution of this quandary:

1. Only here, in 2:14, does Luke ever have a speaker address his audience as *andres Ioudaioi*. Rather, he always uses "Men of Israel" (2:22; 3:12; 5:35; 13:16; 21:28). This would be quite difficult to explain if the two were synonymous ("Jews").[37]

---

scholars (especially Blass [above, n. 32: pp. 828–829], Lake [above, n. 30: pp. 113–114] and
– after Metzger – Güting [above, n. 32], pp. 164–165), and it may be that some ancient scribes acted upon similar reasoning.

[34] A possibility considered by Weiss (above, n. 31), pp. 5–6.

[35] Those who argue that the crowd should be envisaged as wholly Jewish often assume that "Jews and proselytes" should in fact conclude the list, with "Cretans and Arabs" following it due either to error or interpolation (so Harnack [above, n. 30], p. 66), or as a summary flourish meaning "inhabitants of sea and desert" or "inhabitants of east and west;" for that view, see O. Eissfeldt, *Kleine Schriften*, III (edd. R. Sellheim and F. Maass; 1966), pp. 28–34 = *Theologische Literaturzeitung* 72 (1947), cols. 207–212; Schneider (above, n. 22), I, p. 253; W. Stenger, *Kairos* 21 (1979), pp. 212–213. As Kremer (above, n. 32: p. 153), however, I am troubled by the lack of parallels for such rhetorical usage of "Cretans and Arabs." Kilpatrick's reference to Lucianic witnesses (in *Les Actes* [above, n. 26], pp. 92–93, based upon his article in *JJS* 26 [1975], pp. 48–49) does not demonstrate summary usage, and Stenger's declaration (loc. cit.) that "Cretans and Arabs" "unterstehen einem anderen Code als dem ethnographisch-politischen" supplies, if I understand him correctly, only new terminology, but no new argument or evidence.

[36] Both of the latter points are made by S.G. Wilson, *The Gentiles and the Gentile Mission in Luke-Acts* (1973), p. 123; he also refers, in this connection, to 2:36, 39. See also Weiss (above, n. 31), p. 6: "Aber auch dem ganzen Inhalt nach ist die Rede durchaus nur auf Juden zugeschnitten und keine Missionsrede vor Heiden oder Proselyten." For the Jewish orientation of Acts 2, see also Fusco (above, n. 32), pp. 204–209. On the Samaritans and Ethiopian eunuch of Acts 8, see Schneider (above, n. 26), pp. 221–222 ("Zwischenbereich"). On the former, see also Luke 17:18 and J. Jervell, *Luke and the People of God* (1972), p. 124; on the latter, see also Wilson, op. cit., pp. 171–172. Indeed, Fusco (loc. cit., p. 35) suggests that even Cornelius, who was a "God-fearer" and not just any Gentile, is to be viewed as only another gradual step (in ch. 10) before the final across-the board acceptance of Gentiles in ch. 11.

[37] Note that this passage is *not* part of the oft-discussed phenomenon of the preference for "Israel" in the first half of Acts and for *Ioudaioi* in the latter half, on which see, inter alia, Harnack (above, n. 30), pp. 57–58; H. Kuhli, *ExWbNT* (above, n. 4), II, cols. 498–499; cf. 480–482.

2. It is also difficult to imagine that visitors from abroad would be able to identify the apostles specifically as "Galileans" (v. 7)[38] and not simply as "Jews" or "Judaeans" (in the general sense: Palestinians). Such a regional distinction would, however, be quite natural on the lips of Judaeans.

3. While *glōssa* is the word usually used in references to "speaking in tongues," as in Acts 2:4, 11, here, in vv. 6, 8, we instead find *dialektos*, which is used elsewhere in Acts only of spoken "Hebrew" (1:19; 21:40; 22:2; 26:14). While the two terms are at times synonymous, *dialektos* may also be used, as our "dialect," to indicate a regional variety of a language.[39]

Taking our cue from these observations, from Aristotle[40] and from modern Johannine scholarship,[41] we would suggest that *Ioudaioi* in Acts 2:5, 14 originally referred to "Judaeans." Acts 2:5a refers to Judaeans (from various parts of Judaea) living in Jerusalem, and in 2:14 Peter addresses such Judaeans

---

[38] I take "Galileans" to mean simply "people from Galilee," as opposed to the places where the various listeners were "born" (v. 8). Kremer's suggestion (above, n. 32: p. 140) that it meant "followers of Jesus" is based mainly upon the following consideration: "Ist es aber sinnvoll, eine Sprache der Galiläer, auch wenn der Dialekt der Bewohner Galiläas von der der Einwohner Jerusalems verschieden war (Mt 26, 73), mit den Sprachen anderer Nationen zu vergleichen und sie davon zu unterscheiden?" He is quite right; I note, for example, that among themselves the Swiss distinguish "Baseldeutsch" from "Züri[ch]deutsch" and the like, but foreigners, and the Swiss vis à vis them, speak rather of their common "Schweizerdeutsch;" similar examples are available everywhere. However, rather than using this consideration to reinterpret "Galileans," I would suggest that the comparison with foreign languages be eliminated as secondary (see below). Kremer's other argument (ibid.) is that foreigners who heard the apostles speaking their own language would have no way of knowing that they came from Galilee (so "Galileans" must mean something else). But Judaeans, who had heard the apostles speaking in their usual dialects (and were perhaps otherwise familiar with them as well) could easily have known that they were Galileans; this too leads to our suggestion below. As for Kremer's final remark (ibid.), that it is in fact uncertain that all the disciples, or all those who spoke "in tongues," came from Galilee, he himself makes no effort to justify it or to place weight upon it. (For the rejection of yet another reinterpretation of "Galileans," but without any connection to Acts 2, see L. H. Feldman in *ANRW* II/21.2 [1984], pp. 846–847.)

[39] Such as Attic or Ionic; see LSJ, p. 401 s.v. (§ II/2). On the dialects of Palestinian Aramaic, see Ch. Rabin in *The Jewish People in the First Century*, II (edd. S. Safrai and M. Stern; 1976), pp. 1025–1032; J. A. Fitzmyer, *A Wandering Aramean: Collected Aramaic Essays* (1979, pp. 38–43 (= *CBQ* 32 [1970], pp. 71–74). The classic reference is Matthew 26:73. As for the old question, whether "Hebrew" in Acts (and elsewhere) means Hebrew or Aramaic, see Rabin, loc. cit., pp. 1037–1039 (bibliography); Rajak (above, n. 27), pp. 230–232.

[40] As quoted by Clearchus of Soli apud Josephus, *C. Ap.* 1.179 (Stern, *GLA* I, nr. 15, pp. 47–52): ". . . called *Ioudaioi*, taking their name from the place; for the place they inhabit is called Judaea."

[41] See especially M. Lowe, *Novum Testamentum* 18 (1976), pp. 101–130; cf. J. Ashton, ibid. 27 (1985), pp. 40–75. For more on the theme of "Ioudaios" in the sense of "Judaean," see also A. T. Kraabel, *JJS* 33 (1982 = *Essays in Honour of Yigael Yadin*), pp. 454–455 and R. S. Kraemer, *HTR* 82 (1989), pp. 35–53.

in particular, along with all other Jerusalemites.[42] They are mentioned first and especially because it is their very diversity which made the Pentecost miracle what it was said to be.

In other words, we would suggest that an earlier version of this story[43] told of Galileans (the apostles) who astounded the residents of Jerusalem, who came from diverse parts of Judaea, by their ability to speak in the various dialects or accents of Palestinian Aramaic (2:5a[−b? see below],6−8, 13 ff.). Later, however, the addition of 2:5b − or, more probably, the transformation of something like "devout people from all over the land" to "devout people from all nations under heaven" − and vv. 9−11(12),[44] perhaps due to a desire to foreshadow the Gentile mission,[45] turned the account into one which portrays Gentile presence as well − not without leaving traces of the earlier account.

Thus, ascription of Acts 2:5a,14, on the one hand, and 2:5b,9−11, on the other hand, to two different levels of the history of this chapter, removes the objection which might have been raised regarding our interpretation of *katoikeō* in 7:4 and elsewhere in Acts. On the contrary, it was the scrutiny of the latter case which first directed us toward what we believe to be the best solution to some of the difficulties posed by these verses in Acts 2.

Finally, although the suggested analysis of ch. 2 may stand whether Luke added 2:5b,9−12 into a source he found or whether a subsequent editor added them into Luke's Acts,[46] I would like nonetheless to broach the question, for

---

[42] For "Judaea" alongside "Jerusalem," cf. Luke 5:17; 6:17; 21:20−21; Acts 1:8; 8:1; 10:39; 26:20; M. Hengel, *Zeitschrift des deutschen Palästina-Vereins* 99 (1983), p. 151 (in English in *Between Jesus* [above, n. 26], p. 99).

[43] "An earlier" − not "the original," for there was, as often recognized, yet an earlier stage, at which the account referred not to any languages or dialects, but, rather, to unintelligible "speaking in tongues" (glossolalia). See, e.g., G. Lüdemann, *Das frühe Christentum nach den Traditionen der Apostelgeschichte: Ein Kommentar* (1987), pp. 46−49. This earlier stage, however, need not concern us here. On it, see also my essay in the E. Hilgert Festschrift, *Heirs of the Septuagint* (*Studia Philonica Annual* 3; 1991), pp. 256−271.

[44] I.e., the addition of the list of nations in vv. 9−11a engendered vv. 11b−12, a Wiederaufnahme picking up from vv. 7−8. It is widely assumed that the list of nations is based upon some written source; see Kremer (above, n. 32), pp. 157−158; Schneider (above, n. 22), I, pp. 252−255. On the ambiguity of "land," see below, nn. 45 and 47, in connection with Acts 1:8.

[45] After deleting *Ioudaioi* from 2:5, Blass (above, n. 32: pp. 828−829) concludes that "die Idee, die doch in der Pfingstgeschichte liegt, tritt jetzt erst ordentlich klar hervor, nämlich daß bereits die Kirche des ersten Tages eine Weltkirche *in nuce* war." Güting's position above, n. 32: pp. 164−169) is similar, and Wilson (above, n. 36: p. 124) and Kremer (above, n. 32: p. 213), followed by Stenger (above, n. 35: p. 213), say essentially the same, though without the emendation. It may be, however, that the additions were not so much conscious changes as intended improvements upon a misunderstood reference to all the *land* in an original version of 2:5 (see below, n. 47).

[46] By way of comparison, note Kilpatrick (in *Les Actes* [above, n. 26], pp. 81−83), where

it is of critical importance for the structure of Acts. Namely, it is often stated that Acts 1:8 ("you will receive power when the Holy Spirit comes upon you; and you will bear witness to me in Jerusalem, and all over Judaea and Samaria, and away to the ends of the earth" [New English Bible]) sets a plan which Acts follows step by step, and that the Pentecost story, right at the outset of the apostles' history, foreshadows that witnessing "to the ends of the earth." Elsewhere, however, I have argued that Acts 1:8 originally referred to "the end of the *land*," i.e., the Land of Israel, and that this is the meaning which it has in Acts.[47] Note, especially, the facts that the apostles, to whom 1:8 is addressed, do not preach outside of the land (or even to Gentiles in the land, without a new revelation [chs. 10–11]), and that in 13:47, when Paul's response to Jewish hostility is to turn to the Gentiles, he is striking out on his own "to the end of the earth" and quotes in his support from Isaiah (49:6), whose reference is indubitably universal, not from the risen Jesus of Acts 1:8.[48] But if this is the case, then it appears likelier that the minor (but confusing) additions in Acts 2:5b,9–12 were made into Luke's Acts. In his[49] original version, the account dealt not with languages but rather with dialects, and it foreshadowed the evangelization not of the earth, but of all the land. The mandate of 1:8 ran its course not at the end of the book (Rome) but by 9:31, where Luke rounds it off with an irenic summary.[50] Then, as the sequel (chapters 10–11) shows, it was time for a new revelation.

---

he argues the quotation from Joel in Acts 2:17–21 is more universalist than its context in Acts. While Kilpatrick suggests that the former preceded the latter, the author of Acts 2 having taken it from a collection of testimonia more universalist than he was (pp. 89–94), it could just as well be (or so it seems) that the presumably LXX text of Joel used by Luke was later "corrected" by copyists, perhaps on the basis of just such a collection. That suggestion has its difficulties, but so does the notion that Luke would include a text which departed from the LXX and contradicted his own needs in Acts 2. All things being equal, moreover, it is likelier that a universalizing text appeared later in the process than one with its perspectives limited to Jews.

[47] See *JBL* 105 (1986), pp. 669–676. The same understanding of Acts 1:8 seems also to be assumed by H. M. Orlinsky, in *Eretz-Israel* 18 (Nahman Avigad Volume; 1985), p. 52* (non-Hebrew section).

[48] That is, we should probably understand Luke to mean Paul now reinterpreted Jesus' mandate in light of Isaiah.

[49] Not "the" – see above, n. 43.

[50] Cf. Schneider (above, n. 22), II, pp. 40–41, who argues that 9:31 summarizes not only 9:26–30, but, rather, all of 9:1–30. R. Pesch goes one further (*Die Apostelgeschichte*, I [1986], pp. 313–314), viewing 9:31 as a "Zwischenbilanz" since 6:7 (the last such summary), and J. Roloff (*Die Apostelgeschichte* [1981], p. 157) refers us all the way back to 1:8. I believe the latter view is correct, but that – contrary to Roloff – 9:31's failure to bring us to the end of the *earth* does not mean it only partially fulfills the promise of 1:8.

8. On Christian Study of the Zealots[*]

If you check the entry "Zélotes" in the published catalogue of the Dominican École biblique in Jerusalem, which is one of the largest biblical libraries in the world and which lists virtually every book and article of significance in the past century and more, you will find twenty-eight items. Their chronological distribution is very interesting: although the catalogue covers the last century of research, and was up-to-date in 1986, the studies of the Zealots which it lists all appeared between 1958 and 1976. Similarly, if you check the 1954–1985 index to *New Testament Studies*, you will find that between 1954 and 1985 there appeared six articles on the Zealots — all between 1965 and 1972.[1]

It seems, in other words, that the topic rose and fell, in the world of Christian scholarship, during the decade and a half beginning with the late 'fifties, especially flourishing in the last several years of that period. Here, we shall suggest an explanation for this phenomenon. While various factors contributed, some of them fairly obvious, it seems that two in particular, which relate in a not so obvious way to interest in this topic, are in fact the prime explanation for its rise. Namely, it seems that two interrelated problems of the post-war period — the question of Christian anti-Semitism, and the related but distinct issue of the proper Christian attitude vis à vis the State — lent a certain urgency and popularity to a revision of notions concerning Jesus and the early Church in a direction which made ancient Jewish rebels against Rome very relevant. As for the the decline of interest in the topic, it seems to be a case of theological jitters which led scholars to throw out the baby with the bathwater. Namely, when the revision of notions concerning Jesus and the

---

[*] One of my "Joseph and Gertie Schwartz Memorial Lectures" delivered at the University of Toronto in November 1989. A Hebrew version is forthcoming in *The Masada Myth* (ed. D. Bitan, to be published by Keter).

[1] See *Catalogue de la bibliothèque de l'École biblique de Jérusalem*, XII (1986), pp. 608–609; *New Testament Studies: Cumulative Index of Volumes 1–31 (1954–1985)* . . . (comp. I.A. Moir; 1986), pp. 113–114. For thumbnail sketches of scholarship on the Zealots and related themes, see L. H. Feldman, *Josephus and Modern Scholarship (1937–1980)* (1984), pp. 637–672. For surveys of scholarship especially concerned with the Zealots' relevance for early Christianity, see Feldman, ibid., pp. 651–655; M. Gourgues, *Science et esprit* 31 (1979), pp. 125–146; and E. Bammel in *Jesus and the Politics of his Day* (edd. E. Bammel and C.F.D. Moule; 1984), pp. 11–68.

Church got to the overdone point that it required rejection of dearly-held and fundamental notions of them, it was scotched. Thus, study of the fall of interest in this topic will not only encourage a resurrection of some themes which were common twenty years ago but since forgotten due to reasons which have more to do with Christian faith than with historical study. This study will also provide a compact example of a frequent phenomenon in the history of scholarship: when one scholar overdoes the good ideas of others, their baby is often rejected along with his bathwater.[2]

I. From the Fifties until the Mid-Sixties: The Balloon Goes Up

In our discussion of reasons for Christian interest in the Zealots, we will proceed from the superficialities which invited an interest in the subject to the more fundamental issues which gave the interest its direction.

First of all, and most briefly, we may note that the discovery and publication of the Dead Sea Scrolls, which began in the late 1940's, engendered massive Christian interest, and it was only natural that much of that rubbed off onto the study of ancient Jewish sects in general. Similarly, the Masada excavations in the 1960's, which were so widely publicized, directed interest especially toward groups of anti-Roman rebels.

The second factor is more involved. It is the creation of the Jewish state, which, for Christians as for Jews, played an important role for scholarship. The Israeli War of Independence, in 1948, and its success, which broad Christian circles welcomed, invited comparisons with the Maccabean rebellion, and also, more generally, with other Jewish rebellions of antiquity. However, passage from the Maccabees, who have always enjoyed good press among theologians,[3] to the Zealots, the anti-Roman rebels of the first century, was encumbered by one great problem, Josephus. Josephus, the first-century historian who is virtually the only source for the first-century rebels, thoroughly despised them, blamed them for all calamities great and small, denied that they acted upon any legitimate or respectable motives, usually ignored their claim to a religious platform, and when he mentioned it denounced it as totally innovative and, therefore, reprehensible. He refers to them virtually always as plain brigands and criminals seeking their own enrichment and power.

---

[2] For other cases of this, see below, pp. 183, 262.

[3] I refer to the original Maccabean rebels against the decrees against Judaism, not to the Hasmonean state-builders. On the historiography of the Maccabean revolt, see J. Efron, *Studies on the Hasmonean Period* (1987), pp. 1–32.

It is, therefore, not surprising that Christian scholarship might begin to do what nationalist Jewish scholarship had been doing for several decades: rehabilitating the Zealots by showing that Josephus' condemnation of them, far from being the whole truth and nothing but the truth, was in fact an invective resulting from the needs of Josephus' apologetics on behalf of himself and of his nation.[4] On the personal level, Josephus, who had himself been a rebel general, had to convince the Romans that he had truly learned his lesson; this required thorough condemnation of other rebels And on the national level, which is too often forgotten in this context, Josephus was concerned that the Romans believe that those who led a Jewish revolt against Rome were not acting out of any legitimate Jewish motives. For if they were, Rome would have to conclude that Judaism must inevitably clash with Rome, and, therefore, is not to be tolerated.

Thus, to conclude this second consideration, we reiterate that the appearance of the Jewish state, in a war won against great odds, encouraged scholars to re-study the Zealot analogue, and the result of such scholarship was their rehabilitation as legitimate successors of the Maccabees. A 1956 book by W. R. Farmer, entitled *Maccabees, Zealots, and Josephus: An Inquiry into Jewish Nationalism in the Greco-Roman Period*, was the first book ever, I believe, to be devoted to the Zealots, and it − which began as a Union Theological Seminary dissertation, and whose author was soon to become one of America's leading professors of New Testament − was entirely devoted to this theme, the rehabilitation of the Zealots.

However, Farmer's book, on ancient Jewish nationalism, was one which was only indirectly of Christian interest, although he did append a few pages on the topic's relevance for New Testament studies. The third and last factor we shall consider, the Holocaust, in a roundabout way elicited more direct Christian interest.

The Holocaust affected the Christian world in two ways which are relevant to our theme.[5] First of all, it required the churches of Europe, and more generally of the rest of the world, to engage in a certain moral stock-taking:

---

[4] This could be done with more or less sympathy for Josephus. See, for example, the sympathetic evaluation offered by J. N. Simchoni in the introduction to his Hebrew translation of *BJ* (1923), esp. pp. 11−23, on the one hand, and the condemning contrast of Josephus to the Zealots offered by A. Schalit in *Mosnaim* 2 (1933/34), pp. 296−305 (in Hebrew). The latter article was the point of departure for my study of Schalit mentioned in the next note. In general, on the widespread condemnation of Josephus in the "classical conception" of him, which made this particular aspect all the easier, see P. Bilde, *Flavius Josephus between Jerusalem and Rome: His Life, his Works, and their Importance* (1988), pp. 126−128.

[5] For something of the Holocaust's impact upon Jewish historians' views of the first century, especially with regard to the propriety of opposing Rome, compare my essay on Abraham Schalit in *Jewish History* 2/2 (Fall 1987), pp. 9−28.

What had been their response to Hitler? Where had they been? Why had there been so much silence, not to mention collaboration, whether active or passive? But questions such as those, asked by conscientious Christians, immediately raised a normative question: What should be the Christian response to an evil government? May the Church protest? Must it? Or must it rather obey and tolerate injustice? And here, for those conscientious but believing Christians, was the problem, for the central canonical source on the topic seems quite unambiguous, but also quite unconscionable. Namely, according to Paul's oft-quoted pronouncement in Romans 13:1−2, "Every person must submit to the supreme authorities; there is no authority but by act of God, and the existing authorities are instituted by him; consequently anyone who rebels against authority is resisting a divine institution . . ." (trans. New English Bible). And if our conscientious Christians looked rather to Jesus, there too, the best-known statement, that one must render unto Caesar, seems to point in the very same direction. And it was easily supplemented by the other familiar references to Jesus as a pacifist who called for turning the other cheek, loving enemies, walking the extra mile for the authorities, etc.

Thus, it should come as no surprise that post-war Christian scholarship began, alongside of a vigorous reconsideration of the implications of Romans 13,[6] a vigorous reconsideration of Jesus' attitude toward the Rome. The main work to mention here in the early years, the book which is the real point of departure for Christian study of the Zealots, was written by Professor Oscar Cullmann, a prominent professor of New Testament in Basel and Paris. In his *The State in the New Testament*, which appeared in German in 1956 and − as befits a book which meets so pressing a need − in four other languages by 1957, Cullmann confronts the issue head-on and gives what he is fond of terming a complex answer.[7] According to Cullmann, Jesus' eschatological

---

[6] For reviews of its interpretation in the post-war decades, see E. Käsemann, *Zeitschrift für Theologie und Kirche* 56 (1959), pp. 316−376; T. J. Reese, *Biblical Theology Bulletin* 3 (1973), pp. 323−331; and L. Pohle, *Die Christen und der Staat nach Röm 13, 1−7 in der neueren deutschsprachigen Schriftauslegung* (1981).

[7] *Der Staat im Neuen Testament* appeared in English, French, Swedish and Italian in 1956−1957, in a second German edition in 1961, and in Portuguese in 1968. For the World War II church-state context which lies behind it, see the foreword (pp. vii−viii in the English edition). H. G. Wood's short article on the political nature of apocalyptic (*NTS* 2 [1955/56], pp. 262−266) was something of a forerunner. On p. 262 Wood alludes to some other precedents, of which the only post-war work is W. Mensching's short *Jesus im politischen Zeitgeschehen* (1952). Here too, as with Cullmann, the contemporary context of (post-war Germany) is most explicit; the *Vorwort* opens with "Das Buch erwuchs aus Fragen der Gegenwart . . .". But Mensching's volume, which is organized as a Life of Jesus, apparently aroused no significant response. Wood, loc. cit., specifically looks forward to Cullmann's.

perspective, his expectation of an imminent end, relativized all values. With regard to the state, this meant that he could oppose it, and did oppose it, but that he need not, and hence did not, do anything active about his opposition — for the end was near. Thus, on the one hand, Cullmann points out that there were Zealots among the apostles, and that Jesus was sympathetic to their views, and looked forward to the redemption of Israel from Roman rule. On the other hand, however, Jesus himself was not a Zealot, and would not himself actively oppose Rome or allow his disciples to do so. So if Pontius Pilate viewed him as a rebel against Rome, and if many of Jesus' followers viewed him as a political redeemer, they were wrong; they had misunderstood the depth and real import of his message. For, in Jesus' eyes, no state, even a Jewish state, could be so very important when judged from the relativizing perspective of the coming end.

Cullmann's book was exceedingly important. For it focused interest on Jesus himself (not just upon such lesser and wholly Jewish figures as Maccabees, Zealots and Josephus), and it was written in a popular fashion, meant not only for specialists. But his thesis was quite complex, as he says. If you ask, Did Jesus oppose Rome or did he not, you get a yes and no, and that is not too helpful for Christians interested in knowing what they should have done about the Nazis. After all, modern Christians do not live, for the most part, in the expectation of an imminent eschaton. Just as Cullmann explains that Jesus had not been understood, so too, as we shall see, Cullmann would live to complain that he too had been misunderstood.

At this point, we much catch up with a parallel development which reflects another aspect of the Holocaust's impact upon Christians. Namely, as is well known, the Holocaust engendered, among conscientious Christians, serious soul-searching about the role Christianity and its scriptures had played in the origin and development of anti-Semitism. The New Testament, for all of its emphasis upon the Jewish roots of the first Christians, by its very nature had to distance them from Jews. To borrow a phrase from Ephesians 2:14, if the appearance of Christianity destroyed a "wall of hostility" between Jews and Gentiles, it erected one between Christians and Jews. From the Jews as rejecters of Jesus' message (in the Gospels), to the Jews as Christ-killers (in the Gospels) and persecutors of the apostles (in Acts and elsewhere), to the Jews as stubborn rejecters of God's covenant (all over), Christianity's scriptures, and dependent literature, very frequently portray the daughter-religion as one completely divorced from its parent. Conscientious Christians, in the post-Holocaust years, needed to struggle with that just as much as they had to struggle with the question of their attitude toward the State. Books on the topic, in the fifties and sixties, are legion; one thinks, for example, of the books by Father Flannery, Roy Eckhardt, Gregory Baum, John Oester-reicher, etc., as well as the general ecumenical movement and Vatican II . . ., soon to be followed by Rosemary Reuther's *Faith and Fratricide* and much more.[8]

Now, how does this concern the Zealots? The answer is quite simple. If Jesus and the first Christians were Jewish rebels against Rome, then their ideals confirmed those of Jewish nationhood. That, however, meant such an attitude is legitimate, or even authoritative, for modern Christians as well.

This line of thought had its first start in the post-war era in 1951, when S.G.F. Brandon of Manchester University published *The Fall of Jerusalem and the Christian Church: A Study of the Effects of the Jewish Overthrow of A.D. 70 on Christianity* (1957[2]). Here, Brandon tried to do for the early Church what Farmer would do for the Zealots. Brandon argued that the early Church had been involved in rebellion against Rome, and that it was only later literature which tried to cover this up. However, this first start was a false start, for Brandon's case rested on next to nothing, and contradicted the principal piece of evidence on the question: Eusebius (*Hist. eccl.* 3.5.3) claims that the church fled Jerusalem, to Pella in Transjordan, prior to the great rebellion against Rome. It is very difficult to make a case solely on the basis of prior assumptions and the explaining away of contradictory evidence. However, as we have seen, just five years after Brandon's *Fall of Jerusalem* Cullmann was to show that what was nigh impossible to impute to the early Church could at least be reasonably misunderstood about Jesus.[9]

Thus, by the mid-fifties Christian scholarship had become aware that the Zealots could well have been respectable people fighting for a respectable

---

[8] For introductions to this type of literature, see, inter alia, A. Davies, *Antisemitism and the Christian Mind: The Crisis of Conscience after Auschwitz* (1969); idem (ed.), *Antisemitism and the Foundations of Christianity* (1979); C. Klein, *Theologie und Anti-Judaismus: Eine Studie zur deutschen theologischen Literatur der Gegenwart* (1975); E. Fleischner (ed.), *Auschwitz: Beginning of a New Era? Reflections on the Holocaust* (1977); and, with specific regard to the study of ancient Judaism, K. Hoheisel, *Das antike Judentum in christlicher Sicht: Ein Beitrag zur neueren Forschungsgeschichte* (1978), where the second chapter is on post-Holocaust scholarship. (Unfortunately, however, Hoheisel does not deal with the Zealots or with most of the scholars we will cite below). As for the Holocaust's impact on understanding of ancient Judaism and Christianity, we shall focus here on the Zealots. But the Holocaust's impact is evident in many other fields as well, such as, for example, the heavy emphasis upon Romans 9–11 as evidence for Paul's continued love of Israel and belief in the continued validity of its covenant – an approach especially popularized by J. Munck in his *Paulus und die Heilsgeschichte* (1954) and *Christus und Israel: Eine Auslegung von Röm 9–11* (1956); both books also appeared in English. For some indication of the splash these books made, see the long list of reviews in *Studia Theologica* 19 (1965), pp. 17–18.

[9] For Cullman's book as an acceptable moderation of Brandon's unacceptable thesis see, for example, M. Simon, *Les sectes juives au temps de Jésus* (1960), pp. 119–120. As for reviews of Brandon, see, for some typical examples, P. Benoit, *RB* 59 (1952), pp. 451–453; J. Bonsirven, *Biblica* 34 (1953), pp. 536–538; and C.F.D. Moule, *JTS* n.s. 3 (1952), pp. 106–108. Brandon's dependence on R. Eisler (see *Fall of Jerusalem*, pp. x–xi,261) was yet another strike against him; cf. below, n. 35 and p. 183, n. 4.

cause due to respectable nationalist motives, and it had also become aware
that one might make a case for Jesus and/or the early Church having been
misunderstood as being involved in rebellion against Rome. Moreover, on the
background of the Holocaust, there was also a certain interest in emphasizing
Jesus' willingness to oppose an unjust government, and also a willingness to
acknowledge that traditional Christian texts and teachings had played a
significant role in the nurturing of anti-Semitism. What was missing, however,
was a way to close a very important gap between Jesus and the Zealots.
Namely, Jesus was and is conceived of as a religious figure, that is, a figure
whose significance derives from his relationship to and/or teachings about
God. But the Zealots, even the rehabilitated Zealots, were Jewish na-
tionalists. How was the chasm between religion and state to be bridged? It was
this problem which left Cullmann willing to speak only of Jesus being
misunderstood as a Zealot.

Farmer, in his 1956 volume, had begun to chip away at this distinction
between religion and politics. But it entirely disappeared in 1961, when Martin
Hengel published his dissertation on the Zealots, a work which fully put the
topic on the whole on the map, so to speak.[10] As opposed to Cullmann's semi-
popular style, this was a German monograph in the best of its tradition, loaded
with footnotes and citations from all the ancient sources and modern
literature. And the main thesis of this dissertation, submitted for a degree in
Christian theology, was that the Zealots were in fact men of religion. The
book's central chapters focus on the Zealots' philosophy, the tradition of
"zeal" in ancient Israel and in Judaism, and on eschatology and prophecy as
aspects of Zealotism.

A book such as this had to make the world of Christian scholarship take
notice. First-century religion, of the type which tended to eschatology and
renewed prophecy, hits very close to home. True, Hengel denied that Jesus
was a Zealot. In the book's final pages he raises the question, emphasizes
some points of contrast, and concludes that "it is possible to say that, despite
certain points of contact, the proclamation of Jesus and the early Christian
Church represented the real overcoming of the Zealots' attempt to bring
about God's rule on earth by force."[11] But it must be admitted that Hengel's
book made life very easy for those who would claim the opposite. For, first of
all, the very demonstration that the Zealot movement was deeply enrooted in
Israelite and Jewish life and tradition made it all the more possible that Jesus
was party to it. And, secondly, the more religious the movement was, as

---

[10] M. Hengel, *Die Zeloten: Untersuchungen zur jüdischen Freiheitsbewegung in der Zeit
von Herodes I. bis 70 n. Chr.* (1961; 1976²). Cf. below, at n. 46.

[11] Ibid., p. 386 (in both German editions). The formulation "overcoming . . . violence"
will return in the title of a later volume by Hengel; see below, n. 24.

Hengel argued, the more legitimate it could have been for a religious man like Jesus to join it.

And sure enough, the very year Hengel published his dissertation, Brandon was back with the first shot of the second round of his fight to make the early Church zealot. As we have seen, his 1951 book, on the church of Jerusalem, was a bomb. But in 1961 he published his first piece on Jesus and the Zealots, and announced in it that he was working on a book on the subject.[12] As Cullmann had seen, there is more evidence regarding Jesus than there is concerning the church of Jerusalem, and Brandon no longer felt constrained, as Cullmann, to view the evidence as merely circumstantial and misleading, or "complex." Indeed, the next year, 1962, Cullmann himself contributed another tidbit to the collection of data, arguing that the name of Judas Iscariot indicates that this apostle too had been a Zealot: Cullmann suggested deriving his name from the term Sicarius, used of a variety of Jewish rebels against Rome.[13] But Brandon's 1961 article, and Cullmann's 1962 article, were only articles, and in out-of-the-way journals, so they did not make great waves.

At the same time, however, greater waves were being made by Paul Winter's scholarly monograph *On the Trial of Jesus* (1961)[14], and even more by Joel Carmichael's *The Death of Jesus* (1962), which was translated into several languages.[15] Both books emphasize the Roman responsibility for the death of Jesus, thus supporting the assumption that Jesus had been involved in anti-Roman activity; in Carmichael's book, indeed, the picture is painted very fully, if imaginatively. But books by Winter and Carmichael, Jewish writers (and the latter more or less without scholarly pretensions), are not strictly part of our study of Christian scholarship. The same may be said, *mutatis mutandis*, of J.C. McRuer's *The Trial of Jesus* (1964) and of H. H. Cohn's works on the same topic, which began to appear in 1967;[16] written by jurists (justices,

---

[12] S.G.F. Brandon, *Annual of Leeds University Oriental Society* 2 (1959–1961 [1961]), pp. 11–25.

[13] O. Cullmann, *Revue d'histoire et de philosophie religieuses* 42 (1962), pp. 133–140. For a German version of this, and also a lecture on "Die Bedeutung der Zelotenbewegung für das Neue Testament," see his *Vorträge und Aufsätze 1925–1962* (ed. K. Fröhlich; 1966), pp. 214–222 and 292–302.

[14] The second edition (edd. T. A. Burkill and G. Vermes; 1974) includes a select list of more than seventy reviews, out of a total more than twice that number (pp. xii,xxi–xxii).

[15] J. Carmichael, *The Death of Jesus: A New Solution to the Historical Puzzle of the Gospels* (1962); appeared also as a Penguin paperback (1966), as well as in German, French and Dutch. For another round by Carmichael in this debate, see his essay in the Zionist journal he edits, *Midstream* 25/4 (April 1979), pp. 56–69, along with the correspondence ibid. 25/7 (August-September, 1979), p. 69 and 25/10 (December 1979), pp. 66–67.

[16] His "Reflections on the Trial and Death of Jesus" first appeared in *Israel Law Review* 2 (1967), pp. 332–379, and a reprinted version was widely circulated. His volume on the same topic appeared in Hebrew in 1968, and in English in 1971, under the title *The Trial and Death of Jesus*.

respectively, on the highest courts of Canada and Israel), of whom the latter was Jewish, they are not part of the discipline which we have been studying. They are important, however, as part of the background, and functioned as gadflies, keeping the topic on the agenda.

II. 1967–1974:
The Balloon is Inflated until Bursting

In 1967, after the Christian *Vorarbeiten* and Jewish challenges which we have surveyed, and also on the background of the Masada excavations and attendant hullabaloo, and also on the background of the growing calls in the Christian world, especially among students and in the Third World, for a so-called theology of liberation, Brandon published his magnum opus in our field: *Jesus and the Zealots: A Study in the Political Factor in Primitive Christianity*. This book was, for the field of Jesus and the Zealots, what Hengel's book was for the general field of Zealots: a comprehensive monograph with a thesis, supported by a full scholarly apparatus, offered to the world for criticism. Brandon abstained from identifying Jesus as a Zealot (p. 355). But apart from this last word, everything else was here: as Hengel, Brandon emphasized the religious orientation of Zealotism and its continuous tradition of anti-Roman activism (the long third chapter on "Israel's Cause Against Rome, A.D. 6–73" [pp. 65–145] was, at the time, alongside Hengel's and the old one by Schürer, the most detailed account anywhere); he collected, as Cullmann, the evidence for Jesus' close association with Zealots and with the ideals they espoused; he emphasized, as Cullmann and Winter, that the Roman government executed Jesus for Roman reasons; and he set aside as late apologetics, as in his own book on the Church of Jerusalem, the picture of a pacific and universalist Jesus and Church, painted so prominently in the New Testament.[17] It is no wonder that many reviewers either missed Brandon's explicit refusal to label Jesus a Zealot, or chose to ignore it as insincere.[18]

Moreover, before the world could really begin to respond to Brandon's *Jesus and the Zealots*, he followed it up, the very next year, with another

---

[17] Apart from the fact that Jesus was executed by the Roman authorities, alongside "brigands," Brandon, as some of his predecessors, also put great weight on several logia and reports about swords (Matthew 10:34; and 22:36 and 26:51 and parallels), on the by-names of a few of Jesus' disciples which indicate that they were "Zealots" (cf. Cullmann, above, n. 13 and *Agrippa I*, p. 123), and on a very one-sided (Cullmann would say "non-complex") understanding of the nature of Jewish messianism.

[18] See the sharp exchange between Brandon and J. G. Griffiths in *NTS* 17 (1970/71), p. 453; 19 (1972/73), pp. 483–485.

volume, *The Trial of Jesus of Nazareth* (1968), which argues many of the same points. And Brandon also published several articles on the same theme, in journals professional and popular, during the next few years.[19]

The reaction was massive. As Brandon's 1951 book on the Church of Jerusalem, so too his *Jesus and the Zealots* was an easy target for critics, for it was based upon the rejection of so much of what the New Testament has to say about Jesus that it simply failed to convince. Brandon argued that Mark's gospel — which is usually considered the earliest gospel and the source of much of the other two synoptic gospels — was composed during the rebellion against Rome or immediately after it, and, therefore, that the picture of a pacific Christ was a result of apologetics.[20] Any Christian writing then had to do his best to avoid anything that smacked of Jesus and the apostles having been involved in, or having supported, rebellion against Rome. But many reviewers felt that it is irresponsible[21] to hold both that the source of most of what we read about Jesus is unreliable and that a modern historian may validly learn history by turning it all on its head and adding it to the scattered pieces of direct evidence for the opposite picture. Thus, for two central examples, in Luke 22 Jesus recommends that he who has no sword buy one (v. 36), but gives a cryptic response when his disciples show they have swords ("It is enough" — vs. 38) and stops them from using them when the time came to do so (vv. 49–51); which is the real Jesus? Brandon held that the first statement is the most authentic, while the rest consists of apologetic softening and pacifying of the original tradition; Cullmann held that both sides must be accepted. Similarly, for our second example, when John 6:15 says Jesus fled when people would make him a king, Brandon considered the desire authentic and in keeping with Jesus' program, and cast serious doubts about Jesus' purported flight and its import, while Cullmann and others viewed the desire as a result of popular misunderstanding of Jesus, and his flight from it as authentic.[22] Thus, there were plenty of points at which Brandon could be attacked by those who were so inclined. They were legion.

---

[19] S.G.F. Brandon, *The Trial of Jesus of Nazareth* (1968); idem, in *Studia Evangelica* 4 (1968), pp. 8–20, etc. For a complete list of his writings, see *Man and his Salvation: Studies in Memory of S.G.F. Brandon* (edd. E.J. Sharpe and J.R. Hinnells; 1973), pp. 326–334.

[20] See ch. 5 of *Jesus and the Zealots*, also *NTS* 7 (1960/61), pp. 126–141.

[21] Let alone un-Christian. See, for example, A. E. Harvey's review in *JTS* 22 (1971), pp. 200–202, where it is clearly implied that Brandon is not a Christian, and clearly stated that his whole thesis originated in disdain for the Gospels. Brandon was an Anglican priest, and occasionally officiated in that capacity until his death. See the obituary in *The Times* (London), Nov. 2, 1971, p. 17 = *Obituaries from the Times, 1971–1975* (comp. F. C. Roberts; 1978), p. 66, also H. C. Snape in the Brandon memorial volume (above, n. 19), pp. 1–5.

[22] For the latter two examples, see, respectively, Brandon, *Jesus and the Zealots*, p. 317

First of all, those who had started the wagon rolling[23] immediately jumped off of it. Apart from the very numerous review articles, Cullmann published a short *book* against Brandon, and Hengel published two: in these booklets, published in 1970 and 1971 (Cullmann's was published in eight languages, Hengel's in three each), they emphasized the other side of the picture, and that the picture was complex.[24] The spirit of these books (Deuteronomy 21:7) is reflected quite well in the introduction to Cullmann's *Jesus and the Revolutionaries:*

The thesis developed in my previous work concerning the importance of the Zealotist question for Jesus and the understanding of his condemnation has been maintained, since its first appearance in 1956, by a large number of scholars, and indeed naturally also by those who come to conclusions contrary to my own and consider Jesus himself to have been a Zealot or an ally of the Zealots. In view of these one-sided conclusions drawn by those who share my thesis concerning the importance of the Zealot movement for an understandng of the teaching and the life and death of Jesus, it seems to me especially urgent to supplement my investigations of *The State in the New Testament* by showing that, within the framework of an overall view of the consequences of the eschatological proclamation of Jesus, those conclusions not only must not be drawn, but cannot be drawn.

In addition, I count another five full-length books on the trial of Jesus between 1969 and 1973, and several other volumes on Jesus' attitude toward Rome or toward politics in general, virtually all taking their point of departure from Brandon's work, and all virtually unanimous in rejecting his thesis.[25] He did

---

(with n. 4 − 22:51 is Luke's apologetic invention!) vs. Cullmann, *The State in the New Testament*, pp. 31−34, and Brandon, pp. 16, 353−354, vs. Cullmann, p. 21.

[23] It is probably no accident that the immediate post-Brandon years (1970−1972) also saw the appearance of a German edition of H. S. Reimarus' *Apologie* and two (!) English translations of his *Wolfenbüttel Fragments* (1774−1777), which included his "Von dem Zwecke Jesu und seiner Jünger" − perhaps the earliest statement of the "Jesus the Zealot" thesis. See A. Schweitzer, *Geschichte der Leben-Jesu-Forschung* (1984⁹), pp. 56−68, also Bammel (above, n. 1), pp. 11−12 (bibliographical details in his n. 4).

[24] O. Cullmann, *Jesus und die Revolutionären seiner Zeit* (1970); M. Hengel, *War Jesus Revolutionär?* (1970); *Gewalt und Gewaltlosigkeit: Zur "politischen Theologie" in neutestamentlicher Zeit* (1971; the title of the English version is *Victory over Violence: Jesus and the Revolutionies* [1973]). Hengel also published a lengthy critical review of Brandon in *Journal of Semitic Studies* 14 (1969), pp. 231−240. For other prominent Christian critics of the politicization of Jesus and his movement, though not specifically in connection with Brandon, see J. Gnilka, *Bibel und Leben* 12 (1971), pp. 67−78, and E. Grässer, *ZNW* 62 (1971), pp. 266−294.

[25] H. van der Kwaak, *Het Proces van Jezus* (1969); E. Bammel, ed., *The Trial of Jesus: Cambridge Studies in Honour of C.F.D. Moule* (1970); D. R. Griffiths, *The New Testament and the Roman State* (1970); D.R. Catchpole, *The Trial of Jesus: A Study in the Gospels and Jewish Historiography from 1770 to the Present Day* (1971); G. Baumbach, *Jesus von Nazareth im Lichte der jüdischen Gruppenbildung* (1971); W.R Wilson, *The Execution of*

not concede, and continued to answer his critics point for point,[26] but his death in 1971, as Winter's death in 1969, left their thesis orphaned in the scholarly world.

In addition to the criticism of Brandon's one-sidedness, four additional fronts were opened against his thesis. One, a new debate concerning the traditional notion of Markan priority, is not integral to our theme, although it did help undermine Brandon.[27] Another, the possibility — which hit the news in 1971 with the publication of a new Qumran fragment — that the Dead Sea sect approved of crucifixion, which was the first indication that any Jews approved of that mode of punishment, failed to lead anywhere, although some had thought it might buttress the gospels' picture of Jews calling "crucify him, crucify him." The Qumran text turned out to be too fragmentary and ambiguous.[28] A third front, regarding the proper translation of the epithets of a few apostles — was Simon, for example, really known as "the Zealot"? —

Jesus: A Judicial, Literary and Historical Investigation (1970); G.R. Edwards, *Jesus and the Politics of Violence* (1972); and G.S Sloyan, *Jesus on Trial: The Developement of the Passion Narratives and Their Historical and Ecumenical Implications* (1973). See also: G.C. Brauer, Jr., *Judaea Weeping: The Jewish Struggle Against Rome from Pompey to Masada, 63 B.C. to A.D. 73* (1970). All of Edwards' book is directed against Brandon, so too van der Kwaak, pp. 87−96 and 266−279; Baumbach's first chapter; Griffiths, pp. 50−55; Wilson, pp. 222−226; Bammel, pp. 51−54 (by Catchpole) and 83, n. 13 (J. E. Allen); and Brauer, pp. 150−153. Note also that the "erneute and revidierte" fourth edition of J. Blinzler's standard *Der Prozeß Jesu* appeared in 1969, and, on H. H. Cohn's work in these years period, see above, n. 16. For Christian consideration of the question, whether rejection of Brandon must not lead back to blaming "the Jews" for the Crucifixion, see T. Corbishley, *The Month* 227 (No 1220, April 1969), pp. 211−218. Finally, one should note that, probably as fallout from the "Jesus and the Zealots" debate, these same few years also saw an efflorescence of literature on the ancient Church's relations with the Roman state. Note, inter alia, J. Speigl, *Der römische Staat und die Christen: Staat und Kirche von Domitian bis Commodus* (1970); W. Schrage, *Die Christen und der Staat nach dem Neuen Testament* (1971); and the *Wege der Forschung* reader, *Das frühe Christentum im römischen Staat* (ed. R. Klein; 1971).

[26] For his collective settling of accounts of the "aftermath" of *Jesus and the Zealots*, see *Bulletin of the John Rylands Library, Manchester* 54 (1971/72), pp. 47−66. For his other essays, see above, n. 19.

[27] Ironically, one major contribution to the undermining of that traditional notion was made by W. R. Farmer, who had started off the rehabilitation of the Zealots. For the contemporary impact of his *The Synoptic Problem: A Critical Analysis* (1964), see his review in *Perkins School of Theology Journal* 28 (1975), pp. 63−74, also his survey of modern developments of the competing Griesbach theory − in *NTS* 23 (1977), pp. 275−295. By the end of the decade, M.-E. Boismard would dedicate his presidential address at the Society for New Testament Studies annual congress to the "Impass" of the traditional two-source-cum-Markan-priority theory (*NTS* 26 [1979/80], pp. 1−17); as he notes at the outset, questions which twenty years earlier were considered settled were again wide open. For an example of that the very same year, see the reviews in *JBL* 98 (1979), pp. 137−138, 140−145, and 626.

[28] See above, pp. 82−83, n. 10.

turned out to be too lexicographical and too speculative.[29] Of these first three fronts, then, no more need be said.

But the fourth front turned out to be crucial and of very lasting significance for the study of the Zealots. Until now, we have used the term "Zealots" as a general term for Jewish rebels against Rome in the first century. This term, used by Josephus and by the rabbis, has an obvious religious background: it points directly to such biblical heroes as Phineas and Elijah (Numbers 25:10–13; I Kings 19:10). Therefore, Hengel and his followers could argue that the rebels operated out of religious ideals.[30] But Josephus mentions various groups of rebels, and not all may be so easily turned into religionists. Sicarii, or followers of John of Gischala or of Simon ben Giora, for example, seem more motivated by political or social considerations. Therefore, it was important for Brandon to claim, as Hengel before him, that the Zealots in particular had been the standard-bearers of Jewish resistance to Rome. And, at the very least, it was important to know that the Zealots had been in existence at the time of Jesus. But there's the rub: Josephus first uses the term, in *BJ* 2.564, 651, with reference to events in 66 C.E. Whence, therefore, the confidence that they had existed in the days of Jesus?

The truth be said, Hengel and Cullmann, as Farmer and others before them, had ignored this problem, and had simply assumed a continuity in Jewish resistance to Rome. Which is not such an outlandish assumption. But it does lack support at the detailed level of group definition. And already in the wake of Hengel's book, scholars such as S. Zeitlin and G. Baumbach had called attention to the problem, arguing that Josephus distinguished clearly between Sicarii and Zealots.[31] These studies received little notice, perhaps because Baumbach was unknown and because Zeitlin had a reputation for being an oddball, perhaps because the articles were in small print in out-of-the way journals, perhaps because, before Brandon's *Jesus and the Zealots* appeared, the whole topic was still somewhat esoteric and of only marginal interest. But things were different in 1971, at the height of the post-Brandon controversy, when very central journals carried articles making the same precise point.[32] True, Morton Smith, who wrote in *Harvard Theological Review* on "Zealots

---

[29] See J.-A. Morin, *RB* 80 (1973), pp. 332–358; etc. For the similarly continuing lack of consensus concerning "Iscariot," see A. Ehrmann, *JBL* 97 (1978), pp. 572–573.

[30] See especially the fourth chapter of Hengel's *Die Zeloten*.

[31] See S. Zeitlin, *JQR* 51 (1960/61), pp. 165–168 and *JBL* 81 (1962), pp. 395–398; G. Baumbach, *Theologische Literaturzeitung* 90 (1965), cols. 731–740. For another early case of interest in the terminology of "zealots," see B. Salmonsen, *NTS 13* (1965/66), pp. 164–176.

[32] M. Smith, *HTR* 64 (1971), pp. 1–19; M. Borg, *JTS* n.s. 22 (1971), pp. 504–512. For the swift acceptance of this thesis by Christian scholarship, see, inter alia, D.M. Rhoads, *Israel in Revolution: 6–74 C.E. – A Political History Based on the Writings of Josephus* (1976), pp. 52–59 (based on a 1973 dissertation).

and Sicarii: Their Origins and Relation," was not so interested in the question of Jesus and the Zealots; for him, the point that the two groups were not identical was merely another part of his general crusade to prove that ancient Palestinian Judaism was split into many differing factions.[33] But Marc Borg, who wrote in Cambridge University's *Journal of Theological Studies*, was interested precisely in the Jesus-and-the-Zealots question, and, at the end of his article, underlines the lesson: if Brandon thought that the New Testament's silence about the Zealots was due to an apologetic coverup, the truth is that they simply did not exist at the time of Jesus. So Jesus, obviously, could not have been a Zealot. QED.

This last front, in 1971, buried Brandon's thesis along with him. When a few other pieces appeared in 1975/75, and a book in 1976, arguing further that it is even difficult to show any anti-Roman violence in the days of Pontius Pilate (according to Tacitus, "under Tiberius all was quiet" [in Judaea — *Hist.* 5.9.2]), all they did was pile the earth higher over the dead.[34] By 1976, in fact, a Jewish writer who wished it would have been otherwise found himself writing an article, in *Encounter* of all places, entitled "Is the Political Jesus Dead?" As we saw in the bibliographical survey with which we began this survey, most people thought the death of the political Jesus was indeed beyond any doubt.[35] Although a few scholars, such as Hengel and Stern, tried to call back some of the baby which had been thrown out with the bathwater, namely, they tried to restore the notion of a somewhat unified anti-Roman movement over against the attempts to portray the Sicarii and the Zealots as entirely separate groups, neither attempted to associate Jesus of Nazareth

---

[33] See his essay in *Israel: Its Role in Civilization* (ed. M. Davis; 1956), pp. 67–81, and – the year of his *HTR* article – his *Palestinian Parties and Politics that Shaped the Old Testament* (1971). For a recent review of the reception of a major thrust of Smith's thesis, namely, his attack on the notion that first-century Judaism was by and large Pharisaic, see D. Goodblatt, *JSJ* 20 (1989), pp. 12–30. Cf. below, p. 265, n. 60.

[34] See Rhoads (above, n. 32); P. W. Barnett, *NTS* 21 (1974/75), pp. 564–571; and J. Giblet, *Revue théologique de Louvain* 5 (1974), pp. 409–426. Both of the articles were directed against Brandon.

[35] H. Maccoby, *Encounter* 46/2 (February 1976), pp. 80–89. Several responses appeared ibid. 48/4 (April 1977), pp. 83–92. (For Maccoby's own contributions in the course of the *Jesus and the Zealots* debate, see *NTS* 16 [1969/70], pp. 55–60, and his *Revolution in Judaea Jesus and the Jewish Resistance* [1973; a German translation, under the title *König Jesus*, appeared in 1982].) To the topic's last quivering may also be assigned a brief (28-page) and half-baked collection of lecture notes attacking the Jesus-Zealot thesis: J. Hadot, *Histoire des origines du Christianisme: Jésus et les Zélotes — Etude critique des thèses de S. Brandon* (ed. A. Mettewie-Morelli; 1976–1977). Compare H. G. Wood's summary of the result of the previous round of the debate (cf. above, n. 9): "Robert Eisler's bizarre attempt to turn Jesus into a half-hearted Zealot leader, by an absurd over-valuation and fanciful interpretation of the evidence of the Slavonic Josephus, confirmed rather than challenged the current neglect of the study of the political relations of the ministry" (*NTS* 2 [1955/56], p. 262).

with the rebels.[36] So the topic could, and did, remain one of no special interest for Christians.

III. What replaced the Zealots?

Readers may well be wondering if the decline of the Zealot theory didn't leave conscientious Christians back with the post-Holocaust problems which made it popular in the first place. How can one portray Jesus as one who did not accept injustice, and as one who was not alienated from his Jewish world, without portraying him as a rebel? And, on the other hand, what shall one say, if one is interested, about the motivation of the Jewish rebels against Rome, if – despite Hengel, but in the wake of Zeitlin, Baumbach, Smith and Borg – he is not willing to assume that they always acted out of religious motivation?

These vacuums were filled by a trend in scholarship which began, in the modern era, in the seventies, just in time to replace the political approach. The new approach was to focus on the social, intra-Jewish, focus of Jesus' message, as opposed to positing a political, Jewish-Roman focus. With the social focus, Jesus can be viewed as the founder of a social protest movement. As early as 1964, for example, an important volume was devoted to the social message of Luke's gospel; the next two decades saw this and similar lines of research flourish.[37] Again, without any reference to Christianity and the New Testament, the sixties saw the recognition of a phenomenon known as "social banditry" as a form of social protest– I refer especially to books by E.J.

---

[36] Hengel's article dedicated to the basic "Einheit" of the Zealots and Sicarii appeared in 1974 in *Josephus-Studien: Untersuchungen . . . Otto Michel zum 70. Geburtstag gewidmet* (edd. O. Betz, K. Haacker and M. Hengel), pp. 175–196, and was also appended to the 1976 edition of *Die Zeloten* (and its English translation). Note also his criticism of Rhoads (above, n. 32), in *Die Zeloten*[2], p. viii. For M. Stern on the Zealots, see *Encyclopaedia Judaica Yearbook 1973* (1973), pp. 135–152; on pp. 144–145 he defends the notion that there was, at first, a "certain connection" between the Zealots and the Sicarii. For a similar stance, see also H.P. Kingdon, *NTS* 19 (1972/73), pp. 74–81. Even Baumbach, one of the first critics of the Zealots-Sicarii equation (see n. 31), was later to modify his view, and in 1979, in a review of Rhoads, argued that the two groups were fundamentally "einheitlich" (*Theologische Literaturzeitung* 104 [1979], col. 811). But by 1979 the topic was dead. True, in 1984 Bammel's collection (above, n. 1) contained numerous articles arguing against Brandon. But as the 1983 preface to that volume notes (p. xi), it appeared a decade later than planned, and many of the pieces were in fact written a decade earlier. Similarly, M. J. Borg (see above, n. 32), *Conflict, Holiness and Politics in the Teachings of Jesus* (1984) is a revision of an Oxford dissertation completed in 1972.

[37] See H.-J. Degenhardt, *Lukas: Evangelist der Armen* (1965), and, for a review of social interpretation of the New Testament as of the late 'seventies: R. Scroggs, *NTS* 26 (1979), pp. 164–179. For a book which is somewhat between the "Jesus and the Zealots" controversy and the social approach, see R. J. Cassidy, *Jesus, Politics, and Society: A Study of Luke's Gospel* (1978).

Hobsbawn and his disciples[38] — and this line of research, which quickly flourished, was soon applied to the first-century Jewish rebels against Rome. It is perhaps natural that it was a scholar from the Communist bloc, Heinz Kreissig, who wrote the first volume on the social background of the Jewish struggle against Rome, already in 1970; but he had successors, from all around the world, during the succeeding decades.[39]

Thus, when Brandon's thesis was being buried, its replacement was waiting in the wings. The message of Jesus and his followers was portrayed increasingly as one of socio-economic protest — something quite justifiable on the basis of the gospels' evidence, and requiring very little explaining away. The way this thesis replaces the political thesis is obvious, for example, in Cullmann's booklet against Brandon, *Jesus and the Revolutionaries,* where the middle third is devoted to Jesus' social message. Similarly, apart from his two booklets against Brandon, Hengel published, in 1973, a book on property and riches in early Christianity, subtitled "Aspects of a Social History of Early Christianity."[40] This was, moreover, the time when Gerd Theissen began to publish a series of volumes on Christian social history, and they made the topic into a central discipline of New Testament studies for the next decade and more.[41]

Thus, we have arrived at the parallel bottom lines of two ways which parted. On the one hand, the Christian scholar who has written more than anyone else about the Zealots in the past decade, R. A. Horsley,[42] emphasizes frequently that the Zealots and the Sicarii were not messianic and are not, therefore, the

---

[38] See Hobsbawm's *Primitive Rebels: Studies in Archaic Forms of Social Movements in the 19th and 20th Centuries* (1959; 1971³) and *Bandits* (1969). For much further literature, especially with regard to the Roman world, see the review by B.D. Shaw in *Past and Present* 105 (November, 1984), pp. 3–52.

[39] H. Kreissig, *Die sozialen Zusammenhänge des judäischen Krieges* (1970). It is interesting that P. A. Brunt's essay on the same theme likewise appeared in an East German publication: *Klio* 59 (1977), pp. 149–153. Several Jewish scholars wrote studies on this topic as well, but they are beyond the scope of the present study.

[40] For Cullmann's and Hengel's books against Brandon, see above, n. 24. Hengel's new book was *Eigentum und Reichtum in der frühen Kirche: Aspekte einer frühchristlichen Sozialgeschichte* (1973; English translation in 1974).

[41] See G. Theissen, *Soziologie der Jesusbewegung* (1977); *Studien zur Soziologie des Urchristentums* (1979); *The Social Setting of Pauline Christianity* (1982). The first book was translated into five languages. See also, inter alia, A.J Malherbe, *Social Aspects of Early Christianity* (1977); H.C. Kee, *Christian Origins in Sociological Perspective* (1980). I have not seen P. W. Hollenbach's survey of "Recent Historical Jesus Studies and the Social Sciences," which appeared in *SBL Seminar Papers*, 22 (1983), pp. 61–78.

[42] His publications on the topic began in 1979 with "Josephus and the Bandits" (*JSJ* 10, pp. 37–63) and "The Sicarii: Ancient Jewish 'Terrorists'" (*Journal of Religion* 52, pp. 435–458). More recently, see his *Bandits, Prophets, and Messiahs: Popular Movements in the Time of Jesus* (co-authored by J. S. Hanson; 1985) and *Jesus and the Spiral of Violence: Popular Jewish Resistance in Roman Palestine* (1987).

background for understanding Jesus. Rather, he argues, Jesus is to be understood on the background of movements of social protest, movements which he sees as an ancient Judaean variety of social banditry.[43] Similarly, the most recent volume on the reasons for the rebellion of 66–70 against Rome – by a Jew, M. Goodman –downplays religious reasons and focuses on social problems within the Jewish camp.[44] On the other hand, correspondingly, the most recent (?) doctorate on Jesus and the Zealots – a 1985 Pretoria dissertation, in Afrikaans, which may account for the anachronism – denies any connection between them, and a recent volume on Jesus' Jewish background, by a prominent American scholar, mentions the Zealots only twice, and then only in passing, in lists of types of Jews who certainly rejected Jesus' message. Masada, indeed, is mentioned only as a place where Herod built and where there was a synagogue.[45]

Where all this leaves us, however, is at the somehow unsatisfying position that Jewish rebels against Rome were really not primarily anti-Roman, nor were Jesus and his followers. But Jesus was executed by Rome's representative in Judaea, and the rebels fought Rome. Was this really all a result of misunderstanding? Or of some unfortunate misdirection of hostility, by one side or the other, or by both? Somehow, it seems much more likely that, whatever the complexities, so many antagonists couldn't have all been wrong. Rather, current views on the topic seem only to be laboring under the burden of an understandable but overdone backlash to an overdone case, and it is possible that recognition of this will allow for correction.

After I completed the preparation of this paper, it came to my attention that Hengel's *Die Zeloten* (1976[2]) had just been published in English translation (*The Zealots* [1989]).[46] It may be assumed that this will occasion a renewed discussion of the issues involved, and, in the absence of Brandon to stir the pot, it may be that a redressing of the balance may be possible. However, you never know. It is much simpler to determine what extraneous events and scholarly fashions impacted upon debates of the past than how they will impact upon debates of the future.

---

[43] See, for example, his polemic article entitled "Menahem in Jerusalem: A Brief Messianic Episode among the Sicarii – Not 'Zealot Messianism'," in *Novum Testamentum* 27 (1985), pp. 334–348.

[44] See M. Goodman, *The Ruling Class of Judaea: The Origins of the Jewish Revolt Against Rome A.D. 66–70* (1987). My review of this volume is in *IEJ* 40 (1990), pp. 237–239.

[45] See P.J. Maartens, "Jesus als joodse Rebel: 'N teoreties gefundeerde evaluasie" (Diss. theol. Pretoria, 1985; English summary on pp. 454–455); J. H. Charlesworth, *Jesus Within Judaism: New Light from Exciting Archaeological Discoveries* (1988), pp. 59, 109, 118, 207 (n. 13). Charlesworth mentions Brandon only once, in a sentence totally rejecting his thesis (p. 90).

[46] My review of it is in *IEJ* 41 (1991), pp. 219–221.

Nevertheless, I will conclude by hazarding a guess, and use it to put our question into a somewhat broader context. Until now, as perhaps is to be expected from someone like me, I have portrayed Christian interest in the Zealots as if this Christian study of a Jewish topic proceeded only from Christian attention to such Jewish affairs as the Holocaust, the State of Israel, and anti-Semitism. And there is much truth in that; Christian interest in the Zealots before World War II is virtually nil. However, there is a much broader background. Jews, the Holocaust, the State of Israel and anti-Semitism are all real, flesh and blood, in the world. But there has always been, and must always be, a tension in Christianity between the point of view – term it monastic, gnostic, docetic, or the like – which denies the world, and views it as a problem to be avoided as best as possible, and the opposite point of view which affirms the world as a positive arena for Christian life and action.

Above, we presented Cullmann's 1956 *The State in the New Testament*, on the one hand, along with Farmer's *Maccabees, Zealots and Josephus*, which came out the same year, as the real beginnings of modern Christian interest in the Zealots. They were preceded, however, by a 1954 volume by Amos N. Wilder, professor of New Testament Interpretation at Harvard Divinity School (and brother of Thornton Wilder). Wilder, in a series of lectures published in 1954 as *Otherworldliness in the New Testament*, made an across-the-board attack upon the notion that Christianity is, or should be other-worldly. Taking his point of departure from the frequent assessment that Christianity is merely escapist, an opiate for the masses, he admitted that this is too often the case, but argued that it should not be so. In doing so, he repeatedly, if briefly, portrayed Jesus as having been so much involved in his contemporary world that he was very similar to the Zealots (although not to be identified as one of them).

On the other hand, we portrayed another book by Cullmann, his 1970 *Jesus and the Revolutionaries*, as one of the prime squashers of the "Jesus and the Zealots" theme, and so of Christian interest in the Zealots altogether. Now we may add, that the book's opening chapter, perhaps obliquely replying to Wilder, warns that "The fear of the slogan, 'Religion – opiate of the masses,' should not induce us to try to understand the teaching of Jesus *apart* from the eschatological perspective of the coming kingdom." Although he does go on to balance this, as usual ("Furthermore [i.e, "nevertheless" – D.R.S.], the expectation of the coming kingdom, which is not of this world, does in no way detain Jesus from his work *in* this transitory world and *for* this transitory world" [original emphasis]), it is inevitable that the emphasis is on the first statement, which is a denial of Wilder's point of departure. The very last lines of Cullmann's book, significantly, praise the Letter of Diognetus for having properly grasped, better than most observers, the New Testament's double demand from Christians: they "live in the world, but are not of the world."

Now it seems clear to at least one outside observer, that just as Christian interest in the Zealots waxed in the sixties but waned in the seventies and eighties, so too the frequently activist Churches of the sixties were widely replaced by a more sedate and withdrawn Christianity of the seventies and eighties. But it also seems that current developments in eastern Europe and in South America, regions of deeply-rooted Christianity where politics have gone haywire, may change all of that.[47] For the world of scholarship, I would expect that will add a very potent leaven to whatever stir the reappearance of Hengel's work might otherwise arouse.

---

[47] See, for example, the collection of essays on "La théologie de la libération en Amérique latine" in *Archives de sciences sociales des religions* 71 (July–September 1990).

9. On Barnabas and Bar-Kokhba*

There has been quite a bit of debate in recent years, especially in Israel, concerning the causes of the Bar-Kokhba rebellion.[1] The debate, whatever its contemporary wellsprings,[2] is made possible by the lack of concord among the few and problematic sources. Namely, Spartianus claimed that the rebellion broke out in reaction to a Hadrianic decree forbidding circumcision, Cassius Dio instead attributed it to the Roman decision to build Jerusalem as a pagan city and include within it a temple to Jupiter, and Eusebius – who didn't

---

* Hebrew original: *Zion* 46 (1980/81), pp. 339–345. A study by P. Richardson and M. B. Shukster on "Barnabas, Nerva and the Yavnean Rabbis" appeared shortly thereafter, in *JTS* n.s. 34 (1983), pp. 31–55. In my opinion, the two pillars of their interpretation of Barnabas 16, namely, the claims that *Nerva* was expected to rebuild the Temple and that the author of the Epistle would have condemned Jewish participants in such a project as collaborators with ("servants of") the enemy, are far from well-founded. Cf. n. 21.

[1] For the most recent rash of discussions, see A. Linder, *Tarbiz* 44 (1974/75), pp. 126–129 (in Hebrew); J. Geiger, *Zion* 41 (1975/76), pp. 139–147 (in Hebrew); S. Applebaum, *Prolegomena to the Study of the Second Jewish Revolt (A.D. 132–135)* (1976), pp. 5–9; M. D. Herr, *Zion* 43 (1977/78), pp. 1–11 (in Hebrew); G. W. Bowersock, in *Approaches to Ancient Judaism*, II (ed. W. S. Green; 1980), pp. 134–136; A. M. Rabello, *ANRW* II/13 (1980), pp. 699–703, 739–741; P. Schäfer, in *Studies in Aggadah, Targum and Jewish Liturgy in Memory of Joseph Heinemann* (edd. J. J Petuchowski and E. Fleischer; 1981), pp. 74–94 (in German in his *Der Bar Kokhba-Aufstand* [1981], pp. 29–50); L. Mildenberg, *The Coinage of the Bar Kokhba War* (1984), pp. 102–109; A. M. Rabello, in *The Bar-Kokhba Revolt: New Studies* (edd. A. Oppenheimer and U. Rappaport; 1984), pp. 27–46 (in Hebrew); M. Stern, *GLA* II, pp. 401–402, 619–621; B. Isaac and A. Oppenheimer, *JJS* 36 (1985), pp. 33–60 (a survey); D. Golan, *Historia* 35 (1986), pp. 226–239; A. Linder, *The Jews in Imperial Roman Legislation* (1987), pp. 89–102; and D. Rokeah's review of the Hebrew original of the latter: *Zion* 49 (1983/84), pp. 428–431 (in Hebrew). For the previous round of this debate, see especially G. Alon (d. 1950), *The Jews in their Land in the Talmudic Age (70–640 C.E.)*, II (1984), pp. 570–591; E. M. Smallwood, *Latomus* 18 (1959), pp. 334–347 and 20 (1961), pp. 93–96; D. Rokeah, *Tarbiz* 35 (1965/66), pp. 125–131 (in Hebrew); and H. Mantel, *JQR* 68 (1967/68), pp. 224–242, 274–296 and 69 (1968/69), pp. 341–342.

[2] Note that of the scholars listed in the preceding note, all but Bowersock, Schäfer, Mildenberg and Smallwood are (or were) Israelis. For some Israeli reflections on the lessons of this unsuccessful rebellion, see Y. Harkabi, *The Bar Kokhba Syndrome: Risk and Realism in International Politics* (1983), also idem in *Jerusalem Quarterly* 24 (Summer 1982), pp. 64–76 and I. Eldad's response, ibid. 32 (Summer 1984), pp. 113–119.

mention the former decree and thought the latter a *result* of the rebellion —
instead attributed it to the Jews' "madness" (*aponoia*).[3] Faced with such
conflicting direct evidence, scholars have been hard at work at attempts either
to supplement the sources and perhaps also to harmonize them or to prove the
preferability of one or the other. As a modest contribution to these efforts, we
shall offer an interpretation of a few lines of a Christian work which was
composed, apparently, under Hadrian. While this source has at times been
cited in this context, it does not seem that the full and proper conclusions have
been drawn.

The passage is from the Epistle of Barnabas, ch. 16, where there is a
reference to the rebuilding, "now," of the Temple (§ 4). To facilitate our
interpetation of this passage, we shall present here §§ 1—8, according to K.
Lake's translation.[4]

1) I will now speak with you concerning the Temple, and show how the wretched men
erred by putting their hope on the building, and not on the God who made them, as if
it were the house of God. 2) For they consecrated him in the Temple almost like the
heathen. But learn how the Lord speaks in bringing it to naught, "Who has measured
the heaven with a span, or the earth with his outstretched hand? Have not I? saith the
Lord. (Isaiah 40:12) Heaven is my throne, and the earth is my footstool, what house will
ye build for me, or what is the place of my rest?" (ibid. 66:1) You know that their hope
was vain. 3) Furthermore he says again, "Lo, they who destroyed this temple shall
themselves build it."[5] 4) That is happening now. For owing to the war it was destroyed
by the enemy; at present even the servants of the enemy will build it up again. 5) Again,
it was made manifest that the city and the temple and the people of Israel were to be
delivered up. For the Scripture says, "And it shall come to pass in the last days that the
Lord shall deliver the sheep of his pasture, and the sheep-fold, and their tower to
destruction."[6] And it took place according to what the Lord said. 6) But let us inquire
if a temple of God exists. Yes, it exists, where he himself said that he makes and
perfects it. For it is written, "And it shall come to pass when the week is ended that a
temple of God shall be built gloriously in the name of the Lord."[7] 7) I find then that a
temple exists. Learn then how it will be built in the name of the Lord. Before we
believed in God the habitation of our heart was corrupt and weak, like a temple really
built with hands, because it was full of idolatry, and was the house of demons through

---

[3] Spartianus, *Scriptores Historiae Augustae, Hadrianus* 14:2; CD 69.12.1; Eusebius, *Hist.
eccl.* 4.6.1, 3; *Chronicon* (ed. Helm[2]), p. 201. The first two sources may be found in *GLA* II,
nrs. 440 and 511, along with translation, commentary and bibliography.

[4] *The Apostolic Fathers* (LCL; 1912), pp. 397—398. The following translation deviates
from Lake's only in the last eight words of § 1, where Lake, apparently meaninglessly, offers
"and is the true house of God." My translation there conforms to that in the *Sources
chrétiennes* edition: *Épître de Barnabé* (Greek text ed. by R. A. Kraft; intro., translation and
notes by P. Prigent; 1971).

[5] Apparently according to the Septuagint version of Isaiah 49:17. See D. Flusser, *Textus* 2
(1962), pp. 140—142; R. A. Kraft, *JBL* 79 (1960), p. 337, n. 8.

[6] After Ethiopian Enoch 89:56.

[7] Ibid. 91:13?

doing things which were contrary to God. 8) "But it shall be built (gloriously) in the name of the Lord."[7] Now give heed, in order that the temple of the Lord may be built gloriously. Learn in what way. When we received the remission of sins, and put our hope on the Name, we became new, being created again from the beginning; wherefore God truly dwells in us, in the habitation which we are . . .

In the continuation of the chapter, the author develops the notion of the temple found in the believer's heart, and summarizes: "This is a spiritual Temple being built for the Lord" (§ 10).

Thus, the chapter proceeds as follows: following the discussion in §§ 1−5 of the physical Jewish temple, which God does not want and which is, therefore, condemned to be destroyed, the writer asks in § 6 if God really has no temple, and answers affirmatively in §§ 7−10 by pointing to the spiritual temple.

However, there is a problem with this analysis, for while §§ 1−2, 5 do condemn the physical temple and predict its destruction, §§ 3−4 seem to predict its reconstruction. This raises the crucial question: What, according to § 4, will they build?

This exegetical question comes hand in hand with a textual problem in § 4. Although most witnesses speak of rebuilding by the servants of the enemies, one manuscript − but the most ancient one (*Sinaiticus*) − reads "they (= the Jews) *and* the servants of the enemies" shall do the building. This manuscript was only discovered in the midst of the nineteenth century, and many scholars then tended to adopt its reading. Subsequently, however, after the excitement of the new discovery wore off, many scholars returned to the traditional text, according to which only the enemies' servants will do the building.[8] True, the reading which adds the Jews might seem likelier, for the prophecy says that they who destroyed the Temple shall rebuild it, and just as the exegete divided the blame for the destruction (due to *their* fighting it was destroyed *by the enemies*) he ought to divide the labor of rebuilding. But this is a weak basis for fixing the original reading, for it could be that a copyist who had a *Vorlage* which did not mention the Jews added them in due to that very exegetical logic.

Given this textual uncertainty, it is not surprising that there is a lack of unanimity concerning the identity of the temple which is to be built.

1. Some have seen here an allusion to the construction of the Second Temple, with the aid of Persian "servants."[9] On this interpretation, our text refers to Isaiah's prophecy of reconstruction after the destruction of the First

---

[8] So Kraft and Lake (above, n. 4), also SVM I, pp. 535−536. Cf. below, n. 16. According to Schäfer (above, n. 1: pp. 79−81 [pp. 32−34 in German]), even if one inserts the *kai* it may well be that the verse refers only to Romans who, together with their own servants, will do the building.

[9] See Ezra 6:6, 13, especially with the Septuagint: *syndouloi*.

Temple, while the prophecy of destruction, which was realized (§ 5), relates to the destruction of the Second Temple.[10] But this interpretation cannot explain the use of present tense and "now" in § 4.[11]

2. Others, more reasonably, see here a reference to Jewish hopes for a rebuilding of the Temple under Hadrian, with the aid of his officials ("servants").[12] Such hopes are also illustrated by the well-known story in *Genesis Rabbah* 64 and, perhaps, by the positive attitude toward Hadrian in the Fifth Sibylline Oracle (lines 45−48).[13] But this interpretation apparently ignores the unambivalent statement, at the end of § 5, that the prophecy of its destruction has already been fulfilled.[14]

3. Some believe the prophecy of reconstruction relates to the Christians' spiritual temple: after the Jews' physical temple has been destroyed, the "servants of the enemies" − i.e., slaves who became Christians[15] or Christians in general,[16] who, as opposed to the rebellious Jews remained loyal to ("servants of") Rome − continued to build their new, spiritual temple. However, the spiritual temple is not mentioned until § 6, *after* the prophecies of reconstruction and destruction. Moreover, in the absence of other

---

[10] This interpretation was suggested in the nineteenth century by K. Weizsäcker (see Veil [below, n. 12], p. 226), and again by A. L. Williams, *JTS* 34 (1933), pp. 342−343.

[11] The future tense in § 4 ("will build") is equally problematic, unless we are content to assume that it is simply taken over from the prophecy which is being explained.

[12] So, inter alia, A. Schlatter, *Die Tage Trajans und Hadrians* (1897), pp. 61−67; H. Veil, in *Handbuch zu den Neutestamentlichen Apokryphen* (ed. E. Hennecke; 1904), pp. 222−235; H. Bietenhard, *Judaica* 4 (1948), pp. 95−102; L. W. Barnard, *Journal of Egyptian Archaeology* 44 (1958), pp. 101−103; Smallwood, *Jews*, p. 435; and Alon (above, n. 1), pp. 448−452.

[13] Alon (above, n. 1), pp. 453−454 and Bowersock (above, n. 1), p. 134, both in the wake of A. Rzach (*PWRE* II/4 [1923], cols. 2134−2135), hold that these lines were composed by a Jewish writer shortly before the rebellion. However, it is arguable that they were written by a non-Jew; for that claim, and for arguments against the notion that the Jews expected favors from Hadrian, see K. Wengst, *Tradition und Theologie des Barnabasbriefes* (1971), pp. 108−111. For doubts concerning the notion that Hadrian was expected to allow the rebuilding of the Temple, see especially Schäfer (above, n. 1), pp. 75−81 (pp. 28−32 in German).

[14] Most scholars ignore this difficulty. Some (such as Veil [above, n. 12], p. 228) suggest the elimination of the end of § 5 as a late gloss, or that its past tense is "prophetic," bespeaking the author's certitude. So, for example, K. Thieme, *Kirche und Synagoge* (1945), p. 225, n. 84, also L. W. Barnard, *Church Quarterly Review* 159 (1958), p. 214: ". . . and in any case Judaism is totally doomed (16.5)"

[15] J.-D. Burger, *Museum Helveticum* 3 (1946), pp. 118−119. For a somewhat similar view, according to which the "servants" are Roman aristocrats who converted to Christianity, see Williams (above, n. 10), p. 343.

[16] J. J. Gunther, *JSJ* 7 (1976), pp. 150−151. According to Wengst (above, n. 13: p. 107, n. 17), this notion underlies the manuscript which mistakenly added in the Jews alongside of the Romans as Temple-builders, on the presumption that they too will become Christians; cf. above, n. 8.

indications it is methodologically unacceptable to assume, despite the explicit "this temple" in § 3, that the reconstructed temple is essentially different from the destroyed one.

4. Finally, one might apply the prophecies to the destruction of Bar-Kokhba's temple and the construction of Hadrian's temple of Jupiter in its stead. However, there is no hint in the Epistle to indicate it was written after the revolt,[17] and it is just as difficult to establish that Bar-Kokhba even captured Jerusalem, much less constructed a temple there.[18]

All of the above suggestions foundered because they could not coordinate the references to construction and destruction without ignoring their tenses or making them refer to non-similar or non-existent edifices. Only one interpretation — that of Harnack and some others — fits the bill: the author is speaking of a planned construction ("now . . . will build . . .") of a temple which will fulfill the prophecy of destruction of the Jewish temple.[19] This reads just like Cassius Dio's report of Hadrian's foundation of Aelia Capitolina instead of Jerusalem and construction of a temple to Jupiter on the site of the Jewish temple,[20] and we know of no other expected or real event to which Barnabas might be referring. Indeed, several scholars have interpreted Barnabas this way.

---

[17] See Wengst (above, n. 13), pp. 112–113.

[18] Although there are perennial attempts to prove, on the basis of slippery literary evidence, that he did one or the other or both. See, for example, Schlatter (above, n. 12), pp. 40–49; B. Lifshitz, *ANRW* II/8 (1977), pp. 482–483; and, most recently, L. Reznick, *The Holy Temple Revisited* (1990), pp. 151–159 (summarized in *Jewish Action* 50/1 [Winter 1989/90], pp. 36–39). Stern too leaned toward the conclusion that the city was taken by the rebels (*GLA* II, pp. 180, 396). However, the literary evidence is a very weak reed (see especially Schäfer [above, n. 1, in German], pp. 78–101), and the numismatic evidence — the lack of finds of Bar-Kokhba coins in Jerusalem despite thorough excavations — argues strongly against his conquest of the city; see L. Mildenberg, *Schweizer Münzblätter* 27, Heft 105 (Feb. 1977), pp. 1–6; idem (above, n. 1), pp. 62–63. Doubts concerning a Jewish capture of Jerusalem are also expressed by Herr (above, n. 1), pp. 9–10, n. 44; Bowersock (above, n. 1), pp. 136–137; and many others. As for the specific question of his rebuilding of the Temple (which is predicated upon the latter), see also Gunther (above, n. 16), pp. 144–146.

[19] See A. Harnack, *Geschichte der altchristlichen Litteratur bis Eusebius*, II/1 (1897), pp. 410–418; Wengst (above, n. 13), pp. 111–113; SVM I, pp. 535–536; Schäfer (above, n. 1), pp. 79–81 (= pp. 32–34 in German). As for the date of the Epistle, see Harnack, ibid., pp. 410–418 (near end of period between 80–130 C.E.) and Prigent (above, n. 4), pp. 25–27 (second quarter of second century C.E.). Both date it without dependence upon ch. 16, but rather on the basis of such considerations as what it cites and who cites it and the ecclesiastical and theological positions it reflects.

[20] Bowersock (above, n. 1: p. 137) has insisted that *es ton . . . topon* in CD 69.12.1 means not that the new temple was on the site of the Jewish temple, but only that it was instead of it. However, the latter interpretation does not exclude the former, and, in any case, Barnabas could reflect the expectation that the same site would be used.

Thus, the passage's structure is as follows. God does not desire a temple, for the whole world is full of His glory (§§ 1–2). And, indeed, the Temple was destroyed, and now its disappearance will be made irrevocable by the Jews' enemies – in fact by their underlings, and not even by the more respectable ones among them[21] – who will build another temple in its stead (§§ 3–4). All of this corresponds to prophecy (§ 5). However, one should not conclude that there is no such thing as a Temple of God. There is – the spiritual temple in the heart of the believer (§§ 6–10).

One detail demands special attention in the present context: according to § 2, God "abrogates" (*katargōn*) the Temple. This implies that until that point in time the Temple was legitimate. Such a thought corresponds to the Pauline notion that Judaism of law and flesh was legitimate until "the fulness of time," and Paul indeed uses the same verb to describe God's "abrogation" of the old covenant by the Christ-event.[22] But this notion is foreign to Barnabas, which claims time and again that the Jews erred in understanding the Torah as if it gave laws; in truth, it gives moral lessons in the forms of "types" and metaphors.[23] This position is so basic to Barnabas that the commentators have had great difficulty dealing with our passage, which implies that the Temple was formerly legitimate and desirable in God's eyes.[24]

This verb appears five times in the Epistle. Twice, it is clear that it is used of the abrogation of something which formerly existed: death (5:6) and the epoch of Belial (15:5). Neither is a Jewish law, so the above-mentioned theological problem does not arise.[25] In two other passages 2:6 and our 16:2, the reference is to the "abrogation" of the Temple and its cult. The fifth occurrence (9:4),

---

[21] Which makes this final defeat of Judaism's hopes all the more humiliating. This point would seem to allay the objection urged by Richardson and Shukster (above, n. *), p. 37, who argued that the fact that the Epistle speaks of the enemies' servants, instead of the enemies (as in Isaiah 49:17), indicates that the reference is to Jews, not Romans.

[22] See Ephesians 2:15, Romans 7:6 and II Corinthians 3:7, 11, 13–14. Cf. G. Delling, in *Theological Dictionary of the New Testament*, I (1964), pp. 452–454 and F. F. Bruce, *Bulletin of the John Rylands Library* 57 (1974–1975), pp. 259–279.

[23] See, especially, Wengst (above, n. 13), pp. 73–82, also J. Klevinghaus, *Die theologische Stellung der Apostolischen Väter zur alttestamentlichen Offenbarung* (1948), pp. 20–44. More briefly, see also Prigent (above, n. 4), pp. 30–33 and P. Vielhauer, *Geschichte der urchristlichen Literatur* (1975), pp. 604–607.

[24] See Klevinghaus (above, n. 23), p. 20, n. 1, and, in his wake, Wengst (above, n. 13), p. 73, n. 8; Prigent (above, n. 4), p. 84, n. 1, and at greater length in his *Les testimonia dans le christianisme primitif: L'Épître de Barnabé I–XVI et ses sources* (1961), pp. 34–35. Prigent, in both discussions, makes no secret of the circularity: since the usual translation, "abroger," would contradict Barnabas' normal theology, another translation (such as "rejeter" or "refuser") must be provided. So too H. Windisch felt compelled to explain "hier sicher 'einen Irrtum zunichte machen'" (*Der Barnabasbrief* [Handbuch zum Neuen Testament, Ergänzungs-Band III; 1920], p. 387; see also p. 311 [on 2:6]).

[25] And Klevinghaus (above, n. 23: p. 20, n. 1), for example, had no difficulty in viewing these passages as referring to "einen eschatologischen Akt (etwas beseitigen)," as opposed to

interestingly enough, refers to the "abrogation" of circumcision — to which Spartianus tied the outbreak of the rebellion.[26]

It seems, in other words, that while the author of the Epistle could bring only exegetical or *a priori* arguments against the normativeness of the Sabbath, fasts, dietary laws and the like, claiming that God in fact intended only their spiritual meaning, regarding two — circumcision and the Temple cult — he was in a better position. Here, he could point to real historical events — axiomatically directed by divine providence — which "abrogate" these laws and thus show them to be undesirable in the eyes of the master of history. The theological problem disappears: Barnabas holds that these commandments too were never valid in God's eyes, and now, by giving Hadrian free rein, He has made that clear.

Barnabas' argument is very similar to Tertullian's, a generation or two later. That Latin father pointed to the prohibition of Jewish entry into the region of Jerusalem as proof that the Messiah had already come, for he must come from Bethlehem (Micah 5:1/Matthew 2:6) and no Jew can henceforth be there.[27] So too Barnabas asserts that what Hadrian forbids is gone forever, hence the prohibition of circumcision and the pagan takeover of the Temple Mount forever abolish those institutions of Jewish law, which demonstrates that God never wanted them in the first place.

Thus, presuming Barnabas was written before the rebellion, his argument in ch. 16, and his reference to the contemporary "abrogation" of circumcision as well (9:4), support the assumption that both decrees preceded the rebellion. As the other evidence concerning these decrees is so problematic, and many doubt that they — especially the one against circumcision — preceded the rebellion,[28] this additional evidence deserves special attention.

---

the other three appearances (see on), where he was forced to infer "ein Seinsurteil (etwas als unwirksam, falsch und nichtig erklären)."

[26] The possibility that Barnabas is alluding here to the Hadrianic prohibition of circumcision was raised by P. Haeuser, *Der Barnabasbrief, neu untersucht und neu erklärt* (1912), p. 58. It was rejected by Windisch (above, n. 24: p. 352) with the strange argument that Barnabas would not have known or cared (!) about such a decree, and by Smallwood, *Jews*, p. 430, n. 6, who assumes the book was written before the rebellion. In her opinion, the passage means only that "since the real significance of circumcision is spiritual, the physical operation is no longer essential, and verse 4 means, not that the rite has been literally abolished, but that it has been 'superseded', 'made superfluous'." Here, at least, Smallwood admits what the literal sense of the verb is.

[27] Tertullian, *Adversus Iudaeos* 13.1–7. For our present purposes it does not matter whether or not there was, historically, such a prohibition (as is claimed also by Eusebius, *Hist. eccl.* 4.6.3 et al.). For doubts, see Rokeah, *Tarbiz* 35 (1965/66), pp. 122–125 (in Hebrew).

[28] Of those cited in our n. 1, see, for example, Rokeah (*bis*), Geiger, Mantel (pp. 226–236) and Schäfer (pp. 81–94 [34–50 in German]). All four doubt the decree against circumcision preceded the rebellion, and Mantel and Schäfer express similar doubts about the decision to build Aelia Capitolina.

Studies in Josephus and Judaean Chronology

1. Joseph ben Illem and the Date of Herod's Death*

Herod's death, one of the pivotal events of ancient Jewish history, is also, fortunately, one of the most securely dated. On the basis of a few converging lines of evidence, scholars have long agreed to place it somewhere between mid-March and mid-April of 4 B.C.E. Nevertheless, one odd datum preserved by Josephus does not fit in so easily, and has been bothering scholars for a few hundred years. Some have even seen in it reason to posit later dates. In this short study, we shall argue that a proper reading of Josephus, supplemented by some rabbinic and astronomic evidence, will eliminate the difficulty.

The date of Herod's death depends, in general, upon several pieces of literary and numismatic evidence concerning his rule and the respective incumbencies of his sons. These data lead to the conclusion that Herod's years were counted down to 5/4 or 4/3 B.C.E., and that his sons counted their years, accordingly, from 4/3 or 3/2.[1] The specific date of Herod's death, however, results from two Josephan notices. On the one hand, Josephus (*Ant.* 17.167) reports a lunar eclipse shortly before his account of Herod's death. On the other hand, *Ant.* 17.213 ff. and *BJ* 2.10 ff. report that the riots following Herod's death occurred during the Passover festival (when there were enough pilgrims around to riot); with the new moon becoming visible around March 29 in 4 B.C.E.,[2] Passover would have begun around April 12–13. Lunar eclipses were visible in Jerusalem on March 13 and during the night of the

---

* In Hebrew in *Eretz-Israel in the Tannaitic Period: Shmuel Safrai Jubilee Volume* (edd. I. Gafni and M. Stern; forthcoming)

[1] The basic data are as follows. Herod died 37 years after he was coronated (in 40 B.C.E.) and 34 years after Antigonus was executed (in 37 B.C.E. – cf. below, p. 177) – *Ant.* 17.191 = *BJ* 1.665. Archelaus was exiled, after ten (*Ant.* 17.342; *Vita* 5) or nine (*BJ* 2.111) years of rule over Judaea, 37 years after the battle of Actium, which was fought in 31 B.C.E. – *Ant.* 18.26. Philip's years too point to the same conclusion: he is reported to have ruled his territories for 37 years until he died in Tiberius' twentieth year (33/34 C.E.) – *Ant.* 18.106. For all the data, including those for Herod's third heir (Herod Antipas), which are not so decisive, see SVM I, pp. 326–328, n. 165, also J. van Bruggen, in *Miscellanea Neotestamentica*, II (edd. T. Baarda, A.F.J. Klijn and W. C. van Unnik; 1978), pp. 4–12.

[2] See R. A. Parker and W. H. Dubberstein, *Babylonian Chronology, 626 B.C.–A.D. 75* (1956), p. 45.

preceding 15/16 September (5 B.C.E.).[3] Given the fact that Herod was quite ill at the time of the eclipse, according to Josephus, and that the events which occurred between it and Herod's death are not enough to fill the almost seven months between mid-September and Passover, it is almost universally assumed that the eclipse in question was the one of March 13. Hence, according to the nearly unanimous view of scholarship, especially since E. Schürer set out all the data and put his weighty authority behind it, Herod died between mid-March and mid-April.[4] Indeed, when one notes that at least the seven days of mourning (*Ant.* 17.200 = *BJ* 2.200), and probably a few additional days as well, went by between Herod's death and the onset of the festival, the time of death can be narrowed down even more closely, to the period between March 13 and the very beginning of April.[5]

Nevertheless, a nagging problem remains. Just as seven months seem much too long for the events Josephus ascribes to the period between the eclipse and the following Passover, one month seems too short. One would have expected a few months. Anyone who reads Josephus account of this interval (*Ant.* 17.168–212) should be very surprised if he were told that it covers only a

---

[3] See M. Kudlek and E. H. Mickler, *Solar and Lunar Eclipses of the Ancient Near East for 3000 B.C. to 0 with Maps* (1971), p. 156; T. Ritter von Oppolzer, *Canon der Finsternisse* (1887), p. 343. Users should note that these tables follow the astronomers' practice of terming the year prior to 1 C.E. "0" (as in the title of Kudlek-Mickler), so the year they term "−4" is what historians call 5 B.C.E. The historians' practice is followed in F. K. Ginzel, *Spezieller Kanon der Sonnen- und Mondfinsternisse* . . . (1899); see p. 146 of the tables and, on pp. 195–196, the discussion of the eclipse of *Ant.* 17.167. Note also that there is an error in F. Boll's article on eclipses in *PWRE* I/12 (1909), col. 2359: in his discussion of the eclipse mentioned by Josephus, he considers – but rejects, following Ideler (below, n. 8) – the possibility that it was the one which occurred on September "5" of 5 B.C.E. The true date is September 15.

[4] See SVM I, pp. 326–328, n. 165, or, in the last German edition of Schürer's *Geschichte*, vol. I (1901³⁻⁴), pp. 415–417, p. 167. To illustrate the canonical nature of this dating, we shall merely note that neither W. Otto nor A. Schalit, in their massive and detailed monographs on Herod, had anything to add or comment. Both simply gave Schürer's date for Herod's death along with references to Josephus, and, in the former case, a reference to Schürer for the details. See W. Otto, *Herodes: Beiträge zur Geschichte des letzten jüdischen Königshauses* (1913), col. 149 (= *PWRE* Supplementband II [1913], col. 145); A. Schalit, *König Herodes* (1969), p. 643. For the only serious attack on Schürer's dating of Herod's death, see W. E. Filmer, *JTS* n.s. 17 [1966], pp. 283–298; for its unanimous rebuttal, see T. D. Barnes, ibid. 19 (1968), pp. 204–209 (followed by Smallwood, *Jews*, p. 104, n. 158, and by M. Stern, in *The Jewish People in the First Century*, I [edd. S. Safrai and M. Stern; 1974], p. 68) and P. M. Bernegger, *JTS* 34 (1983), pp. 526–531.

[5] Schürer even narrowed the period down to the first days of Nisan, given the data assembled above (n. 1) and the assumption that Herod counted his years from Nisan. Here, we shall ignore this fine point; below, pp. 174–180, and in *Agrippa I*, pp. 57–58, we have argued against the assumption of a Nisan era for the Herodians.

month, and some readers quite familiar with Josephus have refused to accept the notion.[6]

This problem has elicited a few responses. Already J. Kepler, in the early seventeenth century, argued that the assembling of the Jewish elders in Jericho, which Josephus recounts in § 174 and must have been quite time-consuming, in fact occurred prior to the eclipse, and is to be identified with the earlier assemblage reported in §§ 160−161.[7] Similarly, two hundred years later, L. Ideler was to argue that Josephus' narrative is in chronological disorder, some (unspecified) events reported after the eclipse having in fact occurred before it. Josephus did this, according to Ideler, because he wanted to unify his narrative thematically, and therefore closed out the story of the rebels' arrest by immediately recounting their punishment: since the eclipse followed upon the punishment of the rebels, moving up the punishment moved the eclipse up too. In fact, however, a good bit of time transpired between arrest and execution, and events which Josephus reports only after the latter must have occurred before it.[8] Again, in a detailed study in the mid-

---

[6] This narrative includes Herod's deterioration, his seeking of relief at baths near the Dead Sea, his distribution of property to soldiers and friends, assembly of Jewish notables so as to execute them upon his death, the execution of Antipater, Herod's change of testament, his death five days after Antipater (*Ant.* 17.191 = *BJ* 1.665), funeral procession, seven days of mourning (*Ant.* 17.200 = *BJ* 2.1), − and various occasions of negotiation between Archelaus and the people. For the detailed argument that this could not all have fit into a month, see F. Riess, *Das Geburtsjahr Christi* (1880), pp. 16−20, who holds that three months is more reasonable; he is criticized by P. Schegg, *Das Todesjahr des Königs Herodes . . .* (1882), pp. 34−35. More frequently, it is only said that such would be very unlikely − so, for example, Filmer (above, n. 4), p. 284. In the careful wording of T. Corbishley, "A reading of the relevant passages in Josephus would certainly suggest that the events narrated . . . are a little difficult to compress within that space of time [scil. thirty days], unless Josephus is reporting with an unaccustomed fulness" (*JTS* 36 [1935], p. 32).

[7] See J. Kep[p]ler, *De Iesu . . . vero anno natalitio* (1606), p. 22 ("forsan"); idem, *De vero anno quo aeternus Dei filius humanam naturam in utero benedictae virginis Mariae assumpsit* (1614), p. 81 ("Diligenter nota, quod non scribitur demum convocasse primores totius gentis, postquam rediit Ierichuntem, sed *congregatos iam tot et tales concluisse ad necem* [original emphasis].") These two passages may be found in idem, *Gesammelte Werke*, I (ed. M. Caspar; 1938), p. 375, and vol. V (ed. F. Hammer; 1953), p. 61. On Kepler's writings on the chronology of Jesus (and Herod's death), and the attendant controversy, see Hammer, ibid., pp. 397−422. Kepler's view is rejected by Riess (above, n. 6), p. 19, on the basis of the different contexts in which Josephus reports the two assemblages. Given the fact that the second story circulated independently in rabbinic literature (see *Megillat Ta'anit*, ed. Lichtenstein, *HUCA* 8−9 [1931/32], pp. 343−344 [cf. ibid., pp. 271−272; Smallwood, *Jews*, pp. 103−104, n. 155]), however, it could well be that Josephus was led into thinking that the episode was to be distinguished from the assemblage reported by his main source. For a similar situation with regard to Vitellius' "two" visits to Jerusalem, see below, pp. 202−217.

[8] So L. Ideler, *Handbuch der mathematischen und technischen Chronologie*, II (1826), pp. 392−393. Similarly, Schegg (above, n. 6: p. 35) assumed that much of Herod's physical deterioration, though reported after the eclipse, occurred before it.

eighteenth century it was suggested that due to intercalation Passover came
not two weeks after March 29, but two weeks after the next new moon, thus
allowing an additional month for the events of *Ant.* 17.168−212.[9] Finally, in
the twentieth century a few scholars have suggested that the problem be solved
by identifying the eclipse as that of September (5 B.C.E.) or by viewing the
Passover as that of 3 B.C.E.[10]

As far as I see, none of these options can conclusively be disproven,
although each has its own difficulties. In my opinion, however, the whole
problem is only a pseudo-problem, and a proper understanding of Josephus'
report of the eclipse will obviate the need to go to such lengths as positing a
Passover in mid-May, rearranging Josephus' narrative, stretching it beyond its
natural length, or manhandling the other evidence which leads to the spring of
4 B.C.E.

Josephus' narrative in *Ant.* 17 of the period prior to the eclipse and after it
may be divided into five sections:

A. §§ 149−164a: While Herod is very ill, some sages incite youths to take
down and destroy the golden eagle Herod had fixed above one of the Temple's
gates. They are arrested and brought to Jericho, where Herod judged them.

B. §§ 164b−167 (trans. R. Marcus, LCL):

Herod therefore dealt rather mildly with these others but removed the high priest
Matthias from his priestly office as being partly to blame for what had happened, and in
his stead he appointed his[11] wife's brother Joazar as high priest. Now it happened

---

[9] N. Fréret, *Mémoires de l'Académie des inscriptions et belles-lettres* 21 (1754),
pp. 287−288. According to Fréret, that year must have seen the "intercalation
extraordinaire" of an addition of a second Nisan (and cf. pp. 240−241 in the same volume),
which is how he understood the rabbinic phrase "to intercalate Nisan in Nisan" (m.*Pesachim*
4:9 etc.). It is usually assumed that the phrase merely refers to a late decision to intercalate by
the addition of a second Adar, although Fréret's understanding is not isolated; see S.
Lieberman, *Tosefta Ki-fshutah: A Comprehensive Commentary to the Tosephta*, IV (1962),
pp. 622−623 (in Hebrew). But there is no support for Fréret's assumption that this was ever
done in practice. The Mishnah, loc. cit., mentions it only as a practice of "King Hezekiah"
which "the sages" failed to approve; whether any historical event lies behind this report is
anyone's guess. In any case, Fréret's suggestion would work even with a regular intercalation
of a second Adar. My thanks to my friend Dr. Robert Brody, who located Fréret's essay and
copied out a long section of it for me.

[10] For the first option, see Barnes (above, n. 4), p. 209, followed by Smallwood, *Jews*,
p. 104, n. 158. For the latter − Corbishley (above, n. 6). Barnes in fact suggested that Herod
died in December, as is reported in the scholion to *Megillat Ta'anit* for 7 Kislev (ed.
Lichtenstein, *HUCA* 8−9 [1931/32], pp. 293−295, 339). Smallwood, however, doubted that
the events between Herod's death and Passover could have filled that many months, and so
tended to place the king's death in February, leaving the eclipse that in September. Cf. below,
p. 204, n. 8.

[11] I.e., Matthias'. See *Agrippa I*, p. 186.

during this Matthias' term as high priest that another high priest was appointed for a single day — that which the Jews observe as a fast — for the following reason. While serving as priest during the night preceding the day on which the fast occurred, Matthias seemed in a dream to have intercourse with a woman, and since he was unable to serve as a priest because of that experience, a relative of his, Joseph, the son of Ellemus, served as priest in his place. Herod then (*de*) deposed Matthias from the high priesthood. As for the other Matthias, who had stirred up the sedition, he burnt him alive along with some of his companions. And on that same night (*tē̦ autē̦ nukti*) there was an eclipse of the moon.

C. §§ 168–199: Herod's final acts, his death and burial (see n. 6).

D. §§ 200–212: Archelaus opens negotiations with the people.

E. § 213 ff.: Passover arrives and riots begin.

Section B is usually taken to mean that there was a lunar eclipse on the night following the firing of Matthias ben Theophilus and the execution of Matthias the sage and his companions.[12] As the insurrection occurred only when the king was quite ill (*Ant.* 17.148, 150, 161, 168 ff.), this understanding of B leads to the conclusion that the eclipse occurred not long before the king died, that is, in March and not in the preceding September. However, it appears preferable to assume that *Josephus means there was an eclipse the night Matthias ben Theophilus dreamed his fateful dream* — as was argued over a century ago in a little-noticed Latin dissertation by Marcus Brann.[13] For:

---

[12] This understanding is so natural for most scholars that even in detailed discussions of the chronology they simply refer to the eclipse and ignore the story about the high priest. So, for example, Kepler *De vero . . .* (above, n. 7), p. 80 (*Gesammelte Werke*, V, p. 61), where an italicized "quotation" from Josephus reads as follows: "Herodes igitur Matthiae adempto Pontificatu, successorem illi dedit Ioazarum uxoris suae fratrem; seditiosos vivos exussit, et Luna eadem nocte defecit"! The same understanding, and failure even to mention the Joseph ben Illem incident, recurs in Ideler (above, n. 8), p. 391, J. A. van der Chijs, *Dissertatio chronologico-historica inauguralis de Herode Magno, Judaeorum Rege* (1855), pp. xvi, 60–61 (n. 48), Riess (above, n. 6), p. 9 and Schegg (above, n. 6), pp. 26–27, not to mention less detailed accounts. Even Schürer failed to mention Joseph ben Illem in his historical review; his name appears only in the list of high-priests (SVM II, p. 229). Schalit and Otto (above, n. 4) apparently never mention him at all.

[13] M. Brann, *De Herodis, qui dicitur, Magni filiis patrem in imperio secutis*, I (1873), pp. 3–8. Some of the considerations we shall bring below were already adduced by Brann. Apart from the short and sarcastic comments by A. von Gutschmid, *Kleine Schriften*, II (ed. F. Rühl; 1890), pp. 320–321, I have not seen any discussion of Brann's interpretation of this passage. It is also offered, however, although without argument, by G. Hölscher, *Die Hohenpriesterliste bei Josephus und die evangelische Chronologie* (1940), p. 11, n. 1, and by two other scholars, who, however, err concerning the identity of the fast. It was adopted early on by H. Röslin, one of those who sparred with Kepler. According to the latter (in his *Das unser Herr und Hailand Jesus Christus nit nuhr ein Jahr vor dem anfang unserer . . . Jahrzahl geboren sey* [1613], p. 67 = *Gesammelte Werke*, V [ed. F. Hammer; 1953], pp. 168–169), however, Röslin thought the eclipse in question was that of 29 Dec., 1 B.C.E., and therefore

1. The words "that night" refer most naturally to the only antecedent "night" in this story — the one when Matthias dreamed.

2. In the parallel narrative in *BJ* 1.648—2.9 we find virtually all of what we listed in sections A,C,D,E, and the burning of the insurgents is also described, in *BJ* 1.665, very similarly to its description at the beginning and end of section B (§§ 164, 167). That is, only the matters pertaining to the high priest (his removal from office and the erotic anecdote) and the notice concerning the eclipse "that same night" have been added. Now we know, from the parallels in rabbinic literature, that the erotic anecdote circulated independently, and it is reasonable to assume that Josephus received it from some such source, probably a written one.[14] His extract from this source is introduced with the conventional language, "for the following reason," but its end is unclear.[15] From the methodological point of view, it is much more reasonable to assume that the source on the high priesthood supplied the notice of the eclipse as well, than to assume input from *two* new sources. But if the eclipse notice was found with the dream story, then it applies to it.

3. Josephus never says that the firing of the high priest and the execution of the insurgents occurred on the same day, but if he meant the eclipse occurred during the night following those events the reader will have to make that assumption. Otherwise, he will have to ask "Which night?" But that assumption asks quite a lot of the bare words "that night." As a rule, Josephus,

---

concluded that the fast was that of the Tenth of Tebeth! It is not certain that this minor fast was observed during the Second Temple period, and, in any case, there is — as Kepler noted — no evidence for any special service by the high priest on that day. Interestingly, the Brann-Hölscher interpretation is also enshrined in a footnote to the LCL edition of Josephus (vol. 8; 1963, p. 447, n. c). However, the author of that note, A. Wikgren assumed, as is usual, that the eclipse was the one of March 13, and this led him to search for a Jewish fast at that time: he found the Fast of Esther, which, however, is not in evidence prior to the medieval period. On the contrary; its date, 13 Adar, was a holiday, "Nicanor's Day," in the Second Temple period (see II Maccabees 15:36; Lichtenstein [above, n. 7], pp. 279—280, 346, and D. Sperber, *Bar-Ilan Annual* 20—21 [1982/83], pp. 149—150, n. 28 [in Hebrew]; the latter reference was kindly supplied by my friend, Rabbi Dr. David Golinkin). Wikgren's error was already noted by S. S. Miller, *Studies in the History and Traditions of Sepphoris* (1984), pp. 76—77, n. 80. Note that Wikgren erroneously stated the date of the fast of Esther as 11 Adar — which is the case only when 13 Adar falls on Saturday. That occurred in 1960, when, apparently, the note was composed (see the preface to the LCL volume, p. vii).

[14] On the parallels to the dream story, see below, n. 21. As for the general phenomenon of "parallel historical tradition in Josephus and rabbinic literature," see S.J.D. Cohen, in *Proceedings of the Ninth World Congress of Jewish Studies*, B/1 (1986), pp. 7—14. On p. 9, Cohen lists our story as one of the most striking such parallels, alongside Hyrcanus' dream (*Ant.* 13.282—283//Tos. *Sotah* 13:5 etc.) and the accomodating rainfall of *Ant.* 15.425//BT *Ta'anit* 23a. As for the assumption that the source was written, see the literature cited by S. S. Miller, *Studies in the History and Traditions of Sepphoris* (1984), p. 75, n. 75, including Hölscher (above, n. 13), pp. 11—12.

[15] On this type of introduction of snippets from secondary sources, see below, p. 271, n. 76.

as other writers, must be assumed to have told us enough to be able to make sense of his narrative.[16]

4. Indeed, if one applies the words "that night" to the various punitive actions reported in this paragraph, then he should also infer that they were carried out at night[17] — yet another detail we would be expected to infer from between the lines. (Usually, of course, it is supposed that the reference is to the night following the punitive acts. But when Josephus refers to the night following an aforementioned day [English "that night"], he normally uses either the plain *nux* ["night"] or else specifies by using *ekeinē* ["that night"] or even *epiousa* ["the succeeding night"]; but the insistent use of *autē*, as here, seems rather to mean "in the same [=aforementioned] night."[18] Never in *Antiquities*, and only once anywhere [*BJ* 4.640], did I find Josephus using *autē* with regard to the night following an aforementioned day.)

We conclude, therefore, on the basis of these four considerations, that Josephus mentioned the eclipse only apropos of the story of Matthias' dream, which, in turn, he told only as an interesting episode which occurred sometime during that high-priest's tenure. This is, basically, an aspect of Josephus' usual practice, of reporting sundry secondary matters before leaving his account of a given individual.[19]

But can we really find a lunar eclipse "on the eve of the day when the Jews fast," during Matthias' tenure as high priest? Although an interpretation of Josephus on strictly exegetical grounds can stand on its own, we would be all the surer that it is correct if it also corresponds to historical reality.

Let us first postulate that "the day when the Jews fast" is the Day of Atonement, "the fast" *par excellence*.[20] This is also borne out by the several

---

[16] I would agree with F. Hitzig that "Von ihm (scil. Josephus) gilt, was im Allgemein von jedem Schriftsteller, die Präsumtion, er habe sich füglich und seinem Zwecke gemäß ausgedrückt" (*Ostern und Pfingsten* [1837], p. 6), although I disagree with his particular application of this rule, as I explain in a forthcoming essay on the chronology of Antiochus Sidetes' Parthian expedition (in the Menahem Stern memorial volume).

[17] So, for example, Kepler, *De Iesu . . .* (above, n. 7), p. 22 (*Gesammelte Werke*, I, p. 375): ". . . Iudaeorum seditosi . . . qui ea nocte, qua defecit Luna, vivi cremati fuerant . . ."

[18] See K. H. Rengstorf, ed., *A Complete Concordance to Flavius Josephus*, III (1979), pp. 159–160. For just plain *nux*, see, e.g., *Ant.* 10.199; 11.42; 12.306; *Vita* 15, 90; *BJ* 1.330, 437, 585, etc. For the use of *ekeinē*, see *Ant.* 2.313; 6.299; 7.92; 11.247; 13.208; 18.233; 20.91; *Vita* 208; etc. For *epiousa* ("the succeeding night"), see *BJ* 1.98; 5.291; etc.

[19] See below, pp. 188–198 (and pp. 221–222), on how the "external" events which occurred during each governor's term are grouped after that governor's *res gestae*.

[20] The fact that Josephus' reference here is so unambiguous, and supported by rabbinic parallels, eliminates any doubt — if there ever was room for one — that *Ant.* 14.487 ("the festival of the fast") too refers to the Day of Atonement. For that day being "the fast" *simpliciter* see also *Ant.* 18.94; Philo, *De spec. leg.* 1.186; Acts 27:9; Barnabas 7:3–4; etc.; W. H. Brownlee, *The Midrash Pesher of Habakkuk* (1979), pp. 188–189. (For an attempt to

rabbinic parallels to the Joseph ben Illem story (which, however, do not mention the eclipse).[21] Its date is the tenth of Tishri. As for its "eve," it is not clear whether the reference is to the night between the ninth and the tenth — which is already part of the holy day — or the preceding night.[22] Be that as it may, let us ask whether a lunar eclipse coincided with one or the other day during the last years of Herod's reign.

Lunar eclipses are not frequent.[23] During the last decade of the last pre-Christian century there were sixteen, of which seven were visible in Jerusalem. Of them, only three came during months which by any stretch of the imagination could be linked to the Day of Atonement (August—November), and two of the latter, in 9 and 8 B.C.E. (both in November), were certainly too early for Matthias' high-priesthood. That leaves only the one of 15/16 September in 5 B.C.E. Indeed, this seems to be the one Josephus reported.

True, it probably came a few days later than the Day of Atonement. According to the usual tables, the astronomical new moon (conjunction) came during the night of 1/2 September, and would have been visible during the night of 3/4 September.[24] September 4 would therefore have been 1 Tishri, and

---

wiggle out of this, due to real or imagined problems concerning *Ant.* 14.487 [see below, p. 176], see Schalit [above, n. 4], pp. 766—768. And on other notions concerning our "the day when the Jews fast," see above, n. 13.)

[21] Tos. *Yoma* 1:4; BT ibid. 12b—13a; PT ibid. 1:1 (38 c—d). For discussion of these sources and their parallels, see Miller (above, n. 13), pp. 63—88 and G. Larsson, *Der Toseftatraktat Jom hak-Kippurim*, I (1980), pp. 42—49. Both cite much additional literature.

[22] The latter opinion was held by S. Lieberman (above, n. 9), pp. 723—724, notes 22—23. Lieberman argues that the night between 9 and 10 Tishri is already part of the fast and cannot be termed its "eve," and he points to m. *Yoma* 1:6—7 as evidence that the high priest was kept sleepless that night so as to prevent calamities such as the one described by Josephus (and by the rabbis; see above, n. 21). However, it is possible that the latter practice, if it was in fact ever enforced, was only innovated in the wake of our episode. For some criticism of Lieberman on this point see Miller (above, n. 13), p. 77, n. 81, also Larsson (above, n. 21), pp. 44—46, n. 60.

[23] The data in this paragraph are taken from the handbooks listed above, n. 3. For guidelines in calculating which eclipses were visible in Jerusalem, see Oppolzer, p. xxxiii. My calculations based on Oppolzer tally with the data for Babylon given by Kudlek-Mickler; as they note (p. vii) lunar eclipses seen in Babylon were nearly always visible in Jerusalem as well.

[24] For the time of the conjunction, see F. K. Ginzel, *Handbuch der mathematischen und technischen Chronologie*, II (1911), p. 547 = E. Bickerman, *Chronology of the Ancient World* (1968), p. 131. For the start of the month on September 4 in Babylon, see Parker-Dubberstein (above, n. 2), p. 45. The latter, however, list this month as Ululu, and have Tashritu beginning only a month later, on October 4. However, while Judaeans and Babylonians saw the same moon, they need not give the same names to their months; and Rosh HaShana (1 Tishri) on October 4 is unthinkable. For a list of almost 600 years of Jewish holiday dates, prior to the change to the Gregorian calendar in 1582, see the table in *Jewish Encyclopedia* 3 (1903), pp. 505—507 (at the end of M. Friedländer's article on the calendar). During all those years it never came later than September 27. On distinctions between Babylonian and Jewish

the Day of Atonement would have begun on the night of 12/13 September —
three days before the eclipse. However, cloudy nights and other problems
could have narrowed the gap; Brann was willing to accept the conclusion that,
due to cumulative errors, the Day of Atonement indeed began on the night of
the eclipse.[25] But even if that is doubted, it must nevertheless be admitted that
popular and religious memory could well forget the short interval which
separated two such terrible portents as the disqualification of a high priest on
the most holy day and an eclipse; according to rabbinic literature, lunar
eclipses were considered bad omens for the Jews.[26] They could both easily
become part and parcel of one story about a portentous holiday season: from
"the high priest was disqualified on the Day of Atonement and shortly
thereafter there was an eclipse" to "the high priest was disqualified on the Day
of Atonement and it was followed by a lunar eclipse," to what we read in
Josephus, the distance is not great. If religious memory could date the end of
Jewish kingship to the destruction of the Temple, although they were a
generation apart, it could overlook a few days as well.[27]

Moreover, we should note that the September eclipse was much more
impressive than that of the following March. The former was full, the latter
was partial; the former was long (about 220 minutes), the latter was short
(about 135 minutes); and the former was visible begining around 8:50 P.M.,
when many people were about and could not fail to notice it, while the latter
was observable only between about 1:45 and 4:00 A.M. In general, moreover,
we may note that the March eclipse was the smallest seen in Jerusalem in that
decade, while the September eclipse was almost the largest.[28]

calendrical practice, see B. Z. Wacholder and D. B. Weisberg, *HUCA* 42 (1971),
pp. 227–242. In general, on the Jewish calendar in antiquity and its problems, see M. D.
Herr, in *The Jewish People* (above, n. 4), II (1976), pp. 834–864.

[25] Brann (above, n. 13), pp. 7–8.

[26] See the *baraita* in BT *Sukkah* 29a = *Mechilta de-Rabbi Ishmael*, *Bo*, end of *parasha* 1
(ed. Horovitz-Rabin, p. 7): "A lunar eclipse is a bad sign for 'the enemies of Israel' (i.e., for
Israel) who count (months) according to the moon."

[27] On Jewish and Christian memory concerning the death of Agrippa II, see notes 6, 79 and
88 to the final study in this volume. Indeed, for anyone who knows Agrippa II was a Jewish
king during the Second Temple period, and knows of no later Jewish kings, linkage of his
death to the destruction is quite natural. In general, on this type of telescoping, see H.
Delehaye, *The Legends of the Saints: An Introduction to Hagiography* (1907), pp. 12–39.

[28] These data are according to the handbooks cited above, n. 3; the differences between
them are extremely minimal. Note that the moon appears in Jerusalem 37 minutes before
Babylon (Parker-Dubberstein [above, n. 2], p. 25); I corrected, accordingly, the data for
Babylon supplied by Kudlek-Mickler. According to Oppolzer, p. 343, of the seven lunar
eclipses visible in Jerusalem during that decade, four, including the one of September 15 in 5
B.C.E., measured 20–22 *Zoll*; the other three measured 13.2, 5.3 and – in March of 4
B.C.E. – 4.4 *Zoll*. For some older opinions regarding the size (up to 5.5 *Zoll*) and hours of
visibility (beginning as early as 1:17 A.M. and ending as late as 5:15 A.M.) of the March

It appears, therefore, that the exegetical arguments are supported by the astronomical facts: the eclipse mentioned in *Ant.* 17.167, we may assume, occurred in September of 5 B.C.E. But one need not worry about stretching all the events reported ibid. §§ 168–212 out to cover the six months until Passover, for the reference to the eclipse comes in an aside.

Finally, we will note that our assumption that the notice of the eclipse came from a Jewish tradition meshes well with what we know about normal Jewish attitudes toward Herod and eclipses. As we mentioned above (n. 26), Jewish tradition normally views lunar eclipses as bad omens. So too, certainly, was the disqualification of a high priest on the most holy day of the year. But the death of Herod was the occasion of popular celebration, according to both Josephus and rabbinic literature.[29] For a Jewish tradition to link together the high-priestly calamity and the eclipse is fine; for it to link the eclipse to Herod's illness would be a total departure from precedent. It seems, therefore, that it was Josephus himself who so arranged the narrative as to mention the eclipse only after the punitive steps. If one may speculate as to the reason, it would be that, imitating the Greek and Roman tradition of presenting eclipses as signs of coming deaths or catastrophes,[30] Josephus, whose main topic here is the coming death of Herod, moved the eclipse down so as to juxtapose it to the continuation in § 168: "And Herod's illness became more and more acute . . ." This increased the drama of the narrative, but only at the price of causing modern readers some difficulties – which we hope to have alleviated.

---

eclipse, see Ginzel (above, n. 3), pp. 195; he himself, p. 196, held it measured 4.5 *Zoll* and was visible in Jerusalem between 1:51 A.M. and 4:13 A.M

[29] See *BJ* 1.660, *Ant.* 17.176 and Lichtenstein (above, n. 10).

[30] See esp. Boll (above, n. 3), cols. 2331–2336.

2. "Caesarea" and its "Isactium:" Epigraphy, Numismatics and Herodian Chronology*

In an oft-published inscription of 221 C.E. from Laodicea ad Mare (Latakia), Syria, a local pugilist named Aurelius Septimius Irenaeus lists his many victories around the eastern Mediterranean and as far as Italy.[1] In this study, we would like to establish the location of the third-named victory, a point which, in addition to its importance for the history of that city and of sports in its day, seems also, surprisingly enough, to have implications for some controversies regarding Herodian chronology. We shall also suggest an explanation for the apparent error which has prevailed since the mid-nineteenth century with regard to the site of this victory. Indeed, this inquiry shall exemplify a common problem in the history of scholarship: the retention of inferences from hypotheses long after the hypotheses themselves have been superseded. This is especially likely to occur when, as in the present case, the hypothesis and the inference belong to two different disciplines, so practitioners of the one are not so familiar with developments in the other.

I. Which Caesarea?

The list of victories begins, after a vainglorious introduction (lines 1–8), as follows (lines 9–12):

---

* This paper was originally presented in English at the 1986 meeting of the American Oriental Society, and published in Hebrew in *Cathedra* 51 (April 1989), pp. 21–34. It supplies the underpinning for *Agrippa I*, pp. 110–111. My thanks to Professors L. H. Feldman (New York), M. Lämmer (Cologne) and L. Moretti (Rome), who advised me at various points, also to the participants in my seminar at Hebrew University in 1984/85, with whose help much of this paper began to jell.

[1] For the main corpora, see L. Jalabert, R. Mouterde and C. Mondésert, *Inscriptions grecques et latines de la Syrie*, IV (1955), nr. 1265; L. Moretti, *Iscrizioni agonistiche greche* (1953), nr. 85; R. Cagnat and G. Lafaye, *Inscriptiones graecae ad res romanas pertinentes*, III (1906), nr. 1012; W. H. Waddington, *Inscriptions grecques et latines de la Syrie* (1870), nr. 1839; J. Franz, *Corpus Inscriptionum Graecarum*, III (1853), nr. 4472. Moretti's collection will henceforth be cited as *IAG*. For earlier publications of this inscription, see below, nn. 2, 4.

9   Ἐν Αὐγούστῃ Καισαρείᾳ Σεουήρειον οἰκουμενικὸν πυθικῶν[2]
10   πυγμήν ˙ Αὐγούστου Ἄκτια ἐν Νεικοπόλει τῆς περιόδου
11   παίδων πυγμήν˙ ἐν Καισαπείᾳ Ἰσάκτιον παίδων πυγμήν˙
12   ἐν Τύρῳ ...

While the Actian games at Nicopolis are well known,[3] the first and third competitions do not seem to be mentioned by any other source, so we must make our deductions from this text alone. Apparently all scholars who have dealt with this text since the mid-nineteenth century have assumed, without argument, that both games were in Palestinian Caesareas, the former in Caesarea Maritima and the latter in Caesarea Philippi (Paneas).[4]

Now, while the identification of "Augusta Caesarea" as Caesarea Maritima is absolutely secure, on the basis of literary and numismatic evidence,[5] the identification of the "Isactium"'s site as Caesarea Paneas is quite problematic. For, with all due respect to the impressive consensus, it seems indisputable that when an unspecified "Caesarea" follows "Augusta Caesarea" in a list of toponyms, it must refer to the same place. Otherwise, the author of the inscription should have made his intention clear, just as, for example, "Frankfurt" in a list which previous mentioned Frankfurt am Main refers to the same city. Had the author meant Frankfurt an der Oder, he would have said so.[6] There were so many Caesareas in the Roman world that the use of

---

[2] So L. Robert (instead of *Pythikon* of the editions), taking it as a reference to the age-category of the participants in this "Severan" competition: *paides pythikoi* (see *Bulletin épigraphique* 1976, nr. 733, in *Revue des études grecques* 89 [1976], p. 570). This reading eliminates the problem left by the other reading, viz., that while the competitions listed in the inscription are arranged chronologically according to the age of the participants (*paides*, *ageneioi* and *andres*), this first-named competition does not specify the participants' age. In a private communication, Professor Moretti has concurred. Indeed, J. V. Francke already emphasized that "die Richtigkeit der Lesart (scil. with omega) nicht in Zweifel gezogen werden darf" (J. V. Francke, *Griechische und lateinische Inschriften, gesammelt von Otto Friedrich von Richter* [1830], pp. 173–174); as we shall see, this is not the only aspect of Francke's discussion which was to be disregarded.

[3] On them, see the general account in L. Friedländer, *Darstellungen aus der Sittengeschichte Roms*, II (ed. G. Wissowa; 1922¹⁰), pp. 197–198; more literature is cited below, in n. 37.

[4] So L. Robert, *Hellenica* 2 (1946), p. 70, n. 4; F.-M. Abel, *Histoire de la Palestine*, II (1952), p. 160, and all the corpora mentioned in n. 1, above, apart from Waddington's, which makes no comment other than a general reference to Franz's commentary for identification of the various games. The earlier publications of this inscription – collections entitled *Inscriptiones antiquae* edited by R. Pococke (1752; p. 5) and R. Chandler (1774; pp. 92–93), also O. F. von Richter, *Wallfahrten im Morgenlande* (ed. J.P.G. Ewers; 1822; pp. 563–565, 629–630) – have no comment on our "Caesareas."

[5] See J. Ringel, *Césarée de Palestine* (1975), pp. 83–86.

[6] For use of a similar argument in another Herodian connection, cf. L. H. Feldman, *Classical Quarterly* n.s. 35 (1985), pp. 240–241.

distinguishing epithets was unavoidable.[7] Compare, for example, Josephus' accounts of Vespasian's and Titus' trips from one Palestinian Caesarea to the other, where appropriate specifications are used for both (*BJ* 3.443; 7.23); so too another athletic inscription, half a century earlier than ours, which does the same (*IAG* 72, lines 40–43).[8] If anything, moreover, plain "Caesarea" in a Palestinian context – as in Josephus and the New Testament – refers to Caesarea Maritima, which was the provincial capital and by far the more prominent of the two homonymous cities.[9] But concerning this inscription there is a consensus that the unadorned "Caesarea," although following a specific reference to Caesarea Maritima, nonetheless refers to Caesarea Philippi! Clearly, something is amiss.

What is especially puzzling, moreover, is the fact that before the creation of that consensus the above arguments and conclusion had already been fully (if briefly) stated, in what remains until today the most detailed study of this inscription. In his 1830 commentary, after concluding that "Augusta Caesarea" is Caesarea Maritima, Johann Valentin Francke went on to conclude that the other "Caesarea" was the same city:

Denn zu geschweigen, daß diese auch sonst vorzugsweise Cäsarea ohne weitern Beisatz genannt wird, so wäre hier wohl schon zur Unterscheidung ein Zusatz nöthig gewesen, wenn jetzt eine der andern gleiches Namens verstanden werden sollte.[10]

Francke's commentary was used by Johann Franz, whose 1853 commentary in the authoritative *Corpus Inscriptionum Graecarum* (vol. III) apparently lies behind the prevalent view regarding our "Caesarea:"

Urbs quae prima recensetur, est Augusta Caesarea (non Caesaria [sic] Augusta) Palaestinae (cf. Eckhel. D.N.T. III. p. 428. coll. p. 341); Nicopolis Seleucidis est.[11]

---

[7] See the seventeen articles on cities of this name in *PWRE* I/5 (1897), cols. 1288–1295.

[8] Josephus distinguishes between "Caesarea on the coast/sea" and "Caesarea called 'Philip's'," while *IAG* 72 – also found in Waddington (above, n. 1), nr. 1620b – distinguishes between "Strato's Caesarea" and "Caesarea Paneas." It is strange that Moretti, who in his commentary to our inscription (*IAG* 85, p. 250) simply wrote "*Kaisareia* (l. 11) sembra essere Cesarea Paniade (cfr. n. 72 l. 43)," overlooked the striking contrast between the two.

[9] For Josephus, see the references in A. Schalit, *Namenwörterbuch zu Flavius Josephus* (1968), p. 70. In the New Testament, Caesarea Philippi is mentioned twice and identified as such each time (Matthew 16:13//Mark 8:27), while all fifteen references to an unspecified "Caesarea" are to the one on the coast. Comparable accounts of the two Caesareas may be found in SVM II, pp. 115–118, 169–171. On Caesarea Maritima, see especially L. I. Levine, *Caesarea Under Roman Rule* (1975), also Ringel (above, n. 5).

[10] Francke (above, n. 2), p. 174 ("For even if we ignore the fact that this [Caesarea Maritima] is elsewhere usually termed 'Caesarea' without any additional epithet, here some addition would probably be necessary simply to distinguish, if we were now meant to understand the text as referring to another city of the same name.")

[11] The last three words, apparently motivated by the impression that most of the games mentioned in the inscription were in the Syrian region, were deleted in the addenda and

Quae sequitur Caesaria (sic), haud dubie Paneas Trachonitidis est et ipsa Augusta dicta. Succedunt Tyrus . . .[12]

Why did Franz prefer this unnatural interpretation to the simple one stated by Francke?

II. Eckhel's Legacy

One might suspect that Franz assumed that since the victories in "Caesarea" were listed separately, they must have been in different cities. However, it is easy to suggest why they may have been separated: perhaps the victories are listed in chronological order (just as the basic order of the inscription is chronological),[13] or perhaps the pugilist (or the scribe) thought it more appropriate to list the "Isactian" victory only after that at the original "Actian" games. In any case, there are more extreme cases of athletic inscriptions similarly skipping back and forth among names of the same cities.[14] Finally, this partial answer cannot even begin to explain why Franz thought of Caesarea Paneas in particular, after deciding that "Caesarea" *simpliciter* was not Caesarea Maritima.

Another possible explanation is that Franz thought it unlikely that there would be both "Pythian" and "Isactian" youth competititions in the same city.[15] But surprising or not, it is what the plain sense of the inscription requires. Moreover, since another inscription (*IAG* 72, mentioned above) refers to competitions in both Caesarea Maritima and Caesarea Paneas and neither is termed "Isactian," it follows[16] that whichever Caesarea was the site of the "Isactium" was the host of two sets of competititions. Caesarea Maritima, as the larger and more important of the two cities (n. 9), is to be

---

corrigenda, p. 1172. As the first two corpora listed in n. 1 correctly state, the reference is to Nicopolis in Epirus, where the Actia were held. A similar problem formerly led to confusion regarding Tarentum, which is mentioned in line 24; see those same commentaries ad loc.

[12] Franz (above, n. 1), p. 221 ("The city which is first mentioned is Augusta Caesarea [not Caesarea Augusta] of Palestine [cf. J. Eckhel, *Doctrina numorum veterum* I/3 (1794), p. 428; cf. p. 341]; 'Nicopolis' is the 'Seleucid' one [i.e., Nicopolis ad Issum – see our preceding note. D.R.S.]. The 'Caesarea' which is mentioned next is doubtless Paneas in the Trachonitis, which was also called 'Augusta.' There follow Tyre . . .")

[13] See above, n. 2.

[14] See, for example, *IAG*, nr. 73 (Ephesus, ca. 170 C.E.): victories in Ephesus, Miletus, Laodicea, Ephesus, Laodicea, Ephesus, Pergamum, Ephesus, Laodicea . . .

[15] Thus Professor Moretti, in a private communication.

[16] Unless one assumes that the unnamed competition of that inscription is identical with the Isactium or was later replaced by it. The fact that the inscription does mention the names of other competitions militates against the first possibility, and the fact that "Isactium" points to the Augustan period militates against the second, although neither point is conclusive.

preferred. Finally, this explanation cannot explain, any better than the preceding one, why Franz thought of Caesarea Paneas after deciding that our "Caesarea" is not the one on the coast.

The real explanation for Franz's departure from Francke is in fact revealed by his parenthetical reference to Joseph Eckhel, one of the founding fathers of modern numismatics, and his emphatic comment: "non Caesaria Augusta." Franz, it turns out, was building here upon one of Eckhel's hypotheses regarding the coins of Caesarea Paneas, and although the latter has long been superseded and forgotten, Franz's application of it to our inscription has remained as a relic copied from corpus to corpus. In brief, the situation is as follows:

1. Franz's comment indicates his belief that "Augusta Caesarea . . . Caesarea" is not similar to "Frankfurt am Main . . . Frankfurt" but rather to "New York . . . York," where no one would suggest that both toponyms refer to the same city. The order of the terms is not reversible.

2. This belief goes back to Eckhel, who in 1794 laid great weight on the order of the terms of the names of the two Palestinian Caesareas. Eckhel (who did not comment on our inscription) noted that coins of Caesarea Paneas (since Marcus Aurelius) call it "Caesarea Sebaste," which in Latin would be "Caesarea Augusta," while Caesarea Maritima's coins, since the Flavian period, use the Latin name "Augusta Caesarea." According to Eckhel, irreversibility of the names was imperative so as to prevent confusion.[17]

3. To maintain this distinction, however, Eckhel had to trample the literary evidence, for : i) Josephus, in his most formal reference to Caesarea Maritima, calls in "Caesarea Sebaste" (*Ant.* 16.136); ii) Philo, in his only reference to Caesarea Maritima, calls it "Caesarea . . . surnamed Sebaste" (*Leg.* 305); and iii) both Josephus and the New Testament, as noted above (n. 9), frequently call Caesarea Maritima plain "Caesarea," which shows it is comparable to "Frankfurt" and not to "York." Eckhel (ad i) asserted that "Sebaste" is missing from various texts of *Ant.* 16.136, thus greatly overstating the evidence;[18] (ad ii) dismissed Philo as "only Philo;"[19] and ignored the third point altogether. Moreover, Eckhel went so far as to posit an artificial

---

[17] For the reference to Eckhel, see above, n. 12. For the coins of the coastal Caesarea, see L. Kadman, *The Coins of Caesarea Maritima* (1957), esp. pp. 44–45, also Ringel (above, n. 5), pp. 151–160. As for those of Caesarea Paneas, see W. Wroth, *Catalogue of the Greek Coins of Galatia, Cappadocia and Syria [in the British Museum]* (1899), pp. lxxx–lxxxii, 298–299; Y. Meshorer, *INJ* 8 (1984/85), pp. 37–58.

[18] According to Eckhel (above, n. 12: p. 341): "Iosephus uno loco: *Kaisareia Sebastē*, sed posterior haec vox in aliquibus exemplaribus abest." This seems to be based on the comment ad loc. in the great J. Hudson - S. Havercamp edition of Josephus (1726; vol. I, p. 797, note y), where, however, we read only that *Sebastē* is missing from the Latin version. According to Niese's editio maior (1890), this is the only witness which lacks the word.

[19] Eckhel (above, n. 12), p. 429 ("Unus Philo").

distinction between the port of Caesarea Maritima, which, he admitted, was called "Sebaste" (e.g., *Ant.* 17.87, *BJ* 1.613, and coins), and the city itself, to which he denied this epithet.[20]

4. What drove Eckhel to such lengths was the desire to defend and perfect a numismatic thesis offered by Joseph Pellerin in 1765, concerning various bronze coins bearing Augustus' head and the inscription C A; a variety also bears the letters ΛT, normally understood as the numeral (date?) 330. Earlier scholars had ascribed these coins to the Spanish Saragossa (*Caesar Augusta*). Pellerin, however, who basically accepted this decipherment of the letters C A, deduced from the fact that the coins had been found in Syria, and from other considerations, that a Palestinian Caesarea would be more likely. Since Caesarea Maritima was the more prominent one, and its coins showed it was termed "Augusta Caesarea," Pellerin assigned most of these coins to it. However, Caesarea Maritima was founded by Herod, so it is impossible that its coins could call an Augustan date 330 (presuming that the date is according to the municipal era). Therefore, Pellerin found himself forced to assign the dated coins to another Palestinian Caesarea − Caesarea Paneas.[21] Eckhel, more consistently, argued from the general similarity of these coins that if some were from Caesarea Paneas, all were.[22]

Here, then, is the bottom of the matter. In order to make his correction of Pellerin all the more secure, Eckhel posited the irreversibility of the terms of "Augusta Caesarea," so the letters C A could not possibly stand for the name of the coastal city, but only for Caesarea Paneas, which, he assumed, was called "Caesarea Augusta." This was all very tenuous, not only due to the literary evidence summarized above (§ 3), but also because there is no evidence, it seems, for the use of the Latin title "Caesarea Augusta" for Caesarea Paneas. The closest we come is the Greek "Caesarea Sebaste" of its coins. Indeed, one suspects that the use of "Augusta" for Caesarea Maritima, even in Greek characters (as in our inscription), would have precluded use of it for Caesarea Paneas. Nevertheless, this distinction, seconded by Mionnet and others,[23] guided Franz into assuming that "Caesarea" could not be a shorthand second reference to Caesarea Maritima. In the clash between the natural reading and Eckhel's authority, the latter prevailed.[24]

---

[20] Ibid., pp. 341, 428−429.

[21] J. Pellerin, *Mélange de diverses médailles*, I (1765), pp. 36−57.

[22] Eckhel (above, n. 12), pp. 339−341.

[23] T. E. Mionnet, *Description de médailles antiques, grecques et romaines*, V (1811), pp. 311−312; *Supplément*, VIII (1837), pp. 217−218. Eckhel's view was also adopted by other handbooks, such as J. Y. Akerman, *Numismatic Illustrations of the Narrative Portions of the New Testament* (1846), pp. 14−15, and from there into the authoritative *A Dictionary of Roman Coins* (edd. S. W. Stevenson, C. R. Smith and F. W. Madden; 1889), p. 162.

[24] Note that Franz (above, n. 12) cites Eckhel and depends upon him five times in this one

Within a few decades of Franz's publication, the Pellerin-Eckhel thesis was completely undermined and forgotten, for discoveries of the C A coins in England and near Smyrna destroyed the confidence in their Syrian origin, and numerous suggestions regarding the decipherment of the abbreviation soon showed just how fragile their attribution to any Caesarea was. Today, it is most common to read "Commune Asiae"[25] and attribute the coins to Pergamum, although the letters ΛΤ still remain a puzzle.[26]

There thus remains no basis at all for the strange notion (it was never more than that) that "Caesarea" cannot be a shorthand second reference to Augusta Caesarea, i.e., Caesarea Maritima. In other words, there is no reason to reject the natural reading of our inscription, which places the Isactium in Caesarea Maritima.

III. Herodian Chronology

1. The Herodian New Year and Agrippa I's Death

The "world Severan" games mentioned first in our inscription were, presumably, founded in honor of Septimius Severus not too long before this inscription was composed.[27] But it is most likely that the "Isactium" was founded by Herod, more than two centuries earlier.[28] This conclusion results both from the positive consideration that Herod's games at Caesarea — just as Augustus' Actia — are said to have been founded in honor of Augustus and

---

column of *CIG*. For Eckhel's reputation in the mid-nineteenth century, cf. the article on him, by [F.] Kenner, in the *Allgemeine deutsche Biographie*, V (1877), pp. 633–635.

[25] Although the fact that elsewhere this is unambiguously abbreviated as COM ASI or COM ASIAE still gives pause; see J. Deininger, *Die Provinziallandtage der römischen Kaiserzeit* (1965), pp. 52–53, n. 5.

[26] The major studies of these coins include F. de Saulcy, *Annuaire de la Societé française de numismatique* 3 (1868), pp. 259–262; W. Froehner, *Mélanges d'épigraphie et d'archéologie*, [vol. II], XI–XXV (1875), pp. 76–79; H. A. Grueber, *Numismatic Chronicle*, 4th series, 4 (1904), pp. 208–211; B. V. Head, *Historia Numorum* (new ed.; 1911), p. 786; M. Grant, *From Imperium to Auctoritas* (1946), pp. 344–345; C. J. Howgego, *Numismatic Chronicle* 142 (1982), esp. pp. 17–19; and C.H.V. Sutherland, *The Roman Imperial Coinage*, I (1984), p. 37. My thanks to Dr. Hans Voegtli of Münzen und Medaillen AG, Basel, for his help with the bibliography on these coins.

[27] Moretti, in *IAG*, p. 250, suggested that the name of earlier "Pythian" games was expanded in Severus' honor — but see above, n. 2. Abel (above, n. 4: p. 160) and Levine (above, n. 9: p. 57) assume that Septimius Severus founded the games. On Septimius Severus and Caesarea Maritima, see Smallwood, *Jews*, p. 488.

[28] On Herod's Caesarean games, see especially M. Lämmer, *Kölner Beiträge zur Sportwissenschaft* 3 (1974), pp. 95–164. This identification of the Isactium was already made by Francke (above, n. 2), p. 174.

were quadrennial (*Ant.* 16.137—138),[29] and from the negative consideration, that no time was more appropriate than Herod's — who founded Sebaste and Caesarea in honor of Augustus! — for the founding of games in honor of Augustus and the most decisive battle of his career.[30] Furthermore, from the methodological point of view, since we know (from Josephus) that Herod instituted games in honor of Augustus, refusal to identify them with the "Isactium" mentioned in our inscription leads to an unnecessary multiplication of hypotheses.

Identification of Herod's games as an "Isactium" has, it seems, implications regarding two controversial points of Herodian chronology: the use of spring vs. autumn eras for counting regnal years, and the date of Agrippa I's death. It used to be assumed that Herod and his successors counted their regnal years according to a spring era, from 1 Nisan, but — as successive editions of Schürer's handbook show somewhat amusingly — this was never more than an assumption based upon rabbinic law.[31] But the relevance of that law to Herod is more than doubtful.[32] Josephus, at any rate, states in *Ant.* 1.80—81 that 1 Tishri remained the New Year for all purposes apart from religious ones. Again, it is usual to assume that Agrippa I, who received his full kingdom in the early spring of 41 and died "upon completing three years of reign over all Judaea" (*Ant.* 19.343), died in the spring of 44, near the end of his third year assuming a spring era.[33] Lately, however, both views have been attacked: it

---

[29] Josephus says the games were *kata pentaetērida*, which, in ancient "inclusive" terminology (also used, for example, of the Olympic games), is the same as our "quadrennial." See Lämmer (above, n. 28), pp. 142—143, n. 26.

[30] For other similar games, see Suetonius, *Divus Augustus* 59; *Monumentum Ancyranum* 9. For Augustus as Herod's patron, see A. Schalit, *Herodes: Der Mann und sein Werk* (1969), *passim*, esp. pp. 127—131, 554—562 and Chapter IV/4 (on Herod's building projects).

[31] In his *Lehrbuch der neutestamentlichen Zeitgeschichte* (1874), pp. 222—223, n. 5, and in its second edition (now entitled *Geschichte des jüdischen Volkes im Zeitalter Jesu Christi*, I [1890], pp. 343—345, n. 343), Schürer confined himself to stating that the Nisan era was probable, as is indicated by the Mishnah (m.*Rosh HaShana* 1:1). In the third-fourth edition (1901; vol. I, pp. 415—417, n. 167), however, he added references to T. Nöldeke and G. F. Unger. But the former, in a letter quoted by V. Gardthausen, *Augustus und seine Zeit*, II/1 (1891), p. 120, says only that he assumes this to be true (on the basis of the same rabbinic text), while the latter adds only the statement that Schürer, in his second edition, had shown ("nachgewiesen") that Josephus used this system with regard to Herod (*Sitzungsberichte der philosophisch-philologischen und der historischen Classe der k. b. Akademie der Wissenschaften zu München*, Jg. 1896 [1897], p. 361). SVM I, p. 327, is now back to plain "probably," without these references.

[32] And note that alongside the tannaitic view which makes 1 Nisan the new year for kings (m. and Tos. *Rosh HaShana* 1:1), there is also a rabbinic view that non-"Israelite" kings count their years from 1 Tishri, in the autumn (BT ibid., 3a and 8a). Herod may well have been counted among the non-"Israelite" kings; see BT *Baba Batra* 3b—4a, also *Agrippa I*, pp. 165, 222.

[33] On the date of Agrippa's death, see *Agrippa I*, pp. 108—111, 203—207; the present

has been argued that most or all Herodians used an autumnal era,[34] and this has been shown particularly convincingly for Agrippa I. For unless one assumes that he counted "inclusively" from the autumn of 36, which preceded his first enthronement after the death of Tiberius in March 37, it is impossible, or very difficult, to account for his "year five" coins depicting Gaius Caligula, who was killed in January 41![35]

Our ascription of the title "Isactium" to Herod's games at Caesarea fits right into this new trend and lends it support. For Josephus reports that Agrippa died shortly after appearing at Caesarean games in honor of Augustus (*Ant.* 19.343).[36] One need only assume that 1) Agrippa's games were one of the celebrations of Herod's games, and 2) games termed "Isactian" were celebrated in September, the month of the Battle of Actium and of the original Actian games in its memory.[37] The first assumption has already been accepted by numerous scholars,[38] and the second — which no one hitherto had occasion to

---

discussion will deal only with the input from the "Isactium" inscription. The standard discussion, followed by most — e.g., Haenchen, p. 61 — is that of E. Schwartz, *Nachrichten von der königlichen Gesellschaft der Wissenschaften zu Göttingen, Philolog.-hist. Klasse*, 1907, pp. 263–266 (= idem, *Gesammelte Schriften*, V [1963], pp. 124–128). He placed Agrippa's death in early March 44.

[34] See O. Edwards, *Palestine Exploration Quarterly* 114 (1982), pp. 29–42; J. van Bruggen, in *Miscellanea Neotestamentica* . . ., II (edd. T. Baarda, A.F.J. Klijn and W. C. van Unnik; 1978), pp. 1–15.

[35] See A. Stein, *INJ* 5 (1981), pp. 22–26, followed by subsequent authorities (see *Agrippa I*, pp. 57–58, n. 71, where some supportive epigraphic evidence is also cited.) As Stein notes, already U. Rap(p)aport pointed out this problem, in *Revue numismatique*, 6ᵉ série, 10 (1968), p. 72, n. 2. As for the possibility that the coins were dated from Nisan 36 (as the Nisan prior Agrippa's coronation), it seems not to have been suggested by anyone — for good reason. For Tiberius died on 16 March 37, and we are told that Gaius had to wait an appropriate time before crowning Agrippa (*Ant.* 18.237), since the latter had been imprisoned by Tiberius after expressing the hope that the old emperor would soon die (ibid. §§ 168 ff., 186 ff.). It is, therefore, highly unlikely that Agrippa was crowned before the beginning of Nisan, which came on April 6 (see R. A. Parker and W. H. Dubberstein, *Babylonian Chronology, 626 B.C. - A.D. 75* [1956], p. 46). Cf. Stein, loc. cit., pp. 23–24. Moreover, in *Ant.* 19 Josephus reports that Agrippa died at the end of his third year as king of all Judaea (§ 343) and after seven years of rule (§ 350), and these data cannot be accomodated to a spring 36 era.

[36] On the text of this passage, see *Agrippa I*, p. 109, n. 9.

[37] On the date of the Actian games, see Moretti, *IAG*, pp. 205–206. Herod's games would not have clashed with them, for, whether the Actia began in 27 B.C.E. (so Moretti, ibid., also R. Rieks, *Hermes* 98 [1970], pp. 96–116) or in 28 (so others), their quadrennial cycle was removed from that of Herod's games by at least a year. As for their precise date, note that the Actia were not held on the anniversary of the battle (2 September) but, rather, on Augustus' birthday, 23 September (see Rieks, loc cit.). This date is usually very close to 1 Tishri. Thus, for example, in the two years which interest us here, 1 Tishri fell on September 29 in 10 B.C.E. and on 24 September in 43 C.E. (according to Parker and Dubberstein [above, n. 35], pp. 45, 47.)

[38] Such as Schwartz (above, n. 33) and Feldman, p. 377, n. 3. According to Smallwood

consider — is an obvious one. Given the historical associations of "Isactian," "Isactian" games in any season but September would be a contradiction in terms.[39] Thus, Agrippa's death is to be placed ca. September/October 43, "upon completing his third year as king over all of Judaea" — counting "inclusively" from the autumn preceding that final enlargement of his kingdom. This was, according to Josephus, shortly after his appearance at a Caesarean festival, which we may now identify as the fourteenth celebration of Herod's Isactium.[40]

2. Three Counter-Arguments Dismissed

Our conclusion that Herod (or Josephus on his behalf) used an autumnal era has been challenged on three grounds. However, the first two are wrong, and the third, apparently, argues better for the use of such an era than against it.

a) Herod's Conquest of Jerusalem in 37 C.E.

The chronology of Herod's conquest of Jerusalem has been studied in detail by numerous scholars, including, in the past generation, Schalit, "Schürer," Stern, van Bruggen, Smallwood and Baumann. Although Josephus (*Ant.* 14.487) dates it to the Day of Atonement (10 Tishri), all these scholars, as others, agree that the conquest was in fact completed in ca. July 37.[41] Accordingly, on the basis of the usual assumption cited above, that Herod

---

(*Jews*, p. 80, n. 62), it is "surely" correct. Some hold the games were otherwise unattested games in honor of Claudius; see *Agrippa I*, p. 110.

[39] It is not always clear why certain games were termed "*is-*" others: does it refer to the type of competitors? of competition? of prizes? of honoree? See F. Mie, *Quaestiones agonisticae* . . . (1888), pp. 48–53. In the present case, however, in contrast to the case of "Isolympic" and other such games, the obvious historical associations must be given their due weight. For the sake of completeness, we may note that "Isactian" games are also mentioned in an inscription from Aphrodisias (*Bulletein de correspondance hellénique* IX [1885], p. 68). Unfortunately however, it supplies no indication as to the season or the nature of the "identity."

[40] For the foundation of Caesarea in 10/9 B.C.E., see *Ant.* 16.136–137, which dates it to Herod's twentieth year. As Lämmer notes (above, n. 28: p. 130), 10/9 is the usual translation of this date. See, e.g., SVM I, pp. 293, 306, and the many cited by Lämmer and in *Agrippa I*, p. 110, n. 12. Ibid., pp. 204–206, I have explained why I reject Lämmer's own argument (pp. 130–135) for the games having begun in the spring of 11 B.C.E.

[41] See Schalit (above, n. 30), pp. 764–768; SVM I, pp. 284–286, n. 11; Smallwood, *Jews*, pp. 565–567; M. Stern, in *The Jewish People in the First Century*, I (edd. S. Safrai and M. Stern; 1974), pp. 64–68; idem, *GLA*, II, pp. 361–362; van Bruggen (above, n. 34), pp. 13–14; and U. Baumann, *Rom und die Juden . . . (63 v. Chr.–4 v. Chr.)* (1983), pp. 159–163. All list further bibliography on this beloved topic. For the virtually unquestionable assumption that Josephus' "holiday of the fast" refers to the Day of Atonement, see above, p. 163, n. 20.

counted his years from Nisan, it is usual to assume that he counted "inclusively" from Nisan 37. If, as we argued, he used an "inclusive" autumn era, it would have begun in 38. But such a conclusion as the latter is excluded by various considerations which show that Herod counted his years from 37 (see below). As for the possibility that Herod counted from Tishri 37, not "inclusively," we have seen that Agrippa I counted "inclusively," as was usual. In the absence of other considerations to the contrary, it is best to assume that Herod (or Josephus, when writing of him) did too. Here, then, would seem to be a serious contradiction to our conclusion in the preceding section.

First, however, we must note that it is illegitimate to base one's conception of Josephus' chronological system upon a datum with which he disagreed. If he thought the conquest occurred on the Day of Atonement, then, if he dated inclusively from the New Year prior to the conquest, he could have used 1 Tishri 37. More important, however, is a second point: this whole problem is only an illusion, for Josephus did not count Herod's years from the conquest of Jerusalem, although Schürer and numerous others say he did. In fact, if one takes the statement in the scholarly locus classicus on Herodian chronology (SVM I, p. 326, n. 165) that

Josephus states that he reigned 37 years from the date of his appointment (40 B.C.), 34 years from his conquest of Jerusalem, 37 B.C. Cf. *Ant.* xvii 8, 1 (191); *BJ* i 33, 8 (665)

and checks the references, he will find that Josephus in fact counts the thirty-four years *from the execution of Mattathias Antigonus*. But Antigonus was executed in Antioch by Mark Anthony (*Ant.* 14.488−490; Strabo, apud *Ant.* 15.9),[42] and, as is shown by the latter's movements, that occurred in the late autumn of 37, or perhaps early in 36. Anthony was still in Tarentum in September−October 37.[43] Thus, there is nothing here to contradict the usage of an autumn 37 era. Apparently, Josephus, or already Herod, was only willing to count the new king's regnal years after Antigonus was completely removed.[44]

Although it is superfluous in the present context, I will briefly note, moreover, some unease concerning the widespread rejection of Josephus'

---

[42] Apart from these passages, which place the event in Antioch, the fact that Anthony executed Antigonus − despite Josephus' occasional general references to Herod as having killed him (*BJ* 1.665; *Ant.* 17.191) − is also stated in *BJ* 1.357; Plutarch, *Vita Antonii* 36.4; and CD 49.22.6. These passages from Strabo, Plutarch and CD are, respectively, *GLA*, nrs. 108, 266 and 414.

[43] See especially CD 49.23.1; J. Kromayer, *Die rechtliche Begründung des Principats* (Diss. Strassburg; 1888), pp. 51−57, also L. Craven, *Antony's Oriental Policy Until the Defeat of the Parthian Expedition* (1920), p. 67; H. Buchheim, *Die Orientpolitik des Triumvirn M. Antonius* (1960), p. 108, n. 98; and H. Bengtson, *Marcus Antonius* (1977), p. 183.

[44] For Josephus' usual procedure of arranging Judaean history according to successive tenures of rulers, see below, pp. 188−198.

dating of the city's fall to the Day of Atonement. While, if need be, Josephus' dating could easily be swept aside as anti-Herodian folk memory or the like, some good reason should be brought for an earlier date. But careful examination of the aforementioned discussions (n. 41) will show, I believe, that the central argument, nearly the only apparently persuasive one, is from *Ant.* 14.465//*BJ* 1.343, 351, which indicate that the siege began at the end of the *cheimōn* and took five months. On the assumption that *cheimōn* means "winter," this brings us to ca. July; hence the consensus.[45] But it seems that *cheimōn* here should rather be rendered "storm," as is often the case.[46] Readers of Josephus' narrative on the interruption caused by the *cheimōn* hardly gain the impression that a season went by; a day or two is more likely. But if this text refers to a storm and not to winter, then the main pillar of the July dating is gone, for storms, even heavy storms, can come in the spring in this region.[47] I hope to be able to return to this matter in greater detail.

b) Ant. 17.191

U. Rappaport took this passage, which dates Antigonus' death to Herod's *fourth* year since his coronation in Rome in the winter of 40/39, as proof that Herod did not use an autumnal era. Namely, Rappaport assumed that Antigonus was killed only "peu de temps" after the conquest of Jerusalem; since the latter is normally dated to July 37, Rappaport concluded that Antigonus' death came before 1 Tishri — hence only in Herod's *third* year according to an era beginning in Tishri 40.[48] However, as we have seen, in fact at least a few months went by between July 37 and Antigonus' execution.

---

[45] So, for the central example, SVM I, p. 284, n. 11, where ". . . Josephus' account leaves us in no doubt that a winter still intervened before the conquest of Jerusalem" is simply followed by quotes from *Ant.* 14.453, 461, 465 and 473, of which the first three refer to a/the *cheimōn*.

[46] See, for some nearby examples, *Ant.* 14.377, 380, which both Schalit and Marcus render "storm," just as Thackeray (LCL) renders it as "storm" in *BJ* 1.339 and "tempest" in § 343, also Matthew 16:3: every morning one can see not whether it will be winter (for that one needs only a calendar), but whether it will be stormy. The old Latin translation of Josephus (Basel 1524) renders *cheimōn* by *hiems* in *BJ* 1.339, 343 and *Ant.* 14.377, 380, 465; *hiems* can mean "winter" or "storm." At *Ant.* 14.461, however, it has *tempestas*.

[47] According to *Ant.* 6.91, a *cheimōn* is impossible in midsummer. But it is certainly possible in the spring. First-hand knowledge of this is perhaps the only redeeming feature of the heavy rain- and hail-storm which assailed my cousin's outdoor wedding on 17 May 1988 at Kibbutz Qetura, fifty kilometers north of Eilat; the region north of Jerusalem, where Herod was when the *cheimōn* intervened (see Schalit [above, n. 30], p. 96, n. 141), normally gets six or more times as much rainfall annually (see the Survey of Israel's *Atlas of Israel* [1985³], maps 12–13).

[48] See Rap(p)aport (above, n. 35), pp. 65–70 ("peu de temps" — p. 66).

c) The Earthquake in Herod's Seventh Year

Two great students of Josephus and Herod, W. Otto and A. Schalit, took *BJ* 1.370 as decisive proof that Herod used an era beginning in Nisan 37.[49] Here, we read that "the war of Actium was at its peak" in Herod's seventh year, and then, "at the beginning of spring," there was an earthquake in Judaea. The battle of Actium was fought in the first days of September 31, but it was preceded by preparatory clashes beginning in the previous spring.[50] Thus, Otto and Schalit claimed, Josephus' reference is to the spring of 31. On a Tishri 37 era, in contrast, that spring would have been only in Herod's sixth year.

However, this argument is hardly cogent, and, in fact, may be turned on its head. Note, first of all, that the parallel version in *Ant.* 15.121 mentions the earthquake *after* the battle of Actium. Perhaps this more prosaic version should be preferred,[51] whether as a correction or as closer to the language of Josephus' source.[52] Moreover, it is in fact quite difficult to view the preliminary skirmishing as "the peak" of the war of Actium. Finally, note that the whole account in *BJ* here is troublesome, for it states that immediately after ("at the same time" — § 371) the earthquake (which, it will be recalled, occurred "at the beginning of spring"), and because of it, the Arabs attacked Herod, and he went out to war against them and defeated them — and

---

[49] W. Otto, *Herodes* (1913), col. 49, n. * (= *PWRE* Supplementband II [1913], col. 46, n. *); Schalit (above, n. 30), pp. 122–123, n. 98. Otto and Schalit's dating of the earthquake to the beginning of the spring of 31 is followed by many, including, most recently and explicitly, A. Kasher, *Jews, Idumaeans, and Ancient Arabs . . .* (1988), p. 138, n. 25.

[50] See E.G. Huzar, *Mark Antony: A Biography* (1978), pp. 216–219; J. M. Carter, *The Battle of Actium* (1970).

[51] For a remarkable dialogue between the deaf, note that Otto (above, n. 49) depends upon the *BJ* version and cites *Ant.* only with "vgl.," while E. Schwartz (above, n. 33: p. 266, n. 1 [= p. 127, n. 1 in the collection]), with whom Otto argued, who dated the earthquake to the year between autumn 31 and autumn 30, referred to *Antiquities* alone.

[52] For the general assumption that the language of *Antiquities'* account of Herod's reign is closer to that of Nicolaus than is the more elegant version in *BJ*, see S.J.D. Cohen, *Josephus in Galilee and Rome: His Vita and Development as a Historian* (1979), pp. 52–58; M. Stern in *Bible and Jewish History: Studies . . . Dedicated to the Memory of Jacob Liver* (ed. B. Uffenheimer, 1971), pp. 382–387 (in Hebrew); and my essay in *Scripta Classica Israelica* 10 (1989/90), pp. 120–127, where the contrast between a dramatic *BJ* (war at its peak) and *Ant.* (war over) is shown to be typical. As for corrections, note one with regard to this same year: although *BJ* 1.396 places the deaths of Anthony and Cleopatra before Augustus' arrival in Egypt, this incorrect detail was omitted in *Antiquities*. See L. Korach, *Über den Wert des Josephus als Quelle für die römische Geschichte* (1895), p. 76. Similarly, note with Korach (p. 76, n. 1, and p. 83) and Otto (above, n. 49: col. 51 [48]) that *Ant.* 15.196–201 reflects the use of two sources with regard to Augustus' travel through Palestine in 30 B.C.E., unlike *BJ* 1.394–396. In general, on the superiority of *Antiquities'* account in this general context, see A. Kasher, *Proceedings of the Israel Academy of Sciences and Humanities* 7/4 (1985/86), p. 113, n. 6 and p. 115, n. 10 (in Hebrew).

"immediately" thereafter (§ 386) went to Rhodes to make his submission to Augustus. But Augustus seems to have been in Rhodes in the spring of 30.[53] Therefore, it is likelier to date the earthquake and the war to the spring of 30. In any case, those who date the earthquake to the spring of 31 and the campaign to the summer of that year[54] must reject § 386 ("immediately"), and there is no apparent reason to prefer § 371 (even if it could be interpreted to refer to the Actian preliminaries) to § 386.

Given the contradiction between Josephus' parallel accounts and the internal difficulty in *BJ*, no firm conclusions may be drawn here. Nevertheless, it seems more reasonable to depend upon the more prosaic version of *Ant.* 15.121, which has the Actian campaign in the past and not "at its peak." If so, but if *BJ* is correct in placing the earthquake in the spring (a detail missing in *Ant.*), then it came in the spring of 30. That was Herod's eighth year given a Nisan 37 era, but his seventh, as Josephus says, given an era beginning in autumn 37, as we have argued.

Epilogue

As a final aside, we may note that the conclusion that Herod's Caesarean games were known as "Isactian" contributes not only to chronological conclusions. The corollary that the Herodians counted their years from Tishri leads us to recall the rabbinic assumption that "Israelite" kings count from Nisan and pagan ones from Tishri (see n. 32), and the conclusion that Agrippa I died in the wake of his attendance at games in honor of the emperor during the Jewish high holy day season is also worthy of attention. Here, however, we shall content ourselves with the introduction of this third-century inscription into the potential dossier for these first-century questions.[55]

---

[53] This is the usual dating. See, for example, Otto (above, n. 49), col. 50 [47]); Schalit (above, n. 30), p. 127; SVM I, pp. 289, 301. For Augustus' movements after Actium and meeting with Herod in Rhodes in spring 30, see Gardthausen (above, n. 31), II/1, pp. 410–411, also K. Fitzler and O. Seeck, *PWRE* I/19 (1918), cols. 332–334. I note, however, that in 1895 it was suggested to move the Rhodes meeting up to the autumn of 31 (see Korach [above, n. 52], pp. 74–75); no debate of this suggestion is known to me. It is based, primarily, upon Plutarch's narrative, which mentions Herod's submission to Augustus after Actium (*Vita Antonii* 71–72) prior to the winter of 31/30 (ibid. 74). But Rhodes is not mentioned, and Plutarch's reference to Herod's having "gone over to Caesar" need imply no more than acceptance of Augustus' suzerainty, rather than a meeting with him. On the other hand, *Ant.* 15.194–201 indicates that the Rhodes meeting was shortly before Augustus' trip to Egypt in the summer of 30.

[54] So, most recently, Kasher (above, n. 49), p. 138.

[55] For critique of the popular view of Agrippa I as a pious Jew or supporter of the Pharisees, see *Agrippa I*, pp. 116–130, 157–171. One part of that popular view, namely, the claim that

Appendix: *Ant.* 15.354

E. Schwartz, who in general tended to the conclusion that the Herodians used an autumnal era, thought to prove this from *Ant.* 15.354, where it is said that Augustus' visit in Syria in the summer of 20 B.C.E. came in Herod's twentieth year.[56] Schwartz does not cite the text of Josephus, but we may assume that he used Niese's standard edition, which is identical with Naber's: *ēdē . . . proelthontos*. Schwartz's conclusion shows he translated this to mean that Herod's twentieth year had "already progressed (considerably)," which is reasonable. Compare, for example, *Ant.* 19.186, where Josephus says "the night had progressed very much (*proelēluthei . . . epi mega*)." Schwartz apparently assumed that if the year began in Nisan one could not say this of a summer visit, even without *epi mega*. Here, however, there is room for doubt.

Moreover, a manuscript and the epitome, followed by Marcus, read *parelthontos*, which places the visit after the completion of Herod's seventeenth year. This conclusion fits the assumption that Herod counted his years from Nisan 37.[57] While no one should claim a firm rebuttal of Schwartz on the basis of this ill-attested reading, the additional doubt, in addition to the question as to how many months constitute "progressing," force us to leave Schwartz's proof-text aside.

---

rabbinic literature is "generally favorable" (or more) vis à vis "King Agrippa," has recently been restated by S. Schwartz (*Josephus and Judaean Politics* [1990], pp. 160–169), who rejects out of hand my characterization of the image, which he summarizes (p. 160, n. 174) as "largely unsympathetic." Schwartz makes no attempt to deal with the nuances of my account; rather, his condescending note seems to be no more than a way of exempting himself from dealing with a discussion which appeared (in the Hebrew original, which he cites) after he first composed his but three years before he published it. A major difference between our accounts lies in the fact that while both claim to deal with the general theme of "'King Agrippa' in Rabbinic Literature," his is in fact interested in early traditions only, those more or less contemporary with Agrippa II. This leads him to set aside, as late, the condemning traditions cited on my pp. 160–161 and his pp. 163–166, and totally to ignore the midrash (*Leviticus Rabbah* 3:5) I cite on pp. 165–166, where Agrippa is portrayed as ostentatious, in contrast to the true piety of a poor Jew.

[56] See Schwartz (above, n. 33).

[57] So it is not surprising that it was adopted by SVM I, pp. 291–292 and Smallwood, *Jews*, p. 88, n. 97. It is adopted by Gardthausen as well (above, n. 31: II/1, p. 471, n. 43), in the wake of Schürer, but an arithmetic (or printer's) error resulted in the conclusion that the text means Herod's seventeenth year *began* in Nisan 20.

3. Pontius Pilate's Appointment to Office
and the Chronology of Josephus' *Antiquities*, Books 18−20*

This study is primarily an analysis of Josephus' procedure in the arrangement of his narrative in *Ant.* 18−20. Those volumes are, of course, the basis for most of what is known concerning Jewish history from Herod's death until the outbreak of the rebellion of 66−73. However, it often happens that a particular issue may serve as a convenient leverage point for dealing with such a general topic. In this case, the date of Pontius Pilate's appointment to office is just such an issue.

According to Josephus, who attributes to Tiberius a parable comparing new governors to bloodthirsty flies, and veteran governors to sated flies (*Ant.* 18.170−176), that emperor − in order to minimize bloodsucking − sent only two governors to Judaea during his long reign (14−37 C.E.): Valerius Gratus and Pontius Pilate (§ 177). Other data in *Antiquities* confirm this statement: Tiberius appointed Gratus shortly after his own succession to the imperial throne (§§ 32−33), and, after Gratus had spent eleven years in Judaea (ibid. § 35), Pilate was appointed and served another ten years (§ 89), his term ending about the time of Tiberius' death (§ 89). Thus, the virtually unanimous opinion of scholarship is that Gratus served 14/15−26/27 and Pilate − 26/27−36/37.[1]

I. Eisler's Suggestion and its Rejection

"*Virtually* unanimous opinion of scholarship" − the exception was Robert Eisler, who suggested, more than half a century ago, that Pilate was appointed in 19 C.E., or perhaps in late 18.[2] His case rested on two main arguments:

---

* Hebrew original: *Zion* 48 (1982/83), pp. 325−345.

[1] The minor disagreements about 14 or 15, 26 or 27, and 36 or 37 will not concern us here. On them, see U. Holzmeister, *Biblica* 13 (1932), pp. 228−232; E. M. Smallwood, *JJS* 5 (1954), pp. 12−21 (and eadem, *Jews*, pp. 171−172, n. 93); and below, pp. 202−217.

[2] See his *Iēsous Basileus ou Basileusas*, I (1929), pp. 125−130 (in German); idem, *The Messiah Jesus and John the Baptist* (1931), pp. 13−20. The English version of the massive German original is abridged but also corrected.

1) Josephus' short account of Gratus (*Ant.* 18.33–35) deals only with the the appointment and firing of high priests, and since it says three served only a year or "a short time" each and after the fourth appointment we hear of Gratus' return to Rome, it gives the impression that Gratus' tenure in office was only about four years; 2) Eusebius (*Hist. eccl.* 1.9) refers to a report of Jesus' trial which Pilate was said to have sent to Rome during Tiberius' fourth consulate, which was in 21 C.E. While Eusebius saw the date as proof that the report was false,[3] Eisler argued that the report was authentic.

Eisler's suggestion was rejected universally during the first few years after it appeared, in large measure because it came along with a much larger web of revolutionary theory about the Slavonic Josephus and the careers of John the Baptist and Jesus.[4] However, if we ignore the latter and examine our chronological question alone, his approach may now appear to be more worthy of examination.

First of all, let us examine the specific arguments which were adduced against Eisler's case. The first was numismatic: the style of Judaean coins from the years 15/16, 16/17, 17/18, 18/19 and 24/25 is generally stable, but differs from that of the years 28/29–31/32, and this was widely taken to imply a change in governor between the former and the latter.[5] But the numismatic data is ambiguous, because one could with the same justification wonder if the stoppage of annual coinage after 18/19 does not point to a switch in governors.[6]

---

[3] Cf. *Hist. eccl.* 1.11 (end); 9.5, 7.

[4] Numerous reviews of the German original are listed on pp. 629–630 of the English version (above, n. 2). See especially M. Goguel, *Revue historique* 162 (1929), pp. 217–267 (!) and H. Lewy, *Deutsche Literaturzeitung*, 3. Folge, 1 (1930), cols. 481–494. Additionally, three *books* were published in rebuttal of Eisler: A. Goethals, *Anti-Eisler: Un peu de polémique* (1932); J. W. Jack, *The Historic Christ* (1933); and W. Bienert, *Der älteste nichtchristliche Jesusbericht* (1936). For criticism of the chronological aspects of Eisler's theory in particular, see Goguel, pp. 245–253; W. F. Howard, in *Amicitiae Corolla: A Volume of Essays Presented to James Rendel Harris* (ed. H. G. Wood; 1933), pp. 125–132; and G. Ogg, *The Chronology of the Public Ministry of Jesus* (1940), pp. 277–285. As further indication of the total rejection Eisler encountered, note that Holzmeister, in an article on Pilate's chronology (above, n. 1), didn't even mention Eisler, although it is clear that he was aware of his work (see p. 93, n. 2, in the same volume of *Biblica*); cf. above, p. 141, n. 35. It is quite remarkable that recently J. Ernst still thought it necessary to devote a few pages to rejecting "Das Täuferbild des Robert Eisler" (*Johannes der Täufer* [1989], pp. 261–263). On Eisler, who was a fascinating character, see G. Scholem, *Von Berlin nach Jerusalem: Jugenderinnerungen* (1977), pp. 161–169 (pp. 127–132 in English adition).

[5] So P. L. Hedley, *JTS* 35 (1934), pp. 56–57, followed by many, including Feldman, p. 31, n. c.; J. Blinzler, *Der Prozeß Jesu* (1969⁴), p. 40, n. 6; and H. W. Hoehner, *Herod Antipas* (1972), p. 177.

[6] We may note, in passing, that if A. Kindler were right about having found "New Dates on the Coins of the Procurators" (*IEJ* 6 [1956], pp. 54–57), adding in coins for the years 19–22 and 24/25, then this whole argument would disappear. But numismatists tend not to accept

As for the report Eusebius mentioned, scholars generally argued, following Eusebius, that it was a fourth-century anti-Christian forgery.[7] In particular, it was argued that 1) it is doubtful that Pilate would have sent any report on Jesus' trial; 2) it is doubtful that such a report, if sent, would have survived to the fourth century; and 3) if such a report had previously been available, anti-Christian polemicists would not have waited so long to use it. However, convincing as these arguments are, they show only that the report was a fourth-century fraud. They do not explain why the forgers dated the report to a year which anyone who troubled to glance at Josephus, as Eusebius did, could prove wrong. Were the forgers really so stupid?[8] Is it not simpler to assume that their copies of Josephus did not give the numbers "eleven" and "ten" for Gratus' and Pilate's years in Judaea? That is, should we not assume that these numbers in our text reflect corruption or, as Eisler suspected, deliberate Christian rewriting to disprove the false *Acta Pilati*?[9] In any case, it is curious, or suspicious, that, of all seventeen Roman governors of Judaea mentioned by Josephus, only for Gratus and Pilate are we given data regarding the length of their tenures.[10]

---

these readings. See B. Oesterreicher, *IEJ* 9 (1959), pp. 193–195; A. Spijkerman, *Studii Biblici Franciscani Liber Annuus* 13 (1962/63), p. 310; and Y. Meshorer, *Ancient Jewish Coinage*, II (1982), pp. 173–177.

[7] Of those mentioned in n. 4, above, see esp. Goguel, pp. 246–248, Goethals, pp. 29–30, and Jack, pp. 220–229; see also Blinzler (above, n. 5), pp. 39–40, and A. Steinwenter, *Jus* 3 (1952), pp. 473–474. Eusebius (*Hist. eccl.* 9.5) dates the forgery to the reign of Maximin II (305–313 C.E.).

[8] In order to overcome this obvious difficulty, some have suggested that the spurious *Acta* were dated not according to Tiberius' regnal years, but rather to his fourth consulate. According to this theory, it was Eusebius who correctly translated this into Tiberius' seventh year (21 CE.), although the forgers had mistakenly thought that it came in 31 C.E. – which would have tallied with Josephus' data for Pilate. Such an error is indeed found in the *Fasti Idatiani*, and it is possible that a similar source misled the forgers of the *Acta Pilati*. See Ogg (above, n. 4) pp. 284–285, in the wake of R. A. Lipsius, *Die Pilatus-Akten* (1871), p. 31. But this acute suggestion only moves its defenders from the frying pan into the fire, for in order to avoid the notion that Romans were not familiar with Josephus they must assume that they were not familiar with Tacitus, Cassius Dio and Suetonius, for the first two correctly place Tiberius' fourth consulate in 21 C.E. (*Ann.* 3.31.1; CD 57.20), and the third denotes the one of 31 C.E. as his fifth (*Tiberius* 65). There was also much additional epigraphic evidence for the fact that Tiberius' fourth consulate – shared with his son Drusus, who was killed in 23 C.E.! – was in 21 C.E., and the fifth in 31 C.E.; see *Dizionario epigraphico di antichità Romane*, II (1910), pp. 1082–1083. Finally, I shall note that the impression one gets from reading *Hist. eccl.* 1.9 is that Eusebius found the regnal year in the document. Had he computed it himself, we would have expected him to point out the problem and cite evidence concerning the consulate's date.

[9] Eisler (above, n. 2), pp. 128–130 (p. 17 in the English version).

[10] Josephus mentions fourteen governors in *Ant.* (or twelve, if we eliminate Marcellus and Marullus [37–41 C.E.] – *Agrippa I*, pp. 62–66), some of whom in *BJ* as well, and another

Parenthetically, we may exclude from our discussion the fact that Luke 3:1, which places the appearance of John in Tiberius' fifteenth year, and prior to Jesus' public career, contradicts other aspects of Eisler's thesis, as do some less explicit New Testament data.[11] Eisler was forced to claim that these data were wrong, and he invested a good bit of energy and ingenuity in explaining the source of the error.[12] We, however, are not concerned with dating the trial of Jesus and are pointing to the fourth-century *Acta Pilati* only as evidence for what some ancients thought about the beginning of Pilate's tenure.[13] Therefore, we can ignore this matter, since there is nothing in the New Testament to indicate when Pilate was appointed or how far into his tenure the case of Jesus of Nazareth was brought before him.

It thus appears that the chronological question is still open. Over against Josephus' specific data, the facts remain that Gratus' term reads as if it was only four years long, and the annual appointments of high priests and annual coin issues both seem to have ceased around 19 C.E. Were it not for Josephus' numbers, these two points would lead naturally to the conclusion that this is when Gratus was replaced. But Josephus' numbers themselves are somewhat suspect, not only because numbers are very susceptible to corruption, but also because they are the only ones Josephus gives for governors and fourth-century forgers may not have had them in their texts of Josephus.

II. The Chronology of *Ant.* 18–20

Eisler brought one further argument in favor of fixing Pilate's appointment to 18/19 C.E.: after the first events of Pilate's term (*Ant.* 18.55–64), but before the final event of his term, which led to his removal from office (§§ 85–89), Josephus brings, beginning with "and at this time," some scandalous stories culminating in the punishment of Isis-worshippers and expulsion of the Jews of Rome. These events occurred, according to Tacitus (*Ann.* 2.85) and some

three, up to Flavius Silva, in *BJ* alone. For convenient lists of them and references to Josephus, see SVM I, pp. 382–383, 455–470, 515.

[11] For the chronology of Jesus, see inter alia H. W. Hoehner, *Chronological Aspects of the Life of Christ* (1977), with ample references to the data and literature.

[12] See his magnum opus (above, n. 2), II, pp. 123–160 (288–311 in English), also *Revue archéologique*, 5ᵉ série, 32 (1930), pp. 116–126. On the lack of certainty among early Christians concerning the chronology of Jesus and Pilate, see also R. M. Grant, *HTR* 33 (1940), pp. 151–154.

[13] It is noteworthy that T. Mommsen considered the early date assigned to Pilate a sign of the antiquity of the source which lay behind the spurious *Acta*: see his *Gesammelte Schriften*, III (1907), p. 424, n. 2 (= *ZNW* 3 [1902], p. 199, n. 1).

other evidence, in 19 C.E.[14] It follows, therefore, that Pilate was already governor of Judaea "at this time."

However, according to a very widely held view, the last books of *Antiquities*, and especially Book 18, excel in chronological confusion. The fact that, in these books, Josephus brings early events late and late events early shows "Josephus' failure to interweave his sources properly from a chronological point of view,"[15] or, worse, "scarsa cura chronologica;"[16] expressions such as "at that time" are nothing but "Verlegenheitsphrasen;"[17] etc.[18] If so, however, then it is improper to draw any conclusion from the inclusion of the Roman events among the events of Pilate's term.

Moreover, this general rejection has been supported, in this case, by two specific arguments which have suggested *why* Josephus would have departed here from the chronological framework of Pilate's term of office. Neither, however, quite does the job:

The first theory, best known as Ed. Norden's,[19] holds that Josephus' chapter on Pilate has a leitmotiv of *thoryboi*, "tumults" (*Ant.* 18.58, 62, 65, 88 and esp. 85), and, therefore, since he viewed the Roman events as such events, he included them here despite the chronological incongruity.[20] However: a) There is no justification for terming the Roman events *thoryboi*[21] (the

---

[14] See Stern, in *GLA* II, pp. 68–71.

[15] M. Stern, *Zion* 44 (1978/79 = *Yitzhak F. Baer Memorial Volume*, 1980), p. 15 (in Hebrew). As in *GLA* II, p. 70, Stern especially cites the placement of the foundation of Tiberias prior to the death of Phraates IV (*Ant.* 18.36–39), although the latter event preceded the former by two decades. Similarly, others complain about Josephus' placing of the foundation of Tiberias (§§ 36 ff.) after the appointment of Pilate (§ 35), contrary to their true order; see, for example, A. Kindler, in *Jerusalem in the Second Temple Period: Abraham Schalit Memorial Volume* (edd. A. Oppenheimer, U. Rappaport and M. Stern; 1980), pp. 281–282 (in Hebrew) and S. J. D. Cohen, *Josephus in Galilee and Rome: His Vita and Development as a Historian* (1979), p. 65. Cf. below, n. 34.

[16] A. Garzetti, in *Studi in onore di Aristide Calderini e Roberto Paribeni*, I (1956), pp. 217–219. Garzetti cites examples from Otto (see our next note).

[17] So W. Otto, *Herodes* (1913), cols. 186–187,; cf. ibid. 180–181, n. * (= *PWRE* Supplementband II [1913], cols. 179–180; 172–174, n. *).

[18] See, for example, the standard statements in SVM I, p. 58, and in *PWRE* I/18 (1916), col. 1983: "Von Buch XVIII ab lockert sich der bis dahin ziemlich feste Faden der Erzählung . . . Dazu ist die chronologische Ordnung der Erzählungen vielfach sehr mangelhaft . . ." (G. Hölscher).

[19] See his essay on the Testimonium Flavianum in *Neue Jahrbücher für das klassische Altertum, Geschichte und deutsche Literatur* 31 (1913), pp. 638–644, reprinted in his *Kleine Schriften zum klassischen Altertum* (ed. B. Kytzler; 1966), pp. 243–249.

[20] "Josephus hat also . . . mechanisch . . . dem Schema zuliebe zwei Skandale des Jahres 19 aus der einen Quelle herauslöst und sie mit Skandalen der Jahre 26–36 zu einer Serie vereinigt" (Norden, above, n. 19: p. 644 [=249]).

[21] Eisler (above, n. 2), p. 26 (p. 42 in English) similarly notes that the first episode is no *thorybos* (or *stasis*), but rather only a social scandal. Strangely, however, he does admit, but only in the German version (p. 125), that the term can apply to the second affair.

others in this chapter are real riots or almost such), so if Josephus nevertheless pinned the term to them, it must be because he thought they belonged here and therefore took care to make them fit the literary theme as well; and b) if Josephus had thought the Roman events preceded Pilate's term, he could have recounted them just *before* the events of Pilate's term, and thereby kept the same number of successive *thoryboi* without disturbing the chronology. This would have had yet another advantage, namely, it would have allowed Josephus to unify his narrative of Pilate's term in Judaea from beginning to end without interruptions in Rome.

The second theory suggests that Josephus inserted the Roman events here because he wanted to comment, as it were, on his account of Jesus, which immediately precedes them (*Ant.* 18.63−64).[22] According to this theory, the original version of the Testimonium Flavianum referred to the Virgin Birth, and the Roman stories − which both deal with naive women and religious charlatans, one precisely with pretended divine impregnation − were meant as a sort of burlesque of the Christian belief. But it is very difficult to accept this explanation, ingenious as it is, for the current version of the Testimonium says nothing of the Virgin Birth, nor does the medieval Arabic version (which some believe original).[23] Moreover, it is not at all sure that the belief in the Virgin Birth was already current in Josephus' day.[24] Jewish and pagan criticism of the belief is not in evidence before the second century.[25]

Having thus rejected the two theories which were meant to explain why Josephus might have deliberately departed from true chronology in inserting the Roman events of 19 C.E. in the midst of Pilate's affairs, we are left with the general question of the chronological reliability of this part of *Antiquities*. In my opinion, the notion that Josephus did not know the chronology of this period (the two decades preceding his birth) or that he did not care to reproduce it properly is generally mistaken, and derives from a mis-

---

[22] See C. Pharr, *American Journal of Philology* 48 (1927), pp. 142−147; A. A. Bell, *JQR* 67 (1976/77), pp. 16−22. For criticism of this theory, see A.-M. Dubarle, *RB* 84 (1977), pp. 38−47.

[23] See S. Pines, *An Arabic Version of the Testimonium Flavianum and its Implications* (1971); D. Flusser, *Entdeckungen im Neuen Testament* (1987), pp. 216−225. For further literature on this version, see L. H. Feldman, *Josephus and Modern Scholarship (1937−1980)* (1984), pp. 700−703. On research on the "Testimonium Flavianum" in general, see ibid., pp. 679−699, also Feldman and Z. Baras in *Josephus, Judaism, and Christianity* (edd. L. H. Feldman and G. Hata; 1987), pp. 55−58 and 338−348; add, among more recent studies, G. Vermes, *JJS* 38 (1987), pp. 1−10 and J. P. Meier, *CBQ* 52 (1990), pp. 76−99.

[24] This is not to doubt the antiquity of the use of the term "son of God" with regard to Jesus (see M. Hengel, *The Son of God* [1976]). The question is whether it was early understood in the carnal sense, and not only spiritually (of God's primordial or "adoptionist" paternity). See M. Enslin, *JBL* 59 (1940), pp. 317−324; R. H. Fuller, *Biblical Research* 1 (1957), pp. 1−8; and G. Vermes, *Jesus the Jew* (1973), pp. 213−222.

[25] See R. E. Brown, *The Birth of the Messiah* (1979), pp. 534−542.

understanding of his methods.[26] In order to understand this matter properly, one must take cognizance of the variety of subjects with which Josephus had to deal, and of the structural methods which he used to organize his
disparate material.

It is clear that the chronological backbone of this period, beginning with the
death of Herod, was supplied by the succession of rulers of Judaea:[27]
Archelaus (4 B.C.E.−6 C.E.), governors (6−37), Gaius Caligula and
Agrippa I (37−43/44),[28] and again governors (44−66). But, alongside this
central line, there were other personalities and events which Josephus wanted
to include: the Herodians (apart from the rulers of Judaea), high priests,
Parthian kings, Jews of the Diaspora and Roman emperors. How may these
various but chronologically parallel sets of information, frequently deriving
from different sources, be interwoven? A detailed review of *Ant.* 18−20 shows
that Josephus took a very simple course: he defined chapters according to the
successive rulers of Judaea, and in each chapter, after recounting the "central"
events of that chapter (those concerning the rule of Judaea), he then
recounted the other events belonging to the same period of time. It is as if
Josephus organized his files behind major dividers for each of the rulers of
Judaea, and then wrote them up, first recounting the *res gestae* of that ruler,
then whatever else happened "at that time" − i.e., during that same period.
The following table illustrates this. In the notes to it, we will attempt to justify
only those chronological data which are both controversial and affect our
understanding of Josephus' method of arranging the material.

---

[26] For other defenses of Josephus' chronology here, see G. Volkmar, *Jahrbücher für
protestantische Theologie* 11 (1885), pp. 138−145, and S. Giet, *Revue des études
Augustiniennes* 2 (1956), pp. 244−248. From both, I learned the need to understand the
chronology of *Ant.* 18 according to the order of its chapters. However, both used such an
understanding in order to explain why the chapter on Pilate includes episodes which do not
belong there chronologically (Volkmar: the "chapter" is in fact defined not by Pilate's
governorship, but rather by Tiberius' reign [so too J. Kep[p]ler, as early as 1613; see his
Gesammelte Werke, V (ed. F. Hammer; 1953), pp. 161−162]; Giet: Josephus deliberately
applied the literary device of "chronological anticipation" [but he does not explain the rules
or situations which governed the use of such a device]). In my opinion, a broader analysis of
these books will show that the events do indeed belong, chronologically, in a chapter on
Pilate.

[27] For Josephus' obvious strategy of using successive rulers to supply a chronological
backbone for a period, see also, on the Persian period, *JQR* 72 (1981/82), pp. 252−254.

[28] Josephus divided 37−43/44 into three chapters: 37−39 on Agrippa; 39−41 on Gaius (the
Temple-statue affair and his assassination); 41−43/44 on Agrippa. He could not continue the
organization according to governors, for the years 37−41, for, it seems, there were none; see
above, n. 10. Even if there were, however, it is clear that Josephus had no information about
their activities.

Chap.	Ant.	Topic	Years
A	17.399−18.26[29]	Archelaus' rule and exile; reorganization	4 B.C.E.− 6 C.E.
a/1	18.27−28	Antipas and Philip build cities	3−2 B.C.E.[30]
B	18.29a	Coponius' governorship[31]	6−9 C.E.[32]
b/1	18.29b−30	"During C's governorship"− scandal in Temple	6−9
C	18.31a	M. Ambivulus' governorship	9−12
c/1	18.31b	"In his days"−death of Salome	9−12
D	18.32a	A. Rufus' governorship	12−14/15
d/1	18.32b−33a	"In his days"−Augustus dies, Tiberius rules	14

---

[29] Note that here, as in Chapter H, chapters may cut across the divisions between "books" of the *Antiquities*. This corresponds to the fact that Josephus shows no particular awareness of beginning a new book at the onset of *Ant.* 18 and *Ant.* 19. At the beginning of *Ant.* 20, in contrast, Josephus specifically refers to the closing event of the preceding "book" − and according to our analysis too, a new chapter (J) begins at this point.

[30] Four cities are mentioned here: Sepphoris-Autocratoris, Betharamphta-Julias, Paneas-Caesarea (Philippi) and Bethsaïda-Julia. The coins of Paneas show its municipal era began in 3 B.C.E., and, according to Josephus, Bethsaïda was renamed "Julia" in honor of Augustus' daughter, who we know was banished in 2 B.C.E.; if Josephus' statement is correct, then it follows that this city too was founded within a year or two of Herod's death. See SVM II, pp. 170−172. (Lately, A. Kindler has argued from numismatic evidence, with conviction, that the latter city was in fact named after Augustus' widow, Livia-Julia, who died in 29 C.E.; see *Cathedra* 53 [September 1989], pp. 24−26 [in Hebrew]. If this is true, the result is only that Josephus erred in linking the city's name to Augustus' daughter, but not that Josephus departed from his organizational system; cf. below, notes 39, 41.) As for Sepphoris, Hoehner (above, n. 5: p. 85) argues that it too was probably founded in 3/2 B.C.E., for it was Antipas' home prior to the construction of Tiberias. For Betharamphta-Julias, finally, we have no data concerning the date of its foundation, and can only infer from the fact that it is mentioned alongside three founded within a year or two of Herod's death. (Hoehner, ibid., pp. 89−91 suggested 13 C.E., but without any substantial argument; picking an important year in Julia's life or Augustus', at which time it would have been appropriate to honor them, is like picking a year out of a hat.) Note that the summary introduction of this section (§ 27) juxtaposes the accession of Antipas and Philip (after Herod's death) to their foundation of cities, which seems to imply chronological propinquity as well.

[31] In fact, Josephus doesn't mention any central materials concerning Cumanus. These eleven words ("While Coponius . . . was ruling Judaea, the following occurred") come only to maintain the chronological organization of the narrative; it is, as it were, a divider in Josephus' cardfile behind which he found nothing "central" to insert. The same is the case in chapters C and D as well. The fact that Josephus nonetheless maintained such headings testifies to the steadfastness with which he held to this chronological plan.

[32] The conventional division of the years 6−15 C.E. equally among Coponius and his two successors is no more than a guess.

Chap.	*Ant.*	*Topic*	*Years*
E	18.33b−35	V. Gratus' governorship; Pilate appointed	14/15− ?[33]
e/1	18.36−38	Antipas builds Tiberias	19−21[34]
e/2	18.39−54	"At that time"−Parthian affairs, Armenia, Germanicus' mission to East and death there[36]	2 B.C.E.− 19 C.E.[35]
F	18.55−64	Pilate's governorship in Judaea	? − 37[37]
f/1	18.65−80a	"In those days"−Isis scandal	19
f/2	18.80b−84	"At that time"−Jewish scandal in Rome	19
f/3	18.85−89	Pilate suppresses Samaritans and is removed from office	37
f/4	18.90−95	Vitellius and the high-priestly vestments	37[38]
f/5	18.96−126a	Vitellius, the Parthians, Antipas and the Nabateans; Philip dies	34−37[39]

---

[33] This date, which is more or less that of Pilate's appointment (below: F), is at issue in the present study.

[34] Numismatic data show Tiberias was founded ca. 19 C.E.: apart from second-century coins which narrow the range down to 17−23 C.E., the crucial evidence is supplied by a coin of Antipas' twenty-fourth year which apparently celebrates the city's foundation (see Meshorer [above, n. 6] pp. 35−37 and Kindler [above, n. 15]); cf. S. Qedar, *INJ* 9 [1986/87], pp. 29−35). It is not clear whether Antipas' years should be counted from 5/4 B.C.E. or from a year later, so I have left the range as 19−21 C.E. See also below, pp. 267−268.

[35] Some scholars argue that the notice about Orodes' rule of Armenia (§ 52) refers to an event of 35 C.E. (cf. Tacitus, *Ann.* 6.33); so, for example, M.-L. Chaumont, *ANRW* II/9.1 (1976), p. 85. But it is more reasonable to assume, as many others (see her n. 71), that the notice is in place and refers to the years 15/16−18. See esp. E. Täubler, *Die Parthernachrichten bei Josephus* (1904), pp. 9−15, also M. Pani, *Roma e i re d'Oriente da Augusto a Tiberio* (1972), pp. 173−215.

[36] For justification of the view of all these varied events as belonging to one chapter, see below, at n. 55.

[37] The beginning of Pilate's term is at issue in the present study. As for the end of his term, see above, n. 1.

[38] This episode came in the context of Vitellius' goodwill visit to Jerusalem after removing Pilate from office. Thus, although strictly speaking it came after the end of the period defined by Pilate's term as governor, Josephus could include this episode here because it rounds out that story. Cf. below, n. 67. For the chronology, see below, pp. 202−217.

[39] This section also mentions the death of John the Baptist, which probably occurred in 30 or 31 C.E. (see Hoehner [above, n. 5], pp. 131). However, it is clearly a "flashback" (Hoehner, pp. 127−128), and, therefore, does not upset the scheme. See also G. Hölscher,

Chap.	Ant.	Topic	Years
G	18.126b−255	Agrippa I's early career, up until Gaius becomes mad[40]	10 B.C.E.− 39 C.E.
H	18.256−309	Gaius Caligula's rule of Judaea	39−41
h/1	18.310−379 (end of Bk. 18)	Parthian Jewish affairs	20−41[41]
h/2	19.1−274	Murder of Gaius, enthrone- ment of Claudius	41
h/3	19.275−276a	Claudius makes kings (including Agrippa)	41
h/4	19.276b−277	Herodian family affairs[42]	41−43/44[43]
h/5	19.278−291	Claudius and Diaspora Jewry	41

Die Hohenpriesterliste bei Josephus und die evangelische Chronologie (Sitzungsberichte der Heidelberger Akademie der Wissenschaften, Philosophisch-historische Klasse, Jg. 1939/40, 3. Abh.; 1940), pp. 28−30. (There are perennial suggestions to move John's death down to ca. 36, thus eliminating the need to view this passage as a flashback; so, inter alia, W. Schenk, *NTS* 29 [1983], pp. 453−483, criticized by C. Saulnier, *RB* 91 [1984], pp. 362−376, whose argument, however, rests on "les confusions chronologiques de Flavius Josèphe." One way or another, either as flashback or as in its proper chronological context, this paragraph poses no difficulty in our current context. As for its text and authenticity, see E. Nodet, *RB* 92 [1985], esp. pp. 322−331.) As for the negotiations with the Parthians described in §§ 101−105, some scholars believe that they in fact belong to the period after Tiberius' death; so, especially, Garzetti (above, n. 16), pp. 211−229. However, even if this is so, it would not affect our understanding of Josephus' methods, for he clearly thought the events belonged to Tiberius' reign; see the end of § 105. Moreover, many scholars agree with Josephus; see the literature cited by Garzetti, pp. 215−216, n. 18 (esp. Täubler [above, n. 35], pp. 39−46), and add Chaumont (above, n. 35), pp. 90−91.

[40] On Josephus' division of Gaius' rule between sanity and insanity, and comparison with other sources, see Feldman, p. 151, n. b and p. 213, n. b.

[41] See A. von Gutschmid, *Kleine Schriften*, III (ed. F. Rühl; 1892), pp. 52−55; R. H. McDowell, *Coins from Seleucia on the Tigris* (1935), pp. 224−226; N. C. Debevoise, *A Political History of Parthia* (1938), p. 156, n. 54; J. Neusner, *A History of the Jews of Babylonia*, I (1969²), p. 54, n. 1; and, most recently, D. Goodblatt, *Journal of the American Oriental Society* 107 (1987), esp. pp. 616−622. Goodblatt argues that Josephus wrongly combined two episodes, whereas in fact that of Asineus and Anileus transpired somewhat later than the Seleucia affair which ended in 41 C.E. Even if so, however, this − as the cases discussed in our notes 30, 39 and 67 − would not affect our understanding of Josephus' method of organizing his sources; it would mean only that Josephus had his facts wrong here. For him, it was clear that the episode of the two brothers occurred before the Seleucia disaster.

[42] Were it not for the reference to Antiochus IV of Commagene in h/3, it would have been possible to view h/3 and h/4 as one section, dealing with Herodian affairs upon the accession of Claudius to the throne. Given the marriage ties linking Antiochus to the Herodians (*Ant.* 18.140, 19.335 and 20.139), this remains a possibility.

[43] For the death of Marcus Julius Alexander in late 43 or early 44, see A. Fuks, *Journal of Juristic Papyrology* 5 (1951), pp. 214−215 (= idem, *Social Conflicts in Ancient Greece* [1984], pp. 319−320), more fully argued by Fuks in *Zion* 13−14 (1948/49), pp. 14−17 (in Hebrew).

Chap.	Ant.	Topic	Years
I	19.292−366	Agrippa I, King of Judaea; his death; Fadus appointed governor	41−43/44
	(end of Bk. 19)		
J	20.1−5	Fadus' governorship	44−46
j/1	20.6−16	"also then" − Herod of Chalcis and the high priesthood	44−45[44]
j/2	20.17−96	"and at that time" − the conversion to Judaism of royalty in Adiabene	1−60(?)[45]
j/3	20.97−99	"and during Fadus' governor-ship"−Theudas affair	44−46
K	20.100−102	Tiberius Julius Alexander's governorship	46−48
k/1	20.103−104	Herod of Chalcis and high priesthood; Cumanus appointed governor;[47] Herod dies, Agrippa II rules	48/49[46]
L	20.105−137	Cumanus' governorship; his exile and Felix's appointment	48−49[48]
l/1	20.138−147	Agrippa II and his family	52−79
l/2	20.148−157	Claudius dies, Nero reigns	54/55
l/3	20.158−159	Herodians in Armenia, Galilee and Transjordan	55

---

[44] For the date, see *Ant.* 20.14 and below, p. 225, n. 30.

[45] For attempts to reconstruct the chronology of the Adiabene story, which ends in 62 C.E. at the latest (Feldman, p. 439, n. c.; Stern, *GLA* II, p. 86), see N. Brüll, *Jahrbücher für Jüdische Geschichte und Literatur* 1 (1874), pp. 65−72, and H. Graetz, *Geschichte der Juden* III/2 (ed. M. Brann; 1906⁵), pp. 786−790 (= *MGWJ* 26 [1877], pp. 241−255).

[46] The chronology of these events is dealt with below, pp. 224−227.

[47] The presence of this "central" event among the "other" events is surprising. As we have suggested elsewhere (below, pp. 224−225), it may be assumed that this is secondary, reflecting Josephus' decision to correct his original narrative, which followed the order found in *BJ* 2.221−223, according to which Cumanus was appointed after Herod of Chalcis died. That order fits the rules, but was apparently wrong, chronologically, and Josephus apparently decided to rearrange these details so as to reflect their true order.

[48] The usual dates for Cumanus, Felix and Festus are 48−52; 52−60 (or: 52−55); and 60−62 (or 55−62). Elsewhere (below, pp. 218−242), I have argued instead for 48−49; 49−55; and 55−62. These differences do not matter in the present context.

Chap.	Ant.	Topic	Years
M	20.160–178	Felix's governorship	49–55
m/1	20.179–181	"at that time" – Agrippa II and the high priests	49[49]
N	20.182–188	Festus appointed; Jews complain about Felix; Festus' governorship	55–62
n/1	20.189–196	"at that time": Agrippa and high priesthood in Festus' days	55–62
n/2	20.197–203	Agrippa and high priesthood, between Festus and Albinus	62
O	20.204–210	Albinus' governorship	62–64
o/1	20.211–214	"at that time" – Agrippa, his family and the high priesthood	
o/2	20.215	Florus appointed governor; more about Albinus	64
o/3	20.216–218	Agrippa and the Levites	
o/4	20.219–223	"also then" – Agrippa, the Temple and the high priesthood	–[50]
P	20.224–251	summary of high priesthood, from origin to end	–[51]
Q	20.252–258	Florus' procuratorship (brief summary)[52]	64–66
R	20.259–268	Conclusion	

---

[49] Josephus gives no date for the appointment of Ishmael ben Phiabi. See below, pp. 218–242.

[50] There are no explicit chronological data in o/1, o/3 and o/4; only their location indicates that they belong to Albinus' tenure.

[51] This summary of the whole history of the high priesthood, from beginning to destruction, necessarily transcends the borders of the chapter on Albinus, and should be viewed as a part of the book's conclusion. This is confirmed by the brevity of *Ant.*'s narrative of Florus' tenure (Q), which is only a teleological resume concluding with a reference to the detailed account in *BJ* and then, finally, by the formal conclusion of *Ant.* (R). That is, the historical period covered by *Ant.* concludes with Albinus' tenure.

[52] See the preceding note.

As promised, this table exhibits the main rule which Josephus followed in organizing his material. He divided the period into successive chapters according to the rulers of Judaea, and then, within each chapter, first gave the "central" events of the period, then, as if "appendices," the other events of the period. His conception is made particularly clear by the way he frequently introduces "other" material with the words "in his days" or the like, referring to the previously-named ruler.

However, it is true that there are a number of exceptions to this rule, apparent or otherwise. One chapter, G, begins long before the previous one; seven appendices (e/2, h/1, h/4, j/2, l/1−3) go beyond the chronological bounds of the chapter to which we assigned them; and in two cases (j/3, o/2) Josephus returns to "central" events of a chapter after he had already dealt with them and had even finished the "other" events of the same chapter. Do not these exceptions destroy our claim that a serious and systematic chronological framework informs these books?

Let us begin by acknowledging that we see no way of explaining, within the system, the two last-mentioned difficulties (j/3 and o/2). As we have suggested elsewhere, o/2 (*Ant.* 20.215), a confused and self-contradictory paragraph, was composed due to a special reason and reflects Josephus' confusion in the course of attempting to combine two contradictory sources.[53] It is not surprising that Josephus departed here from his usual practice. No such excuse regarding j/3 (*Ant.* 20.97−99) suggests itself. Perhaps here too we must simply allow Josephus less than perfection; or perhaps we should give him some benefit of doubt, in light of the fact that this section is not listed in an ancient "table of contents" which was transmitted along with his manuscripts.[54]

Apart from these two, it seems that all the other exceptions may be understood on the basis of two guidelines which Josephus followed in applying his basic rule.

The first guideline is, that a long story is to be inserted at its chronological focus, not necessarily at its beginning or end. Thus:

1. e/2: There is no chronological focus to this long discussion of the Parthian kings, until its end links it up with Armenia, Commagene, Germanicus' mission to the east (17 C.E.) and his death there (in 19): as Tacitus explains (*Ann.* 2.42.7−43.1), the situations in Armenia and Commagene were among the prime reasons for the mission.[55] Therefore, 17−19 C.E. is to be viewed as

---

[53] See *JQR* 72 (1981/82), pp. 258−262.

[54] See Feldman, pp. 548−549. It is perhaps noteworthy that Acts 5:35−37 makes a crass chronological error concerning Theudas, placing him before Judas the Galilean although the latter preceded him by forty years. However, even if j/3 had appeared in its proper place, before j/1, it would not account for this mistake. For an explanation − not at all original − of the genesis of Acts' error, see *Agrippa* I, p. 215, n. 12.

[55] And they were, accordingly, the scene of Germanicus' most impressive accom-

the chronological focus here — years in the course of Gratus' term by any reckoning. Everything earlier is only background information.

2. G: While it is true that the story of Agrippa I begins with his birth (11/10 B.C.E.), the chapter's opening (*Ant.* 18.126b), as a heading, places the story at the point of Tiberius' death (37 C.E.). Everything which precedes this point is only background information.

3. h/1: Although the story of Asinaeus and Anilaeus begins ca. 20 C.E., the story's opening (*Ant.* 18.310) defines it as one about a terrible disaster which befell the Jews of Babylonia. This plainly refers to the slaughter of the Jews of Seleucia, which concludes this long "appendix." It occurred, apparently, in 41 C.E., as various factors indicate.[56] It was according to this focus that the whole story was inserted.

4. h/4: The focus of the story, as the preceding one, is upon what Claudius did upon ascending to the imperial throne in 41 C.E., including the release of Alexander the Alabarch from prison, just as the preceding sections reported Agrippa I's enthronement. When Josephus here records the subsequent marriage of Agrippa's daughter to Alexander's son, and her remarriage after being widowed, these are only marginalia to the main story.

5. j/2: This long account of the royal house of Adiabene is introduced, in its heading (*Ant.* 20.17), as an account of how Izates and his mother, Helene, "adopted the Jewish way of life," i.e., how they converted. When did this occur? To determine the answer to this question, we must note that Josephus distinguishes between Izates' willingness to "fear" God as the Jews do, as some women did (§§ 34—35), on the one hand, and full conversion.[57] Helene's conversion is mentioned in § 35, and Izates, we read in § 38, considered doing the same (*einai bebaiōs Ioudaios*), via circumcision. But because there were those who were leery of his taking such a step, some unspecified period of time

---

plishments: he enthroned a new king in Armenia (*Ann.* 2.56) and attached Commagene, which had previously been an independent kingdom, to Provincia Syria (ibid.). On Germanicus in the east see, in general, E. Koestermann, *Historia* 7 (1958), pp. 331—375; W. Orth, *Die Provinzialpolitik des Tiberius* (1970), pp. 37—39; and D. Hennig, *Chiron* 2 (1972), pp. 354—358.

[56] See above, n. 41, esp. von Gutschmid, who on p. 54 explains that the slaughter occurred in 41 C.E. and that it was this "Hauptsache" which gave Josephus the "Anlaß . . . auch die früheren Vorfälle unter diesem Jahre zu erzählen."

[57] In recent years, especially in the wake of Jewish "Who is a Jew?" debates (cf. above, p. 5, n. 12) and the publication of the Aphrodisias inscription (J. Reynolds and R. Tannenbaum, *Jews and God-Fearers at Aphrodisias* [1987]), much has been written about the distinction between God-fearers and converts. See, inter alia, Stern, *GLA* II, pp. 103—106, S.J.D. Cohen, *HTR* 80 (1987), pp. 409—430 (especially on Josephus' usage; pp. 424—425 on the Adiabene episode), idem, ibid. 82 (1989), pp. 13—34, and L. H. Feldman, *Revue des études juives* 148 (1989), pp. 265—305 (bibliography ibid., pp. 275—276, n. 36). On the Adiabene episode in particular, see also L. H. Schiffman's discussion in *Josephus, Judaism, and Christianity* (above, n. 23), pp. 293—312.

(§ 43) went by before he took the plunge and was circumcised (§§ 46–47). The terminology and the facts indicate that it was this to which Josephus' opening summary for this affair (§ 17) referred.

After a few general comments in § 48, which Josephus himself brackets within his narrative,[58] Josephus continues his story (§§ 49 ff.), and reports Helene's trip to Jerusalem. This is crucial for our question, for elsewhere (§ 101) we learn that this took place during the governorship of Tiberius Julius Alexander (ca. 46–48 C.E.). Now, according to § 49 she made this trip only after she saw her son Izates' continued success even after and despite his conversion. On the other hand, it is likely that after converting she would not have waited too long before going to sacrifice in Jerusalem.[59] Hence, it is quite natural to infer that the king's conversion took place during the years before Alexander, when Fadus was ruling Judaea – which is just where Josephus places the story.

6. 1/1 : This group of notices appears here apropos of the affairs of Agrippa II and his sisters during the governorship of Felix. (Although Felix himself plays a role in this story [§§ 141–144], it is as a spouse and not as governor, so its placement in an "appendix" does not violate the basic scheme.) Just as in the case of h/4, the fact that Josephus gives some additional family details regarding the results of these affairs should not be allowed to obscure his procedure here.[60]

However, 1/1 raises another problem, of course, for it is placed after the chapter on Cumanus but, along with the next two appendices (1/2–3), clearly refers to events which occurred during the term of his successor, Felix. Why wasn't this material added in as an appendix to the next chapter (M), on Felix?

---

[58] "But we shall report these events later." Josephus did not fulfill this promise, a fact which, along with other considerations, points to the conclusion that Josephus used for this Adiabene story a pre-existent written narrative (which probably included and fulfilled the promise). See F. Schemann, *Die Quellen des Flavius Josephus* . . . (1887), esp. pp. 19–26; Täubler (above, n. 35), pp. 62–65. Cf. below, n. 60.

[59] On sacrifices by new converts, see m.*Kelim* 2:1 and *Sifré* to Numbers 15:14 (§ 108; ed. Horovitz, p. 112; for annotated German translation, see K. G. Kuhn, *Sifre zu Numeri* [1959], pp. 300–301); B. J. Bamberger, *Proselytism in the Talmudic Period* (1939), pp. 44–45; L. H. Schiffman, *Who Was a Jew?* (1985), pp. 30–32 (his Hebrew article cited there has since appeared in English in *Josephus, Judaism, and Christianity* [above, n. 23]; see its pp. 305–306); also S. Safrai, *Die Wallfahrt im Zeitalter des Zweiten Tempels* (1981), p. 106. The latter three scholars all assume that Helene's sacrifices included those completing her conversion. (Although Schiffman refers to Helene's trip as having been in ca. 30 C.E., he makes no attempt to justify this and explicitly renounces, on p. 294 of his article in *JJC*, any attempt to deal with the episode's chronology.)

[60] The unfulfilled promise to return "later" to the details of an event in 79 C.E., a period Josephus hardly could have contemplated covering in *Ant.*, is – as in the case mentioned in n. 58 – an indication of the use of a source, in this case, one on the Herodians. In my article mentioned above, n. 53, I attempted to characterize this source.

This question leads us to the *second guideline* promised above, according to which Josephus applied his major rule: When there was a gap in the chain of Judaean government, due to a ruler's death or removal from office prior to the arrival of his successor, Josephus will mention the appointment of the new ruler, but the narrative of his events will be postponed until after some "other" events of the period. This postponement, as P. Villalba has recently noticed in a similar case, reflects the passage of time before the new ruler's arrival.[61]

Such gaps are not usual, for a governor usually stays in his post until his successor arrives. Josephus' language frequently reflects this normal procedure.[62] In the period we are studying, there were only five such gaps: after Archelaus and Cumanus were removed from office,[63] and after Gaius, Agrippa I and Festus died. And it is very interesting, that in four of these five cases,[64] and only in them in *Ant.* 18–20, "other" events divide the notice of the new ruler's arrival from the narrative of the events of his term:[65]

Chaps.	New Appointment	"Other" Material	"Central" Material
A–B	*Ant.* 18.2a: Cumanus appointed after Archelaus exiled	18.2b–28	18.29a[66]
H–I	19.274–275: Agrippa enthroned after Gaius dies	19.276–291	19.292–366[67]

---

[61] Cf. P. Villalba i Varneda, *The Historical Method of Flavius Josephus* (1986), p. 171, on *BJ* 3.505–522, where Josephus stops the narrative for a while to allow for the construction of rafts.

[62] As a rule, he announces the end of a governor's term of office only when reporting the appointment or arrival of a new one (see, for example, *Ant.* 18.33; 20.100, 103, 182, 252). See esp. 20.215: Albinus hears a new governor is on his way, but naturally continues serving until the latter arrives.

[63] Even if one assumes, on the basis of Tacitus (*Ann.* 2.54 [*GLA* II, pp. 77–82]; see below, pp. 231–237), that Felix was serving in some local capacity prior to his elevation to the governorship instead of Cumanus, there still must have been something of an "interregnum" while Cumanus went to Rome and was tried there, and before the decision to appoint Felix in his stead made its way back to Judaea.

[64] Again, it is chapter J (on Fadus, who was appointed after the death of Agrippa I) which is exceptional, just as with regard to Theudas (above, n. 54).

[65] This also happens in chapter K, but there the "other" material, which separates Cumanus' appointment from his *res gestae*, takes up only one short paragraph (20.104). See above, n. 47. In the cases mentioned here the "other" material is much longer (between seven and twenty-seven paragraphs).

[66] See above, n. 31.

[67] These paragraphs also include events which occurred immediately after Agrippa's death and due to it. For a similar rounding-out of the chronological framework, see above, n. 38. For the argument that §§ 292–299 in fact refer to the period before Gaius died, see *Agrip-*

Chaps.	New Appointment	"Other" Material	"Central" Material
L–M	20.136–137: Cumanus sent to Rome for trial; Felix appointed	20.138–159	20.160–178
N–O	20.197a: Festus died, Albinus appointed	20.197b–203	20.204–210

III. Pilate's Appointment –
Its Insertion and Circumstances

Having seen Josephus' main rule for organizing his material, the two reasonable guidelines which he followed in problematic cases, and the fact that – with only two significant exceptions (j/3 and o/2) – he did succeed in organizing his material properly from a chronological point of view, let us now return to Pontius Pilate. It is, I believe, more than a little interesting to note that Josephus' narrative concerning Pilate follows the pattern of the narratives which we just charted, those where there was a break in continuity:

Chaps.	New Appointment	"Other" Material	"Central" Material
E–F	*Ant.* 18.35: Gratus returns to Rome and Pilate appointed	18.36–54	18.55–64

That is, the structure of Josephus' narrative here suggests that there was a gap between the end of Gratus' service and Pilate's arrival in Judaea. And the same is implied, in fact, by Josephus' wording: "Gratus returned to Rome, after serving eleven years in Judaea, and Pontius Pilate came as his successor." Gratus' return to Rome is mentioned before Pilate's arrival, in contrast to Josephus' usual practice of referring to the appointment of X instead of Y. And, indeed, although Josephus does not mention such a break in continuity (as he does, for example, with regard to the suspension of Cumanus or the death of Festus), it is in fact simple to suggest how one would have come about.

During the years 17–19 C.E., Germanicus was touring the East as a special troubleshooter charged with resolving various issues in the client kingdoms and provinces (see above, n. 55). Alongside of the problems in Armenia and Commagene, Tacitus also mentions, as background for the mission, Syrian

---

pa I, pp. 11–14. Josephus, however, thought they dealt with the period after Claudius had ascended to the imperial throne; cf. above, n. 41.

and Judaean complaints about oppressive taxes.[68] We have no information regarding what was done about these complaints, but they were part of Germanicus' mandate and he had ample time to deal with them: we hear that he visited "many provinces" in the course of 18 C.E., and stayed a long time in Syria, whence he went to Egypt and back in 19 C.E.[69] If he did deal with the Judaeans' complaints, as he should have,[70] he may well have sent Gratus back to Rome for a review of the matter. If Tiberius then decided to send in a new governor, the result would have been a gap, probably of a couple of months or more, between Gratus' departure and the arrival of his replacement.

As support for this reconstruction, we may note that while Tacitus records complaints about taxes alone, it may be assumed that Judaeans would also take umbrage at Gratus' high-handed approach to the high priesthood: he apparently appointed and fired high priests every year (*Ant.* 18.34—35). But this stopped with the fourth appointee, Joseph Caiaphas, who remained in his post during the remainder of Gratus' term and and during all of Pilate's term as well (18/19 C.E.—37 C.E.!). Since no one seems to have offered a convincing explanation for this abrupt reversal of policy,[71] I would venture to suggest that Germanicus (or Tiberius), in order to assuage the angry Judaeans, not only removed Gratus from office but also denied his successor the right to interfere with the high priesthood. This step would have been one in the direction of separation of religion and state in Judaea: after the Hasmoneans had run the state as high priests, and Herod had run the high-priesthood, now the Romans began to back away. The next step would come at the end of Caiaphas' term, with Vitellius' agreement to return to priestly custody the high-priestly vestments (*Ant.* 18.90—95), thus reversing another

---

[68] *Ann.* 2.42.5. For text, translation, commentary and bibliography, see Stern, *GLA* II, pp. 67—68.

[69] On the date of the visits to many provinces ("pluris pro provincias transigitur" — *Ann.* 2.62.1), see Koestermann (above, n. 55), p. 351, n. 47, who notes "das bekannte Prinzip der gebrochenen Linienführung, das hier wiederum bei Tacitus begegnet." Failure to appreciate it may lead to chronological misunderstandings, just as with regard to Josephus.

[70] And it is clear that he did handle the other items with which he was charged; see above, n. 55. Similarly, note that two predecessors of Germanicus, Marcus Vipsanius Agrippa and Gaius Caesar, whose oriental trips were precedents for his, visited Judaea despite the fact that in contrast to Germanicus they, as far as we know, had no specific problems to deal with there. For the sources on their visits, see Stern in *GLA*, II, p. 111.

[71] Some, including E. M. Smallwood (*JTS* 13 [1962], p. 22), P. Gaechter (*Petrus und seine Zeit* [1958], p. 71) and J.-P. Lémonon (*Pilate et le gouvernement de la Judée: Textes et monuments* [1981], pp. 99—100, 274—275), have sought to explain Caiaphas' long service on the basis of his friendship with the governor or bribes. However, the former explanation, along with the usual chronology, assumes extraordinary friendship with two governors, and the latter assumes that it is more profitable to take bribes from an incumbent than from a competitor, which is hardly likely. According to II Maccabees 4:7—10, 24 and PT *Yoma* 1:1 (38c), the office-seeker's bribes are usually more impressive than the incumbent's.

Herodian measure designed to keep the Jewish religious authorities firmly under the ruler's thumb.[72]

IV. Summary

With regard to our specific question, the year Pilate was appointed, we have suggested that the location of Josephus' notice concerning the appointment, before the foundation of Tiberias (19—20 C.E.) and before the narrative culminating in Germanicus' death (19 C.E.), indicates that it too is to be placed ca. 19 C.E. The same is also implied, apparently, by the inclusion of the Roman scandals of 19 within the chapter on Pilate. Moreover, this suggestion is also based upon a few specific considerations — the impression given by the narrative of Gratus' term, the cessation that year of annual minting and annual appointments of high priests, and Eusebius' report about fourth-century forgers — and upon an analysis of the relationship of structure and chronology in the last three books of the *Antiquities*. To my mind, all of these considerations carry enough weight to overcome the presumption of authenticity of the specific numerical data in our texts of Josephus (*Ant.* 18.35, 89), which so smoothly give 26 or 27 C.E. as the year in which Pilate succeeded Gratus. Especially in light of the exceptional nature of Josephus' numerical data here, and the presence of Germanicus with a mandate to do something in Judaea, it seems to us that the question, so long considered closed, should now at least be considered open, and that the weight of evidence points to the earlier dating.

But we can go beyond that with regard to the larger question at stake here — Josephus' way of arranging his materials. In order to illustrate the importance of a proper understanding here, let us briefly recall a dispute of four centuries ago: the positions taken then are, basically, the same ones held variously today, but it may be that a new resolution is now possible. Toward the end of the sixteenth century, C. Baronius took Josephus to task for mentioning the Roman scandals of 19 C.E. (*Ant.* 18.65—84) after the Crucifixion of Jesus (§§ 63—64), although, as Tacitus shows, they really preceded it by more than a decade. According to Baronius, such chronological

---

[72] Vitellius' concession is also reported in *Ant.* 15.405—409 and 20.12; as evidence for the halting nature of these Roman concessions, note, however, that Vitellius, around the same time that he returned the high-priestly vestments to the Jews, twice removed and appointed high priests (*Ant.* 18.95, 123). On this episode, see below, pp. 202—217. After Vitellius, however, the right to appoint and remove high priests was deposited in Jewish (Herodian) hands (see *Ant.* 19.297; 20.15—16, 222, etc.). In general, on Rome's attempt to back away from Herod's policy of supervising the institutions and authorities of the Jewish religion, see also above, p. 14, n. 31.

errors were typical of Josephus.[73] A couple decades later, I. Casaubon, in the course of his all-embracing attack upon Baronius, took up the cudgels on Josephus' behalf:[74]

But Josephus did not intend to tell the history of our savior according to the years in which the events occurred. He briefly summarized his life, passion and resurrection within the context of the period within which he (Josephus) was sure he had lived, but he did not have the precise chronological data. This is the frequent practice of great historians – Thucydides, Polybius, Livius –especially in matters about which they did not wish to be delayed. And even in the chapters of the history proper (*"in partibus legitimae historiae"*) they often took this liberty . . . and, nevertheless, no one condemns them for this . . .

Our approach is similar to Casaubon's, but our conclusion fits Baronius' basic assumption. Namely, we have suggested, as did Casaubon, that one must distinguish between "central" and "other" events, and that this distinction has implications for the chronological structure of Josephus' narrative. But, as opposed to Casaubon, we did not abandon the assumption that Josephus arranged his material in chronological order. Rather, we assumed, as did Baronius, and as naturally results from such introductory formulas as "then" and "at that time," that Josephus did indeed intend to bring his various episodes in chronological order. The proper response to Baronius' strictures is, in our opinion, that Josephus reported "central" events of a governor's term (such as Pilate's execution of Jesus) before the "other" events of the same period of time (such as events in the Diaspora), so that "central" events which occurred late in a procurator's term of office will be reported before "other" events which occurred earlier in the same period. If, indeed, events of 19 C.E. occurred during Pilate's term of office, as we have suggested, then no problem remains.

On the basis of the above analysis and suggestions, it seems that Josephus' narrative in *Ant.* 18–20 may be redeemed from the widespread condemnation which has so long been its lot, at least as far as chronology is concerned.[75] And Josephus' redemption is ours as well, for without this narrative the historian and chronologist of first-century Judaea doesn't even have a leg to stand on, much less enough rope to hang himself.

---

[73] C. Baronius, *Annales ecclesiastici*, I (1593), p. 82 (Annus, 21 § II) (first published in 1588): ". . . more suo plurimum a veritate temporis discrepat . . ." For the dating of the Roman scandals, see above, n. 14.

[74] I. Casaubon, *De rebus sacris et ecclesiasticis exercitationes XVI. ad Cardinalis Baronii prolegomena in Annales et primam eorum partem* . . . (1654 [first published in 1614]), p. 206.

[75] See above, at nn. 15–18.

4. Pontius Pilate's Suspension from Office: Chronology and Sources*

It is not at all surprising that scholars have directed more attention to Pontius Pilate and his Judaean governorship than to any other period of ancient Jewish history. It is remarkable, however, that Josephus devoted such a great deal of attention to him (*BJ* 2.169–177; *Ant.* 18.55–64, 85–89), a fact especially striking when one recalls that he has nothing in *BJ*, and next to nothing in *Ant.*, to say about Pilate's predecessors, the first four Roman governors of Judaea. As opposed to his modern heirs, however, there is nothing to indicate that Josephus' interest in Pilate stemmed from any special interest of his in the birth of Christianity.[1] Nor, however, in contrast to some of Josephus' material about later governors, did his account of Pilate stem from first-hand knowledge: Josephus was only born the year Pilate was dismissed (*Vita* 5; *Ant.* 20.267). Thus, Josephus' account must reflect the relative richness of material available to him.

But despite the richness of the material and the intensity with which it has been studied, several problems remain. Some of these, it seems, are in fact a result of the richness of Josephus' narrative; the more material, the more questions legitimately raised. In the present study, we shall suggest that a troublesome chronological difficulty concerning Pilate's removal from office is the result of Josephus' failure to coordinate two sources reporting the same event. The natural result of this failure is the erroneous notion that there were two such events, and the difficulty in making room for both of them is notorious. If, however, we can show that the two accounts describe the same event, we can both resolve the chronological conundrum and also give a fuller account of that event. Moreover, tracing of the two separate accounts to two separate sources will enrich our knowledge of contemporary Jewish historiography and of Josephus' procedures in handling his sources.

---

* Hebrew original: *Tarbiz* 51 (1981/82), pp. 383–398.

[1] It is, however, possible that the richness of sources stemmed from Christians' attempts to collect and preserve as much as possible about this period; perhaps Josephus had access to such a collection. Note, in this connection, that the only other ancient writer to refer to Pilate, apart from Philo (*Leg.* 299–305), Josephus and the New Testament writers, does so in a Christian context (Tacitus, *Ann.* 15.44 – *GLA* II, pp. 88–93).

I. The Problem

According to *Ant.* 18.89, L. Vitellius, the Roman governor of Syria, removed Pilate from office and sent him to Rome so as to answer various complaints against him, but, although Pilate hurried to Rome, by the time he arrived Tiberius had died. Tiberius died on 16 March 37 (Tacitus, *Ann.* 6.50).[2] Immediately thereafter (§§ 90—95), Josephus records that Vitellius visited Jerusalem during the Passover festival. Passover probably fell on April 19 or 20 that year,[3] so these two reports coordinate well; the first datum means Pilate was suspended sometime around February-March, while the second regards a visit in April. The problem comes with Josephus' report a few pages later, in §§ 122—126, of Vitellius visiting Jerusalem during a Jewish festival, at which time he received notice of Tiberius' death. Given the importance of this news and Vitellius' stature as the supreme Roman official in the East, he probably received this news within a few weeks, which would lead us to assume that the visit of §§ 122—126 was during Passover 37, in mid-April. But, if this is the case, and the earlier Passover visit, of §§ 90—95, is therefore moved up to the spring of 36 C.E., then what shall we say of Josephus' notice that Pilate, although he hurried to Rome,[4] arrived only after Tiberius died — about a year later?! This is the problem.

Various solutions have been proposed.[5] Some suggest that Josephus erred in dating the first visit to Passover, and that it really came during the preceding week-long festival, Tabernacles, in the autumn of 36.[6] But, even apart from assuming the mistake, this solution requires us to assume that Pilate, although

---

[2] See E. Koestermann, *Cornelius Tacitus: Annalen*, II (1965), pp. 363—364, where further evidence is cited and evaluated.

[3] This is the usual assumption, presuming that in Jerusalem, as in Babylon, the month which began ca. 6 April 37 was considered to be Nisan; see R. A. Parker and W. H. Dubberstein, *Babylonian Chronology, 626 B.C.—A.D. 75* (1956), p. 46. On the notion — which arose under the pressure of the problems to be discussed here — that the Jews instead viewed the *preceding* month as Nisan, see below, n. 11.

[4] While some scholars have accepted this as natural, in light of Pilate's desire to get there before his accusers, E. M. Smallwood perhaps more reasonably assumes he would not have been enthusiastic about the trip (*JJS* 5 [1954], p. 13). Nevertheless, she too agreed that Pilate could not have procrastinated too long and that, in any case, Josephus' explicit testimony, and CD 53.15.6 (below, n. 7), may not be overlooked without cause.

[5] For summaries, see M. Stern in *The Jewish People in the First Century*, I (edd. S. Safrai and M. Stern; 1974), pp. 68—70; H. Hoehner, *Herod Antipas* (1972), pp. 313—316. Strangely, SVM I, pp. 387—388, which dates the first visit to 36 and leaves Pilate on the road for about a year, seems to be unaware of the problem or of the literature; so too W. Schenk, *NTS* 29 (1983), p. 461.

[6] So U. Holzmeister, *Biblica* 13 (1932), pp. 228—232; P. Gaechter, *Petrus und seine Zeit* (1958), pp. 85—86.

he "hurried," didn't get to Rome within six months.[7] Therefore, some simply reject Josephus' dating of the first visit, placing it rather ca. December 36 or January 37.[8] This, however, is quite radical, as is the suggestion that Vitellius visited Jerusalem before either of the two visits recorded in *Ant.* 18.[9] Yet others would resolve the problem from the other end, suggesting that the visit of §§ 122–126 was during the Pentecost (Shavuot) festival, seven weeks after Passover.[10] But who can imagine that almost three months went by before Vitellius heard of Tiberius' death?![11]

---

[7] And note CD 53.15.6: Augustus ruled that every governor must return to Rome within three months of the arrival of his replacement.

[8] So, especially, Smallwood (above, n. 4), pp. 12–21 (and *Jews*, p. 171), followed, inter alia, by P. L. Maier, *Hermes* 99 (1971), pp. 365–366, in his imaginative study of Pilate's fate. For the same suggestion, argued in less detail, see already E. von Dobschütz, *Realencyklopädie für protestantische Theologie und Kirche* XV (1904³), p. 398. This approach to such Gordian knots is typical of Smallwood; cf. above, p. 160, n. 10 and below, p. 221, n. 15.

[9] This suggestion, offered – as a refinement of Smallwood's – by Hoehner (above, n. 5), p. 315 and by J.-P. Lémonon, *Pilate et le gouvernement de la Judée: Textes et monuments* (1981), pp. 243–244, was meant to resolve an ancillary problem: if Vitellius first visited Jerusalem during Passover of 37, then, while he might have written to Tiberius about the Jews' requests, he could not have received a response from Tiberius – but *Ant.* 15.405, in a proleptic review of the story, asserts that he did. Smallwood allowed this problem to set aside Josephus' explicit dating of the first visit to Passover, but these other scholars instead conclude that the visit reported in *Ant.* 15.405 is to be distinguished from that of *Ant.* 18.90–95. It seems, however, extravagant to assume an additional visit; the mention of Tiberius' involvement, in the summary account in *Ant.* 15, is either a simple unmotivated error (as the reference in § 407 to Vitellius instead of Longinus obviously is) or to be chalked up to the author's apologetic desire to involve the emperor himself in the protection of Judaism. Cf. below, at n. 41.

[10] J. Jeremias, *Jerusalem in the Time of Jesus* (1969), p. 195, n. 153; J. Blinzler, *Der Prozeß Jesu* (1969⁴), pp. 271–273.

[11] For literature and examples concerning the speed of travel between Rome and the East, see Lémonon (above, n. 9), p. 242, nn. 4–5; Stern (above, n. 5), p. 70; and Holzmeister (above, n. 6), p. 229. None of Blinzler's examples (above, n. 10: pp. 272–273) of slower mail has to do with anything remotely as important as the death of an emperor, except for one in the depths of winter; and even that notice, of Pertinax's accession to the imperial throne on 1 January 193, reached Egypt within sixty-three days. Hoehner (above, n. 5: pp. 314–315) defends the Pentecost thesis, but only on the assumptions that 1) notice of the emperor's death was sent by land and 2) Passover came a month earlier than usually supposed, so Pentecost was already on May 11 – less than two months after Tiberius died. But the period of "mare clausum" ended on March 10, and, although sea travel might have been somewhat hazardous until May (see Vegetius, *Epitome rei militaris* IV, 39), such an important datum as the emperor's death would have been sent by sea. Cf. *BJ* 2.203, according to which news of Gaius Caligula's death, although in mid-winter, was brought to the East by sea, in a "good journey." It is usually assumed – on the basis of *Megillat Ta'anit* to 22 Shebat (ed. Lichtenstein, *HUCA* 8–9 [1931/32], pp. 344–345 [cf. ibid. 301–302]) and other considerations – that this trip took about a month; see P. Bilde, *Studia Theologica* 32 (1978), p. 90. As for Hoehner's assumption, also shared by Blinzler (above, n. 10: p. 273), that Passover came a month earlier, i.e., around March 22 (assuming 1 Nisan was 8 March – see

All of the aforementioned proposals entail either rejecting part of Josephus' account or accepting assumptions contrary to common sense and experience. Another solution, proposed nearly eighty years ago by W. Otto, deserves more attention than it has received: Otto suggested that the two accounts refer to one and the same visit, during Passover 37.[12] Such a solution resolves all of our difficulties: Pilate was suspended from office shortly before the festival and hurried off to Rome, but Tiberius died before he arrived (perhaps even before he was suspended!); news of Tiberius' death reached Vitellius within about five weeks, during his Passover visit in Jerusalem.

Apart from Otto's failure to supply a thorough examination and defense of this thesis (which came only as an aside in a monograph about Herod), two specific problems must immediately be noted: 1) Josephus reports, near the end of each visit narrative (§§ 95, 123), that Vitellius removed a high priest from office and appointed his successor — but the names are different; 2) Vitellius' first visit is also mentioned in *Ant.* 15.405, and there we read that he not only sent a letter to Tiberius but also received his reply, which is impossible if the first visit came in April 37. Otto recognized the first problem, but solved it by assuming that it arose due to conflicting traditions concerning the high-priestly appointments;[13] he did not notice or deal with the passage in *Ant.* 15 or with the difficulty it raises.[14]

Parker and Dubberstein [above, n. 3]), while it may be somewhat exaggerated to state that it is "durch die Klimaverhältnisse ausgeschlossen" (Holzmeister, above, n. 6: p. 229), it is not a likely point of departure. For while the rule that Passover must come after the vernal equinox was not without exception (on both rule and exceptions see M. D. Herr, in *The Jewish People in the First Century* II [edd. S. Safrai and M. Stern; 1976], pp. 853–856, also F. K. Ginzel, *Handbuch der mathematischen und technischen Chronologie*, III [1914], pp. 212–213), we have no right to assume, unless forced to do so, that the year we are considering was exceptional. But the vernal equinox in 37 C.E. was on March 23; see the clear exposition by P. Couderc in *Encyclopedia Americana* V (international edition; 1974), pp. 187–188.

[12] W. Otto, *Herodes* (1913), cols. 192–194, n. * (= *PWRE* Supplementband II [1913], cols. 185–187, n. *). Otto was followed by G. Hölscher, *Die Hohenpriesterliste bei Josephus und die evangelische Chronologie* (Sitzungsberichte der Heidelberger Akademie der Wissenschaften, Philosophisch-historische Klasse, Jg. 1939/40, 3. Abh.; 1940) pp. 15–16, 24, and the same idea was briefly suggested, independently (?), by J. Felten, *Neutestamentliche Zeitgeschichte*, I (1925²⁻³), p. 172, n. 4, and by C. Saulnier, *RB* 91 (1984), p. 374. Finally, note that F. F. Bruce, *New Testament History* (1972), p. 65, n. 39, identifies the two visits as being one, on Passover 37 — but he also subscribes to the position that there was an additional visit which preceded it (see above, n. 9). See ibid., p. 31, also his essay on Herod Antipas in *Annual of the Leeds University Oriental Society* V (1963–1965), pp. 18–19. However, neither of Bruce's discussions goes into any detail.

[13] See the end of his discussion cited above (n. 12); part of Otto's statement is quoted below, at n. 33.

[14] He did deal with that passage in another context; see cols. 13–14 of the book (= cols. 11–12 in the *PWRE* edition).

Such an hypothesis, that a historical work contains two uncoordinated accounts of the same event, should have led to source-criticism. But the decades following the publication of Otto's *Herodes* happened to witness a dramatic decline in interest in Josephan source criticism, for various reasons.[15] In this specific connection, it suffices to note that Otto's suggestion is not mentioned by Holzmeister, Smallwood, Hoehner or Lémonon, although they discussed our problem in detail,[16] and that those who mentioned it were content to reject it out of hand due to one or both of the two problems we mentioned.[17] It seems, however, that a detailed analysis of the passages in question will improve upon Otto's insight and demonstrate its basic validity.

II. Four Passages, How Many Sources?

According to *Ant.* 18.90–95, during Vitellius' "first" visit Vitellius returned the high-priestly vestments to priestly custody.[18] Elsewhere, Josephus refers to this same gesture, both prospectively and retrospectively. It is worthwhile to compare these three narratives, which we will label as follows:

A – *Ant.* 15.403–408 (which § 409 terms a "digression")
B – *Ant.* 18.90–95
C – *Ant.* 20.6–14

In general, these accounts tell a single and simple tale in three acts. According to A, the Hasmoneans had built a fortress near the Temple and made a practice of depositing their high-priestly vestments there; Herod – who, § 409 reports, strengthened the fortress and renamed it "Antonia"– maintained the practice, keeping the high-priestly vestments there under lock and key (so as

---

[15] See below, pp. 262–265.

[16] See above, notes 5, 6, 8, 9.

[17] So, inter alia, Stern (above, n. 5), p. 70, n. 4, and A. Garzetti, *Studi in onore di Aristide Calderini e Roberto Paribeni*, I (1956), p. 218, n. 27. Blinzler (above, n. 10: pp. 271–272) devoted somewhat more attention to Otto's thesis before rejecting it, arguing that the two "Jerusalemreisen des Vitellius werden durch Josephus so einleuchtend motiviert, daß die Annahme einer Dublette durchaus nicht angezeigt, geschweige erforderlich ist." However, Josephus gives no reason for either visit; rather, he only describes Vitellius' doings during each. (Blinzler goes on to explain that the first visit "diente der Klärung der durch die Enthebung des Pilatus entstandenen Probleme," while the second was motivated by Vitellius' desire to cultivate Jewish goodwill on the eve of his expedition against the Arabs. So werden die Jerusalemreisen des Vitellius durch *Blinzler* so einleuchtend motiviert . . .)

[18] On the political significance of this gesture, see P. Winter, *On the Trial of Jesus* (new ed. by T. A. Burkill and G. Vermes; 1974), pp. 21–26. In explaining the Jews' desire to control the vestments it would be mistaken, I think, to focus – with Feldman, p. 68, n.a. – on the problem of their ritual purity. Indeed, § 93 apparently indicates the Romans' efforts to preserve the vestments' purity even while under their control; cf. below, n. 23.

keep these high religious officials under his thumb). This practice was continued by the Roman governors prior to Vitellius, whose return of the vestments to priestly custody constitutes the second act. Finally, after the death of Agrippa I, Fadus, the new governor of Judaea, tried to restore governmental custody of the vestments, but the Jews appealed to Claudius and he ratified the existing practice, in his response citing Vitellius' act as a binding precedent.

This story is told by all the sources (although this or that detail is absent here or there), as follows: A tells the whole story, B gives only the first two stages and C the third alone, apart from the allusion to Vitellus. However, detailed consideration uncovers the following remarkable points:

i. A reports that the fortress was built by the Hasmonean kings and high priests. B, however, says it was built by "one of the priests, named Hyrcanus." (C does not relate to this).

ii. B treats *baris* as a common noun, meaning "large house" or "tower." This Greek term is similar to the Hebrew word *birah* which was, apparently, used for the fortress as early as the Persian period (Neh. 2:8; 7:2). However, the Greek noun is very rare, and most of the references to it in LSJ are to Josephus and the Septuagint. Therefore, it is interesting that Josephus, in A, explains that the fortress was *named* Baris. While paralleled elsewhere in Josephus (*BJ* 1.75, 118; *Ant.* 13.307), this is contrary to B.[19]

iii. A and C speak of "the holy (or "priestly") vestment," but B speaks of "the vestment" *simpliciter*.[20]

iv. A terms Herod "King Herod," but B calls him plain "Herod." (C doesn't mention him).

v. One step down in prominence, B mentions Archelaus and terms him "king," but A and C fail to mention him.

vi. A reports that the vestments were kept in the Antonia under the seal of the high priest and the (Temple's) treasurers, but B, although it agrees about the treasurers, refers to the priests, not the high priest. (C says nothing on the subject.)

vii. According to A the treasurers would receive the vestments from the Roman commander, but B says the recipients were the priests. (No comment in C.)

---

[19] B's usage is paralleled by *BJ* 1.353 (= *Ant.* 14.481), where Josephus uses *baris* without indicating that it is the name of the fortress, just as elsewhere, and with regard to other fortresses, he uses the word as a common noun (*Ant.* 10.264–265; 11.99; 12.230; etc.). B's usage is also paralleled by 15.409b, just after the end of the digression we termed A – another point in favor of viewing A as based on a distinct source. Cf. below, Part IV, § 6.

[20] *Hē stolē* – 18.91, 92, 95; § 93 adds "of the high priest." In § 90, Josephus refers to the *stolē* of the high priest and all his ornaments (*kosmos*); below, at note 29, we shall distinguish between § 90 and the rest of B. We will return to this terminology below, Part IV, § 5.

viii. According to A and C, at issue was the *exousia* ("authority") over the vestments, this term appearing several times.[21] But neither it nor any similar term appears as a legal term in B.[22] The one time *exousia* appears here (§ 91), it refers to the "permission" given the high priest to wear the vestments, not to authority over them.

ix. According to A, it was customary to hand over the vestments before each festival, but B specifies this happened before "the three festivals and the fast." (Nothing on this topic in C.)

x. B also mentions the need to purify the garments for seven days after their removal from the fortress, before they were worn, and includes, in § 93, a few obscure details concerning, apparently, the preservation of the vestments' purity while in the fortress.[23] None of this, apart from the seal (above—vi), appears in A or C.

xi. B mentions no emperor, but attributes the entire gesture to Vitellius alone. According to A, in contrast, although Vitellius wanted to allow the Jewish request, he nevertheless first asked for, and received, Tiberius' permission. (C does not specify, but only has Claudius say that he does as Vitellius did.)

xii. B records that Vitellius' visit came during Passover, while A does not date the visit to any festival at all and C does not even mention Vitellius' visit, but only his gesture.

xiii. A and C only generally report that Vitellus gave the vestments to the Jews, and do not report where they kept them, but B says he gave them to the *priests* and they kept them in the Temple.

xiv. A and C speak of the Jews in the third person, but B, once, uses the first person ("according to our custom"—§ 95).

These observations lead to a number of conclusions.

First, B's point of view is clearly quite different from A's. B's point of view is Jewish: it is interested in details about the Hasmoneans (i), Jewish holidays (ix,xii) and purity arrangements (x), uses Jewish Greek (ii) and even refers to the Jews in the first person (xiv), but has no need to identify Herod or to dignify him (iv), mentions Archelaus but makes a typical Jewish mistake by

---

[21] *Ant* 15.405 (twice),407; 20.6, 7, 12. On this term and its equivalence to *potestas*, see H. Zucker, *Studien zur jüdischen Selbstverwaltung im Altertum* (1936), p. 149; H. J. Mason, *Greek Terms for Roman Institutions* (1974), pp. 44, 132—134.

[22] Apart from once in § 90; see above, n. 20.

[23] The statement that the vestments were kept in a house built of stone apparently stands in some relationship to m.*Parah* 3:1 ("stone house"), where too the "seven days" of purifying are mentioned (as also in m.*Yoma* 1:1). The lamp lit daily in the fortress, according to Josephus, remains a riddle. Cf. A. Büchler, *Die Priester und der Cultus im letzten Jahrzehnt des jerusalemischen Tempels* (1895), pp. 69—70, n. 2.

referring to him as having been "king"[24] (v); this failure to use the correct Roman term (ethnarch), as in viii (*exousia*) as well, and the failure to mention any emperor (xi), shows what part of the world is *not* this source's concern. Rather, B's point of view is that of the Jerusalem priesthood, as is indicated by the details in vi, vii, and xiii, and also, probably, by the special attention to purity (x) and the lack of need to explain which vestments were at issue (iii).

The assumption that B is based upon a source emanating from the Jerusalem priesthood may be further supported both by the probability that a similar source was used by Josephus later in *Antiquities* (in Book 20),[25] and by the fact that Josephus presents this passage in the summary+"and this is the reason"+story format which he frequently uses when inserting, into a narrative built on something else, an excerpt from an auxiliary source.[26] Thus, § 90 is Josephus' summary of the extract of the source which follows; it is this which accounts for the occasional points at which § 90 agrees with A and C against the body of B (see above, notes 20 and 22). Below, at the end of Part II, we shall show further evidence for Josephan responsibility for the composition of § 90.

A, in contrast, has a Roman point of view. It speaks of the Hasmoneans without caring to be specific (i) and similarly lacks details concerning Jewish holidays (ix,xii) and purity (x), but properly identifies Herod's status (iv) and omits his second-class heir who played no significant role in this story (v), involves the emperor (xi), and uses the appropriate legal terminology to describe the issue (viii), taking care to clarify, for the uninitiated, a term of Jewish Greek (ii) and the nature of the vestments at issue (iii). Similarly, when it speaks of the Jewish representatives it refers only to administrative officials or to the most salient religious functionary, the high priest (vi,vii; cf. xiii).

But A, so different from B, is quite similar to C, although it contains only the last part of the story. We have already noted similarities between A and C with regard to terminology (iii,viii) and point of view (xiii,xiv). Moreover, there are verbal similarities: both say Fadus wanted the Jews "to deposit" (*katathesthai*) the vestments "as was formerly the case" (*kathōs kai proteron ēsan/katha dē kai proteron ēn*) and that Agrippa (A) or the Jews (C) "requested" (*aitēsameno(u)s*) "authority" (*exousia*) over them; both explain that "only the high priest" (*monos ho archiereus*) is allowed to wear the vestments, and both identify Agrippa II, who intervened in the dispute, as "the younger" (*neōteros*), explaining that he "happened" (*tugchanōn/ etugchanen*) to be in Rome at the time. None of these appears in B. It is quite

---

[24] For Josephan and New Testament evidence for popular terming of Archelaus and Herod Antipas as "kings," see Hoehner (above, n. 5), pp. 149–150.

[25] See *JQR* 72 (1981/82), pp. 241–268.

[26] See below, p. 271, n. 76.

interesting, moreover that both A and C credit emperors with the resolution of the disputes to the Jews' satisfaction (A reports this concerning Tiberius and Claudius, C refers to the latter alone). In general, finally, it may be said that the whole story is identical in A and C (as far as the latter goes), except that there is one crass error in A (Claudius is said to have sent his response to Vitellius, instead of to Longinus) and C includes a few details absent from A (Longinus' troops, his permission for the Jewish delegation, and the taking hostage of the delegates' children) – which is only natural, given the fact that C is the natural locus for this part of the story, which A only summarizes prospectively.

Thus, if B seems to derive from a priestly source, A and C both seem to derive from another source, which had Roman readers in mind. At the end of our study we will make a suggestion about its authorship. First, however, we must investigate Josephus' account of Vitellius' "second" visit, *Ant.* 18.122–126, which we shall dub D.

D is the last of a series of stories which follow upon B, stories which share a common interest in Herod Antipas and Provincia Syria (and its governor, Vitellius):

§§ 96–105: After a Roman-Parthian squabble, Vitellius first schemed against the Parthian king, but later makes peace with him; Herod Antipas serves as their host but also hastens to report the agreement to Rome, thus arousing Vitellius' wrath.

§§ 106–108: The death of Philip, here identified as "Herod's brother," referring to Herod Antipas, rather than as "Herod's son;" identifying Philip this way, rather than by reference to his more famous father, is surprising and underlines the context. Following Philip's death, his tetrarchy was attached to Provincia Syria.

§§ 109–126: A clash between Herod Antipas and his father-in-law, the Nabatean king. (Here Josephus inserts a short flashback [§§ 116–119] on John the Baptist, whose execution, he says, was viewed by some as the reason for Antipas' defeat.[27]) Vitellius, ordered to intervene on Antipas' behalf, came with a large army, and, detouring from his campaign, visited Jerusalem with the tetrarch. During this visit, he hears of Tiberius' death and, therefore, dispersed his army and returned to Antioch.

After these stories, Josephus opens a new chapter, on Agrippa I and his history (§§ 126 ff.).

It is quite difficult to imagine that these three stories, which focus upon Antipas and Vitellius, derive from the source which lies behind the account of the first visit (B). Whether one choses to attribute them to a comprehensive *Herodäergeschichte*, or rather prefers to be wary of such inclusive theories,[28] it

---

[27] Cf. above, pp. 190–191, n. 39.

[28] In Chapter I of *Agrippa I* I posited Josephan usage of a *Vita* of Herod Antipas (dubbed *Antip*) in his account of Agrippa I; of the supportive arguments from differential vocabulary (pp. 177–178), the second, third and sixth also apply to the sections we are now studying. Moreover, in general, these sections are hostile toward Antipas, just as *Antip* is, and § 105

is nevertheless the case that the interests of these stories are far removed from the priestly horizons, uninterested in Rome and in the details of the tetrarch's regime, which characterize B. And if the assumption that they derive from different sources helps resolve the chronological problem with which we began, so much the better.

Here, one more point is of special significance. While it is true that B and D are quite dissimilar, this is not at all true regarding the opening sentence of B (§ 90). We have already noted that § 90 agrees a few times with A and C against B, and that its formulation shows it to be Josephus' own summary of the folowing extract from his priestly source.[29] *But in this opening "summary," Josephus inserted a number of points and phrases which indicate that he saw this visit as identical with the one described in D (§§ 122–126).* Namely, § 90 and D both refer Vitellius' arrival in Judaea (and not just to his being there), his "ascent" to Jerusalem (*eis/epi Hierosolymōn anģei*) on "a traditional festival" (*heortē patrios/heortēs patriou*) of the Jews, at which time he was "received magnificently" (*dechtheis megaloprepōs/dechtheis . . . ekprepōs*) These agreements are quite impressive. Taken together with the fact that Josephus, in neither narrative, indicates that Vitellius visited Jerusalem another time, it seems simplest to assume that the historian knew of but one visit. Had he thought there were two such visits, he too should have been bothered by the chronological conundrum which bothers his modern students. Rather, just as Tiberius' death ends both our Vitellius story and also the long and separate story of Agrippa's imprisonment (*Ant.* 18.224–237), and just as the long story of the conspiracy to assassinate Gaius Caligula (*Ant.* 19.17 ff.) ran parallel to the end of the Temple-statue narrative, which ended with the same assassination (18.307) but is told separately (and separated by the events of the end of Book 18, which also culminated in 41),[30] so too here, Josephus simply brought the two accounts of Vitellius' visit separately.

However, while no one could possibly fail to realize that it is the same Tiberius whose death is mentioned in *Ant.* 18.89 and who dies in 18.224, or that it is the same Gaius who dies in *Ant.* 18.307 and who is assassinated at such length in Book 19, concerning Vitellius' visit the case is not the same. The foci of the two accounts are very different. Indeed, as our review of scholarship showed, most readers assume that the two accounts refer to two different visits. Now we must add that, surprising as it may seem, Josephus

---

seems to indicate that Josephus' source for the present narrative knew about Antipas' fall – narrated in *Ant.* 18.238–255 on the basis of *Antip.* From a methodological point of view, finally, it is more reasonable to assume Josephus used the same source for all of this Antipas material. Nevertheless, our present case does not require that assumption.

[29] See above, notes 20, 22 and 26.
[30] See above, p. 191, n. 41.

himself seems to have forgotten that the two accounts refer to the same visit. This occurred during a later stage of his work when, as we shall now see, he returned to his narrative and inserted the data on the high-priestly succession.

III. Josephus' Method of Composition

As we have seen in the preceding study, Josephus divided his narrative according to the successive rulers of Judaea, inserting, in the latter part of each "chapter," information about other topics of interest. It is as if he had a card file in which the main dividers bore the names of the successive rulers of Judaea (in the first century − governors and Agrippa I), and behind each divider he put first whatever he had on the ruler and his *res gestae* and, thereafter, whatever else applied to the period. Both stories about Vitellius' visit(s) appear in the latter category, after the conclusion of Pilate's *res gestae* (§ 89) but before the beginning of the next new chapter, on Agrippa I.[31] This is appropriate, for they have to do with the affairs of the high-priesthood, Herodians and Provincia Syria, which are all "external" from the point of view of the government of Judaea. It is probable that Josephus, as he worked, inserted such stories in what he believed to be their proper places; and if some of them came to him in a larger framework, such as histories or a history of the Herodians, he broke them up and inserted segments as he worked.

But we know Josephus had another source, which covered not this or that ruler or even this or that century, but, rather, more than a milennium. I refer to the chronicle of the high priesthood, which Josephus mentions in *Ant.* 20.261 and *C. Ap.* 1.36 and which was, apparently, the basis for the summary in *Ant.* 20.224−251.[32] It seems that understanding of this source will help us deal with the first of the problems which we noted with regard to Otto's thesis, namely, the fact that B and D close with different high-priestly appointments by Vitellius.

For it is not likely that the sources which supplied the visit stories in B and D supplied the names of the high priests appointed by Vitellius. While B, on the one hand, is interested in high-priestly affairs, it is clear, from numerous notices in Josephus, that the high-priestly chronicle which he used for the

---

[31] See the table above, pp. 190−191.

[32] On this list, see especially Hölscher (above, n. 12) and J. von Destinon, *Die Quellen des Flavius Josephus*, I (1882), pp. 29−39; unfortunately, however, von Destinon does not consider the high-priestly notices after *Ant.* XV. As he shows, in the Hasmonean period − the period of a high-priestly dynasty! − the data on the high-priesthood scattered through the narrative are usually taken from sources other than the chronicle summarized in *Ant.* 20. In the Roman period, however, a period in which high-priests were much less central to the main flow of history, Josephus needed that chronicle more. Cf. below, p. 222, n. 19.

succession notices did not tell stories, but only gave the names of the high priests and the names of those who appointed and deposed them. Note, for nearby examples, *Ant.* 18.34–35 (!) and 20.16, 103. As for D, it is not concerned with the Jerusalem high-priesthood. Thus, one may doubt that "es verschiedene Traditionen über die Zeit der Entsetzung der beiden Brüder als Hohepriester gegeben hat, Traditionen, die uns beide vorliegen."[33]

Moreover, given the way our two notices on the high priesthood are not integrated organically into the narrative,[34] it is highly likely that Josephus inserted these notices after drafting or completing the rest of his narrative. This is especially the case with high priests such as the ones appointed by Vitellius, who are only names; they do not appear elsewhere in Josephus' narrative, apart from these allusions to their appointment and deposition. Suppose, therefore, that after completing his narratives Josephus then turned to the high-priestly chronicle and found in it the following two successive entries:

Vitellius, the governor of Syria, removed Joseph Caiaphas from the high priesthood and appointed Jonathan ben Ananus in his stead.

Vitellius, the governor of Syria (or: He) removed Jonathan from the high priesthood and appointed his brother Theophilus in his stead.

If Josephus then returned to his narrative, some time after composing it, he may well have forgotten that the two accounts refer to the same visit. As the experience of readers, even historically-oriented readers, shows, that point is not obvious. Consequently, there was nothing to stop him from inserting one of these notices at the conclusion of "each" visit. For our part, however, we would suggest that Vitellius in fact fired Caiaphas at the same time he suspended Pilate, which would have been reasonable, given Caiaphas' long tenure and his association with Pilate.[35] The second appointment, of Theophilus instead of Jonathan, may well have come shortly thereafter, at the time of the visit to Jerusalem, as Josephus wrote in D. This accords with the statement that Jonathan wore the high-priestly vestments only once (*Ant.* 19.314). That would have been on Passover of 37.

The second objection to Otto's thesis is the fact that, according to A, at the time of his "first" visit Vitellius wrote Tiberius and received his reply: according to our chronology, Tiberius was dead when Vitellius wrote.

---

[33] This is the conclusion of Otto's long note cited above, n. 12.

[34] ". . . sehr lose und ohne pragmatische Verknüpfung in den erzählenden Zusammenhang eingefügt . . ." (Hölscher [above, n. 12], p. 15).

[35] Caiaphas, appointed ca. 19 C.E. and replaced in 37, served longer than any other high priest in the Roman period. While some scholars have assumed this was due to his good relations with Pilate, I have argued (above, p. 199) that Pilate simply lacked the authority to appoint and replace high priests. Nevertheless, friendship may well have developed over the long years of parallel tenure.

However, neither B nor C reports that Tiberius wrote Vitellius, and we may note that Claudius' letter in C, which states that Vitellius "did" what he did and makes no allusion to Tiberius, is generally accepted as basically authentic.[36] Thus, it may be that A is simply in error on this point.[37] That conclusion will become more convincing upon examination of the question of its authorship.

IV. Who Wrote A?

As we have seen, Josephus seems to have used four sources for the narratives we have considered. One supplied A and C, another supplied B, another supplied D (and influenced Josephus' summary introduction of B), and entries from the high-priestly chronicle were inserted at the conclusions of B and D. Concerning most of these sources, one may characterize the point of view but hardly attempt to specify the authorship. Concerning the identity of the author behind A and C, however, a probable case can be made.

It is clear that Claudius' letter, quoted in C, was not the source for Josephus' narrative in A, for most of the story in A, which details the history of the high-priestly vestments from the Hasmoneans until Claudius, is absent from C. On the other hand, we do have another source which refers to Vitellius' presence in Jerusalem at the time Tiberius' death became known: Philo, *Legatio ad Gaium* 231. And, as is well known, that composition, or the larger historical work of which it is a part, has only partially been preserved.[38] Could this work, which was written under Claudius (see its §§ 107, 206), be the source Josephus used for A and C?[39]

In cautiously positing an affirmative answer, the following considerations may be adduced:

1. Philo, in *Leg.* 231−232, reports not only Vitellius' presence in Jerusalem at the time Gaius' succession became known but also the sacrifices offered

---

[36] See, for example, M. Stern in *Literatur und Religion des Frühjudentums* (edd. J. Maier and J. Schreiner; 1973), pp. 198−199 ("keinerlei Probleme"); M. P. Charlesworth, *Documents Illustrating the Reigns of Claudius and Nero* (1951), p. 2 ("Josephus' version of a Claudian edict").

[37] Cf. above, n. 9.

[38] See J. Morris in SVM III/2, pp. 859−864.

[39] For the suggestion that the lost end of the *Legatio* included events under Claudius, see, inter alia, F.H. Colson, *Philo* X (LCL; 1962), pp. 186−187, note e. More recently, there has been a tendency to ascribe more and more of the Philonic corpus to the Claudius years. See A. Terian, *Philonis Alexandrini De Animalibus* (1981), p. 34; further literature cited in *Studia Philonica Annual* 1 (1989), p. 65, n. 9, in the context of my argument that *De Somniis* was composed after that emperor's succession to the imperial throne.

there on Gaius' behalf; the latter are also mentioned ibid. § 356. That is, Philo knew about this occasion and thought it was noteworthy.

2. Philo had every interest in recording imperial protection of Jewish religious privileges; their infringement, by Flaccus and Gaius, was the occasion of his historiography, and an important apologetic point of his book(s) was the assemblage of precedents for that imperial policy.[40]

3. Indeed, Philo's interest was so great that, as we have argued elsewhere, in *Leg.* 299–305 he improperly credited Tiberius with a concession to Jerusalem's sacrosanct status in fact made by Pontius Pilate himself, as is shown by *BJ* 2.169–174//*Ant.* 18.55–59.[41] The introduction of Tiberius into A, which chronology excludes, serves the same apologetic purpose.

4. Philo, whose family intermarried with Herod's,[42] records that prominent Herodians interceded on the Jews' behalf in the dispute with Pilate (*Leg.* 300); Josephus does not mention them. Similarly, Agrippa I's intercession with Gaius is a prominent centerpiece in the *Legatio* (§ 261–329). The references in A and C to Agrippa II's intercession with Claudius, in the dispute about the vestments, would have fit right into a Philonic account.

5. As we noted (iii), the term "the holy vestment" (*hē hiera stolē*) appears in A and C (*Ant.* 15.405; 20.6, 7, 9), but not in B. Philo uses it in *Leg.* 296, i.e., in the very book which, in its lost ending, may have covered the Claudian part of the vestments story. In contrast, while in *Ant.* 3.211 and 11.62 Josephus does use the same words to describe the high-priestly vestments, his regular usage more specifically defines it as "of the high priest" (3.151, 158, 180), or with an adjective, *archieratikē* (4.83, 6.115, 13.46), which distinguishes it from

---

[40] See esp. *Leg.* 140–161 and 291–332 (for the obviously Philonic authorship of "Agrippa's" epistle, see *Agrippa I*, pp. 200–202), also *In Flaccum* 106 ff. In general, cf. *Agrippa I*, p. 80, n. 53, including the reference to G. Delling, *Klio* 54 (1972), pp. 171–192 (on Philo on Augustus). In this respect, a serious difference should be noted between *Leg.* and *In Flaccum*: while the latter is concerned to show that God providentially cares for the Jews, the former is more concerned with making a legal and political case the Romans could accept. Thus, *Leg.* seems clearly to be aimed at a Roman readership (as we concluded in Part II concerning A [and C]), while *In Flaccum*, which frequently reads like the Book of Esther, had a Jewish readership in mind. This may account for much of the overlapping and contradictions between the two books Cf. my study of Philonic and Josephan dramatics in *Scripta Classica Israelica* 10 (1989/90), esp. p. 120, n. 13.

[41] See my essay in *The Jerusalem Cathedra* 3 (1983), pp. 25–45, along with *Agrippa I*, p. 74, n. 33. For my response to A. Kasher's repeated criticism of my position – which was formerly quite popular – see the 1987 Hebrew original of *Agrippa I*, pp. 86–87, n. 37.

[42] On the short-lived marriage of Philo's nephew and Agrippa I's daughter Berenice, see *Ant.* 19.276–277. As Graetz suggested (*Geschichte der Juden*, III/2 [ed. M. Brann; 1906⁵], pp. 428, 650) it may well be that also Demetrius the Alabarch, who married another daughter of Agrippa (*Ant.* 20.147), was a member of Philo's family. Cf. my essay on Philo's family in *Nourished with Peace: Studies in Hellenistic Judaism in Memory of Samuel Sandmel* (edd. F. E. Greenspahn, E. Hilgert and B. L. Mack; 1984), pp. 155–171, esp. pp. 161–164.

the vestments of the regular priests (of which Josephus uses *hieratikē*: 3.107, 6.359, 8.93[bis],9.223, 15.390; on 15.403, see below). Thus, given his usual diction, and given the references just before A to *priests'* vestments (15.390), we would have expected Josephus to use *archieratikē*. The fact that he did not, and that he instead uses the same general terminology Philo uses in the very book we suspect Josephus used here, is noteworthy. [43] Indeed, in 15.403 Josephus refers to the *high*-priestly vestment merely as *tēn hieratikēn stolēn* – a complete departure from his usual practice. But Philo, who never uses *archieratikos* (which Josephus should have used here), uses *hieratikos* five times in his extant writings.

6. Similarly, in connection with the observation (ii) that A treats *baris* as the fortress' name, while B, as frequently in Josephus (including right after A – see n. 19), sees it as a common noun, note that Philo, whose Greek is purer, never uses *baris* at all. Here too, in other words, A's usage is what we would expect from Philo.

7. Just as, according to Philo (*Leg.* 179), Agrippa I just "happened" to be in Alexandria (*ek tuchēs*) and could help out with the struggle of the city's Jews, so too, according to A and C, Agrippa II "happened" to be in Rome (*tugchanōn/etugchanen*) at the time of the vestments dispute under Claudius.

8. A detail of titulature: apart from *Leg.* 206, *Ant.* 19.304 and *Ant.* 20.11, which latter is in C, I know of no other cases in which Claudius is termed "Claudius Caesar Germanicus," which is either too formal (the inclusion of Germanicus) or negligent (omits Tiberius). But the first is in a book by Philo and we have attributed the second to him as well, so it is likely that the third too is Philonic. [44]

9. Finally, we may note in general that Josephus' use of his forerunner's historiography is quite natural and to be expected, and that it has often been posited and demonstrated with conviction. Lately, we have argued that Josephus made considerable use of it in *Ant.* 18–19, where the problems considered in this paper begin. [45]

Thus, it seems that Josephus used lost Philonic historiography in preparing A and C, summarizing the long story in A [46] and bringing in C, in detail, the Claudian part of the story. This conclusion bolsters, in general, our conclusion

---

[43] Cf. *hē hiera esthēs* in *Vita Mosis* 2.131 and *De specialibus legibus* 1.95, 97; see also ibid. 4.69. Here, and in the next paragraph, I have made use of G. Mayer, *Index Philoneus* (1974). The Josephan data in the preceding paragraph have been corrected and amplified with the help of the fourth and final volume (1983) of the Josephus concordance (ed. K. H. Rengstorf), which appeared after the original Hebrew version of this study.

[44] See *Agrippa I*, p. 31, n. 38.

[45] See ibid., Chapter I, esp. pp. 18–23.

[46] In the course of this summary he also made an error, stating in § 407 that Claudius wrote to Vitellius (instead of that Claudius wrote to Longinus and referred to Vitellius).

that Josephus used written sources for his different accounts — which facilitates the creation of doublets, as we have argued.

Epilogue

In his 1913 monograph on Herod, W. Otto developed the thesis that Josephus had access to a source — which included our A — on the Herodian period written by that ubiquitous character of ancient historiography, Anonymus. This author, he stated, was a priest who wrote in the forties of the first century. In a footnote, Otto mentioned that he had an idea as to who the author was, but preferred to reveal it only after further study.[47]

Three years later, in addenda in an odd corner of *PWRE*,[48] Otto returned to the subject and revealed that he was thinking of Philo and planned to devote a detailed study to the question of Josephus' sources on the period. But such a study seems never to have been published, perhaps because Otto turned to other areas of study.[49]

As his suggestion concerning Vitellius' visit, so too Otto's nomination of Philo seems not to have been noticed.[50] I ran across it only after completing this paper, and found it encouraging to see that Otto was thinking in the same direction. While one may well doubt that everything Otto ascribed to Philo was his, or even that everything Otto attributed to him was necessarily written by the same individual and that he was a priest,[51] it is clear that the question of Josephus' use of Philo is worthy of renewed attention. In this general field too, as with regard to our specific question, Otto's remarks, as unsubstantiated as they were, may prove quite seminal and on target.

---

[47] See Otto (above, n. 12), cols. 14 (12), n. *.

[48] Vol. I/18 (1916), col. 2515. These addenda to his article on Herod appeared at the end of a volume with the keywords "Imperium"–"Iugum."

[49] Search in H. Schreckenberg's and L. H. Feldman's volumes of Josephus bibliography, and elsewhere, failed to uncover any such study; what seems to have been Otto's last article on Josephus was published in 1916, the year he published the above-mentioned addenda. On Otto, see H. Bengtson, *Kleine Schriften zur alten Geschichte* (1974), pp. 599–618.

[50] Although — contrary to my statement in the Hebrew original of this article — Otto's addenda were noticed and listed, along with his entry for *Herodes*, by H. Schreckenberg in his *Bibliographie zu Flavius Josephus* (1968), p. 169.

[51] Although it does in fact seem quite likely that Philo was a priest; see my study in *Nourished* (above, n. 42).

5. Ishmael ben Phiabi and the Chronology of Provincia Judaea*

I. The Problem

Two high priests named Ishmael ben Phiabi are known.[1] The first was appointed by the Roman governor Valerius Gratus ca. 15 C.E., and was replaced "not long thereafter" (*Ant.* 18.34). The second one, who will concern us here, was probably his son or grandson.[2] He was appointed by Agrippa II, but after running into difficulties with the king and with the Roman governor he was sent to Rome and replaced (*Ant.* 20.179, 189–196). As it seems, his chronology is something of an Archimedean point, with implications for a number of questions concerning Judaean and Pauline chronology.

When was Ishmael ben Phiabi II appointed, and when was he sent to Rome? Josephus gives no dates, but various clues given in his writings may be of use. Ishmael's appointment is mentioned at the end of Josephus' account of Felix's procuratorship (20.179) and before the notice of the appointment of a new procurator, Porcius Festus (20.182). On the basis of the usual assumption that Felix ruled Judaea until ca. 59–60 C.E.,[3] it would seem that Ishmael acceded to the high priesthood around that time. On the other hand, Ishmael was retained in Rome due to the intervention of Poppaea, who is termed Nero's "woman" (*gynē* – 20.195). This could fit any of the years between 58 and 65 C.E.[4] However, since Ishmael was sent to Rome during Festus' term and

---

* Hebrew original: *Tarbiz* 52 (1982/83), pp. 177–200.

[1] For a lonely view that there was only one, see below, n. 8.

[2] For priests named after their fathers, see Mattathias ben Mattathias (Josephus' brother – *Vita* 8); Ananus ben Ananus (*Ant.* 20.197 etc.); Zechariah ben Zechariah (intended for John the Baptist – Luke 1:59). Johanan ben Johanan (*Ant.* 20.14) was probably a priest, given his name (for Johanan as a priestly name, see *Sinai* 88 [1980/81], pp. 37–39 [in Hebrew]) and his prominence.

[3] So, e.g. SVM I, p. 460; Smallwood, *Jews*, p. 269; M. Stern, in *The Jewish People in the First Century*, I (edd. S. Safrai and M. Stern; 1974), pp. 74–76; A. Schalit, *Roman Administration in Palestine* (1937), p.147, n. 84 (in Hebrew).

[4] Poppaea married Nero in spring/summer 62 C.E., but was his "mistress" (Feldman, p. 492, n. c) as early as 58. As Ishmael's trip to Rome can hardly be postponed to as late as 62 (see immediately below, on *BJ* 6.300–305), we are forced to accept *gynē* in its more general

Festus' successor, Albinus, began ruling Judaea no later than the fall (feast of Tabernacles) of 62 C.E. (*BJ* 6.300–305),[5] it follows that he could not have been sent to Rome later than 62 C.E.

Thus, Ishmael was appointed ca. 60 C.E. and deposed no later than 62 C.E. This conclusion is very widespread, as all the handbooks will show.[6] Nevertheless, acceptance of it requires the rejection of two ancient data. While it is possible that we might find ourselves forced to do so, this should only be done after careful consideration of the problem.

First, we note that there has been preserved, in the name of Rabbi Johanan (the central Palestinian sage of the third century), a list of high priests who served for long periods (BT *Yoma* 9a). While this list does include some obviously exaggerated data about the earlier and more legendary figures ("Simon the Just" and "Johanan the High Priest," who are said to have served for forty and eighty years, respectively), this does not justify the out-of-hand rejection of its datum concerning the more recent and lesser-known Ishmael – to whom it ascribes a ten-year incumbency. "Ten years" does not seem to be a standard round or hyperbolic period of time in rabbinic literature, and the basic claim of the list, namely, that most high priests of the Second Temple period hardly averaged a year each in office, is well supported by the Fourth Gospel (John 11:49, 51; 18:13) and other evidence concerning the last decades of that period.[7] Thus, there is a prima facie case on behalf of the credibility of R. Johanan's datum concerning Ishmael – but it flatly contradicts the consensus described above, which grants this high priest only a year or two. This problem becomes even more difficult when we note that R. Johanan's list does not include Ishmael's immediate predecessor, Ananias ben Nedebaeus, although current opinion gives him about eleven years (48–58/59 C.E.).[8]

---

sense, woman." Cf. *Ant.* 17.34, where Josephus uses the more specific *gametē* when he wants to distinguish between married women and *gynaikes*. SVM I, p. 466, offers another solution: Poppea is termed "wife" proleptically, although at the time she was only a "concubine." On Poppaea, see R. Hanslik in *PWRE* I/43 (1953), cols. 85–88.

[5] Here it is stated that Albinus was in office four years before the start of the rebellion – which *BJ* 2.284 dates to the fall of 66.

[6] See, for example, SVM II, p. 231; Stern (above, n. 3), pp. 366–369; and the tables in E. M. Smallwood, *JTS* n.s. 13 (1962), p. 32 and D. M. Rhoads, *Israel in Revolution: 6–74 C.E. – A Political History Based on the Writings of Josephus* (1976), p. 185.

[7] On round and hyperbolic numbers in rabbinic literature, see J. Bergmann, *MGWJ* 82 (1938), pp. 361–376. As for nearly annual changes of the high priest, see G. Alon, *Jews, Judaism and the Classical World* (1977), pp. 61–65, also U. Holzmeister, *Zeitschrift für katholische Theologie* 44 (1920), pp. 306–312.

[8] I have noticed only one attempt to deal with this difficulty: S. Munk's suggestion (*Palestine* [1845], p. 563b, n. 1) that there was only one priest named Ishmael ben Phiabi, who served eight years under Gratus and another two in the fifties. But this entails not only that his second tenure was at quite an advanced age, but also that Josephus failed to remark upon the highly unusual circumstance, and that, on the contrary, Josephus' statement that Ishmael

Second, Josephus reports a famine which afflicted Judaea "in the days of Claudius the emperor of the Romans, and of our high priest Ishmael" (*Ant.* 3.320). Claudius died in 54 C.E., about five years before the usual dating of Ishmael's accession to the high priesthood. Moreover: it is usual, and probably correct, to identify this famine with the one of the late forties mentioned in *Ant.* 20.51–52, 101 and in Acts 11:27–30.[9] But this heightens the discrepancy between Josephus' statement and the usual dating of Ishmael's high priesthood. In order to solve the problem, scholars have either assumed that Josephus is referring to another Ishmael[10] (but our list of high priests is full and includes no Ishmael other than ben Phiabi)[11] or emended the high priest's name or that of the emperor[12] (and, in the latter event, assumed that the famine in question is otherwise unknown), or suggested that Ishmael was appointed in the late forties and subsequently deposed, only to be reappointed ca. 59–60 (without Josephus mentioning these vicissitudes).[13] All of these solutions are, of course, merely counsels of desperation, but the only other

---

served "not long" under Gratus (*Ant.* 18.34) refers to eight years. Two other high priests mentioned there are each said to have served a year each, and the impression gained is that Ishmael served even less. (Above, pp. 182–201, I have argued that Gratus himself was only in office for about four years.) The notion that there was only one Ishmael ben Phiabi reappeared in the 1969 Hebrew version of S. Applebaum's *Jews and Greeks in Ancient Cyrene* (p. 191), but not in the 1979 English edition.

[9] On this famine, see J. Jeremias, *Jerusalem in the Time of Jesus* (1969), pp. 141–143; further literature is cited below, n. 68. Certainty that the reference is to the same famine is bolstered not only by the lack of reference to other famines under Claudius, but also by the specific detail that both *Ant.* 3.321 and 20.51–52 refer to the import of grain from abroad.

[10] So K. Lake, in *The Beginnings of Christianity*, I/5 (edd. F. J. Foakes Jackson and K. Lake; 1933), p. 455. Lake suggests that this high priest is not mentioned elsewhere, or that he is to be identified with the one "called Cantheras" (*Ant.* 20.16); in any case, he admits that Josephus forgot to note his appointment. But it is clear, and nigh-universally agreed, that the high priest "called Cantheras" is to be identified with Eliehoeinai ben Cantheras, whose appointment is the preceding one in *Ant.* (19.342). See, for example, SVM II, p. 231, also G. Hölscher, *Die Hohenpriesterliste bei Josephus und die evangelische Chronologie* (Sitzungsberichte der Heidelberger Akademie der Wissenschaften, Philosophisch-historische Klasse, Jg. 1939/40, 3. Abhandlung; 1940), p. 16. On the identity of this Eliehoeinai, see *Agrippa I*, pp. 185–195 (including contribution by Dr. Robert Brody).

[11] Josephus reports (*Ant.* 20.250) that there were twenty-eight high priests from Herod until the Destruction of the Temple, and, indeed, that is the number mentioned in *Antiquities*. Lists of them, with references to Josephus, may be found in Jeremias (above, n. 9), pp. 377–378; SVM II, pp. 229–232; Hölscher (above, n. 10), pp. 9–19; and Smallwood (above, n. 6), pp. 31–32.

[12] Changing the high-priest's name: Jeremias (above, n. 9), p. 143. Change of the emperor's name (to Nero): H. St. J. Thackeray's note to *Ant.* 3.320 in the LCL *Josephus* (vol. IV, 1930; pp. 474–475, n. a.).

[13] H. Graetz, *Geschichte der Juden* III/2 (ed. M. Brann; 1906⁵), pp. 726–727; cf. table, p. 754.

approach to date, simply to reject *Ant.* 3.320 out of hand,[14] is hardly more satisfactory.

So long as we assume that Ishmael was appointed at the end of Felix's term of office, there is no way to overcome the problems posed by these sources. They may be resolved only by the assumption that Ishmael was appointed in the late forties.[15] This would allow him to serve ten years, beginning with the famine, and be to sent to Rome at a time when Poppaea was Nero's "woman." There are, of course, some problems with this alternative assumption, and they moved scholars to prefer the late chronology, at the price of rejecting the two data adduced above. Below, we will argue that, in fact, those problems are illusions or of only minimal weight, and should not be allowed to overcome the plain meaning of the sources. Along the way, we will also suggest a few other revisions of first-century Judaean chronology, and we will also have some observations about the chronology of Paul, whose career crossed those of Felix and Festus and who was tried in the presence of a high priest.

II. Under What Circumstances was Ishmael Appointed?

Ishmael's predecessor, Ananias ben Nedebaeus, was appointed by Herod of Chalcis (Agrippa I's brother) — *Ant.* 20.103. Herod died in 48 C.E.,[16] and Claudius bequeathed to Agrippa II the right to appoint high priests (*Ant.* 20.16, 104, 222). As we have noted, it is only at the conclusion of his account of Felix's term that Josephus reports Agrippa II's appointment of Ishmael, his first such appointment: "At that time King Agrippa gave the high priesthood to Ishmael; he was the son of Phiabi" (*Ant.* 20.179). This location of the notice, and the words "at that time," have engendered the natural and usual assumption that Ishmael was appointed at the end of Felix's governorship.

However, two observations must be made. First, Josephus usually bunches notices about the high priesthood at the end of his account of a governor's term of office. Thus, for example, we read in *Ant.* 20.103 of Ananias ben Nedebaeus's appointment just before we read of the arrival of a new governor, and so too, regarding other high priests and governors, in *Ant.* 20.196,

---

[14] So Hölscher (above, n. 10: pp. 17–18) and several others, including E. Meyer, *Ursprung und Anfänge des Christentums*, III (1923), pp. 166–167, n. 6, and J. Dupont, *RB* 62 (1955), p. 53 (= idem, *Études sur les Actes des Apôtres* [1967], pp. 163–164).

[15] As was indeed suggested by Smallwood, *Jews*, p. 262, n. 23, who suggests that Ishmael was appointed during Cumanus' governorship, the notice of it being wrongly located in the narrative of Felix's term of office. An explanation which resolves the chronological conundrum without assuming a mistake on Josephus' part is preferable. Cf. above, p. 204, n. 8.

[16] "In the eighth year of Claudius Caesar" (*Ant.* 20.104); Claudius became emperor in January of 41 C.E.

213—214 and 223. Should we conclude that all of these high priests were appointed at the end of a governor's period of service? Aparently not, for there is no logic which should have brought Agrippa II to do such a thing. Rather, we should view this arrangement of data as a reflection of Josephus' procedure for interfiling material of differing origin and relating to differing themes. Namely, within each "chapter" of his narrative, defined by the successive terms of the governors of Judaea, he first gives the material relating to the governor and his administration of the province, and then various other matters are covered, including the history of the high priesthood in the period in question.[17] The words "at that time" are simply a convenient way of making the narrative flow, and mean nothing more that "within this period of time" — namely, in our case, during Felix's term as governor of Judaea.[18] We need not assume it happened at the end of that term.

The second observation is, that Josephus' notice about the appointment of Ishmael does not mention the name of his predecessor, whom he succeeded. This is a deviation from Josephus' usual practice, according to which he states that the relevant authority took the high priesthood from X and gave it to Y;[19] here, he states only that Agrippa gave it to Ishmael. This may indicate that it was not Agrippa, or not Agrippa alone, who removed Ishmael's predecessor from office. Thus, for example, we find a similar exception in the case of Ishmael's successor, Joseph ben Simeon, where Josephus uses identical language for Agrippa's "giving" the high priesthood and does not mention it having been "taken" from Ishmael (*Ant.* 20.196) — and in that case we are explicitly told that Ishmael lost his position because he was detained in Rome (§ 195), and that Agrippa appointed a replacement when he learned of the situation. It is probable that something similar happened to Ishmael's predecessor, Ananias ben Nedebaeus.

Indeed, we need not look far in order to substantiate this probability. According to Josephus, there was a violent clash between Jews and

---

[17] Only after writing the Hebrew version of this paper did I realize that this procedure is only part of a more general practice Josephus followed in *Ant.* 18—20; see above, pp. 188—198.

[18] On the looseness of "at that time," see *JQR* 72 (1981/82), esp. pp. 246—252; S.J.D. Cohen, *Josephus in Galilee and Rome: His Vita and Development as a Historian* (1979), p. 55, n. 108; W. Otto, *Herodes* (1913), cols. 180—181, n. * (= *PWRE* Supplementband II [1913] cols. 172—174, n. *); and *JSJ* 21 (1990), p. 191. In the present context, it does not matter whether or not the connection of different themes also involves the connection of extracts from different sources, as is frequently the case.

[19] See *Ant.* 15.41, 322; 17.78, 164, 339, 341; 18.26, 34—35, 95, 123; 19.297, 312, 316, 342; 20.1, 103, 197, 203, 213, 223. All of these cases mention the removal of the predecessor along with the appointment of the new high priest. Only with regard to two of the twenty-eight high priests from Herod to the Destruction (above, n. 11) did Josephus omit notice of their removal and the appointment of their successors: Hananel the Babylonian (*Ant.* 15.56, 322) and Jesus ben Seth (17.341; 18.26). Cf. above, p. 212, n. 32.

Samaritans during the term of Felix's predecessor, Cumanus, and representatives of the antagonists were sent to Rome to have the dispute adjudicated. Among these, in chains, was Ananias ben Nedebaeus (*BJ* 2.243; only somewhat less specific in *Ant.* 20.131).[20] The Jews won their case, and Ananias returned to Judaea, but it is nowhere stated that he resumed the high priesthood.[21] And, indeed, one may wonder: when the high priest was absent, and being treated as a criminal, would it not have been natural for Agrippa to have appointed a replacement? Moreover, the right to appoint high priests was a source of power and, apparently, of income as well, and it is likely that Agrippa would have exercised it as soon as possible after he received it.[22] So it is probable that Agrippa II appointed Ishmael shortly after Ananias was sent to Rome. But since Cumanus too was sent to Rome at the same time, and Felix appointed in his stead, the result is that Agrippa appointed Ishmael about the same time Felix began serving as governor of Judaea.[23] When was that?

III. When was Felix Appointed to Office?

Josephus gives no dates regarding the date of Felix's appointment or length of his service, nor does he give such data regarding Felix's predecessor (Cumanus) or his successor (Festus). We will, therefore, have to proceed on

---

[20] The latter source does not explicitly say Ananias was sent to Rome, only that his faction was, but it is not unreasonable to infer (as Feldman, in his translation) that Ananias went too. It is likely that the accounts of Cumanus' governorship, in *Ant.* and *BJ*, are based upon the same source; cf. below, n. 27 and Part IIIc.

[21] See *Ant.* 20.205−210, 213; *BJ* 2.409, 441 (his death). All agree that these references are to a time after Ananias was no longer high priest, and that the title "high priest" is to be read generically; see below, n. 23.

[22] So already Graetz (above, n. 13), p. 726; Smallwood, *Jews*, p. 262, n. 23. As Smallwood notes, Agrippa's father (*Ant.* 19.297) and uncle (20.16) did the same. For high-priestly appointments as sources of income, cf. above, p. 199, n. 71.

[23] The conflict between this result and Acts 23:2 and 24:1, according to which Ananias (ben Nedebaeus) was high priest during Felix's term of office, is not a serious difficulty. For Acts, as Josephus, uses "high priest" in a broad social sense; see Jeremias (above, n. 9), pp. 175−181; SVM II, pp. 232−236; and Stern (above, n. 3), II, pp. 600−603. This is indicated, for Acts, not only by the use of the plural ("high priests" − 4:23; 9:21; 23:14; etc.), but also by the fact that of the other two named individuals termed "high priest" in Acts (4:6; 19:14), neither was *the* high priest at the time. As Ananias' continued prominence after his service in that capacity is well-documented (see n. 21), we need not conclude that Acts 23:2 and 24:1 are to be taken as a reference to his incumbency. On the contrary: note that Paul's protestation in Acts 23:5, wherein he states that he did not know that Ananias was the high priest, may in fact support the notion that he was not the official incumbent at the time of the trial. If so, then Paul's trial would not be a *terminus post quem* for Ananias' dismissal, but rather a *terminus ad quem*. However, given the enigmatic nature of Acts 23:5, one should not push this consideration.

the basis of indirect evidence. Felix was appointed (*Ant.* 20.137) sometime
between the death of Herod of Chalcis in 48 C.E. (§ 104) and the expansion of
Agrippa II's territories in 53 (§ 138). We begin by attempting to define a
terminus post quem for Felix's appointment:

a) When was Cumanus Exiled?

Just before the notice of Cumanus' appointment, Josephus reports Ananias'
appointment, and just after Cumanus' appointment we read of Herod of
Chalcis' death in 48 C.E. (*Ant.* 20.103–4). It would seem, therefore, that all
three occurred in close chronological proximity. However, it is instructive to
read the passage in question (trans. Feldman):

> Herod, king of Chalcis, now removed Joseph, the son of Camei, from the high
> priesthood and assigned the office to Ananias, the son of Nedebaeus, as successor.
> Cumanus also came as successor to Tiberius Alexander. Herod, the brother of the great
> king Agrippa,[24] died in the eighth year of the reign of Claudius Caesar. He left three
> sons – Aristobulus, born to him by his first wife, and Berenicianus and Hyrcanus, born
> to him by Berenice, his brother's daughter. Claudius Caesar assigned Herod's kingdom
> to the younger Agrippa.

In my experience, anyone reading this paragraph assumes that Josephus
distinguishes between two individuals named Herod: King Herod of Chalcis
and Agrippa I's brother. But they were in fact one and the same. Why, then,
did Josephus add identifying words the second time he is mentioned, and not
simply say "Herod"? Or, if for some reason he wanted to re-identify the man,
why not "King Herod" or "Herod of Chalcis," as the first time? The most
probable explanation is that Josephus has spliced notices taken from two
different sources: one deals with the high priesthood and the other with the
Herodian family (as the details show).[25] But this means that the impression of
close chronological proximity between the events mentioned in this passage is
undermined.

As for Cumanus' appointment, reported here *between* the two notices about
Herod, it is interesting to note that in the parallel narrative, in *BJ* 2.223, it is
mentioned only *after* the report of Herod's death and Agrippa II's succession
to his kingdom. It has been suggested that *BJ*'s version is correct and *Ant.*'s is
only a clumsy rewriting of it.[26] However, it seems more probable that, in this

---

[24] On this title, see *Agrippa I*, pp. 136–137
[25] In *Ant.* 20.261 and *C. Ap.* 1.36, Josephus mentions a list of high priests; cf. above,
p. 212, n. 32. As for the Herodians, Josephus seems to have a number of sources; see *Agrippa
I*, ch. I. For another case in which problems arise due to the apparent combination of priestly
and Herodian materials, see above, pp. 202–217.
[26] V. Burr, *Tiberius Julius Alexander* (1955), pp. 30–31.

section of *Antiquities* Josephus returned to his source and did not base his account on *BJ* alone.[27] Moreover, while the account in *BJ* is smooth from a literary point of view, the chapter on Chalcis (§§ 221–223) being completed before the chapter on Cumanus begins, the account in *Antiquities* jumps around. Why would Josephus abandon both literary quality and chronological truth? Is it not more likely that he reordered the material in order to restore the proper chronological order?[28]

Proceeding, therefore, on the assumption that Cumanus was appointed before Herod of Chalcis died, we may now ask when that occurred. Two data will help us here. The first: According to *Ant.* 20.138, Claudius enlarged Agrippa II's kingdom upon the completion of his own twelfth year, but at the same time took Chalcis from the Jewish king after he had ruled it for four years. The end of Claudius' twelfth year was the end of 52 or very outset of 53 C.E., and this indicates that Agrippa's four years as king of Chalcis began in late 48 or early 49. And the second datum: According to *BJ* 2.284, the great rebellion broke out in the month of Artemisios in 66 C.E., in the seventeenth year of King Agrippa. This points to an era between April/May 49 and April/May 50. These two data may be coordinated one with another on the presumption that Herod died in late 48 or in the first weeks of 49 (before Claudius' ninth year began on January 25), and after a few months – due to the winter and decision-making processes – Agrippa II was appointed in his stead, in ca. April–May of 49.[29]

This means that Cumanus was appointed by 25 January 49, but we don't know how long before that date. The last absolute date in Josephus' narrative, sometime in the course of 45 C.E., appears in a document cited in the course of the narrative concerning Cumanus' second predecessor, Fadus (*Ant.* 20.14),[30] but we don't know how much longer Fadus served or how long his successor (Tiberius Julius Alexander) served, before being replaced by

---

[27] On the Cumanus narrative in *Antiquities*, see esp. Cohen (above, n. 18), pp. 62–63; F. Schemann, *Die Quellen des Flavius Josephus in der jüdischen Archaeologie Buch XVIII–XX = Polemos II, cap. VII–XIV,3* (1887), pp. 11–18; and Meyer (above, n. 14), pp. 44–45, n. 4. See also G. Hölscher, *PWRE* I/18 (1916), col. 1988.

[28] So too Cohen (above, n. 18), p. 63. Cf. above, p. 192, n. 47.

[29] For emphasis upon the fact that BJ 2.284 leads us to 49, not 50, see H. Seyrig, *Revue numismatique*, 6ᵉ série, 6 (1964), p. 56 = idem, *Scripta Numismatica* (1986), p. 126. Smallwood (*Jews*, p. 262, n. 22) assumes an interregnum of a year or more between Herod's death and Agrippa's appointment, and SVM (I, p. 472, n. 6) goes even further, assuming that Agrippa II's years were counted, as those of a Jewish king, from Nisan 50. However, there is nothing to indicate an interregnum, and, in addition to the other doubts pertaining to the use of a spring era (see above, pp. 174–180), we may note that SVM is forced (ibid. n. 7), in consequence of its assumption, to assume that the datum in *Ant.* 20.138 applies to the *end* of 53 C.E., although the formulation, as noted, points rather to the beginning of that year.

[30] The precise date is corrupt; see Feldman ad loc., also Smallwood, *Jews*, p. 261, n. 18; Lake (above, n. 10), p. 453.

Cumanus. (The usual assignment of 44–46 to Fadus and 46–48 to Tiberius Julius Alexander is simply a convention, similar to the symmetric apportionment of 6–9, 9–12 and 12–15 to the first three Roman governors of Judaea).

Perhaps we will have better luck with another question: How long did Cumanus serve? Josephus begins his account of Cumanus' term with an ugly incident which occurred during a celebration of the Passover festival; we next hear of a clash during a pilgrimage festival (*BJ* 2.232; *Ant.* 20.118), and when the governor of Syria, Ummidius Quadratus, then intervened and sent Cumanus and the main antagonists to Rome, he thereafter visited Jerusalem – again during a Passover festival (*BJ* 2.244; *Ant.* 20.133). The way these stormy events are interwoven has led many scholars to assume that they all took place during one year.[31] Building upon this reasonable impression, all we have to know, in order to determine the length of Cumanus' service, is how long went by between his appointment to office and the Passover of the first incident.

Since, as we will later see, it is usual to assume Felix was appointed in 52 C.E., it is also usual to suppose that Josephus' account portrays the last year of Cumanus' governorship, between Passover 51 and Passover 52. But no reader of Josephus would suppose that more than two years had passed between his appointment and the outbreak of trouble: Josephus' accounts, in both books, open with the first stormy Passover. Moreover, commenting upon the sacrilegious behavior of a Roman soldier during that first incident, Josephus notes that Cumanus' predecessors too had posted soldiers in the Temple during the festivals (*Ant.* 20.107). This appears to imply that this was Cumanus' first festival as governor; otherwise, Josephus could have pointed out that Cumanus himself had done so in previous years.

As we have seen, Cumanus' first Passover in Judaea could have been in 49, or in any one of the three previous years (although in decreasing probability, the further back one goes), for we do not know until when his predecessor served. Here, we would suggest a hypothesis which, although it cannot be proven at this point, will account for a number of details we have so far assembled: Cumanus' first Passover was that of 48. If this was the case, then he was removed from office and sent to Rome shortly before Passover 49, along with Ananias ben Nedebaeus and the others – i.e., around the time Agrippa

---

[31] So, for example, in the notes to *BJ* 2.244 in the translations by H. St. J. Thackeray (English [LCL] – 1927), G. Ricciotti (Italian – 1949), O. Michel and O. Bauernfeind (German – 1962) and A. Pelletier (French – 1980). This unanimity of the translators is quite a good recommendation, for it means that those who are most familiar with Josephus' style, and have less occasion than historians to consider extraneous factors, agree that this is the plain sense of Josephus' narrative.

II inherited his uncle's kingdom, as we have seen. Then Agrippa appointed Ishmael, around the same time that Claudius was appointing Felix to take Cumanus' place.

To see if this was indeed the case, we will attack the problem from the other direction, from the *terminus ad quem* for Felix's appointment to office. Our point of departure will be Paul's statement to Felix, according to Acts 24:10, that he is confident because he knows that Felix has been judging the Jews "for many years." Of course, it is possible that these words are conventional and empty of historical value; but while we could live easily with such a judgement as a conclusion, there is no reason to assume it *a priori*.[32] Let us therefore ask:

b) When was Paul Tried by Felix?

The linchpin of Pauline chronology is Paul's visit to Corinth, for after he remained there a year and six months a new governor, Gallio, arrived (Acts 18:11−12): thanks to a famous inscription, it is known that L. Iunnius Gallio's term as governor began ca. May 51.[33] If Paul left Corinth "several days" later (18:18),[34] then this happened in the late spring or early summer of 51. Thereafter, we hear of trips to Palestine and Syria (18:18−22), followed by a voyage to Ephesus where Paul stayed about two and a quarter years (19:8 + 19:10),[35] and then of Paul's return to Jerusalem via Macedonia, Greece (staying there three months − 20:3), and Macedonia again (where he celebrated Passover); Paul hoped to arrive in Jerusalem in time for Pentecost (20:16), fifty days after Passover, and apparently succeeded in doing so or in arriving only shortly thereafter;[36] and twelve days later he was already on trial before Felix (24:11). There is no scholarly consensus regarding the length of these journeys since Corinth,[37] but for reasons which will become apparent it seems that the following short chronology is to be preferred:

---

[32] As was the procedure in *Beginnings* (above, n. 10), IV, p. 300; so too Ed. Schwartz, *Nachrichten von der königlichen Gesellschaft der Wissenschaften zu Göttingen, Philologisch-historische Klasse* (1907), pp. 294−295 (an important essay reprinted, with original pagination shown, in his *Gesammelte Schriften*, V [1963], pp. 124−169.)

[33] On "the Gallio inscription," see A. Plassart, *Revue des études grecques* 80 (1967), pp. 372−378; G. Luedemann, *Paul, Apostle to the Gentiles* (1984), pp. 163−164.

[34] "In view of the riot we may think that this was hardly the 'many days' of the RSV but more probably the 'several days' of the Berkeley Version" (J. Finegan, *Handbook of Biblical Chronology* [1964], p. 507).

[35] Acts 20:31 refers to "three years," but this is rounded and exaggerated to fit the argument. As commentators agree, the figure was closer to two (19:10) and a quarter (19:8) years. See, for example, Haenchen, p. 67, and H. Conzelmann, *Die Apostelgeschichte* (1972²), p. 120.

[36] On the text of Acts 21:26−27, see Schwartz (above, n. 32), pp. 290−291, n. 2.

[37] For a table comparing various opinions, see Lake (above, n. 10), p. 473. As there are more or less specific data for other parts of Paul's travels, the main question is how much time

May/June 51 — Paul leaves Corinth
By Autumn 51 — visits in Palestine and Syria and arrival in Ephesus
Until mid-winter 53/54 — in Ephesus
Until Passover 54 — Macedonia, Greece, Macedonia
Pentecost 54 — Jerusalem

According to such a reconstruction, Paul was tried by Felix in the early summer of 54.[38] Let us see how this will fit in with what we know of events subsequent to the trial.

The trial ended without a decision and Paul remained in prison. After two years, according to Acts 24:27, a new Roman governor of Judaea arrived: Festus. If we knew when this happened, we could check our dating of the trial. However, precisely this question is one of the most debated questions of first-century Judaean chronology: while some scholars date Festus' appointment ca. 59−60, others peg it to 55−56.[39] This thorny problem is created by the discord among four data: 1) Acts 24:27, as noted, says that, after his trial, Paul stayed in prison for two years before Festus arrived to take Felix's place; 2) Paul was tried in 54 C.E. (according to our short chronology; the many who date the trial later make the problem worse); 3) Josephus reports that after Festus replaced Felix the Jews of Caesarea sent a delegation to Nero to complain against Felix, but the latter was not punished thanks to the intervention of his brother Pallas, "who was then very highly respected by Nero" (*Ant.* 20.182); but 4) Tacitus (*Ann.* 13.14) reports that Pallas was removed from his office in late 54 or early 55,[40] a year or two earlier than the date resulting from the first two data.

Various solutions have been proposed. Some would ignore Josephus' statement about Pallas or reject it,[41] while others prefer to attempt (quite hopelessly) to bring Pallas' removal from office down to a somewhat later

---

to allot the visits in Palestine and Syria. Given the fact that both are mentioned in one verse (18:22), it is reasonable to infer that they did not take long. I see no reason to assume, with Haenchen (p. 67), that Paul arrived in Ephesus only in the autumn of 52.

[38] So too, for example, C. Saumagne, in *Mélanges d'archéologie et d'histoire offerts à André Piganiol*, III (ed. R. Chevallier; 1966), p. 1386.

[39] For a survey of the problem, see Stern (above, n. 3), pp. 74−76. On some inconclusive arguments, see Appendix II.

[40] The date results from the fact that Nero, who succeeded Claudius in October 54, fired Pallas before planning to kill Britannicus; the latter was murdered before his fourteenth birthday (*Ann.* 13.15), which came in mid-February of 55 (cf. below, n. 42). On Pallas, see S. I. Oost, *American Journal of Philology* 79 (1958), pp. 113−139.

[41] It is ignored by G. B. Caird, *The Apostolic Age* (1955), p. 210 and denied significance by Conzelmann (above, n. 35), p. 139; Schwartz (above, n. 32), pp. 285−286; and Smallwood, *Jews*, pp. 270−271, n. 46. (Smallwood, as SVM I, p. 466, also considers the possibility that Josephus' testimony should be viewed as proof that Pallas regained his influence, despite the fact that this is not documented elsewhere.)

date[42] or suggest that despite his removal from office Pallas retained some influence with Nero (but Josephus says "very highly honored").[43] Again, yet others would reinterpret Acts 24:27 as if it referred to Felix's having completed two years as governor, but this interpretation[44] ignores both the narrow context (the previous verse describes the conditions of Paul's imprisonment) and the fact that the narrative of Acts is following Paul's career, not Felix's.[45]

In order to resolve this conundrun, I suggest two revisions of the third datum:

a. It is doubtful that Pallas was ever very highly respected *by Nero*. Nero, who ascended to the throne in mid-October 54 and within two or three months found an occasion to fire the rich freedman who was his mother's lover, probably tended to do so from the outset.[46] But if we settle for Pallas being simply influential, and not necessarily honored by Nero, we need not limit ourselves to the period prior to his removal from office. According to Tacitus, Pallas left his post arrogantly and with good conditions, taking with him many slaves and a promise of immunity (*Ann.* 13.14).[47] He did not disappear from the stage of history until he was made to stand trial, despite his immunity, in

---

[42] As noted above (n. 40), Pallas was removed from office before Britannicus' fourteenth birthday; according to Tacitus, who reports the event in the course of his narrative for 54/55 C.E., that birthday came in February of 55. According to Suetonius, however, Britannicus was born to Claudius "vicesimo imperii die inque secundo consulatu" (*Claudius* 27). Suetonius' two data apparently contradict one another: the former points to February 41 but the latter – to 42 C.E. Haenchen, pp. 70–71, n. 3, argues that "imperii die" refers only to the date, January 25, and the year is indicated only by the reference to the second consulate; the result is that Britannicus was born in February 42, so Pallas, according to Suetonius, was removed from office late in 55 or early in 56. However, even if that were Suetonius' opinion, it would still contradict Tacitus' report, which is to be preferred. Moreover, it could not deal with the Alexandrian coin which honors Britannicus in 41 C.E. See J. Vogt, *Die alexandrinischen Münzen*, I (1924), pp. 24–25, and the detailed discussion by F. Giancotti in *Atti della Accademia Nazionale dei Lincei, ser. 8, Rendiconti* (Classe di scienze morali, storiche e filologiche) 9 (1954), pp. 587–591.

[43] So, for example, Stern (above, n. 3), p. 76; Meyer (above, n. 14), p. 53. Our solution will be similar, but it will nevertheless allow Pallas' final fall to be earlier.

[44] Argued especially by Saumagne (above, n. 38), pp. 1384–1386; Schwartz (above, n. 32), p. 294; and Haenchen, pp. 71, 661.

[45] Indeed, Haenchen (ibid.) argues that the author of Acts thought the reference to two years, which he found in his source, was to the time Paul spent in prison prior to his trial; the true reference, however, according to Haenchen, was to Felix's service as governor. Although such an error is of course possible, we would prefer a reconstruction which does not need to posit one.

[46] Compare the case of Agrippina (Nero's mother): although Nero and his advisers probably plotted against her from the outset, she at first enjoyed great honor, and her position only gradually deteriorated until she was murdered in 59. See C. Lackeit in *PWRE* I/19 (1918), cols. 912–913.

[47] See Oost (above, n. 40), pp. 133–135.

late 55 (*Ann.* 13.23).[48] Although he put in an arrogant appearance at that trial too, it seems that it was nevertheless his downfall, and we hear nothing more about him until his death in 62 (*Ann.* 14.60).[49] The end of 55 may thus be taken as a *terminus ad quem* supplied by our third datum.

b. Although *Ant.* 20.182 states the Caesarean delegation to Nero set out only after Festus was appointed, *BJ* 2.270, apparently speaking of the same delegation (see below), says it was sent during Felix's governorship. *BJ* claims that Felix sent delegations from both sides to Nero, while *Ant.* holds the Jews made their peace with Felix and mentions no complaints to Rome as long as he was governor. Which version shall we prefer?

On the one hand, the account in *Ant.* is not convincing: if the riots ended the way it claims, why did the Jews complain against Felix after he was replaced? And if there were two separate delegations (one under Felix and one after him), why does each narrative report one alone? Moreover given Josephus' report of Felix's hostility toward the Jews of Caesarea, "both" Jewish delegations would have attacked him, and not only the "Greeks" of Caesarea. That is, the topics discussed by "both" delegations were probably the same. So we conclude that there was only one Jewish delegation, which was sent while Felix was still governor.[50] Josephus probably narrated it in *Ant.* under Festus due to the continuation of the story, which played itself out under that governor.

On the basis of these two revisions of the third datum, it is not difficult to support the following chronology:

early summer 54 — Paul's trial before Felix
autumn 55 — Caesarean delegations to Rome
end of 55 — Pallas' trial
spring/summer 56 — Festus arrives in Judaea, two years after Paul's trial[51]

Thus, our examination of the events after Paul's trial indeed corresponds with our conclusions on the basis of its antecedents: Paul's trial was shortly after Pentecost of 54. If we now return to Acts 24:10, it appears impossible to accept the statement that Felix had been serving for "many years" if, as is usually

---

[48] On this trial, see Oost, loc. cit., pp. 135–137. The date results from the placement of the story toward the end of the events of 55 C.E. and from the beginning of the next sentence: "Fine anni."

[49] See Oost, loc. cit., p. 138.

[50] So too SVM I, pp. 465–467; Smallwood, *Jews*, p. 287, n. 101; L. I. Levine, *Caesarea Under Roman Rule* (1975), p. 29. Stern (above, n. 3: p. 368), however, assumed there were two delegations.

[51] It thus seems, we may note, that just as Felix was appointed after Pallas came to enjoy high honor (*Ann.* 11.29 — 48 C.E.), and Pallas could still save his brother at the time of the Caesarean complaints, so too Felix was removed from office shortly after his brother's downfall. As for Festus' appointment in 56, see above, n. 39.

assumed, he only assumed office in 52 C.E. Consequently, as we have seen
(n. 32), many simply discount this statement. But it would be acceptable if
Felix had in fact been in office since 49 C.E., as we suggested.

The time has come, therefore, to ask why it is universally assumed that Felix
began his term of office in 52 C.E. This consensus rests upon two pillars, one
each from Josephus and Tacitus. Josephus reports Felix's appointment
between Cumanus' removal from office and the 53 C.E. expansion of Agrippa
II's territories (*BJ* 2.245−247; *Ant.* 20.136−138), and from the juxtaposition
of these latter two notices it is inferred that Cumanus administered Judaea
until ca. 53. However, one might just as well infer from the fact that Josephus
does not give a date for Felix's appointment but does give one for the
expansion of Agrippa's kingdom, that the latter event occurred some time
after the former one, thus requiring a new beginning, as it were. And, in any
case, we have already brought our argument for Cumanus not having served
more than a year in the late forties.

The argument from Tacitus requires more attention. It seems that rather
than contradicting our reconstruction, it in fact supports it.

c) Tacitus and Josephus on Judaea, 49−52 C.E.

An expression similar to Acts 24:10's "many years" appears in *Ann.*
12.54.1−4.[52] In the context of his account of 52 C.E., Tacitus mentions Felix
as one who had ruled Judaea "already for some time" ("iam pridem Iudaeae
impositus"). According to Tacitus, the Jews had always been agitating since
the traumatic days of Gaius Caligula, and Felix, moreover, played a role in
fomenting unrest. Cumanus and Felix, we read, were procurators at the same
time in different parts of Palestine, Felix ruling Samaria and Cumanus − the
Galilee. Together, they let the Jews and the Samaritans fight one another as
long as they let them share the booty, but when matters got out of hand
Quadratus, the governor of Syria, intervened. He punished those locals who
had killed Roman soldiers, but he also took care to have Cumanus punished.
"Thus was quiet restored to the province" is Tacitus' conclusion of this
intriguing report.

Before evaluating the reliability of this account, we must first interpret it.
Tacitus does not say that the episode he describes − in which Felix was not
governor of Judaea, but only of Samaria − took place in 52 C.E. On the
contrary, he states that it took place sometime between ("interim" − § 2)
Gaius' days and 52 C.E. By the latter year, in fact, Felix had "already for some
time" been governor of Judaea. Tacitus tells the story in his account of 52 C.E.
not because it happened then, but only because he needed it then to help

---

[52] Text, translation, commentary and bibliography in *GLA* II, pp. 76−82.

condemn Pallas. Tacitus despised Pallas and missed no opportunity to besmirch him.[53] But in *Ann*. 12.53, just before our passage, Tacitus was forced to tell a story which redounded to Pallas' credit: Pallas turned down a large cash prize for service to the state. Tacitus solved the problem in two ways: he added some ironic comments about Pallas' generosity,[54] and he appended a story about Pallas' corrupt and rapacious brother. This point and context are made quite clear by Tacitus' introduction of his account here: "But his brother, Felix, did not show such moderation . . ." Thus, we should not infer from Tacitus, as is usual, that Felix was appointed in 52 C.E. On the contrary, if we may accept his testimony, we may see in it support for our claim that Felix had been governor of Judaea "already for some time," about three years, by 52 C.E.

But may we accept Tacitus' testimony? What shall we say of his claim that Cumanus and Felix served side by side, and not one after the other as Josephus claims and as fits our usual picture of the Roman administration of Judaea? And what shall we say of his failure to refer to a "procurator" of Judaea (in the limited sense) at the time of the disturbances he describes? (He refers only to the governors of Samaria and the Galilee). Due to these difficulties, some scholars simply reject Tacitus' account here out of hand,[55] while others would harmonize it with Josephus by inferring that Felix filled some secondary role in the administration of the province while Cumanus was governor. Even Tacitus' firmest advocate here, Ed. Schwartz (see below), admitted that there is almost no hint in Josephus of the type of situation described in our account.[56]

However, it appears worthwhile to reexamine Schwartz's theory. It may be improved, and support from Josephus may be adduced. Schwartz's point of departure was another passage in the *Annales*, in the context of 49 C.E.: "Ituraea and Judaea were joined to the province of Syria upon the deaths of their kings, Sohaemus and Agrippa" (*Ann*. 12.23.1).[57] Accordingly, Schwartz postulated that Claudius tried an administrative experiment (*"Verwaltungsexperiment"*) in 49, attaching Judaea — in the limited sense — to Syria. Thus, Schwartz explains, there was no "procurator" of Judaea at the time Cumanus and Felix ruled other parts of Palestine. According to Schwartz, this experiment continued until 52 C.E., when it was canceled, Cumanus was exiled, and Felix was appointed governor of all of Provincia Judaea.[58]

---

[53] See *Ann*. 11.29; 12.65; 13.2, 14, 23 (according to Oost [above, n. 40], p. 135, Tacitus reports the trial only in order to exemplify Pallas' arrogance); 14.2.

[54] On this irony, see Oost, loc. cit, pp. 131–132; R. Syme, *Tacitus*, II (1958), p. 539.

[55] So, for example, Schalit (above, n. 3), p. 147, n. 82; SVM I, pp. 459–460, n. 15.

[56] Schwartz (above, n. 32), p. 287.

[57] *GLA* II, pp. 75–76.

[58] Schwartz (above, n. 32), pp. 286–287.

As is, on the one hand, this theory is not at all convincing. First of all, too much is missing: if there had been such a Verwaltungsexperiment, we should have heard about when and why it was instituted and when and why it was canceled. Such questions, much less answers, are not suggested by Josephus or Tacitus. Moreover, from Josephus' account it is clear that Cumanus was in fact governor of Provincia Judaea (*BJ* 2.223; *Ant.* 20.105, 107). And again, we must underline that Tacitus does not say Felix was appointed governor of the province in 52, but that by then he had for some time held the post.

On the other hand, however, I would agree with the many scholars who assume that Tacitus did not simply create his account out of whole cloth while daydreaming. Such scholars argue, as noted above, that one should salvage from Tacitus' account at least the datum that Felix served in Judaea in some subordinate position during Cumanus' governorship of the province. And they have even pointed out that a similar inference may be drawn from *BJ* 2.247's report of Felix's appointment: "Claudius afterwards sent Felix, Pallas' brother, as the governor of Judaea, Samaria, the Galilee and Peraea." As no other governor's appointment is detailed in this way, it may be inferred that, prior to his appointment to governorship of the entire province, Felix had exercised authority in one or more of its constituent areas.[59]

But, even if this was the case, we must still ask what led Tacitus to err and assume that Cumanus had not been governor of the province, and what made him think that Judaea had been attached to Syria in 49 C.E. The obvious answer is that he had a source which misled him to such conclusions. Suppose he had a source which reported rioting in Palestine in 49 C.E. and the involvement of the Roman provincial officials, quiet returning to the province only after the intervention of the legate of Syria. If the source did not report that Cumanus was governor of Judaea, but did report that the riots were between Galileans and Samaritans, it would be natural to infer that Judaea was administratively linked to Syria and that the two officials mentioned in the source, Cumanus and Felix, had been rulers of the two districts in question, but not of Judaea. The same conclusion would tend to be supported by the fact that the two Herodians connected with the years 48–49, Herod II (who died) and Agrippa II (who succeeded him), were not kings of Judaea. If, in other words, Tacitus thought he knew of Roman officials who ruled regions of Palestine but not Judaea proper, and knew of Herodians who, although the natural rulers of Judaea, did not rule it, and if he also knew of intervention in Judaea by the Roman governor of Syria, the most likely inference was that Judaea proper was ruled by the governor of Syria – as previously regions of Palestine had been so ruled.[60] This is the conclusion which Tacitus drew in

[59] See Stern, *GLA* II, pp. 79–80; idem (above, n. 3), pp. 374–376.
[60] On Philip's territories, see *Ant.* 18.108. As for Lysanias' territories, and Judaea under

Ann. 12.23.1. The details of his source on Cumanus and Felix, however, he reserved for his narrative on 52 (12.54), as we have seen, in order to use it against Pallas.

Was there really such a source as this? There is, of course, no point in claiming certainty on such matters, but it seems that a number of oddities in Josephus' account may be explained on the assumption that he too used such a source:[61]

a. Although *BJ* 2.223 reports that Cumanus was sent to replace Tiberius Julius Alexander as the governor of the province, the parallel in *Ant.* 20.103 says only that "Cumanus came as the successor of Tiberius Julius Alexander," without specifying his title. This may be explained on the assumption that *Ant.* is closer to the language of its source than *BJ*, and that the source too did not specify Cumanus' title.

b. Neither *BJ* 2.247 nor *Ant.* 20.137, which report Felix's appointment, note that he was Cumanus' "successor" − in contrast to Josephus' practice regarding almost every other governor.[62] It is said only that Felix was sent to Judaea, without mentioning Cumanus. A source for such a statement could well give the impression that both served at the same time.

c. *Ant.* 20.116 reports that after one of the riots the Jews went to complain to Cumanus in Caesarea, "since Cumanus chanced to be (*etugchanen*) there." Such a statement reinforces the impression that Cumanus was not governor of Judaea, for, if he were, Caesarea would have been his usual residence.

d. *BJ* 2.223 reports Cumanus' appointment after Herod's inheritance of Chalcis, saying "Cumanus took over from Alexander the governorship *of the rest of the province*." For us, this is a troublesome remark, for Chalcis had never been part of the province. But for one who was not familiar with the detailed history and geography of the region, a reasonable conclusion would be that Cumanus was not entrusted with the governorship of all of Judaea. And, indeed, it is not said here or anywhere else in *BJ*'s long narrative on him

---

Gaius, see *Agrippa I*, pp. 60−65. In general, on Syrian oversight of Provincia Judaea, see Stern (above, n. 3), pp. 311−315; J.-P. Lémonon, *Pilate et le gouvernement de la Judée* (1981), pp. 60−71. Cf. *Ant.* 17.355, 18.2, and 19.363, which show how natural it was to think of Judaea as a district of Syria.

[61] Cf. above, n. 27.

[62] See *Ant.* 18.31, 32, 33, 35; 20.100, 103, 182, 215, 252; *BJ* 2.223, 271, 272, 277 (several of the early governors are not mentioned in *BJ*). Josephus does not use such language with regard to Coponius and Fadus, of course, because they replaced Herodians and did not simply "succeed" governors. Neither is there any such language with regard to Marcellus (*Ant.* 18.89) and Marullus (§ 237) − which jibes well with the argument that neither was a governor of Judaea (see *Agrippa I*, pp. 62−65). Thus, apart from Felix, the only governor who succeeded one who is not said to have done so is Albinus. He, however, is exceptional in that his predecessor died in office, which Josephus specifically points out in *Ant.* 20.197.

(BJ 2.223–246) that Cumanus had been the governor of Judaea; this opening sentence is the closest we get.

e. In the *Antiquities*, in contrast, Cumanus is once called "governor" (20.132 – *epitropos*), but "of Judaea" is not added. His name is twice linked to "Judaea," but both (20.105, 107) seem to be from Josephus' additions to what he found in his source. Namely:

i. In *Ant.* 20.105, the opening "When Cumanus administered the affairs of Judaea there was an uproar in the city of Jerusalem, on account of which many Jews died" is followed by "But first I shall report the reason, on account of which it occurred." Such language is typical Josephan language when inserting material from a written source.[63] In other words, these opening sentences reflect *Josephus'* knowledge that Cumanus had been governor of Judaea, but not, necessarily, details stated by his source.

ii. In *Ant.* 20.107, Josephus states that Cumanus stationed soldiers in the Temple just as had previously been done by "those who had served as governors of Judaea before him," thus indicating that Cumanus had indeed been a governor. But in the parallel in *BJ* 2.224, while the fact that soldiers had in the past too been stationed there is stated, we are not told who had stationed them. Again, therefore, it seems that Josephus has, in *Antiquities*, amplified the statement of his source with his own knowledge that Cumanus was a governor of the whole province.

Thus, these five observations point to the existence of a written source on the period which did not know that Cumanus had been governor of Judaea, or didn't make the point clear. Moreover, literary arguments for the use of a written source for this part of Josephus' narrative have already been adduced.[64] Josephus used the source at length, since he was interested in the history of Judaea, and he amplified it now and then with his knowledge regarding Cumanus' true post. Moreover, he omits reference to Felix under Cumanus, thus leaving the latter the sole villain.[65] Tacitus for his part, used

---

[63] See below, p. 271, n. 76. For a nearby example in *Ant.* 20, see §§ 141–144: the concluding unfulfilled cross-reference ("as we shall relate below") is another sign that Josephus took this passage from a written source (where it was fulfilled), for it is unbelievable that here, in the middle of the final book of his *Antiquities*, Josephus did not know that his own narrative would not cover events of 79 C.E. In *JQR* 72 (1981/82), pp. 241–268, we have attempted to characterize this source.

[64] See above, n. 27.

[65] One may speculate as to why Josephus did not report Felix's role as a sub-gubernatorial official in the events, evidently identical with those of *Ann.* 12.54, which he narrates in *BJ* 2.232 ff. and *Ant.* 20.118 ff. Perhaps he did not understand the situation reflected by the source, or thought, perhaps correctly – Josephus was already in his young teens at the time the source portrayed! – that it was in error. Or perhaps inserting Felix under Cumanus would have caused Josephus too much difficulty in following his usual procedure of dealing with governors only successively (see above, pp. 188–198). Finally, pitting Cumanus against Felix would have made it more difficult to portray them both as villains.

only one story from the source, to serve his purposes regarding Pallas, and improperly drew some false (if natural) conclusions regarding the relations of Judaea and Syria and the positions held by Cumanus and Felix.

Summary regarding the date of Felix's appointment: From Josephus, we determined that it is possible, and indeed probable, that Cumanus' governorship was no longer than a year, and began no later than the very beginning of 49 C.E. We suggested, in fact, that it began in the spring of 48. To this we added Paul's statement, apparently in 54 C.E., that Felix had already been judging the province for "many years" and Tacitus' statement that by 52 C.E. Felix had already been governor of Judaea for some time; both fit a 49 C.E. start for his governorship. Moreover, we suggested that Tacitus' statement regarding the annexation of Judaea to Syria in 49 C.E., although wrong, gives the point of reference for his other statement, a few pages later, that by 52 Felix had been governor of Judaea for some time. These statements may be traced to a lost source which Josephus too seems to have used.

Now, if we return to Ishmael ben Phiabi, and recall that our opening discussion placed his appointment around the same time as Felix was appointed, i.e., in the spring of 49, then it will no longer be difficult to accept R. Johanan's ascription of ten years to him and the same sage's failure to list Ananias ben Nedebaeus among the high priests who served for more than a year or so. For Ishmael, on the one hand, would have been in the high priesthood about ten years, as R. Johanan says, if he was appointed in 49 C.E. and sent to Rome in the late fifties, when Poppaea was Nero's "woman." And Ananias ben Nedebaeus, on the other hand, who was appointed just before Cumanus was and replaced at the end of Cumanus' term, would indeed have served for just about a year, in accordance with the norm reported by R. Johanan (and the Fourth Gospel, etc. − above, n. 7). While it would have been easy to live with the conclusion that this third-century sage erred regarding first-century high priests, there does not seem to be any particular reason to assume that he did. This leaves only one problem:

IV. Was Ishmael High Priest at the Time of the Famine
(*Ant.* 3.320)?

If we agree to place Ishmael's appointment in the spring or summer of 49 C.E., this problem is not at all difficult. As stated in Part I, we accept the usual assumption that the famine in question is the well-known one in the days of Claudius. Josephus, it is true, mentions the famine in the context of his discussion of the governorship of Tiberius Julius Alexander (*Ant.* 20.101), Cumanus' predecessor. If we were to assume that the famine ended in the days of this procurator, we would have to admit that at least a year (the rest of his term + all of Cumanus') passed between that time and Ishmael's appointment to office. However, two reasons lead us to assume that the famine in fact continued at least until the spring of 49: a) either, as is usually assumed, the year 47/48 was a sabbatical year, in which case the results of a famine that year would have been felt until the new harvest in 49,[66] or else the year 48/49 itself was a sabbatical, with even worse results;[67] and b) various literary and archaeological data from the Mediterranean basin testify to a general famine in the late forties, until as late as 51 C.E.[68]

This leaves only a marginal difficulty. Josephus' reference to the famine in *Ant.* 3.320 reports that Ishmael was the high priest *on Passover* at the time of the famine, but according to our reconstruction of the events (above, Part III/a) it seems that Ishmael could have been appointed only after Passover 49. We could resolve this difficulty either by assuming that the Pasover in question was that of 50, or by assuming that — since Josephus' source on the high priesthood did not, apparently, give exact dates for the appointment of high priests, but only the names of the appointers[69] — he wrongly inferred from Ananias ben Nedebaeus' removal before Passover that Ishmael was also appointed at that time. Indeed, it is possible that the Jerusalem priesthood provisionally appointed Ishmael so as not to leave the high priesthood vacant during Passover 49, and Agrippa's later "appointment" of him was really only a ratification of that move.

---

[66] "The famine must, therefore, have run the following course: Summer 47, the harvest failed; the sabbatical year 47−48 aggravated the famine, and prolonged it until the next harvest of spring 49" (Jeremias, above, n. 9: p. 143).

[67] For the debate concerning the sabbatical cycle, see the literature cited in *Agrippa I*, p. 107, n. 4.

[68] See Dupont (above, n. 14), pp. 52−55 (= *Études*, pp. 163−165); K. S. Gapp, *HTR* 28 (1935), pp. 258−265.

[69] As one may see from the notices scattered around *Antiquities* (cf. above, n. 19), the high-priestly chronicle gave the names of the high priests and often the names of those who appointed them, also, at times, the priest's length of service and his family connections; but no absolute dates. Therefore, short interruptions would not immediately be evident. Cf. Hölscher's characterization of the chronicle (above, n. 10: pp. 19−22). Correspondingly, there is virtually no evidence for usage of high-priestly lists for dating. I Maccabees 13:42 and BT *Rosh HaShana* 18b (cf. above, p. 48), which report such for the Hasmoneans, are exceptions which prove the rule, for it was done insofar as they were temporal rulers, not qua high priests. So far, I believe the only evidence we have for dating according to the high priest's name, apart from *Ant.* 3.320 and Luke 3:1, is the disappointingly fragmentary votive inscription published by B. Isaac in *IEJ* 33 (1983), pp. 86−92 − and none specifies which year of the high priest. Although many high priests served only a year each (see above, n. 7), the cases of Caiaphas and Ishmael, among others who served for longer periods, show such specification would be necessary if the high priest's name were to be used eponymously for dating.

V. Summary

Our discussion has been directed, primarily, against two widespread opinions: the assumption that Ishmael was appointed only at the end of Felix's term of office, and the assumption that Felix was appointed to office in 52 C.E., leaving Cumanus four years (48–52). The first assumption was based on the location of the notice of Ishmael's appointment in Josephus' narrative and its introduction by the words "at that time" (*Ant.* 20.179): we argued that neither consideration carries much specific chronological weight. Rather, they are mere by-products of Josephus' editorial procedures, and show only that Ishmael was appointed *sometime* during Felix's tenure. The second assumption too, on the date of Felix's appointment to the Judaean governorship, is based upon the juxtaposition of notices in Josephus, and also upon Tacitus' narrative for 52 C.E.: we argued that Tacitus was not referring to events of that year, but rather to events some time past, and that, in any event, Josephus' narrative of Cumanus' term of office appears to refer to a period of one year.

Accordingly, instead of those two widespread opinions, we argued that both Ishmael and Felix were appointed in 49 C.E., after their predecessors – Ananias ben Nedebaeus and Cumanus – were sent to Rome. This reconstruction is supported by the assumption that Agrippa II would have exercised his authority to appoint high priests at the earliest opportunity, and also by Acts 24:10, which indicates that Felix had been governor for several years by the time of Paul's arrest – which we placed in the spring/summer of 54 C.E. Correspondingly, we placed Festus' arrival in Judaea, to replace Felix, in the summer of 56, "two years" after Paul was arrested (Acts 24:27).

This reconstruction allows us to accept at face value not only the two data about Ishmael with which we began – BT *Yoma* 9a and *Ant.* 3.320 – but also to accept Acts 24:10 ("many years") and the main point of *Ant.* 20.182 (Pallas was quite respected at the time of Felix's trial). While we could have lived easily with the notion that any of these data had been disproven, it is improper method to discard them *a priori* and, as we have argued, there seems to be no good reason to do so *a posteriori* either. Finally, we have also shown that a proper reading of Tacitus' information of Judaea in the years 49–52 does not contradict our reconstruction, and, on the contrary, despite its confusion, it in fact supports the notion that Felix was in Judaea as early as the late forties. The value of Tacitus' testimony is enhanced by the probability that it was drawn from the same source which served Josephus for this period.

The following table sets out our chronological conclusions:

Before Passover 48	Cumanus appointed procurator of Judaea
Late 48/January 49	Herod of Chalcis dies
Before Passover 49	Cumanus and Ananias sent to Rome; Cumanus exiled, Felix appointed
April/May 49	Agrippa II given Chalcis and appoints Ishmael
Early summer 54	Paul arrested in Jerusalem; trial by Felix
Autumn 55	Caesarean delegation to Rome
Late 55	Pallas' trial
Spring 56	Festus appointed to replace Felix
58 or 59	Ishmael sent to Rome and detained there

The appendices detail inconclusive debates on two issues.

Appendix I:
On Longinus' and Quadratus' Syrian Governorships

The chronology suggested above, which assumes that Ummidius Quadratus was governor of Syria in the spring of 49 (when he intervened in Judaea and suspended Cumanus), contradicts the usual assumption that his predecessor, Cassius Longinus, was still in the post at that time. That assumption, found, for example, in SVM I, p. 264 and *GLA* II, p. 81 (both cite additional bibliography), depends upon the fact that Tacitus mentions Longinus as the governor of Syria (*Ann.* 12.11–12) during his account of 49 C.E. (*Ann.* 12.5–24). It seems, however, that there is no room for certainty concerning the matter.

In *Ann.* 12.10–14, Tacitus reports Meherdates' attempt to wrest the Parthian crown from Gotarzes. This attempt came in the wake of a Parthian mission to Rome: Claudius gave his approval to the mission's request, and sent Meherdates, along with Longinus, to the Euphrates, where the two parted. Meherdates crossed the river, but rather than directly proceeding on to attack Gotarzes, he spent "many days" in Edessa and then, upon his departure, did not take the direct route to Mesopotamia but rather detoured via Armenia — where passage, in the early winter, was, however, quite difficult. Given this poor beginning, it is not surprising that Gotarzes defeated Meherdates and captured him. However, Tacitus concludes, Gotarzes died soon thereafter.

When did these events occur? As we have noted, they are reported in the context of 49 C.E. It is clear, however, that not all of these events took place during that year. For, first of all, Meherdates only began passing through

Armenia at the beginning of a winter, and his campaign certainly extended into the next year. Moreover, we know that Gotarzes did not die until 51 (or even 52; see R. H. McDowell, *Coins from Seleucia on the Tigris* [1935], pp. 190–191, 227; N. C. Debevoise, *A Political History of Parthia* [1938], p. 174; E. Koestermann, *Cornelius Tacitus: Annalen*, III [1967], p. 133). It is apparent, therefore, that Tacitus summarized a long story here, one which is basically external to his main topic (Roman affairs). The question is, is 49 C.E. the year in which the story *began* (with the Parthian delegation to Rome) – in which case it is clear that Longinus was the Roman governor of Syria that year; or is 49 C.E. the year of the *main story*, Meherdates' defeat?

I find the latter option more reasonable, for two reasons. First, according to *Ann.* 11.10 the Parthian delegation went to Rome in 47 C.E., and it is difficult to imagine that two years went by before it was heard. In order to resolve this difficulty, Koestermann (ibid., p. 123) suggested that the delegation was in fact sent later, Tacitus' narrative in the *Annales* having run over beyond 47 C.E. But by the same token the problem may be resolved from the other direction, by the assumption that Tacitus' narrative for 49 began its review of Parthian affairs with a background event which preceded that year – the hearing of the Parthian delegation, just as it obviously ends with an event well after that year – Gotarzes' death. Second, McDowell (op. cit., p. 227) has noted that the emphasis on Gotarzes' person in coins of 46/47 and 47/48 indicates that Meherdates was already competing with him then. (McDowell notes that the usual dating of Meherdates' campaign, 49 C.E., "presents difficulties" – and left the matter at that. U. Kahrstedt's response [*Artabanos III. und seine Erben* (1950), p. 26, n. 15], that it is improper to attribute such a mistake to Tacitus with regard to maters of Roman history, is beside the point, both because the matter is tangential to Roman history – Longinus left Meherdates at the Euphrates! – and because the question is not, "Did Tacitus err?" but, rather, "Which part of his narrative caused him to locate it in the course of his narrative for 49 C.E.?")

Accordingly, we would suggest that the Parthian delegation was received in 47 or 48, and Meherdates was then sent out with Longinus. The winter preceding his downfall was thus the winter of 48/49. Tacitus chose to insert the story at its culmination, supplying the background retrospectively, a procedure we have elsewhere observed in Josephus; see above, pp. 194–196. Tacitus, therefore, presents no obstacle to the assumption that Quadratus was governor of Syria in the spring of 49 C.E.

Appendix II:
On the Date of Festus' Appointment

That Festus was appointed ca. 56 C.E., as argued above, is maintained by various scholars (including Haenchen, pp. 70–71; Conzelmann [above, n. 35], p. 139; Lake [above, n. 10], pp. 466–467; Schwartz [above, n. 32], pp. 285–286), but their arguments are not always cogent. Stern (above, n. 3: pp. 74–76) lists and rejects three of their arguments. We did not use two of those (another interpretation of Acts 24:27 [cf. above, at nn. 44–45] and Eusebius' testimony), and the third, which links Pallas' fall from influence to his removal from office, we have corrected, linking it rather to his trial. As for Stern's three arguments in favor of the more usual dating of Festus' appointment to ca. 60, they are not persuasive. The first is the fact that Josephus relates numerous events under Felix after the death of Claudius in 54, thus indicating – Stern argues – that Felix served long under Nero. However, since prior to his notice of Claudius' death Josephus reports nothing which occurred under Felix (apart from his marriage to Drusilla, which is reported in *Ant.* 20.141–144 as part of the Herodian narrative, not part of Felix's *res gestae* [see above, p. 196, on 1/1]), it is hardly justified to conclude that all which is reported after Claudius' death occurred after that date. See Saumagne (above, n. 38) p. 1341 and especially Schwartz (above, n. 32), p. 285. Stern's second argument is from the fact that the incident of the Egyptian prophet (*Ant.* 20.169–172), which was not among the first events under Felix, was already "before these days" by the time of Paul's trial under Felix (Acts 21:38). This too argues for a longer tenure for Felix. According to the chronology we have proposed here, which too lengthens Felix's term of office (but by making it begin earlier, not end later), this point requires no debate. Finally, Stern argues from the fact that Josephus, when he was twenty-six years old (i.e., ca. 63 C.E. – see *Ant.* 20.267 and *Vita* 5), went to Rome in order to obtain the release of priests who had been sent there by Felix (*Vita* 13). This is more reasonable on the assumption that Felix served as late as 60 C.E. However, it is not impossible that Josephus went seven or eight years after the priests had been sent. On the other hand, if one is to insist that Josephus was sent shortly after they were arrested, even two years is a long wait (so Smallwood [*Jews* p. 281, n. 84] has suggested that "Albinus" should be substituted for "Felix" here). In any case, there are other problems with the chronology of the first paragraphs of *Vita* (missing link[s?] in the stemma in §§ 3–5; 16 years + three considerable periods + 3 years = 19 years in §§ 11–12 – see SVM I, p. 46, n. 3; Cohen [above, n. 18], pp. 107–108), so the datum concerning Josephus' age at the time of his Roman mission cannot be considered very probative.

Finally, although those who adhere to the late date for Festus' appointment usually place it in 59 or 60, Stern in fact raised the possibility of moving Festus' appointment up to 58/59, so as to account for a procuratorial coin minted that year. While others who hold to the late dating for Festus had consequently ascribed the coin to Felix, Stern suggests that − since Felix had last minted coins in 54 − the new issue marked the arrival of a new governor. In all this, Stern was followed by Y. Meshorer (*Ancient Jewish Coinage*, II [1982], pp. 182−183), who quotes him at length. However, even according to the usual chronology, followed by Stern and Meshorer, the two Judaean governors who preceded Festus in minting (Pilate and Felix) waited two or three years before minting (much more according to the chronology suggested in this volume), so the inference does not seem warranted. For a table summarizing the provincial coinage, see Meshorer, pp. 173−174. Stern, indeed, in a note (p. 76, n. 5) which Meshorer did not copy, left open the possibility that Felix had minted the coin, after an interval of a few years during which he had not done so. That would have been a response to a need for new coinage. But such a need could have been dealt with by Festus too.

6. Texts, Coins, Fashions and Dates:
Josephus' *Vita* and Agrippa II's Death*

> "Historians usually find what they are
> looking for — a fact that makes me
> uneasy."
> *Morton Smith**

In 1606, J. J. Scaliger published his magnum opus on Eusebius' *Chronicon*. Among his notes was the observation that although Josephus, when completing his *Antiquities* in Domitian's thirteenth year (93/94 C.E. — *Ant.* 20.267), announced (§ 266) that he would continue to write a brief autobiography, he must have waited a few years. This emerges from the fact that his *Vita* (§ 359) mentions Agrippa II's death, an event which Photius, in his account of Justus of Tiberias (*Bibliotheca* 33), dated to Trajan's third year (100 C.E.). For Scaliger, who had been deeply involved with the production of the first (1601) edition of Photius, this was not a problem, but rather only an observation of an obvious fact.[1]

Almost three hundred years later, in the standard edition of his standard handbook on the period, Emil Schürer said the exact same thing.[2] But it now required a footnote of more than half a page of small print to dispose of all the doubts which had been raised in the intervening centuries and which had given rise to a consensus that the *Vita* appeared under Domitian (d. 96) and Agrippa

---

* An abridged version of this paper was presented as a "Joseph and Gertie Schwartz Memorial Lecture" at the University of Toronto in November 1989.
**M. Smith, *The Secret Gospel: The Discovery and Interpretation of the Secret Gospel According to Mark* (1973), p. 96.
[1] See the "Animadversiones in chronologica Eusebii," in his: *Thesaurus Temporum, Eusebii Pamphili Caesareae Palaestinae Episcopi, Chronicorum canonum* . . . (1606 [reprinted 1968]), p. 187 (ad ann. Abr. 2109). For the relevant passage from Photius, see vol. I, pp. 18—19 in R. Henry's 1959 edition of the *Bibliotheca* (translated below, n. 16). Cf. Henry, p. xxxvii, on Scaliger's contribution to the 1601 Photius edition in which, correspondingly, no emendations were suggested regarding the date of Agrippa's death.
[2] E. Schürer, *Geschichte des jüdischen Volkes im Zeitalter Jesu Christi*, I (1901³⁻⁴), pp. 599—600, n. 47.

II had died even before the publication of *Antiquities* in 93/94. And another seventy years later, in the revised English version of this handbook, the same footnote is more than double the length and comes to the conclusions Schürer himself had resisted.[3] Those conclusions, in fact, are very widely held, and today one almost never finds Photius' date for Agrippa's death.[4] In what follows, we propose to analyze the discussion of this issue, which — precisely because it is so circumscribed — offers a paradigmatic case of the interplaying effects of the piecemeal discovery and assimilation of knowledge, of the changing integration and disintegration of related disciplines, and of changes in philological fashions. Moreover, understanding the history of the debate will help us understand why the time has now come to reconsider Photius' dating — which, indeed, many have assumed to be taken from Justus' lost work itself.

I. From the Seventeenth Century to the 1890's

At first, as we have seen, Scaliger noted only the contradiction between Photius' date for Agrippa's death and the assumption that the *Vita* was written immediately after the *Antiquities*; therefore, he rejected that assumption. This adoption of Photius' date was prepared, however, a few pages earlier, by the rejection of some evidence in earlier Church literature: Eusebius states that Agrippa II reigned only twenty-six years and Scaliger assumed that Syncellus too, whose newly-discovered text read "twenty-three," should be corrected to the same.[5] Since Agrippa received his kingdom in 49 C.E. (Josephus, *Ant.*

---

[3] SVM I, pp. 481–483, n. 47.

[4] Other currently standard reference works and central discussions with this date include, for some examples, the detailed discussions in Smallwood, *Jews*, pp. 573–574; *Prosopographia Imperii Romani saec. I.I.III.*, pars IV/3 (ed. L. Petersen; 1966²), p. 134 (nr. 132, Agrippa II) and p. 363 (nr. 872, Justus of Tiberias); T. Rajak, *Josephus: The Historian and His Society* (1983), pp. 237–238; E. Migliario, *Athenaeum* n.s. 59 (1981), pp. 98–101; and, especially, S. J. D. Cohen, *Josephus in Galilee and Rome: His Vita and Development as a Historian* (1979), pp 170–180. For just as heavy a consensus three-four generations ago, despite Schürer, see below, n. 22. Nothing much changed in between. See, for two prominent examples, R. Syme, in *Cambridge Ancient History*, XI (edd. S. A. Cook, F. E. Adcock and M. P. Charlesworth; 1936), p. 138, and A. H M. Jones, *The Herods of Judaea* (1938), p. 259.

[5] See Eusebius, *Chronicon*, p. 179 (ed. Helm²); Georgius Syncellus, *Chronographia*, vol. I, pp. 629, 647–648 (ed. Dindorf [Bonn]; 1829). Dindorf's, as already J. Goar's 1652 edition (which was available to Dodwell — see below), gives "twenty-three" in both passages, but Scaliger, in his reconstruction of Eusebius' lost first book, based upon Syncellus, has "twenty-six" (as Eusebius) in the first (above, n. 1: p. 65, line 3). In the second (his p. 65, line 28), however, he has "twenty-three," as Goar and Dindorf. For Scaliger's discussion, see "Animadversiones," p. 182. Cf. vol. II, p. 333 of Dindorf's edition, where Scaliger's reading is noted, and ibid., p. 540, where Dindorf acknowledges the logic of Scaliger's explanation of

20.103−4; *BJ* 2.284), these writers thus date his fall to 75 C.E. Scaliger had noted, however, that both writers, in these same passages, assume Agrippa II succeeded his father immediately upon the latter's death in 44 C.E., so he concluded that the twenty-six year reign was merely a calculation based upon the misconception that the end of the last Jewish king came at the same time as the destruction of the Temple: 70−44=26.[6] Therefore, when Scaliger came to discuss the dates of the *Vita* and of Agrippa's death, he had no difficulty in following Photius.

It was only natural that someone would take the opposite course, and, in the late 1680's, Henry Dodwell, the English historian, did just that. Scaliger had emended Syncellus into agreeing with Eusebius and rejected their joint statement as a result of calculation on the basis of an erroneous assumption (reign since 44), leaving Photius unchallenged. But while Eusebius' figure might well be so rejected, Syncellus' figure, if left uncorrected, is not so readily dismissed; and the first edition of Sycellus, in 1652, indeed left "twenty-three" unchanged.[7] Dodwell noticed, moreover that twenty-three years from Agrippa's enthronement in 49/50 bring us to 72 C.E. − *Vespasian's* third year. Therefore, he suggested that Photius' reference to Agrippa's death be emended so as to refer, in fact, to Vespasian's third year instead of Trajan's.[8]

This was quite an attractive solution, but, apart from the lack of manuscript or other internal support for the emendation, three more difficulties should be mentioned: 1) it flatly contradicted Cassius Dio's notice (66[65].15.3 [Xiphilinus]) that Agrippa II was alive and in Rome in 75 C.E.; 2) it just as

---

Eusebius but nevertheless reasserts the reading of "twenty-three" in Syncellus. The same reading, "twenty-three," is also found in Anastasius Bibliothecarius' excerpts from Syncellus, reprinted in Migne, *Patrologia Graeca* 108, col. 1197. Most of Scaliger's emendations of Syncellus were unannounced ("stillschweigend"), according to J. Bernays, *Joseph Justus Scaliger* (1855), p. 222.

[6] The same misconception lies behind the story found in several medieval Jewish sources about Agrippa's execution at the time of the Destruction. See, inter alia, *Josippon*, vol. I, p. 450 (ed. Flusser; cf. ibid., vol. II, pp. 32−42); *Zemah David*, pp. 83−84 (ed. Breuer); A. Posnanski, *Schiloh: Ein Beitrag zur Geschichte der Messiaslehre* (1904), pp. 217, 223, 228, 238. Cf. below, nn. 79 and 88.

[7] See above, n. 5.

[8] Dodwell's discussion may be found in J. Pearson, *Opera posthuma chronologica &c.,* II (1688), pp. 173−175. Dodwell's main argument, apart from the evidence of Eusebius and Syncellus, is from Photius/Justus' failure to say anything about Agrippa's fate after Vespasian (for the text, see below, n. 16). His suggestion is not quite as wild as it sounds ("Vespasian" for "Trajan"), for due to the immediately antecedent reference to Vespasian in Photius' text, the emendation requires only *tou autou* instead of *Traianou*. For the assumption that the Epaphroditus who was Josephus' patron was the one executed in 95 C.E., and that Josephus himself (who had many enemies) probably died shortly thereafter, see also Dodwell's *Dissertationes in Irenaeum* (1689), p. 468.

flatly contradicted Josephus' claim (*Vita* 359–360) that Justus had waited for
twenty years, until Agrippa II died, before publishing his history of the Jewish
war; and 3) it was apparently contradicted even by the minimal numismatic
evidence which was then available. I do not know how anyone dealt with the
first problem. The second was adroitly sidestepped by the foremost scholar of
the next few years, S. Lenain de Tillemont, whose discussion remained the
standard one for the next two centuries.[9] But the third problem was to bring
about a lasting revision of Dodwell's approach, as we shall now see.

Chr. Noldius' 1660 discussion of Herodian chronology, which accepts
Photius' date without difficulty (and rejects Eusebius' and Syncellus' à la
Scaliger), shows no knowledge of any relevant coins. But a decade after
Noldius, E. Spanheim, one of the pioneers of numismatics, would publish
coins dated not only to Agrippa's nineteenth and twenty-fourth years, but also
to his twenty-sixth and twenty-ninth.[10] On the natural assumption that their
era was Agrippa's 49/50 C.E. enthronement, these showed that Agrippa was
still minting as late as 78 C.E. – five years later than Vespasian's third year.
What is one to do when an elegant emendation is contradicted by mere coins?
Dodwell's solution had been to manhandle the coins: he postulated that
Agrippa II used his father's death (44 C.E.) as the era for his coins, although
he was not to become a king until five years later. This was nice in that it again

---

[9] Dio's reference to Agrippa being in Rome was already noted, and juxtaposed with
Photius' notice on Agrippa and with Josephus' statement that the Herodian line survived
Herod by a century (*Ant.* 18.128), by J. Ussher, *Annales* II (1654), p. 702 (a.M. 4076, the very
last lines of the volume); it was applied against Dodwell's suggestion (that Agrippa died in 72
C.E.) by S. Basnage, *Annales politico-ecclesiastici* I (1706), p. 783. As for Josephus' "twenty
years," E. Spanheim's note on *Vita* 359–360 in the great 1726 Hudson-Havercamp edition of
Josephus (vol. II, p. 33, n. 1) only refers the reader back to his opening note on the *Vita*,
where no mention is made of the twenty years. Tillemont, for his part, summarizes Josephus'
text here until just before the reference to the twenty years, covering it with "etc.". That is,
Tillemont informs the reader only that Josephus complained that Justus had waited until
Vespasian and Titus died. Then, having suppressed the number of years, Tillemont has the
nerve to claim that Josephus' statement "n'est pas neanmoins si exprès, que nous ne pussions
mettre sa (= Agrippa's) mort dès auparavant, si nous en avions quelque preuve"! See S.
Lenain de Tillemont, *Histoire des empereurs*, I (1690), Note XLI, p. 731 = p. 30 of notes in
second ed., 1732.

[10] See Chr. Noldius, *Historia Idumaea, seu de vita et gestis Heodum diatribe* (1660),
reprinted in the 1726 Hudson-Havercamp Josephus, vol. II, pp. 333–395 (see esp.
pp. 383–384; this section of the essay is not included in the English translation included in
various old editions of Josephus); E. Spanheim, *Dissertatio de praestantia et usu numismatum
antiquorum* (1671[2]), pp. 447, 863–864 (the 1664 first edition does not mention Agrippa's
coins). Spanheim published pictures of these coins, and the same year a picture of a "year 26"
coin was also published in C. Patin, *Imperatorum Romanorum numismata . . .* (1671), p. 164.
Already Scaliger (above, n. 1: p. 182 – ad ann. Abr. 2086) cited coins of Agrippa's twenty-
first (see below, n. 35!) and twenty-sixth years as additional proof, apart from Photius, for
Eusebius' (and Syncellus') error.

pointed to 72 C.E. (Vespasian's third year), but is patently absurd, as Tillemont was soon to note.[11] A humbler, if less satisfactory, approach was taken by Spanheim's own brother, Friedrich: in his learned chronological discussion published in 1701, he rehearsed the arguments in favor of Dodwell's emendation and adopted his conclusion, but then lamely added the notice that "my brother, who is familiar with coins," had informed him that there were coins from up to Agrippa's twenty-ninth year. No further comment was added.[12]

Others did better. Dodwell's emendation of Photius became available just a couple of years before S. Lenain de Tillemont began publishing his monumental *Histoire des empereurs* and, in response, he managed to add, in the very last pages of his first volume (1690), an extended appendix about the dates of Agrippa's death and the composition of the *Vita*.[13] Here, on the one hand, Tillemont recognized that the coins, if not already Scaliger, had disposed of Eusebius and Syncellus. On the other hand, however, in a few closely-printed columns, Tillemont set out the arguments which, instead of Eusebius and Syncellus, were to become the heart of the new anti-Photius dossier, based on evidence which was not only much more ancient but also from a source as close as possible to Agrippa II – Josephus himself. Tillemont's arguments were, in a nutshell, several indications that the *Vita*, which mentions Agrippa's death, was written before Domitian's (September, 96 C.E.). First, the way in which Josephus notes that Vespasian, Titus and Domitian were gracious toward him (*Vita* 414–429), but makes no mention of Nerva or Trajan, implies that he wrote under Domitian. Second, the fact that the *Vita*, as *Antiquities* and *Contra Apionem*, is dedicated to one Epaphroditus (*Vita* 430), would indicate the same, on the supposition that this man was the prominent freedman and secretary (*a libellis*) executed by Domitian in 95 (CD 67.14; Suetonius, *Domitian* 14).[14] Third, the enclitic beginning of *Vita* (*emoi de*) seems to imply that the book is a direct continuation of *Antiquities*, so its date should be about the same as that of the latter – Domitian's thirteenth year. And, finally, the same conclusion seems to emerge also from the facts that the *Vita* follows the *Antiquities* in all but one manuscript, and that

[11] See Tillemont, as above, n. 9.

[12] F. Spanheim, *Opera, quatenus complectuntur geographiam, chronologiam, et historiam sacram atque ecclesiasticam utriusque temporis* (1701), *Chronologia sacra*, cols. 584–585, 591. Already in 1675, this Spanheim had noted the end of the Herodian line about the same time ("circa haec fere tempora") as the destruction of the Temple: *Introductio ad historiam et antiquitates sacras* (1675), p. 299. On his one argument apart from the evidence from Syncellus, see below, n. 33.

[13] Tillemont (above, n. 9), pp. 730–732 (= 29–30).

[14] On this Epaphroditus, see *Ant.* 1.8, *C. Ap.* 1.1, 2.1 and 2.296, and A. Stein, in *PWRE* I/10 (1905), cols. 2710–2711.

Josephus, in the last paragraph of the *Vita*, announces that he herewith concludes his narrative of the Jews' *antiquities*. (Tillemont was here developing a line of scholarship with its own history: if in 1569 J. Christophorson had felt it neccessary to replace Eusebius' reference to "in the end of the *Antiquities*" with "in the *Vita*" in his Latin translation of Eusebius' *Hist.eccl.* 3.10.8−11 [where he cites *Vita* 361−364], and Scaliger too, a half century later, still thought Eusebius' text was corrupt here, by 1659, H. Valesius' standard edition was pointing out that the *Vita* is, indeed, the conclusion of the *Antiquities*.[15])

But if the *Vita* was written before 96 C.E. and mentions Agrippa's death, then it appears obvious that Photius, or his copyists, must be wrong. So if Dodwell's suggestion to make Photius refer to *Vespasian*'s third year was eliminated by the coins of Agrippa's twenty-ninth year, the next best suggestions were to let the patriarch refer to Titus' third year or to Domitian's − and, indeed, Tillemont closed his discussion by leaving both possibilities open. And that was the way things would stay for the next two hundred years, one scholar after another adopting one or the other of these possibilities. The only new suggestions were that of C. Müller to make Photius refer to *Justus'* death in Trajan's third year, and that of N. Brüll who, as late as 1885, emended "Trajan" into "Domitian" and "third" into "thirteen," thus allowing Agrippa to die the same year Josephus finished his *Antiquities*.[16] The only thing which

---

[15] For the debate on *Hist. eccl.* 3.10, see Scaliger (above, n. 1), p. 188 and Valesius' 1659 edition, reprinted in Migne, *Patrologia Graeca* 20, col. 243, n. 84; Christophorson had rendered *tēs Archaiologias tou telous* with "in libello . . . de sua ipsius vita."

[16] Already in 1687, in fact, H. Aldrich had opted for *Domitian*'s third year, in his comment on *BJ* 2.14.4 on the very last page of his *Fl. Josephi Historiarum de Bello Judaico, Liber primus et pars secundi* (1687 [perhaps first released in 1700 − cf. I. A. Fabricius, *Bibliotheca Graeca*, V (1796³), pp. 42−43]), p. 132; the gist of his comment was later reprinted in vol. 2, p. 180 of the 1726 Hudson-Havercamp Josephus. I. M. Jost, a century later, preferred *Titus'* third year (*Geschichte der Israeliten*, II [1821], pp. 103−4, n. 12). Both suggestions are repeated frequently, including in the apparatus to Codex 33 in I. Bekker's 1824−25 edition of Photius (vol. I, p. 6 = Migne, *Patrologia Graeca* 103, cols. 65−66). For Brüll's suggestion, see *Jahrbücher für Jüdische Geschichte und Literatur* 7 (1885), pp. 51−53. As for interpreting Photius so as to have him mean *Justus* died in Trajan's third year, see C. Müller, *Fragmenta historicorum graecorum*, III (1849), p. 523, where this understanding is presented quite matter-of-factly; Müller was followed by H. Graetz, *MGWJ* 26 (1877), pp. 338−339, who deliberately used this interpretation to resolve our problem. To the present writer, as to almost all readers of Photius − including those cited in n. 21, below − it is clear that the text means that Agrippa died in Trajan's third year. In the statement, "The history [of Justus of Tiberias] begins (*archetai*) with Moses and concludes (*katalēgei*) with the death (*teleutēs*) of Agrippa, the seventh of the house of Herod and the last of Jewish kings, who received rule under Claudius, was granted additional territory by Nero and even more by Vespasian, and died (*teleutą*) in Trajan's third year, where also the history concludes (*katelēxen*)," the chiastic correspondence of the underlined words clearly distinguishes between Agrippa's life and Justus' history. (For the same way of characterizing a history, see the end of Photius' codex

might be said for this audacity is that it at least had the virtue of accounting for Josephus' notice about the minimum of twenty years which had passed between the war and Agrippa's death.

None of these suggestions was at all convincing or transcriptionally likely, and they were all dropped when, in the late nineteenth century, stronger evidence that Photius was wrong became available.[17] It seems, in other words, that when the evidence against Photius' dating of Agrippa's death was only inferential, scholars preferred to avoid attacking Photius directly and concentrated upon his copyists alone, but when the case for an earlier death became direct and more solid, they were willing to give up the groundless emendations and simply pronounce Photius to be in error. This was also, of course, a particular case of two more general developments: 1) the establishment of disciplined text criticism, in the course of the nineteenth century, left emendations very much on the defensive and often in disrepute — if already A. Boekh, in mid-century, guessed that at most five emendations in a hundred were correct, by 1921, U. von Wilamowitz-Möllendorf was opining that one in a thousand was a more accurate estimate;[18] and 2) under the weight of increasing archaeological, papyrological and epigraphic discoveries, Byzantine works had become increasingly marginal in the study of antiquity, so why bother emending them?

31, just a few lines before our passage: Theodoret of Cyr's history begins [*archetai*] with the Arian controversy and ends [*katalēgei*] with the death [*teleutēs*] of Diodorus.) For more criticism of Müller, see Brüll (above) and A. Baerwald, *Flavius Josephus in Galiläa, sein Verhältniss zu den Parteien insbesondere zu Justus von Tiberias und König Agrippa II.* (1877), pp. 19—20, n. 6.

[17] For the wholesale rejection of the emendations and misinterpretation, see not only Schürer (above, n. 2), p. 88, n. 20, who therefore accepts Photius, but also various scholars who nonetheless reject Photius as well, such as H. Luther, *Josephus und Justus von Tiberias: Ein Beitrag zur Geschichte des jüdischen Aufstandes* (1910), p. 64, n. 2. For some earlier doubts, see M. Brann, *MGWJ* 20 (1871), pp. 26—28. SVM I ignores the whole possibility of emendation: compare its p. 54 to the original version mentioned at the outset of this note. Similarly, no emendations of the date are mentioned in the apparatus to Henry's edition of Photius (above, n. 1), in contrast to Bekker's (above, n. 16).

[18] Boeckh's assessment (*Enzyklopädie und Methodologie der philologischen Wissenschaften*, I [ed. E. Bratuscheck; 1886²], p. 175) is cited, along with some others, at the outset of the chapter on emendation in a standard handbook of the day: F. W. Hall, *A Companion to Classical Texts* (1913), p. 151. For the more pessimistic estimate, see U. von Wilamowitz-Möllendorff, *Geschichte der Philologie* (1921), p. 61 (= *History of Classical Scholarship* [1982], p. 136). For another straw in the wind, see *The Classical Papers of A. E. Housman*, III (collected and edited by J. Diggle and F. R. D. Goodyear; 1972), p. 903 (a 1915 review of a reedition of Ovid's *Tristia*, in which the editor had eliminated two-thirds of the emendations he had offered in 1889; Housman thought almost all of the rest should go too.) On the especial riskiness of emendation due to historical considerations, see Boeckh, op. cit., pp. 207—210. In general, on the decline of conjectural emendation in the late nineteenth century, see E. J. Kenney, *The Classical Text* (1974), pp. 125—127.

The new and stronger case against Photius was based upon the discovery that passages in Josephus' *Antiquities* 17 and 20 indicated that Agrippa was already dead. As late as 1877, most scholars who discussed our problem, even in detail, knew of only *Vita* 359, in all of Josephus' writings, as an indication of Agrippa's death.[19] This left room for the conservative Scaliger-Schürer solution, which allowed for the passage of several years between the *Antiquities* (93/94 C.E.) and the *Vita*. But, beginning with an article by H. Graetz in that same 1877, and especially in the next two decades — a period of very lively Josephus studies accompanying the preparation and publication of B. Niese's critical edition — a number of scholars noticed that *Ant.* 17.28 referred to the beginning of Roman rule over (some of?) Agrippa II's former territories. And they also noticed several passages in *Antiquities* 20 which are so nasty with regard to Agrippa and his sisters that it is difficult to believe Josephus would have written them if the king were around to read them.[20] Therefore, the 93/94 C.E. date for *Antiquities* now came to be taken as a firm *terminus ad quem* for Agrippa's death. So firm, in fact, that it now became acceptable to stop emending Photius into line and to begin admitting that he had erred. At most, one needed only suggest the source of his error.[21]

---

[19] See Baerwald (above, n. 16), pp. 17–19; Brüll (above, n. 16); Brann (above, n. 17); E. Schürer, *Lehrbuch der neutestamentlichen Zeitgeschichte* (1874), p. 322.

[20] B. Niese rested his case for Agrippa dying by 93/94 C.E. on *Ant.* 17.28, commenting on the way it had previously been overlooked (*Historische Zeitschrift* 76 [1896], p. 227. For the record, we note, however, that E. Spanheim, in the 1706 edition of his *Dissertatio* [above, n. 10: p. 532], had already pointed out this passage and its implication. Schürer too [above, n. 19: p. 321] had noted the passage, but concluded only that Agrippa's rule of this particular military colony had ended by 93/94.) Elsewhere, however, the passage most frequently cited is *Ant.* 20.145–147, where Josephus reports rumors of incest between Agrippa and Berenice; see also ibid., §§ 141–144, 189–196, 211–214, 216–218. See Graetz (above, n. 16), pp. 340–341; A. von Gutschmid, *Kleine Schriften*, IV (ed. F. Rühl; 1893), pp. 354–355 — see below, at n. 37!; A. Schlatter, *Der Chronograph aus dem zehnten Jahre Antoninus* (Texte und Untersuchungen XII/1; 1894), pp. 40–44; C. Erbes, *Zeitschrift für wissenschaftliche Theologie* 39 (1896), esp. pp. 425–427; Luther (above, n. 17), pp. 55–59. It is all this literature in the 1890's which accounts for the length of Schürer's 1901 discussion (above, n. 2) in contrast to his brevity in 1874 (above, n. 19); indeed, even in the 1891 second edition of his *Geschichte* (I, pp. 501–502, n. 43), Schürer still failed to relate to any *Ant.* argument for an early death.

[21] I have encountered three theories, none particularly convincing. The first, offered by Basnage (below, n. 35: pp. 105–6) and then again by Niese (above, n. 20: p. 226, n. 4) and his disciple (Luther [above, n. 17: p. 52]), and more recently by B. Z. Wacholder (*Eupolemus: A Study of Judaeo-Greek Literature* [1974], p. 302) and his disciple (D. A. Barish [*HTR* 71 (1978), pp. 71–72]), assumes that Photius *found* the date "third year of Trajan" in Justus' text but mistakenly thought it referred to the year of Agrippa's death; in fact, according to this theory, the date was that of the completion or publication of Justus' work. The second theory, offered by Th. Frankfort on p. 53 of her 1961 article mentioned in n. 45 below, suggests that Photius *calculated* the regnal date from a Christian date, and that his error is similar to many Byzantine errors regarding first-century chronology. But there is

II. From the 1890's to the 1930's:
A Sleeper and a Backfire

Thus, by the early twentieth century, the pre-93/94 dating for Agrippa's death, and the resultant Domitianic date for the *Vita*, had carried the field; Schürer's 1901 protest (n. 2) was buried under the flood of names of prominent scholars who now confidently rejected Photius. Wherever one turned in those years, whether to the standard repository of classical knowledge, or to the standard prosopographical handbook, or to the standard edition of Josephus, or to the standard handbooks on Roman and ancient history and literature, not to mention many other works, he would find the same statement.[22] Moreover, these same decades were to see two new developments which — the one naturally but only after a long incubation, and the other despite itself but immediately — would combine to make this view all the more regnant in the twentieth century.

The natural contribution to the regnant view is quite simple: there were published, in 1895 and 1934, two inscriptions which, although apparently coming from parts of Agrippa's eastern territories (Trachonitis and Auranitis), were dated by imperial dates to 96 and 97 C.E. without reference to Agrippa. Moreover, in 1939 it was noted that the very name of the Cohors I Flavia Canathenorum (known from inscriptions from N. Africa and elsewhere) similarly indicates that this unit from Canatha (in the Trachonitis) was organized as part of the imperial army by one of the Flavians, i.e., no later than Domitian's death. The obvious inference from these epigraphic

---

every reason to doubt that Photius found a Christian date in his text of Justus; see Cohen (above, n. 4), p. 173, n. 223, also below, n. 69. The third theory, which appears in the new "Schürer" (SVM I, p. 482, n. 47, part (1)), notes that the entry on Justus (ch. 14) in Jerome's *De viris illustribus* is followed by one (ch. 15) on Clement of Alexandria, who died, according to Jerome, in Trajan's third year: perhaps Photius got his information from Jerome and conflated information from the two entries. But this is highly speculative, especially since Jerome's entry on Justus focuses upon a book by him which Photius ignores and, on the other hand, says nothing about Agrippa, upon whom Photius focuses. That is, there is nothing in common between Photius' and Jerome's accounts of Justus. One can well understand Y. Dan's throwing up his hands in impatience at these explanations: "In any case, it seems that Photius erred for some reason . . . in the end, it doesn't matter very much how Photius arrived at this date" (in *Josephus Flavius: Historian of Eretz-Israel in the Hellenistic-Roman Period — Collected Papers* [ed. U. Rappaport; 1982], p. 61 [in Hebrew]).

[22] See A. Rosenberg, *PWRE* I/19 (1917), cols. 149–150; F. Jacoby, ibid. I/20 (1919), cols. 1345–1346; B. Niese, p. v (the very opening) of the Praefatio to his edition of Josephus (vol. I, 1887); K. Wachsmuth, *Einleitung in das Studium der alten Geschichte* (1895), p. 448; and W. von Christ - O. Stählin, *Geschichte der griechischen Literatur*, II/1 (1920²), p. 593, n. 1 and p. 597 (§§ 640, 643). H. Dessau too, in *PIR* (above, n. 4), pars II (1897), p. 164 (nr. 89, Agrippa II), leans toward Domitianic dates for the *Vita* and for Agrippa's death; cf. ibid., p. 36 (nr. 51, Epaphroditus), p. 69 (nr. 189, Josephus) and p. 254 (nr. 581, Justus).

observations is that Agrippa was dead by then and his territories annexed, as held by the consensus. But since these three bits of evidence were buried in collections of inscriptions and gain relevance here only because they *fail* to mention Agrippa, it is, perhaps, not surprising that several decades would go by, until 1939 and then again the early 1960's, before they were associated with our problem.[23]

The contribution despite itself to the regnant view, which had immediate results, has to do with philological fashion. Beginning in the mid-to-late nineteenth century, classical philologists began to apply the scalpels of source criticism to distinguishing different layers ("editions") of an author's own work: just as an author might add a paragraph based upon one source to something based upon another, so too might he add a new paragraph of his own to a text he had earlier composed.[24] With regard to Josephus, this was soon applied to our problem, for the *Vita*'s allusion to Agrippa's death comes in the course of a long chapter (65 = §§ 336–367) which Josephus himself introduces and closes as a "digression" (§ 367 – *parekbasis*). Therefore, while as late as 1910 and 1911 detailed discussions of our subject could still argue or assume that all of the *Vita* appeared at once, it was becoming fairly common, in the margins of the consensus on a Domitianic *terminus ad quem* for Agrippa's death, to maintain the Photian date for Agrippa's death and assume that the *Vita* reference to it was added in a second edition after 100. First-rank scholars such as A. Stein (1905) and Fr. Rühl (1916) espoused this theory, and G. Hölscher (1916) thought it at least worthy of consideration.[25] A few years

---

[23] See W. Ewing, *Palestine Exploration Fund Quarterly Statement*, 1895, p. 157, nr. 109 = *Inscriptiones graecae ad res romanas pertinentes*, III, 1176; M. Dunand, *Le musée de Soueïda: Inscriptions et monuments figurés* (1934), pp. 49–50, nr. 75; and, on the unit from Canatha, G. C. Richards, *Classical Quarterly* 33 (1939), p. 37, n. 1. Richards, who writes that A. H. M. Jones had pointed out the implications of the cohort's name, seems to have been the first to apply this point, and the first-mentioned inscription, to our question: he accepted Photius' dating for Agrippa's death, along with a second-edition theory (see below), and emphasized that the epigraphic evidence reflects only on the question of Agrippa's end of rule, not on that of his death. Frankfort referred to the first-mentioned inscriptions in 1962, but not to the cohort (see below, n. 45), and was followed by others, and finally in 1967/68 Y. Dan referred to all three pieces of evidence in his unpublished 1967/68 Hebrew University M.A. thesis: "Agrippa II: King and Kingdom," p. 11 (in Hebrew).

[24] See H. Emonds, *Zweite Auflage im Altertum* (1941); on p. 3, Emonds traces the beginning of the blooming of this approach to the latter years of the nineteenth century. It seems first to have been applied to Josephus in a brief comment (anticipating Laqueur's theory on *Antiquities'* second edition) by H. Ewald, *Geschichte des Volkes Israel*, VII (1859[2]), p. 96.

[25] See Stein (above, n. 14); Fr. Rühl, *Rheinisches Museum für Philologie* n.F. 71 (1916), p. 297; G. Hölscher, *PWRE* I/18 (1916), cols. 1941–1942, n. *. For the continued assumption that all of our *Vita* appeared at once, see Luther (above, n. 17), pp. 55–65 and H. Vincent, *RB* n.s. 8 (1911), p. 380.

later, indeed, in 1924, B. Motzo would publish a detailed defense of this thesis.[26]

However, as so often happens, this baby was thrown out with someone else's bathwater. Namely, this modest theory had the bad luck to be similar to a much more far-reaching and reckless one which appeared around the same time, and the revulsion with which the scholarly world rejected the latter affected the former as well. In 1920, just as scholars were beginning to be able to sit back and read what had appeared during the war, R. Laqueur published *Der jüdische Historiker Flavius Josephus: Ein biographischer Versuch auf neuer quellenkritischer Grundlage*, a book dedicated to showing that Josephus was constantly revising his works. As his foremost critic complained: "alles wird flüssig." Laqueur's theses included the propositions that the *Vita* was based upon a report Josephus wrote in 66/67 C.E. concerning his activities in the Galilee; that he used this report in writing the *Jewish War* in the seventies; that the book underwent later revision; that the early report is more or less reproduced in the *Vita*, but here too there was much revision, including the addition of all passages relating to Justus of Tiberias and, among them, the passage alluding to Agrippa's death (§ 359); and that this *Vita*, which is thus Josephus' earliest and latest book, first appeared with a second edition of the *Antiquities*, the existence of which Laqueur deduced from what he saw as a double conclusion of the work (20.259, 267), comparable to the modern practice of adding a new preface to a book's second edition.

Laqueur's theory is so involved and so frequently unfounded that it won general rejection, and, in falling, tore down the whole type of theory to which it had been dedicated. The years following Laqueur saw not only the general rejection of his theory and approach,[27] but also, in particular, the publication of some detailed studies dedicated to showing the unity of the *Vita*, both

---

[26] [R.] B. Motzo, *Saggi di storia e letteratura giudeo-ellenistica* (1924), pp. 214–226 = idem, *Ricerche sulla letteratura e la storia giudaico-ellenistica* (1977), pp. 685–697. He was followed by A. Momigliano, *Cambridge Ancient History*, X (edd. S. A. Cook, F. E. Adcock and M. P. Charlesworth; 1934), p. 886.

[27] First, foremost, and sufficiently by R. Helm, in *Philologische Wochenschrift* 41 (1921), cols. 481–493, 505–516 (who opens with the comment on "flüssig"). Among the other condemnations, especially notable is that by Fr. Münzer, *Orientalistische Literaturzeitung* 24 (1921), cols 213–216. That R. Eisler basically approved of Laqueur (*Iēsous Basileus ou Basileusas*, I [1929], esp. pp. 261–264 and 412, n. 3) did not exactly help the latter's reputation, given the former's; for a notion of the way in which Eisler was received, cf. above, p. 183, n. 4. For a review of the reception of Laqueur's work on Josephus, see Migliario (above, n. 4), pp. 100–101. The only significant support Laqueur received for his thesis on the relation of the *Vita* and the *War* was from M. Gelzer, *Hermes* 80 (1952), pp. 67–90 = idem, *Kleine Schriften*, III (1964) pp. 299–325. Laqueur's theory about *Antiquities'* two editions did much better; see below, n. 55.

linguistically[28] and thematically: even in those parts where Justus is not mentioned, the latter studies claimed, the *Vita* is to be understood as a response to the Tiberian's invective.[29] These studies undermined the basis for separating parts of the *Vita* written before Agrippa died from those added after that time; by 1941, a compendious work on the phenomenon of "second editions" in antiquity did not even bother to mention Laqueur's work on Josephus, contenting itself with a summary rejection of his similar work on Polybius.[30] This, then, is the backfire, the contribution despite itself: although Laqueur's point of departure had been an indignant protest against the "Kunststücke" of German scholarship which had been mobilized against Photius, his attempt to support Photius' date resulted in confirming the confidence of those who rejected it.[31] Below, we will see that Laqueur also contributed in another more intended way to the same result.

III. On Numismatics and History, 1693—1965

> "Bad money drives out good money."
> *Gresham's Law*

At this point, we must return to a discipline and body of evidence which we last saw in 1701, when F. Spanheim mentioned it but did not attempt to deal with it. As we saw, Tillemont (1690) and his followers knew of coins of up to Agrippa's twenty-ninth year, and could live with them on the reasonable presumption that their era was Agrippa's enthronement in 49 C.E. Namely, they could suppose that Agrippa was dead by Titus' or Domitian's third year. However, around the same time Tillemont and the Spanheims wrote, two new

---

[28] The contemporary Josephan authority repeatedly argued that the language of the *Vita* is so similar to that of *Antiquities* 20 that it too must have been composed in the nineties, not in the sixties: see H. St. J. Thackeray, *Josephus*, I (LCL; 1926), pp. xvi—xvii; idem, *Josephus: The Man and the Historian* (1929), pp. 18—19; and idem, *A Lexicon to Josephus*, I (1930), p. ix. For more of the same type of argument, see *JQR* 72 (1981/82), p. 259, n. 53.

[29] See H. Drexler, *Klio* 19 (1923), esp. pp. 293—299, and A. Schalit, ibid. 26 (1933), esp. pp. 67—68. For the assumption, on the basis of these studies and similar considerations, that all of the *Vita* was directed against Justus, see Migliario (above, n. 4), pp. 92—137, along with her corresponding criticism of Cohen (above, n. 4) in the same volume of *Athenaeum*, pp. 242—244. But see below, n. 72.

[30] See Emonds (above, n. 24), p. 3.

[31] Laqueur's first chapter is dedicated to the relationship of the *Vita* to the *Antiquities*; the protest against the "Kunststücke" used to overcome Photius occurs in its second footnote (p. 2). Of these, it is an open question whether the most remarkable was Brüll's (above, n. 16) or von Gutschmid's (below, at n. 37). On the baby and bathwater boomerang effect of Laqueur's book, cf. Wood's comments on Eisler (above, p. 141, n. 35) and our own on Aptowitzer (above, p. 44).

numismatic data upset the situation entirely — or should have. First, there came to light coins of Agrippa's "year 26" dated according to Domitian's twelfth consulate — 86 C.E. This showed that he used a 61 C.E. era, no matter how reasonable it had previously been, on the basis of Josephus, to postulate a 49 C.E. era. Second, a coin of his "year 35" was discovered, and this, when applied to the newly-found 61 C.E. era, showed that Agrippa was alive and minting as late as 95 C.E. These coins were published, respectively, in J. Harduin's 1693 booklet on Herodian coins and chronology and in a 1700 volume by J. Vaillant, and the conclusions were already made clear in the new 1706 edition of E. Spanheim's magnum opus and in Harduin's 1709 *De numis Herodiadum*, discussed and defended in detail in E. Frölich's 1752 monograph on ancient royal coins, and written large in the appropriate section of J. Eckhel's authoritative compendium of 1794, which here depends largely upon Frölich.[32]

For numismatists, therefore, it was now clear that Josephus' reference to Domitian's thirteenth year could not be a *terminus ad quem* for Agrippa's death (or for the *Vita*, if it interested them), so there was no reason to doubt Photius. In 1752, it is true, Frölich still felt a need to argue the matter, showing that the arguments from Josephus (silence re emperors after Domitian and dedication to Epaphroditus) were insufficient, and even adding another argument from Josephus in favor of a late date for Agrippa's death.[33] But by

---

[32] See J. Harduin (sometimes spelled Hardouin), *Chronologiae ex nummis antiquis restitutae prolusio de nummis Herodiadum* (1693), pp. 19—20; idem, *Opera selecta* (1709), pp. 333—334; J. Vaillant, *Numismata Imperatorum, Augustarum et Caesarum, a populis, romanae ditionis, graece loquentibus* . . . (1700²), p. 25; E. Spanheim (Spanhemius) (above, n. 10 — editio nova, vol. I [London 1706 — I used the 1717 Amsterdam reprint]), pp. 532—534 (in the second edition of 1671, pp. 447, 863—864, he knew only of coins up to "year 29" and reserved judgement re Photius, but in this new edition he accepted the latter); E. Frölich, *Regum veterum numismata anecdota* . . . (n.d. [1752]), pp. 93—98 (the title-page attributes this book to F. A. de Khevenhüller, but later writers knew it was by Frölich; cf. C. von Wurzbach, *Biographisches Lexikon des Kaiserthums Oesterreich*, IV [1858], pp. 376—377); and J. Eckhel, *Doctrina numorum veterum*, I/3 (1794), pp. 493—496. J. Pellerin helped complete the picture by publishing a coin of Agrippa's thirty-fourth year: *Recueil de médailles de rois* (1762), p. 176. Already A. Pagi (d. 1699) had heard of the coin identifying Agrippa's twenty-sixth year as that of Domitian's twelfth consulate, but for some reason improperly identified the latter as 80 C.E., although elsewhere in the same volume he properly identified it as 86 C.E. See his *Critica historico-chronologica in universos annales ecclesiasticos* . . . *Baronii*, I (1705), pp. 46, 75 (first published in 1689, and later reprinted beneath Baronius' text in vol. I of the 1738 edition of the *Annales*, pp. 588, 714 [ad ann. Chr. 60 and 86]).

[33] Frölich (above, n. 32: pp. 94—96) 1) noted that H. Grotius had identified Josephus' Epaphroditus with one still alive under Trajan (*Opera theologica*, II/1 [1679], p. 332 —Grotius makes this suggestion as an aside, without relating it to any chronological problem; he apparently refers to the *grammaticus* mentioned by the *Suda* — see below, Part V); 2) underlined that Josephus might well recall Domitian's favors even in Trajan's day; and 3) points to *Ant.* 18.128, where Josephus says that within a century of Herod's death *almost all*

1794 Eckhel simply rejected Tillemont's early dating out of hand, and by the nineteenth century the discipline had so grown that numismatists could comfortably live in a world all their own. Cavedoni (1856), Madden (1864), de Saulcy (1874) and Reinach (1887) all take it for granted, without even mentioning any doubt at all, that Agrippa II died in 99 or 100 C.E. Indeed, although Tillemont enjoyed great authority among historians, in 1881 Madden, a prominent numismatist, had no compunctions about concluding a long note citing authorities for Photius' date with the mere notice that "I do not know on what authority" Tillemont, cited by Eckhel, argued for an earlier date. He apparently did not care to find out − Tillemont's book is not at all rare. And so it goes: while Reinach's 1903 edition already fell in with the historians' consensus for an early dating, the standard numismatic works by Head (1911) and Hill (1914) still show no awareness of any doubt or argument concerning Photius' date.[34]

In thus ignoring the historians, numismatists were returning a compliment. We have already noted how Dodwell manhandled the numismatic evidence and F. Spanheim left it in isolation. J. Basnage, in 1707, who knew only of the "year 26" coin of 86 C.E. but not of that of "year 35," simply doubted the former's reading, supposing it should be "year 36" as required by the 49/50 C.E. era; it is not clear whether this satisfied S. Deyling, who in 1711 followed Basnage in every other way and simply ignored the fact that the "year 26" coin was dated to 86 C.E. But historical scholarship's fate was sealed, for almost two hundred years, by the inclusion of some old notes by E. Spanheim (prominently, at the very outset and at the very end of the *Vita*), and of C. Cellarius' 1696 tract on Herodian chronology, in the 1726 Hudson-Havercamp edition of Josephus. This made these discussions widely available, although both of them, as Tillemont and F. Spanheim, knew only of coins up to Agrippa's twenty-ninth year and nothing of the 61 C.E. era. In fact, both were

---

of his posterity had died out, as proof that Agrippa II was still alive after Domitian's death, since he was the last of the Herodians. I do not know who would want to press this latter point. But it is better than the recurrent claims that all the Herodians' reigns, including Herod's, add up to one hundred years (so, e.g., Syncellus [n. 5] and Spanheim [n. 12 − 1701]), if this is meant to be based upon Josephus' statement. For Josephus, as Frölich understood, more probably refers to the passage of time since Herod's death.

[34] Eckhel (above, n. 32: p. 496) concludes his discussion of Agrippa's death by pointing to the coins of his thirty-fourth and thirty-fifth years, quoting Photius, and simply pronouncing "Haec non vidit Tillemontius, qui Agrippam circa annum P.X. 93 mortuum conjecit." See also D. C. Cavedoni, *Biblische Numismatik*, II (1856), pp. 35−39; F. W. Madden, *History of Jewish Coinage* (1864), pp. 113, 133; idem, *Coins of the Jews* (1881), pp. 143−144, n. 12; F. de Saulcy, *Numismatique de la terre sainte* (1874), pp. 316, 335; Th. Reinach, *Les monnaies juives* (1887, p. 37 (cf. idem, *Jewish Coins* [1903], p. 37); B. V. Head, *Historia Numorum: A Manual of Greek Numismatics* (1911²), p. 809; and G. F. Hill, *Catalogue of the Greek Coins of Palestine (Galilee, Samaria, and Judaea)* (1914), pp. xcviii−c.

terribly out of date: Cellarius, although responding to Harduin, wrote on the basis of Spanheim's 1671 edition and ignores Harduin's evidence for the 61 C.E. era, and Spanheim himself, as we have seen, had lived to revise his views, in the light of the new evidence, in the 1706 edition of his work. Nor was the matter helped by Bishop Ussher's oft-quoted claim, in 1652, that there was a Greek "Judaea Capta" coin dated to Agrippa's twenty-first year, which just happens to fit the 49/50 C.E. era. While a hundred years later Frölich was to conclude that this coin was either forged or misread, and no one seems to have seen it, nevertheless, for historians, it reinforced the inclination to maintain the 49/50 C.E. era.[35] With this state of knowledge in the great authorities, it is not surprising that for the next two hundred years historians, by and large, did not know what was common knowledge among the numismatists.[36] Graetz, for example, in 1856, made no mention at all of coins in adopting Dodwell's emendation of Photius (Agrippa died in *Vespasian's* third year), and even M. Brann, who wrote a long and detailed monograph on Agrippa II in 1870−1871, depended upon Cellarius alone; others simply ignore the coins altogether. But perhaps this was just as well, for when one prominent historian of the late nineteenth century noticed that the coins showed Agrippa alive in 95 C.E., his only response was to conclude that the king must have gone crazy, so Josephus could freely malign him as if he were already dead . . .[37]

---

[35] See J. Basnage, *L'histoire et la religion des Juifs*, I (1707), pp. 102−109 (esp. p. 107), followed very closely (as far as he goes) by S. Deyling in his *Observationes sacrae* (1711), pp. 265−266. (Both, as some others, also refer to Ussher's "Judaea Capta" coin dated to Agrippa's twenty-first year [Ussher, above, n. 9, ad 70 C.E.], which, indeed, Scaliger too had cited [above, n. 1: p. 182]; on this "coin," see Frölich [above, n. 32], p. 110.) E. Spanheim's notes, which make no reference to coins, may be found in vol. II of Hudson-Havercamp, p. 1 (n. a) and p. 39 (notes b−c). Chr. Cellarius' 1696 "Dissertatio . . . qua Flavii Josephi de Herodibus historia a *notheias* suspicione contra cl. v. Joannem Harduinum justis vindiciis adseritur, et nummis antiquis conciliatur" was reprinted ibid., pp. 324−329; see esp. pp. 328−329. It may be read in English in many printings of Whiston's translation of Josephus, e.g.: *The Works of Flavius Josephus* (1841), pp. 998−1007 (here: pp. 1004−5.)

[36] I have not found any detailed account of historians' reception of numismatics. The *Dialogues Upon the Usefulness of Ancient Medals, Especially in Relation to the Latin and Greek Poets* by J. Addison (d. 1719) were frequently reprinted, and also published in German and Spanish translations, in the course of the eighteenth century. On the other hand, it was only in 1836, *after* the publication of his *Geschichte Alexanders des Großen* and *Geschichte der Nachfolger Alexanders*, that J. G. Droysen announced that he was planning to begin to study coins: *Johann Gustav Droysen: Briefwechsel*, I (ed. R. Hübner; 1929), pp. 90, 108. A systematic account of this topic is a desideratum.

[37] See von Gutschmid (above, n. 20). For nerve, this may be compared to Dodwell's assertion that Agrippa II counted the years of his reign from five years before it began (above, at n. 11), or to B. G. Niebuhr's assertion, in a similar case, that coins of Antiochus Sidetes were minted for three years after his death (*Kleine historische und philologische Schriften*, I [1828], pp. 251−252). In all fairness, however, we should note that von Gutschmid's suggestion comes only in an unpublished lecture which appeared posthumously. The other

But this situation had to change. The great Th. Mommsen published an article about Agrippa's coins in 1872,[38] and, although he did not address the question of the date of Agrippa's death, the very fact of his studying the coins was enough to arouse historians' interest. Thus, a few years later, on the one hand, Graetz tried to support the early death-date by substituting an earlier era for the 61 C.E. one accepted by numismatists; on the other hand, this was the generation in which E. Schürer's handbook on the period first appeared, and he pointed to the coins with the 61 C.E. era as the mainstay of his support for Photius.[39] Schürer was quite isolated, as we have noted, but his authority required that the matter be addressed.

Scholars who held to the early dating for Agrippa's death took two tacks in overcoming the coins. The first was to claim that Agrippa's coins show mistakes, and are, therefore, not to be trusted.[40] But of the three "mistakes" cited, two are only the absence of full imperial titulature, and one is no mistake: the fact that Agrippa's coins portray Vespasian and Titus after they died shows only, as Eckhel had noted, that Agrippa remained intent upon honoring the whole Flavian family. There is no reason to think any of these three "mistakes" invalidates the dates read clearly on Agrippa's coins, and, indeed, those familiar with ancient coins seem not to have any trouble taking these irregularities in their stride.[41]

The other tack taken to defend the early date against the coins was somewhat more serious. While eighteenth-century scholars, including Eckhel, had known of the 61 C.E. era alone, in the course of the nineteenth century there became known two coins and an inscription which used a double date, the additional era beginning five years earlier — 56 C.E.[42] While there was no evidence for the use of this era alone, it nevertheless became possible to

---

references in the preceding lines are to Brann (above, n. 17), p. 25 (and cf. p. 28, n. 1 where he refers to the possibility of coins from "as late as" 83 C.E.!) and H. Graetz, *Geschichte der Juden*, III (1856), p. 453. Th. Lewin, *Fasti Sacri* (1865), pp. 338, 356 (§§ 1983, 2111) is an exception: a historian who follows Eckhel (above, n. 32) and has Agrippa die in Trajan's third year.

[38] Th. Mommsen, *Numismatische Zeitschrift* 3 (1871 [1872]), pp. 449–457.

[39] See Graetz (above, n. 16), pp. 341–351; Schürer (above, n. 19).

[40] See Niese (above, n. 20), p. 226, n. 4 and Luther, (above, n. 17), pp. 64–65 ("Aber die Münzen sind in diesem Falle von geringer Beweiskraft, da sich Inkorrektheiten darin finden").

[41] See, e.g., Eckhel (above, n. 32), p. 495, who simply notes the coins' failure to reflect Vespasian's and Titus' posthumous deification; Mommsen (above, n. 38), p. 455, who is content to note that backwoods Galileans might not always get imperial titulature right; and Hill (above, n. 34), p. xcix, who rejects the propriety of assuming that all titulature is accurate and all people portrayed are still alive, for such assumptions result only in hopeless confusion.

[42] See Schürer (above, n. 2), p. 589, n. 7. In 1924, a new inscription with this double dating was added to the dossier: *Syria* 5 (1924), pp. 324–330, nr. 5 = *Supplementum Epigraphicum Graecum* VII, nr. 970.

postulate its use for the "year 34" and "year 35" coins, thus allowing Agrippa to die in the early nineties. And so, indeed, was argued by Graetz in 1877 and briefly suggested by H. Luther in 1910.[43]

Below, shortly, we will see that this option was indeed to become popular for a time, but only in the 1960's and 1970's. It is noteworthy, however, that the main response to the discovery of the use of a second era was instead to use it as justification for the assumption of yet a third: 49/50 C.E. For historians, Agrippa's 56 and 61 C.E. eras were (and remain) riddles. On the one hand, it is very difficult to discover what events (of his career?) explain them;[44] on the other hand, it is quite disconcerting that Agrippa's coins are not based upon the year of his ascent to the throne (49 C.E.), the era which seems obvious and which Josephus uses for him. So it is not surprising to find historians pouncing upon the evidence for the 56 C.E. era as proof that more than one era was admissible, and therefore turning back to the 49 C.E. era for the "year 35" coins — thus allowing the early dating of Agrippa's death and the *Vita* to stand. That this was the case was argued in detail by C. Erbes in 1896, suggested by G. MacDonald in 1905, echoed by A. Rosenberg in 1917, argued at length by A. Schalit in 1932/33, and more or less taken for granted, in 1961, by Th. Frankfort.[45]

This incursion by historians into numismatics could not go unchallenged by the numismatists, who, not too strangely, found it difficult to view evidence for the use of a 56 C.E. era as proof for a 49/50 C.E. era. On the other hand, it had also become clear to them that the historians really had a problem here. So, three years after Frankfort wrote, H. Seyrig stepped in and finally did what was obvious: he argued, as Graetz had, that Agrippa's "year 35" coins

---

[43] See Graetz (above, n. 39); Luther (above, n. 17), p. 65.

[44] Usually it is assumed that one or the other era has something to do with the refoundation of Paneas as Neronias, but there are complications. For a recent contribution, see A. Stein, *INJ* 8 (1984/85), pp. 9–11.

[45] See Erbes (above, n. 20), pp. 419–425; G. MacDonald, *Catalogue of Greek Coins in the Hunterian Collection, University of Glasgow*, III (1905), pp. 290–291; Rosenberg (above, n. 22), cols. 147, 150; A. Schalit, *Zion* o.s. 5 (1932/33), pp. 184–196 (in Hebrew); and Th. Frankfort, *Revue belge de philologie et d'histoire* 39 (1961), pp. 55–56 (where she adds an iconographic argument). Cf. Frankfort's essay in *Hommages à Albert Grenier* [II] (ed. M. Renard; 1962), pp. 659–672; on p. 58 of her former article and p. 667 of the latter, Frankfort pointed out the significance of the inscriptions mentioned in n. 23, above (although, in the latter, she mistakenly refers to *IGRR* III, 1127 instead of III, 1176). Around the same time, J. Meyshan (in *Eretz-Israel* 6 [1960/61], pp. 111–114 [Hebrew, with a detailed English summary, pp. 33*–34*]) and M. Weisbrem (*Israel Numismatic Bulletin* 2 [April–July, 1962], p. 50) assumed the use of a 50 C.E. era, but the former explicitly defended Photius' date for Agrippa's death and maintained the 61 C.E. era for the "year 35" coins, while the latter did not address the question. (B. Kanael replied with a detailed study reasserting the 56 and 61 C.E. eras, ibid. 5 [July 1963], pp. 8–13). For the record, note that already J. Basnage (above, n. 35: p. 107) supposed the use of three different eras on Agrippa's coins.

(and many others) were based upon the 56 C.E. era – and that was that. Numismatists and historians were happy and all chimed in: as late as 1979, in a detailed account of our subject, S. J. D. Cohen could properly leave the matter by noting that Seyrig's view "has gained wide support."[46]

With all due respect, however, this wide acceptance is nothing less than amazing, at least in retrospect, because Seyrig simply ignored one of the most important numismatic data, one which Mommsen and others had noted long before him: coins of Agrippa's "year 24," which Seyrig assigned to the 56 C.E. era, refer to Domitian as "Germanicus," a title which the emperor assumed only in 84 C.E. or late in 83.[47] This accords well with a 61 C.E. era, but impossibly with a 56 C.E. era. Inexplicably, the very title "Germanicus" does not appear in Seyrig's article.

Moreover, since even Seyrig admitted that some coins of Agrippa's "year 26" are based upon the 61 C.E. era, as is shown by the dating according to Domitian's twelfth consulate = 86 C.E., he was faced with the difficulty of explaining why Agrippa, between 79 and 86 C.E., would pass from a 56 C.E. era to the 61 C.E. era, only to return later to the earlier era in time to date the "year 35 coins" according to it. But this difficulty, which he did notice, did not hold him up much more than the previous one ("Germanicus"); he simply asserted that the 61 C.E. era was some local quirk.[48]

The truth is, it seems, that Seyrig's choice of the 56 C.E. era was based on nothing more than a scholar's wish to tidy up the data concerning Agrippa's death, on the one hand, and his great experience and respect for the chanciness of the preservation of data, on the other. Namely, he rebelled at the thought that Agrippa's last coins, his death, and the annexation of his territories – to which we may add the publication of Justus' history and Josephus' *Vita* – could all fit into 95/96 C.E., and that we would just happen to have evidence for all of this: "Ce n'est pas impossible, mais c'est un peu juste."[49] Therefore, he preferred to move Agrippa's death up a few years. Correspondingly, the widespread acceptance of Seyrig's view seems to have resulted not so much from any argument which he offered as from his prestige

---

[46] See H. Seyrig, *Revue numismatique*, 6ᵉ serie, 6 (1964), pp. 55–65 (reprinted in idem, *Scripta Numismatica* [1986], pp. 125–135, where the original pagination is also shown); Cohen (above, n. 4), p. 173 (with references to the post-Seyrig literature).

[47] See H. Mattingly, *Coins of the Roman Empire in the British Museum*, II (1930), pp. lxxxiv–lxxxv; J. von Ungern-Sternberg, in *Festschrift Robert Werner zu seinem 65. Geburtstag* (edd. W. Dahlheim, W. Schuller and J. von Ungern-Sternberg; 1989), pp. 166–167, n. 1 (where much literature is cited). This consideration had been dealt with, one way or another, by some scholars on both sides of our question; see, e.g., Mommsen (above, n. 38), p. 455 and Schalit (above, n. 45), esp. p. 192.

[48] Seyrig (above, n. 46), p. 61.

[49] Seyrig, loc. cit.

and from his solution's status as a welcome final nail in Photius' coffin, allowing the other arguments on Agrippa's death to stand unchallenged.

IV. 1965–1986:
New Discoveries and Old-New Fashions in Philology

What next happened is quite ironic. Seyrig himself, the very next year (1965), published an inscription from which the natural inference is that Agrippa lived until at least 98 C.E.: a general proudly notes his eighteen-year service as a centurion under Agrippa, followed by ten years as a *strategos* under Trajan.[50] Although, as Seyrig immediately noted, it is possible that there was a gap between the two periods of service, even the new Schürer admits that no one would imagine this were it not for the 1895 and 1934 inscriptions which indicate that Agrippa was not ruling by 96–97.[51]

Again, just as Cohen (n. 46) was noting the widespread acceptance of Seyrig's 56 C.E. era for the "year 35" coins, D. Barag was publishing his case for restoring the 61 C.E. era, on the basis of the two aforementioned weaknesses of Seyrig's analysis and, especially, of a hitherto unassociated body of evidence: comparison with "Judaea Capta" coins indicates that coins of Agrippa's "year 14" imitate exemplars of the former which could not have been minted before 71 C.E., which is impossible if Agrippa's were dated according to the 56 C.E. era. And, in any case, it is nigh impossible to admit that Agrippa could mint coins celebrating the Roman victory in Judaea as early as 69/70, which is the result if we assume a 56 C.E. era for these coins. Hence, Barag argued for a return to the 61 C.E. era.[52] And his view has swept the field, including those who formerly accepted Seyrig's case.[53] But this means that once again, just as in the two and a half centuries preceding

---

[50] H. Seyrig, *Syria* 42 (1965), pp. 31–34 = *L'année epigraphique* 1966, p. 156, nr. 493 (where, however, the natural inference that Agrippa died in 98 [i.e., not before 98] is mistakenly attributed to Seyrig).

[51] SVM I, p. 483, n. 47, part (8). Cf. our preceding note.

[52] See D. Barag, *Numismatic Chronicle*, 7th series, 18 (1978), pp. 14–23; idem, *INJ* 5 (1981), pp. 27–30. Barag's first article was published in Hebrew, along with the comments of Y. Meshorer, U. Rappaport and A. Kindler, in *Cathedra* 8 (July, 1978), pp. 47–68.

[53] For Y. Meshorer's detailed discussion, settling upon the 61 C.E. era (instead of his former support for Seyrig, cited by Cohen), see his *Ancient Jewish Coinage*, II (1982), pp. 65–73. Cf. pp. 78–79 for the suggestion that the maritime images on coins of Agrippa's nineteenth year reflect Berenice's trip to Rome in 79 C.E. – on the basis of the 61 C.E. era. Barag is also followed by I. Carradice, in *INJ* 6–7 (1982/83), pp. 17–18, and A. Kindler, in *Israel – People and Land* 1 (= Museum Ha'Aretz yearbook, 1983/84), pp. 67–84 (in Hebrew), already takes the 61 C.E. era for granted, as do S. Schwartz (in his 1986 article, and pp. 19–20 of his 1990 book, cited below, n. 61), and S. Qedar, *INJ* 9 (1986/87), pp. 29–35.

Seyrig's article, *the date at the end of Antiquities (93/94 C.E.) may not, according to the numismatic evidence, be used as a terminus ad quem for Agrippa's death*, so that all that now remains to contradict Photius are three considerations: 1) Josephus' silence about Nerva and Trajan in *Vita* 414–429; 2) the two inscriptions' failure to date by Agrippa's reign in 96–97 C.E.; and 3) the *Vita*'s dedication to Epaphroditus. The first two being mere arguments from silence, it is apparent just how weak the anti-Photius dossier now became.[54] We will return to this below.

Moreover, these numismatic and epigraphic developments played right into the hands of an old-new direction in philological fashion. As stated in the subtitle of his book, Laqueur used the tools of source-criticism in order to study Josephus himself, not the history he recounts. On the one hand, his book gave Josephan source-criticism a very bad name, just as, elsewhere as well, source-criticism was declining; for several decades it would be a very daring scholar who would be willing to engage in taking Josephus' works apart and putting them back together.[55] On the other hand, however, Laqueur had applied those tools not to source-criticism but rather to composition criticism, to Josephus' repeated reediting of his own work: Laqueur thus directed scholarship toward Josephus himself, viewing him as an author much more

---

[54] For the ease with which the argument from Josephus' silence about Domitian's successors (and reference to Domitian's protection) may be set aside, see Frölich (above, n. 33), Rühl (above, n. 25), p. 297, and now Schwartz (below, n. 61 [1990]), p. 20, n. 84. As for the inscriptions' silence, see below, Part VI and n. 81. On Epaphroditus, see below, Part V.

[55] On the decline of Josephan source-criticism, see, in general, the comments of H. Lindner, *Die Geschichtsauffassung des Flavius Josephus im Bellum Judaicum, gleichzeitig ein Beitrag zur Quellenfrage* (1972), p. vii, along with a review of its history, ibid., pp. 3–16. The general "waning of Quellenforschung" is also noted, for example, by T. J. Luce, *Livy: The Composition of his History* (1977), p. xv; see also H. F. Hahn, *The Old Testament in Modern Research* (expanded edition, 1966), pp. 226–249, on the way in which theology took over biblical studies beginning in the 1920's, largely replacing source-critical study of the history of Israelite religion. Compare A. E. Housman's 1922 parody of typical English prejudice against German source-critics (above, n. 18: p. 1061). However, it may be noted that Laqueur's theory that the *Antiquities* appeared in two editions had a surprising longevity (hence Barish's article — above, n. 21). See, for example, H. W. Attridge, *The Interpretation of Biblical History in the Antiquitates Judaicae of Flavius Josephus* (1976), p. 52, n. 2, who lists several scholars who adopted the view. But virtually no one put the theory to work with regard to our problem. (For an exception, see Richards [above, n. 23].) Note, for the most significant example, the fact that R. J. H. Shutt (*Studies in Josephus* [1961], pp. 77–78, 90–92), who adopts the two-edition theory and applies it to problems in *Antiquities* 14–19, seems not to have been aware of the fact that any, not to mention most, scholars, rejected Photius' dating of Agrippa II's death. That same year, H. R. Moehring specifically pointed to Laqueur's book as the turning point in the modern abandonment of Josephan source-criticism; see *Early Christian Origins: Studies in honor of Harold R. Willoughby* (ed. A. Wikgren; 1961), p. 121.

than as an editor and compiler.[56] This caught on, and much of the work of the next five-six decades derived from the perspective that Josephus was an author; that his works, whatever their sources and stages of development, should be viewed as his own; and that he, and his works, are at least as interesting objects of scholarly attention as the events which they describe.

This new orientation of Josephan scholarship took two main directions: "Josephus, the Man and the Historian." A few scholars (such as H. St. J. Thackeray, F. J. Foakes Jackson, R. J. H. Shutt and, especially, T. Rajak) wrote books about both aspects, but most concentrated upon the latter, which is much more accessible. Their studies, in turn, divided according to the two main components of Josephus' historiographical tradition: some examined Josephus as a representative of Jewish theology (e.g., books by H. Guttmann and A. Schlatter in the early period and by H. Lindner and H. W. Attridge in the 'seventies), while others concentrated upon analyzing him as a Hellenistic writer (this approach, opened especially by B. Brüne a few years before Laqueur, flourished in the decades after him; we may note, especially, studies by E. Stein, H. Spródowsky, M. Braun, I. Heinemann, A. Schalit, P. Collomp, H. R. Moehring, M. Stern, A. Pelletier, P. Bilde and L. H. Feldman).[57] None of this was totally new, of course. What was new was its

---

[56] See especially the concluding methodological chapter of his volume, also, for example, his critique of W. Weber in cols. 1105–1114 (esp. 1113–1114) of the same volume of *PhW* in which Helm's review (above, n. 27) appeared.

[57] We shall not, of course, attempt to review here all of Josephan scholarship in the sixty years between Laqueur and Cohen, but only to exemplify some of what appear to be its main lines. And it is also obvious that, in generalizing trends and lumping many different works together, we have trampled a great many nuances. An in-depth review of currents in Josephan scholarship is a desideratum, and I doubt that it will merely confirm S. Sandmel's pronouncement, on p. vi of his introduction to the 1967 reprint of Thackeray's *Josephus: The Man* . . . (above, n. 28), that Josephan scholarship has seen no "great upheavals" or "major novel interpretations." Chapter IV of P. Bilde's *Flavius Josephus Between Jerusalem and Rome* (1988) is a good start, and S.J.D. Cohen, in *The State of Jewish Studies* (edd. S.J.D. Cohen and E.L. Greenstein; 1990), pp. 59–60 interestingly puts Josephan studies into a much broader context; cf. *Agrippa I*, pp. xiii–xiv. The works mentioned: Thackeray (just now cited); F. J. Foakes Jackson, *Josephus and the Jews* (1930); Shutt (above, n. 55); Rajak (above, n. 4 – based on a dissertation of the mid-1970's); H. Guttmann *Die Darstellung der jüdischen Religion bei Flavius Josephus* (1928); A. Schlatter, *Die Theologie des Judentums nach dem Bericht des Josefus* (1932); Lindner and Attridge (above, n. 55); B. Brüne, *Flavius Josephus und seine Schriften in ihrem Verhältnis zum Judentume, zur griechisch-römischen Welt und zum Christentume* . . . (1913); E. Stein, *Eos* 33 (1930/31), pp. 641–650 (in Hebrew in *Sneh* 1/5–6 [1928/29], pp. 1–14); H. Spródowsky, *Die Hellenisierung der Geschichte von Joseph in Aegypten bei Flavius Josephus* (1937); M. Braun, *History and Romance in Graeco-Oriental Literature* (1938); I. Heinemann, *Zion* n.s. 5 (1939/40), pp. 180–203 (in Hebrew); A. Schalit, *Joseph ben Mattathias [Flavius Josephus]: Antiquities of the Jews*, I (1943/44), pp. xi–lxxxii (in Hebrew); P. Collomp, in *Mélanges 1945, III: Études historiques* (Publications de la Faculté des Lettres de l'Université de Strasbourg, 106; 1947), pp. 81–92 (in German in A. Schalit, ed., *Zur Josephus-Forschung* [Darmstadt, 1973], pp. 278–293); H. R. Moehring,

intensity and its increasing exclusiveness: if previous scholars had usually seen the detailed analysis of Josephus' narrative as part of the process of studying the events which he describes, now, history and literature to a large extent parted ways. To take only an extreme example, but one dealing with three quite central Josephan scholars: while, as late as 1913, W. Otto's fundamental monograph upon Herod deals with Josephan source-criticism in every other footnote, using it to support his reconstruction of events, fifty years later, A. Schalit's massive work on the Jewish monarch has almost nothing similar. Schalit managed to write almost eight hundred pages on Herod, based almost entirely upon Josephus, virtually without addressing the question of his source's sources and interests. A few years later, on the other hand, Schalit would be severely attacked by H. R. Moehring, who preferred to study Josephus as literature and as evidence for himself alone, and thought it remarkable, and reprehensible, that Schalit — in another work — had, *mirabile dictu*, "abused [Josephus' writings] as a mine to be quarried for positive information . . ."[58] Thus, Otto, Schalit and Moehring well illustrate the fact that Laqueur's work separated a period characterized by history with source-criticism from one in which those who studied history often did so without source-criticism, and in which Josephus was more often studied for his own sake and not as a source for the history of the events he describes.

But source-criticism, and its tools, are potentially important for historical reconstruction. A historical conundrum posed by an ancient source may at times be resolved by the recognition that we are, in fact, not reading *an* ancient source but rather more than one, parts of which having been improperly juxtaposed. People like Otto and Laqueur knew that, and applied their knowledge. In the fifty-sixty years after Laqueur, however, too many students

---

"Novelistic Elements in the Writings of Flavius Josephus" (unpublished dissertation, Chicago, 1957); M. Stern, in *Historians and Historical Schools: Lectures Delivered at the Seventh Convention of the Historical Society of Israel, December 1961* (1962), pp. 22—28 (in Hebrew); A. Pelletier, *Flavius Josèphe: Adaptateur de la Lettre d'Aristée* (1962); and P. Bilde, *JSJ* 10 (1979), pp. 179—202. For L. H. Feldman's studies of Josephus as a Hellenizing historian, see his study in *JQR* 75 (1984/85), pp. 212—252, with the references in his notes 12, 32, 33, 36, 50, 67, and 88.

[58] See W. Otto, *Herodes: Beiträge zur Geschichte des letzten jüdischen Königshauses* (1913; originally in *PWRE* Supplementband II [1913]; for his continued interest in Josephan source-criticism, see above, p. 217, n. 48); A. Schalit, *König Herodes: Der Mann und sein Werk* (1969 expanded version of 1960 Hebrew original); and H. R. Moehring, *ANRW* II/21.2 (1984), esp. pp. 917—944 (the condemnation of "quarrying" appears on p. 925). On Moehring's criticism (of Schalit's essay in *ANRW* II/2 [1975], pp. 208—327) see *Jewish History* 2/2 (Fall 1987), pp. 9—28. Compare, in contrast, Moehring's praise for Attridge's study of Josephus' *theology* (above, n. 55): *JBL* 97 (1978), pp. 459—460. (It should be noted, however, that Schalit did devote one section of his book [pp. 575—586 in the German edition] to Josephus' narrative on an especially romantic episode, Mariamme's death, and in a note there [p. 583, n. 37] announced that he hoped to devote a separate study to Josephus' sources concerning Herod.)

of Josephus forgot that or became uninterested in it, so they either studied Josephus as history or as literature but not, for the most part, as both. In such a climate, it is obvious that "second-edition" theories, however modest they might be, were not needed by many students of Josephus or of Judaean history, not only because Laqueur had given them a bad name, but also because problems such as ours, which such a theory could solve, were not considered very interesting.

However, just as epigraphic and numismatic developments of the nineteen-sixties and 'seventies were beginning to invite a reexamination of the rejection of Photius' date (see above, nn. 50–53), the wind was beginning to shift with regard to the above-mentioned approach to Josephus as well. This was certainly, in part, a reflection of the general reaction, outside of Josephan studies as well, against excesses of solipsism and historicistic skepticism which had led so many historians to abandon the hope of retrieving positive history on the basis of our sources.[59] More specifically, however, for Josephan studies the impetus came from way out in left field: the discovery of the Dead Sea Scrolls, beginning in the late nineteen-forties. These demonstrated, much more forcefully than anything previously known, the variegated nature of Judaism in the last centuries of the Second Temple period, and thus placed a question mark alongside Josephus' repeated claims that the Pharisees were the most popular party (especially: *Antiquities* 13.288, 298; 18.15, 17). One way of dealing with this problem was suggested by M. Smith in 1956: noting that virtually all of Josephus' claims to this effect are in the *Antiquities*, Smith proposed that Josephus had become a Pharisee between the seventies (the *Jewish War*) and the nineties (*Antiquities* and *Vita* – where he claims he was a Pharisee [§ 12]), and that his statements regarding the popularity of this sect are, insofar as they regard the pre-Destruction period (of which Josephus wrote), to be discounted as pro-Pharisaic propaganda.[60] In other words, Smith

---

[59] For contemporary complaints about the widespread tendency to view ancient historical sources simply as another type of literature, see, especially, A. Momigliano's 1974 and 1981 essays reprinted, respectively, in his *Sesto contributo alla storia degli studi classici e del mondo antico*, I (1980), pp. 23–32 and in his *Settimo contributo* . . . (1984), pp. 289–296, also M. Hengel's *Acts and the History of Earliest Christianity* (1979). See also G. Lüdemann, *Das frühe Christentum nach den Traditionen der Apostelgeschichte: Ein Kommentar* (1987), p. 11.

[60] M. Smith, in *Israel: Its Role in Civilization* (ed. M. Davis; 1956), esp. pp. 74–77. For criticism of this theory, see S. N. Mason, *Studies in Religion/Sciences religieuses* 17 (1988), pp. 455–469. (I have not yet seen Mason's *Flavius Josephus on the Pharisees: A Composition-Critical Study* [1991], and will, therefore, reserve judgement on his claim, in *JJS* 40 [1989], pp. 31–45, that Josephus, in *Vita* 12, didn't even claim to be a Pharisee.) Josephus' Pharisees have also been discussed recently by S. Schwartz, on pp. 172–200 of his book mentioned in our next note. For my own source-critical criticism of the Josephan part of Smith's theory – only this part – see *JSJ* 14 (1983), pp. 157–171. (Cohen [above, n. 57: p. 60] is wrong to summarize that paper as attributing the differences between *Ant.* and *BJ* on the Pharisees to "Josephus's discovery of new sources." Rather, I suggest that Josephus used the same source,

redirected scholars toward Josephus' personal development — what Laqueur
had called "Der Werdegang des Josephus" — as a key to understanding
problems in his writings, and, *nolens volens*, the questions and tools of source
criticism returned along with it. This was pursued in depth by Smith's student,
S. J. D. Cohen, in his doctorate published in 1979, and then again by S.
Schwartz, who wrote, under Smith's direction (and "strongly influenced" by
Cohen), a 1985 Columbia University dissertation on "Josephus and Judaism
from 70 to 100 C.E." In these works, we find a clear revival of Laqueur's
approach, banned for two generations, including such theories as the *Vita*
being based upon a draft (*"hypomnēma"*) of the sixties which was used in the
Jewish War as well (Cohen) and that the seventh book of the *War* itself was
twice revised, under Domitian and Trajan, after first appearing under Titus
(Schwartz).[61]

V. Back to Photius' Threshold

In his 1986 study dealing with the three editions of *BJ* 7, S. Schwartz also
addressed, if only briefly, the questions of the dates of Agrippa's death and the
composition of the *Vita*. Writing in the wake of the new numismatic
consensus, he used 95 as the *terminus post quem*. As for the *terminus ad quem*,
he did not take Domitian's death, however, but rather Nerva's — based upon
the assumption that Josephus' Epaphroditus was not the freedman secretary
executed by Domitian, but rather a well-known *grammaticus* of the same
name, described by the *Suda*. This allows Schwartz to avoid the necessity of
concluding that Agrippa was still minting in 95 but died in time for Justus and
Josephus to write and Epaphroditus to be executed all in the year or so before
Domitian died — which would be, as Seyrig said, "un peu juste." Since the
Suda says the *grammaticus* was prominent in Rome from Nero until Nerva,

---

Nicolaus of Damascus, in parallel sections of *BJ* and *Ant.*, but was less careful in editing it in
Ant. As for his comment, ibid., p. 70, n. 18, that "Schwartz practices source criticism with a
fervor and a certainty seldom seen outside of German dissertations of the nineteenth century"
— while his general essay was admittedly not the place, I do hope that he will somewhere
discuss my arguments.) On Smith's reconstruction in general (and not just with regard to
Josephus), cf. above, p. 141, n. 33.

   [61] Cohen (above, n. 4) frequently acknowledges his debt to Laqueur, also in his essay cited
above, n. 57 (but cf. n. 75, below), and Schwartz uses language which would have been nigh
unthinkable a generation ago: "this . . . [conclusion] makes it possible (! — D.R.S.) to accept
for this book the theory proposed by Laqueur . . ." (*HTR* 79 [1986], p. 376.) Schwartz's
dissertation has now appeared, under the title *Josephus and Judaean Politics* (1990); his debt
to Smith and Cohen is written large in the preface, p. ix. For a critique of Cohen's book as only
a "remake" of Laqueur's "most absurd" theory, which greatly overstates the matter, see P.
Vidal-Naquet, *L'antiquité classique* 51 (1982), pp. 408–9.

Schwartz concluded that the *Vita* was written between 95 and 98 (Nerva died in January 98), and he settled for the latter part of this period, 97/98, apparently in order to leave enough time for Justus and Josephus to write.[62]

This *terminus ad quem* is quite problematic. First of all, we should note that most earlier scholars were sure that Josephus' Epaphroditus was the freedman secretary;[63] the ease with which the numismatic evidence junked that assumption should leave us skeptical about other identifications. After all, as many scholars have noted, the name itself is not uncommon. Moreover, the *Suda* does not say that the grammarian died under Nerva, but only that he "was prominent in Rome" until Nerva; perhaps he moved, perhaps he fell from prominence. And, finally, Laqueur has already argued, with conviction, that the *Suda* frequently uses a very schematic dating for *floruit*s, which should not be pressed.[64] If, on the basis of the *Suda*, we are willing to let the *Vita* be written as late as 97/98, can we really be so confident that it could not have been written a mere three years or so later, as results from Photius' explicit testimony concerning Agrippa II's death? Is it not the case that the real reason preventing us from accepting Photius' date is simply the inertia of a scholarly tradition which arose when the numismatic evidence was unknown and was preserved by generations of scholars who ignored it?

Moreover, three additional arguments may be adduced in Photius' favor, one from numismatics and two from philology. The numismatic one is simple: already de Saulcy and Hill noticed that Roman coinage of Tiberias began in the eightieth or eighty-first year of the municipal era, and, based upon Photius' date for the death of Agrippa II, they deduced that the city had been founded in 19 or 20 C.E.[65] In the past generation, independent numismatic

---

[62] In Schwartz's article and book cited in the preceding note, see, respectively, p. 385, n. 45, and pp. 19–20. Vincent too (above, n. 25: pp. 376–379) alludes to the *Suda* as if it says this Epaphroditus died during Nerva's reign. For the passage, see *Suidae Lexicon*, II (ed. A. Adler; 1931), p. 334. Schwartz's *HTR* essay began as an appendix to his 1985 dissertation.

[63] See Schürer (above, n. 2), p. 80, n. 8, who cites several authorities; add Stein (above, n. 14). Schürer's own preference for the *Suda*'s *grammaticus* was only a function of his isolated position maintaining Photius' date. For Grotius and Frölich, see above, n. 33.

[64] See Laqueur, *Jüdische Historiker*, pp. 26–28; so too, in general, A. I. Baumgarten, *The Phoenician History of Philo of Byblos: A Commentary* (1981), pp. 32–35 (pp. 34–35: "In any case, Pliny's letter is a reminder of the inconclusiveness of any chronological conclusion based on the entries in Suidas . . .").

[65] See de Saulcy (above, n. 34), p. 335 and Hill (above, n. 34), p. xiv. On Tiberias' municipal coinage, see Y. Meshorer, *City-Coins of Eretz-Israel and the Decapolis in the Roman Period* (1985), pp. 34–35. That the coins of Tiberias' eighty-first year were issued no later than 101/2 is confirmed by the absence of "Dacicus" from Trajan's official titulature, as is noted by Smallwood, *Jews*, p. 573; cf. Mattingly (above, n. 47), III, p. lviii. (De Saulcy also mentions a similar coin, in his private collection, from Tiberias' eightieth year, but Y. Meshorer has kindly informed me that such a coin has not come to light and most probably the

evidence has confirmed that Herod Antipas founded the city in his twenty-fourth year, i.e., 19/20 or 20/21 C.E.[66] We may now, therefore, reverse the argument and use it to support Photius' date for Agrippa's death. Cohen apparently sensed this, but, locked in as he was, by the post-Seyrig consensus, to Agrippa dying in the early nineties, he was forced to theorize that the city was in limbo for six or more years, before it finally achieved the right to mint.[67] But the date of the beginning of Roman coinage in Tiberias corresponds so well with Photius' date for Agrippa's death that it appears far more reasonable simply to view the former as confirming the latter.

As for the two philological arguments, one is simple, the other only somewhat more complicated. Studies by T. Hägg (1975) and W. T. Treadgold (1980) have greatly contributed to the classification of Photius' diverse "codices" and the understanding of his working methods.[68] Codex 33, on Justus of Tiberias, where the details about Agrippa's career and death are given, belongs to what Treadgold calls Class IIA: "Descriptions probably composed by referring back to the original text (or possibly to notes on it): Precise references," a category which is generally accurate, as both Hägg and Treadgold note, apparently since Photius wrote these short entries by referring back to the beginning and/or end of the work in question in order to give such data as the book's limits and the number of volumes.[69] The *Bibliotheca* includes nine Class IIA codices on historical works which have been preserved, and of them six, discussing books which cover long periods, are comparable to the one on Justus.[70] I checked them all, and found them,

---

alpha making 80 into 81 had simply worn off. There are, in contrast, numerous specimens of coins from the eighty-first year.)

[66] See Meshorer (above, n. 52), pp. 35−36; further literature is cited above, p. 190, n. 34. The doubt (19/20 or 20/21) stems from unclarity about the precise beginning of the era (Herod's death or Antipas' ratification by Augustus) and the beginning of the year (fall or spring); these problems are immaterial here. On them, see above, p. 157, n. 1 and pp. 173−180.

[67] See Cohen (above, n. 4), pp. 138−141.

[68] T. Hägg, *Photios als Vermittler antiker Literatur* (1975); W. T. Treadgold, *The Nature of the Bibliotheca of Photius* (1980).

[69] On this type of what Hägg called a "Kurzreferat," see Treadgold (above, n. 68), pp. 84−85, 118; ibid., pp. 118−168, Treadgold classifies all the codices. With regard to the Kurzreferate, Hägg too notes "Die Informationen sind meistens korrekt" (p. 199); ibid., n. 25, he adds that "kurze Angaben über die chronologischen Grenzen eines Geschichtswerks dessen Anfang und Ende direkt entnommen sind." So too I. Klinkenberg, *De Photi Bibliothecae codicibus historicis* (1913), pp. 27−28.

[70] Of the nine codices which, according to Treadgold's list, represent Class IIA reports on preserved historical texts, two (codices 15 and 88) are on Gelasius's history of the council of Nicaea and one (codex 91[2]) is on Arrian's *Indica*. Justus' book was a chronicle covering a long period, and should rather be compared with the church histories by Eusebius, Socrates, Evagrius, Sozomenes, Theodoret and Nicephorus (codices 27, 28, 29, 30, 31, and 66; note the proximity of codex 33, on Justus, to the first five of these).

indeed, to be totally accurate, with one exception which proves the rule: Codex 31, on Theodoret of Cyr, states that his *Church History* went up to the death of Diodorus (of Tarsus, d. ca. 390), in the days when Sisinnius was bishop of Constantinople (426−427). In fact, however, while the last lines of the book (Migne, *Patrologia Graeca* 82, cols. 1277−1280) do list Sisinnius as the last bishop of Constaninople, they also tell us that the history ends with the death of Theodore of Mopsuestia (d. 428). But the latter is identified here as a disciple of "the great Diodorus." In other words, here too it seems that Photius' summary was based upon a check of the last page of the book; while here his skimming failed him, the other five cases show that he was usually very accurate. It is likely, therefore, that he may be trusted with regard to Justus as well.

The other, somewhat more complicated philological argument proceeds from the oft-observed fact that Josephus' main attack upon Justus, in ch. 65 of the *Vita*, is quite easily separated from the rest of the work. Indeed, as we have seen (n. 25), even before Laqueur several scholars had suggested that it was secondarily added to the *Vita* after Justus' work appeared. These suggestions did not catch on, because it was then thought that several statements in *Antiquities* 17 and 20 indicate that Agrippa was dead by 93/94, when the *Antiquities* was completed. Now, however, we know that Agrippa was alive as late as 95 C.E., which means either that the inference drawn from those passages is incorrect[71] or that they were added into the *Antiquities* subsequent to the 93/94 completion of the work's first "edition." Be that as it may, the way is again open for a "second edition" theory for the *Vita* as a solution for our problem.

As will be remembered, Laqueur's solution was so all-inclusive and radical that it fell by its own weight. He thought that *all* references to Justus were secondary (see below, n. 75), and that the core of the *Vita* was written without any reference to the Tiberian. These claims were easily refuted (see above, nn. 27−29), by scholars who showed just how arbitrary it often was to dissect out references to Justus, and just how widespread Josephus' apologetic stance is throughout the *Vita*. This was taken to mean that all of the *Vita* was written as a response to Justus.

However, the fact that Josephus is apologetic all through the *Vita* does not mean that he is always responding to Justus. The very fact that, as Laqueur's critics showed, Josephus is everywhere replying to the standard political invective of his period, means that he might easily have had to respond this

---

[71] That is, Josephus could write such statements although Agrippa was still alive. This conclusion engenders thoughts about Josephus' sources or other reasons for writing in this way about Agrippa, but they need not concern us here. Cf. my article cited at the end of n. 28, above.

way to any critic at all. Why, then, should we disbelieve him when he tells us in several passages that he had various critics, not only Justus?[72]

As for the question of the organic or secondary nature of the *Vita* references to Justus, it seems that one circumstance must be taken very seriously: of all the references to Justus, those two which refer to Justus' historical work are clearly part of secondary passages (as is indicated by compositional fingerprints) and both passages attack him, contradicting, in doing so, other references to Justus in the *Vita*. The obvious implication of this is that the latter reflect Josephus' first edition or draft of the *Vita*, and the former were added only after Justus published his work. Since that happened only after Agrippa died (*Vita* 359), it becomes all the easier to accept Photius' dating of that event. We will now briefly demonstrate these statements.

Only two passages of the *Vita* explicitly refer to Justus' history: §§ 40–41 and §§ 336–367. The latter is clearly a digression, as Josephus states at its beginning and end. It also contradicts § 410 where, despite the cross-reference ("as has been narrated above"), the details of Justus' imprisonment are not identical with those in §§ 342–343. Moreover, the digression's version accuses Justus of attacking the villages of the Decapolis (§ 341), and asserts that both Vespasian and Agrippa condemned Justus to death; the version in § 410 says only that the Decapolitans accused Justus (Josephus not opining as to the truth of the accusation) but the good king Agrippa preserved him from death. Thus, it seems that Josephus first wrote nicely or neutrally about Justus (note their common problems in §§ 174–177), and only later, after Justus attacked him after Agrippa died, did Josephus add the "great digression"[73] and, in the course of it, give another version of this episode as well. This brought him to add the cross-reference in § 410, but not to otherwise bring it into line with the new version.[74]

---

[72] See especially *Vita* 6 and 336 and *C. Ap.* 1.46, 53–56, also *Antiquities* 20.266. That Josephus' counterattack in the *Vita* need not have been directed against Justus alone has recently been acknowledged by T. Rajak, in *Josephus, Judaism, and Christianity* (edd. L. H. Feldman and G. Hata; 1987), pp. 85–87.

[73] I.e., §§ 336–367. For the record, and lest it seem that the term "great digression" was coined by Cohen (as Rajak, loc. cit., p. 85 suggests) and reflects this section's effect upon the reader's mood, we will note that already Motzo (above, n. 26–p. 222 [= 693]), long before the Great Depression, wrote about "la grande digressione".

[74] It should be added that also the only other passage of the *Vita* which explicitly attacks Justus, apart from the two which refer to his historical work, namely, §§ 390–393, seems quite clearly to be an insert: it is introduced with "about this time" and presented with the summary + "for the following reason" + details structure (on which two criteria see, respectively, my article cited in n. 28 and Williamson's cited in n. 76), and it gives another version of part of the preceding story: whereas there (§ 381) we read only of the leading councilmen of Tiberias approaching Agrippa, here, at the end of the story (§ 393), we read, specifically, of Justus' doing the same. Moreover, the body of §§ 390–393 agrees with both of our other secondary passages in that they portray Justus as responsible for leading the

As for §§ 40−41, five considerations show that it too is part of a secondary inlay.[75] First, here too, as in the "great digression" (§ 341), Josephus himself tells us roundly that Justus led the attack on the villages of the Decapolis (§ 42). Second, as in the case of §§ 342−343//410, we have a contradiction: whereas § 41 has Justus' brother being one of the prime *villains* of the rebellion, §§ 177 and 186 have him being one of its prime *victims*. Third, this whole section on Tiberias is surrounded by the signs of what has been shown to be a typical Josephan way of introducing outside material into a narrative: summary + "for the following reason" at the outset (§ 31b), rounding-off concluding phrase at the end (§ 43a).[76] Fourth, right after this section on Tiberias, Josephus says some very nice things about John of Gischala (§§ 43−45), whereas everywhere else, in *Vita* and the *Jewish War*, he makes him the vilest of villains and Josephus' own worst enemy.[77] As Laqueur, I can think of no reason for this rehabilitation of John, other than a Josephan desire to make the foregoing picture of Justus all the more damning. In other words, the fact that the section on Tiberias (which denounces Justus' history) is immediately followed by another passage which seems to be secondary reinforces the conclusion that it is too. And fifth, finally, the arrangement of *Vita* 30 ff. is quite strange. We read of Josephus' departure for the Galilee, then, successively, of his learning of the situation in Sepphoris, Tiberias,

---

Tiberians into rebellion, even against their will; cf. below, n. 78. However, for our purposes it is unnecessary to show secondary any passages other than the two which mention Justus' historical work.

[75] See pp. 37−42 of Laqueur's book, where, in his discussion of this passage, we find "the usual Laqueurian brew of fact and fantasy" (Cohen [above, n. 4], p. 129). This section is part of a larger argument, which Laqueur concludes, on pp. 46−47, with the following chain: "Ist nun aber 32−62 ein späterer Einschub in einen älteren Text, dann müssen alle diejenigen Partien, welche auf diesem Berichte beruhen oder sonst irgendwie mit ihm in Zusammenhang stehen, ebenfalls sekundär sein und sich anstandslos beseitigen lassen . . .," which a page later becomes "unser ja schon festehendes Ergebnis, daß alle Justusstücke nachträglich eingeschoben sind."

[76] See H. G. M. Williamson, *JTS* n.s. 28 (1977), pp. 50−55. For studies of cases of this in the latter half of *Antiquities*, see above, p. 162 (on *Ant.* 17.165−167), p. 209 (on *Ant.* 18.91−95), and p. 235 (on *Ant.* 20.105−112); *Agrippa I*, pp. 5−6 (on *Ant.* 18.151−154), and *JQR* 72 (1981/82), pp. 241−268 (on *Ant.* 14.268−270; 18.39−54; and 20.141−144).

[77] Drexler (above, n. 29: p. 299) makes this point quite forcefully. Helm (above, n. 27: col. 486) pointed to *BJ* 2.590, just as Gelzer (above, n. 27: p. 74 [307], n. 30) pointed to *BJ* 2.575 and 2.615, as evidence that Josephus at first got along with John, thus arguing against the secondariness of *Vita* 43−45 (which, in addition, Helm termed "sehr kahl"). But this is beside the point. The question is not whether John originally cooperated with Josephus but rather how Josephus, after the war, would write about John: in *BJ* 2.590 and 2.615, Josephus makes it clear that the wicked John had originally deceived him. Nothing like this appears in *Vita* 43−45. For similar rhetoric, note how Josephus has only good things to report about Festus in *BJ* 2.271, where he is followed immediately by an explicitly contrasted wicked Albinus. In *Ant.* 20, in contrast, where the account of Festus ends at § 188 and that on Albinus begins only at § 204 and there is, therefore, no such direct comparison, Festus is not praised.

Gischala and Gamala, and then of his departure from Sepphoris to learn the situation in Tiberias and Gischala. Why does he twice learn of the situation in Tiberias and Gischala? And why are they so different, first with bad Justus and good John, then with no Justus[78] and villainous John? It seems, as Laqueur argued, that here too is an indication that the first account of Tiberias and Gischala is an inlay.

VI. Conclusions

Apart from some worthless Jewish and Christian traditions linking Agrippa's death to the destruction of the Second Temple,[79] the only explicit statement anywhere regarding the year of Agrippa II's death is offered by Photius, in the

---

[78] Justus is mentioned fleetingly in § 65 and has no role in the narrative; as Laqueur (p. 47) notes, his name hangs "völlig in der Luft." This may well indicate that it was stuck in secondarily; so Gelzer (above, n. 27), p. 75 (=309). See also Cohen (above, n. 4: p. 137), who accounts it among "Josephan glosses" "which have no organic connection with their contexts and seem to intrude on the narrative;" Cohen leaves open the possibility that, as Laqueur thought, they are interpolations into an earlier text. Even if not, the fact remains that there is no comparison between the passing reference to him here and the passionate condemnation in §§ 32–42, 336–367, and 390–393. (As for the difficult question, why Josephus would add Justus' name into § 65, the best Cohen can suggest is that "most likely he wanted to implicate him in the negotiations concerning the destruction of the palace." However, the continuation makes clear that the leaders of Tiberias at first opposed that destruction, and when it was finally accomplished and accompanied by looting they opposed the latter as well; Josephus makes no attempt to distinguish between Justus and the others. Perhaps Justus' name in § 65 is meant only to support Josephus' general claim that Justus was prominent in Tiberias, a claim he puts to work elsewhere; cf. above, n. 74.)

[79] On some Jews and Christians who thought Agrippa II died in the early seventies, see above, notes 5–6 and Cohen (above, n. 4), pp. 170–172. They would seem to reflect no more than folk or religious memory's tendency to assume that Jewish royalty disappeared when the last remnants of Jewish statehood did. This assumption died hard: even C. Baronius, who knew that Agrippa outlived the destruction, nevertheless insisted on linking the end of his monarchy, as *rex Iudeorum*, to the Destruction (*Annales ecclesiastici*, I [1601], p. 901 [ad ann. Chr. 73]). Although I. Casaubon would correctly brand this as "mera . . . hallucinatio" just a few years later, since Agrippa had never been *rex Iudeorum* (*De rebus sacris et ecclesiasticis exercitationes xvi ad cardinalis Baronii Prolegomena in Annales & primam eorum partem* [1614], p. 22), the same natural misconception would often reappear; see, for example, F. Spanheim (above, n. 12). Cf. below, n. 88! I have also ignored speculations (e.g. Schürer, above, n. 2: pp. 598–599, n. 45 = SVM I, p. 481, n. 45; von Gutschmid, above, n. 20: p. 355), to the effect that the letters S.C. (= senatusconsulto) on some of Agrippa's coins of 86 C.E. indicate a Roman takeover. The fact that Harduin (above, n. 32: pp. 19, 82–83 [= *Opera selecta*, pp. 333, 349]) could instead infer that Rome then gave Agrippa certain military powers, and Basnage (above, n. 35: p. 108) could prefer to infer that Rome then reconfirmed his monarchy, indicates just how arbitrary this type of speculation is. On the lack of evidence for anything special happening in Palestine in 86 C.E., see Smallwood, *Jews*, pp. 353–355.

course of his account of Justus of Tiberias. It seems likely, as many scholars have assumed, that Photius took the date from Justus' work itself (where else?), and recent study of the bibliophile's working methods bears this out. But, even if that were not the case, we should demand strong reasons to set the date aside. Earlier generations of scholars thought that they had such a reason, namely, Josephus' date of 93/94 for the conclusion of *Antiquities*: at first only because the *Vita* was taken to be an *immediate* continuation of the *Antiquities*, and later also because passages in the *Antiquities* were thought to imply that Agrippa was dead when they were written, this date, in a composition by a contemporary and friend of Agrippa's, was taken to override Photius'. Numismatists have long known, however, that Agrippa was alive until at least 95 C.E., and after centuries of ignoring this evidence and a few generations of trying to overcome it, historians have now begun to realize that Josephus' date for the *Antiquities* cannot serve as a *terminus ad quem* for Agrippa's death and the *Vita*.

In the meantime, however, philologists had pointed to three other reasons to date the *Vita*, and hence Agrippa's death, to no later than Domitian's death: the *Vita*'s dedication to a man identified as one killed by Domitian in 95 C.E., its failure to mention emperors after Domitian when referring to the ones who had been gracious toward Josephus, and its willingness to say something positive about Domitian (who was so widely condemned after his death). But there is no certainty regarding the identity of Josephus' Epaphroditus, and the value of the psychological arguments about Domitian, of which the first is *ex silentio* to boot, is doubtful.[80]

Again, in the twentieth century, some inscriptions (n. 23) were held to clinch the case against Photius, for they seem to indicate that, by 96−97 C.E., Agrippa was no longer ruling in his kingdom. The obvious inference is that he was dead. But, here too, the *argumentum ex silentio* is not decisive: perhaps the failure to mention Agrippa is only a quirk of the authors of the inscriptions or of the stonecutters, or perhaps Agrippa lost possession of some of his lands a few years before he died. And perhaps the doubts regarding the extent of Agrippa's territories and the provenance of one of the inscriptions should also be recalled.[81] I confess to not being satisfied by any of these suggested ways of overcoming these inscriptions, but it does seem clear that arguments from their silence are of less force than the explicit testimony of Agrippa's coins and of Photius, along with the other evidence − the 1965 inscription, the coins of Tiberias, and the editorial fingerprints in the *Vita* − which we have adduced.

---

[80] See above, n. 54.

[81] Note that Dunand roundly states "provenance inconnue" with regard to his inscription (above, n. 23); Seyrig (above, n. 46), pp. 60−61 assumes that it is probably from the vicinity of the museum (in the Auranitis). For a reminder concerning the doubts pertaining to the borders of Agrippa's kingdom, see Rappaport (above, n. 52), p. 64.

In other words, we are back in the vicinity of Photius' date, not because his authority is unassailable but because the reasons to assail it have become undermined and Photius' credit on this type of matter has been restored, because the circumstantial evidence against him now seems to be outweighed by that in his favor, and because the surgery on Josephus which Photius' date requires has again become permissible, after having served time for almost sixty years because of Laqueur's abuse of it.

This conclusion may lead us, on the one hand, to speculate on the circumstances of the end of Agrippa's rule. How, and when, did it happen that Rome "received the rule" of some of Agrippa's lands, as Josephus states in *Antiquities* 17.28 and may be supported by the epigraphic evidence? Before his death or after? Was it due to a failure to maintain order? (Is it only a coincidence that soldiers were drafted into the Roman army precisely from the town where Agrippa − or his father − had published an edict denouncing "wild" guerillas [*OGIS* I, nr. 424]?) Or did he fall prey to accusations of secretly supporting the rebels a generation earlier?[82] Or to Domitian's anti-Jewish streak?[83] Were there accusations that Justus, Agrippa's secretary, had secretly colluded with him in anti-Gentile raids, accusations which Justus − with the passing of Tiberias from Agrippa's to Roman rule − attempted to rebuff by shifting them to Josephus?[84] Is this the polemical context which gave these matters an urgency thirty years or more after they were over and done with? These suggestions seem reasonable, but, for the present, the absence of harder information must perforce leave them somewhat in the realm of speculation.

On the other hand, finally, our analysis of the history of scholarship on this question may lead us to more than speculation. We have seen how violent and unfounded emendations were widespread so long nothing stronger could be found to settle a problem, and then disappeared overnight; we have seen a

---

[82] Various scholars (such as Rühl [above, n. 25], pp. 300−301 and Baerwald [above, n. 16], pp. 27−41) have attempted to portray Agrippa II as a secret rebel against Rome, but their arguments are, by and large, far from convincing. See Cohen (above, n. 4), p. 13, and, in general *Agrippa I*, p. 171. Nevertheless, ancient enemies of Agrippa II, no less than modern Zionists, could have tried to portray him as an enemy of Rome; note, inter alia, *Vita* 46−53, especially with the problematic text of § 52.

[83] The question of a Domitianic persecution of Judaism, or rather only a generally unsympathetic climate vis à vis Jews, has often been debated on the basis of meager and problematic sources. See, inter alia, P. Keresztes in *Vigiliae Christianae* 27 (1973), pp. 1−15; S. Applebaum, *Scripta Classica Israelica* 1 (1974), pp. 116−123; Stern, *GLA* II, pp. 128−131, 380−382; and G. Stemberger, in *Christlicher Antijudaismus und jüdischer Antipaganismus: Ihre Motive und Hintergründe in den ersten drei Jahrhunderten* (ed. H. Frohnhofen; 1990), pp. 16−17.

[84] Cohen (above, n. 4: pp. 138−141) sees this as part of the Sitz im Leben of Justus' work: in an attempt to improve Tiberias' credentials in Rome's eyes, blame for its participation in the rebellion had to be shifted elsewhere.

good modest theory discarded merely because someone incorporated it into an extravagant one; we have seen numismatic evidence assimilated as long as it was harmless and thereafter trampled or ignored; and we have seen the very same numismatist who thought he laid the matter to rest in 1964, at the price of ignoring an obvious difficulty or two, being forced by new discoveries to reopen the question the very next year.

But if the latter observations lead to humility and self-criticism, the synchronism of some of these developments also leads the present writer, at least, to wonder. We have seen the general demise of emending on historical grounds just around the same time as, on the one hand, greater familiarity with Josephus gave supporters of an early dating arguments sufficient simply to proclaim Photius wrong, and, on the other hand, the appearance of second-edition theories for the first time allowed Photius' partisans Josephan arguments. We have, again, seen a baby-and-bathwater phenomenon in our corner coincide with a general decline of source-criticism and its tools, but we also saw a revival of Laqueur coincide not only with a general reaction against the treatment of ancient historiography as if it were only literature,[85] but also with epigraphic and (especially) numismatic advances which demanded a reopening of the books and a more sympathetic treatment of Photius — and this just as students of Photius were readying the material necessary to support him here. Is this all just coincidence? How usual is this in historical scholarship? I wonder.

Appendix: On the Chronographer of 354

In 1850, Theodor Mommsen published a long essay on the Chronographer of 354, along with an edition, including a "Liber generationis" from a single Viennese manuscript.[86] The latter, a Latin translation from a lost Greek

---

[85] See above, n. 59.

[86] Th. Mommsen, in *Abhandlungen der philologisch-historischen Classe der königlichen-sächsischen Gesellschaft der Wissenschaften* 1 (1850), pp. 547–668 (pp. 585–598 about the chronicle, pp. 637–643 — its text). The text may also be found, with a new introduction, in Th. Mommsen, ed., *Chronica Minora saec. IV.V.VI.VII.*, vol. I (Monumenta Germaniae Historica, Auctorum antiquissimorum IX; 1892), pp. 78–140. In the 1892 edition, Mommsen rearranged the order so as to print this text in parallel with others (which do not contain anything parallel to the two concluding paragraphs of this chronicle, upon which we shall focus here). To facilitate matters for those for whom only one or the other edition is accessible, and also to provide an antidote for mistaken references, I shall refer below to both: references to the text will be to page and line of the 1850 edition followed, after a slash, with the page and paragraph (or line) in the 1892 one. The text may also be found in C. Frick, *Chronica Minora* (1892), pp. 80–111. Mommsen's 1850 essay was reprinted, but without the text and without the discussion of our chronicle, in his *Gesammelte Schriften* VII (1909), pp. 536–579, 606–632.

original, ends with a paragraph which bears upon the chronology of Agrippa II. The text is, however, obviously corrupt in a number of places, to such an extent that various scholars, from Mommsen to Cohen, have despaired of extracting anything coherent or reliable from it.[87]

In 1896, however, Carl Erbes published an acute study of this part of the text, suggesting a number of emendations which result in Agrippa dying in 86 C.E., a date which he attempted to support with numismatic arguments as well, and which he tried to show was not contradicted by Josephus; Photius, he argued, should be explained away one way or another.[88] While advances and discoveries have since abrogated Erbes' numismatic arguments,[89] it seems that no one has answered Erbes' argument based upon the Chronographer of 354 (apart from wholesale rejection of anything based upon this corrupt text). Schürer, in fact, agreed to consider the date of 86 C.E., if only as that of Agrippa's loss of some of his territories.[90] In fact, however, it appears that examination will show that − if anything may be deduced from this corrupt text − it most probably only confirms Josephus' date for Agrippa's enthronement, and says nothing of the date of his death.

The data in the concluding section of this chronicle (p. 643/140) are as follows:

A. From Creation to Cyrus ("ad cyrum")   4916
B. Persian Rule   230
C. Macedonian Rule   270

---

[87] See Mommsen's 1892 discussion, pp. 87−88, along with, inter alia, Rosenberg (above, n. 22), col. 150 and Cohen (above, n. 4), p. 172, n. 222.

[88] Erbes (above, n. 20), pp. 415−432. Erbes disposes of Photius, on pp. 431−432, by suggesting either the Müller-Graetz approach (above, n. 16) or Niese's (above, n. 21); as another possibility, he also casts doubt on the authenticity of Justus' book used by Photius. (In an earlier study of our text − in *Jahrbücher für protestantische Theologie* 5 [1879], pp. 624−628 − Erbes had assumed Agrippa died in 70 C.E.; he was misled by Mommsen, who in his 1850 edition [above, n. 86], p. 586, apparently dates Agrippa's death or fall to 71 C.E. The misconception was, indeed, quite popular at the time; see, for another example in a serious work, A. Weiss' essay in the *Jahres-Bericht über das k. k. akademische Gymnasium in Wien für das Schuljahr 1882−83*, p. 6. Cf. above, n. 79!)

[89] I refer not only to Barag et al. (above, notes 52−53), but also to Erbes' emphasis upon Domitian's not being termed "Germanicus" on coins between Agrippa's 26th and 35th years, when the epithet reappears, from which he inferred that these coins must have been dated according to a 50 C.E. era. Schalit (above, n. 45: pp. 188, 192) echoed this argument. Both depended upon Madden's 1881 work (above, n. 34). But in the meantime two new counter-examples have come to light: Meshorer (above, n. 53), p. 257, nrs. 47 and 50.

[90] Schürer (above, n. 2), p. 598; SVM I, pp. 480−481.

D. Jewish Monarchy until Agrippa   345
  ("sub suis regibus fuerunt usque ad
  agrippam, qui nouissimus fuit rex
  iudeorum")
E. From Agrippa until Consulate of   5870
  Septimius Severus (194 C.E.)
F. From Latter until 249   57[91]
G. From Latter until 304   55
H. From Latter until 334   30
I. Total From Creation Until 334   1017 (sic!)

Erbes' procedure was as follows:

1. He assumed, quite reasonably, that the number appearing as E was meant to give the total since Creation instead of the period between Agrippa and 194.

2. Since $A+B+C+D = 5761$, which is 109 less than 5870, he concluded that E should have said Agrippa died 109 years before 194, i.e., in 85−86 C.E.

3. The same result was reached from the other direction with the aid of another bit of emendation. Namely, Erbes subtracted 100 each from C and D, thus creating fairly acceptable figures for Macedonian rule (Alexander to Judas Maccabaeus − ca. 170 years) and Jewish monarchy (245 years): if the latter begins in 159 B.C.E. − where Eusebius begins Jonathan's rule (*Chronicon*, ed. Helm,[2] p. 142) − then it ends in 86 C.E.[92]

A major problem with this approach is that previous sections of this chronicle give different figures and view the Hellenistic period differently, as Erbes himself clearly stated:

We note, moreover, that our concluding section of the universal chronicle has 4916 years from Creation until Cyrus, while elsewhere . . . it has 4841; that here the Persian period is 230 years long, while earlier it was 222 (or 272); and that here the Macedonians are followed in the Syrian line, but previously − in the Egyptian line . . .[93]

---

[91] In F−H consular dates are given. Mommsen (above, n. 86: p. 586/140) suggests that "LVII" here is a mistake for "LVIT," i.e., "LV item."

[92] In an apparent misprint, Erbes (p. 418) states Eusebius had Jonathan's rule begin "mit dem Jahre 1857 ab Abr. = 159 v. Chr.;" read 1859. It is not clear how Erbes wanted to use Eusebius in order to support our chronicle's claim that Jewish kings ruled for 245 years. For Eusebius, Jonathan was not a king but only a "dux," and Judas Maccabaeus was one before him; the first Hasmonean "rex," according to Eusebius, was Johanan Hyrcanus I. See *Chronicon* (ed. Helm[2]), pp. 141, 142, 144, 145.

[93] Erbes (above, n. 20), pp. 418−419 (my translation). In the space represented by three dots, Erbes referred to 640[4]/130[138] and 641[28]/130[182] for the 4841 years from Creation to Cyrus. As for the length of Persian rule, since its end is said to have come in a.M. 5113 (641[35]/131[198]), it would appear that it was 272 years (5113−4841), but the individual reigns listed in 641[29−35]/131[184−198] add up to 271. The total given in 641[34]/131[196] is 222, evidently missing an L (see below).

Erbes' conclusion was that this concluding section must, therefore, have been based upon another source and not upon the foregoing data. He further guessed that that source was Justus' lost chronicle, a point supported by the similarity of this chronicle's characterization of Agrippa as "qui nouissimus fuit rex Iudaeorum" to Photius'/Justus' "last (*hystatou*) of the Jewish kings."

However, it is certainly much more likely to assume, unless and until the opposite is proven, that this concluding section of the chronicle, which begins with "Ex quo ergo" ($643^{23}/140^{11}$), is indeed based upon the previously assembled data. This is especially the case in that the obviously corrupt state of the document's numbers makes it difficult to be confident that different data indicate different sources. Thus, for one of Erbes' examples, the ease of confusion beteen CCXXII, CCXXX and CCLXX makes them a doubtful support for distinguishing sources.[94] Let us, therefore, proceed upon the assumption that this concluding section of the chronicle is based upon the foregoing data, and see whether the emendations required will not be more minimal, and better founded, than those required by Erbes.[95]

---

[94] One may compare, for example, the years each of the nine antediluvian fathers is said to have lived before fathering his firstborn, according to $638^{8-11}/91^{27}-92^{35}$, with the figures in the summary in $642^{2-10}/139^{3-11}$, just before the section which concerns us. There is exact agreement only with regard to three: Enos, Cainan amd Enoch. While the figures in the summary all agree with the Septuagint's (Genesis 5), those in the earlier section differ as follows: Adam is missing a C; Seth is missing a V; Malaleel has an extra I; Iareth is missing II but has an extra C (according to Mommsen's 1850 text) or has a V instead of an I and an extra C (according to Mommsen's 1892 text); Mathusala has two extra X's; and Lamech is ascribed CLXXII instead of CLXXXIX. Would anyone suggest that we are dealing here with different sources? For some comparable cases of corruption in Roman numerals and a reasonable willingness to correct them, Professor Amnon Linder kindly referred me to O. Seeck, *Regesten der Kaiser und Päpste für die Jahre 311 bis 476 n. Chr.* (1919), pp. 96–97.

[95] In general, one may say that the text is frequently corrupt but may usually be restored with fair certainty, due to the overlapping nature of the calculations. Note, for example, that the reigns of twenty kings of Judaea from Saul to Joachim ($639^{21-42}/120^{112}-126^{135}$) total exactly 462 years and 12 months, i.e., 463 years – the figure which is restated two pages later ($641^{19}/129^{180}$). Also the reigns of fifteen Ptolemaic kings all add up properly in $641^{37-44}/137^{199-217}$. Again, of the forty numbers given for the twenty generations between Adam and Abraham, two numbers per generation ($642-643^{2-22}/139^{3-23}$), all but seven correspond exactly with the Septuagint's text in Genesis 5 and 11: three are off by one or two years only, two are off by exactly one hundred years, one (the very last one) has no counterpart in the Septuagint, and one ($643^{5}/139^{6}$ – 711 instead of 740) is only a case of an I instead of an L: DCCXI for DCCXL. Similarly, in $641^{17-18}/129^{179}$, 412+30 is said to be 462 instead of 442: CCCCLXII for CCCCXLII (simple metathesis). Or, for a final example, if one merely omits the first I so as to turn the unintelligible XIVIII in $639^{7}/116^{94}$ into XVIII, as in Judges 3:14, the nineteen figures (including one written out, not in numerals) in this long section ($639^{4-19}/114^{91}-120^{110}$) indeed total 441, as is stated at its conclusion.

Returning, therefore, to the first four items in the table, we suggest:

A. Instead of 4916, let us read 4841: IIIIDCCCXLI for IIIIDCCCCXVI — a C was added and the L became a V. The year a. M. 4841 is, as Erbes noted, the chronicle's usual date for Cyrus' ascent to the throne, or, more precisely, for Cyrus' ending of the seventy years of Babylonian exile (see n. 93).

B. Instead of 230 (CCXXX), let us read 270 (CCLXX), substituting an L for an X. This is based upon the fact that the separate reigns of the Persian kings given in $641^{29-35}/131^{184-198}$ add up to 271 years, from which one must subtract 1 since the Return came in Cyrus' second year, as our chronicler noted just after this section (in $642^{31}/140^9$).

C. Let us retain the Chronographer's figure of 270 years for Macedonian rule. Erbes is somewhat misleading when he states, in the inset passage quoted above, that the concluding section of the chronicle follows the Seleucid line: in the text as we have it, there is no awareness of the different types of Macedonians. In the extant text the Chronicle counts 335 years of Ptolemaic kings (p. 641/137) and then begins "post ptholomeum dyonisi" — at this point the text breaks. Clearly something is missing,[96] and we have no reason to suspect that it was anything other than a statement culminating in 270 years between Alexander and the Hasmonean monarchy. That this figure is wrong, historically, is beside the point.

D. Similarly, let us retain the Chronographer's figure of 345 years for Jewish monarchy.

In other words, all we have suggested is that we change two letters so as to substitute for A the number which this chronicle itself, twice, gives in its stead, and that we substitute in B one L for one X, in order to restore here the number which also emerges from this chronicle itself. If we now return to Erbes' argument, and accept his quite logical step 1, we may continue as follows:

2. A+B+C+D = 5726, which is 144 years less than 5870, so if the latter is equivalent to 194 C.E., the former is equivalent to 50 C.E.. Which is right where Josephus puts the beginning of Agrippa's reign (*Ant.* 20.103–4; *BJ* 2.284). And here we may note that our text does not give the length of Agrippa's reign; contrast, for example, $639^{18-19}/120^{109-110}$, "post hunc samuhel sacerdos iudcauit populum annis XXI et unxit Saul primum regem in israel. fiunt anni CCCCXLI," or $641^{19}/129^{180}$, "A saul usque ad ioachim qui regnauit annis XL fiunt anni CCCCLXIII." That is, when our author counts a period to the end of a king's reign, he says so. In other words, there is nothing to indicate that D takes us to the end of Agrippa's reign. On the contrary, *it is*

---

[96] As Mommsen notes on p. 137 of the 1892 edition, the latter half of this page of the manuscript is blank. It seems that the scribe (author?) hoped to go back and fill in more Hellenistic (and Roman?) history, but did not manage to do so.

much more likely that "ad agrippam," here, just like "ad cyrum" at the outset of our passage (A) refers to the beginning of his reign.

Apart from the above, which shows just how simply and directly the last paragraph of this chronicle fits into the usual scheme of Agrippa's chronology, one might still wonder why the numbers it gives for A and B are wrong. Perhaps there is no point in asking the question, given the fact that the document is so frequently corrupt. And certainly the correction of B, from CCXXX to CCLXX, is nothing to give us pause. But the correction of A from IIIIDCCCCXVI to IIIIDCCCXLI is somewhat more complex, and it would be nice if some better explanation than mere unmotivated scribal error could be adduced to explain it away. The following seems to fit the bill.

The chronicle begins summing up in the penultimate paragraph, which, after recapitulating the twenty generations from Adam to Abraham, goes on as follows:

A'   Abraham fathered Isaac at age 100.
B'   "Ergo" – 1000 years between Noah and Abraham.
C'   From Abraham to Jacob's descent into Egypt – 180 years.
D'   In Egypt – 430 years.
E'   In desert – 40 years.
F'   Joshua rules – 32 years.
G'   Book of Judges – 490 years,
H'   Book of Kings – 34 years.
I'   Judaea lasts – 374 years.
J'   Exile – 70 years.
K'   Judaea and Temple deserted – 710 years.
L'   Cyrus permits Jews to return – in his second year.

At this point the concluding paragraph begins from Cyrus, as we saw above, stating that, "ex quo ergo," there were 4916 years from the Creation until his reign. We have already seen that the chronicle's true figure for this period is 4841 years. The question now is, Can these figures be turned into the erroneous 4916, so as to obviate the need for supposing another source (Erbes) or mere scribal error (as suggested above)?

It is likely that the chronicler, desirous of having an "ex quo ergo" notion of the years which passed between Creation and Cyrus, would use the subtotals previously obtained. So, to begin with, A' would be superfluous, superseded by B'. In order to know the years from Adam to the birth of Isaac, he would need only add the years from Adam to the Flood – 2242 according to our chronicle[97] – to B'. But B' (1000) is corrupt; adding the data given just

---

[97] This date for the flood is given in 638[14]/93[38] and in 641[11]; in 643[11]/139[13] an extra C appears (2342).

before this section, which corresponds exactly with the Septuagint of Genesis 11, gives 1170 years. In contrast, C', D', E' and F' are almost impeccable; the only quibble might be with F', which gives Joshua 32 years while elsewhere he is given 30 ($639^4/115^{91}$ and $641^{16-18}/129^{178-179}$).

G' introduces an interesting problem. While the chronicle had referred to the *period* of the Judges, G' states the *Book* of Judges covers 490 years. I don't know why it does so. Nevertheless, if we review its data on the period of the Judges ($639^{4-19}/114^{91}-120^{110}$), a total of 441 years, and exclude Joshua (30 years) and Samuel (21 years) for they do not appear in the Book of Judges, the result is precisely 390 years. I assume, therefore, that G', CCCCXC, contains one C too many, and should be 390.

H' is another problem; how can one say that the Book of Kings covers only 34 years? But since the next item (I') is the duration of Judah, it seems likely, as Mommsen saw, that H' only means to give the duration of the United Monarchy.[98] According to $639^{21-23}/120^{112}-121^{115}$, that would be 40 years (Saul) + 40 years and 6 months (David) + 41 years (Solomon) = 122 years. It is not difficult to imagine H', XXXIIII, being a corrupted form of CXXIIIT, i.e., "CXXII. item," the same mistake which Mommsen convincingly discovered elsewhere (see n. 91). Alternatively, if one takes H' to refer to all of the *Book* of Kings (including I–II Samuel, as in the Septuagint) before the division of the Monarchy, then one must add in 21 years for Samuel (which we excluded from G'), for a total of 143; XXXIIII will thus have lost a C and traded an X for an I.

I', 374 years for the separate existence of Judah, should have resulted from a simple calculation. If the period of all the kings from Saul to Joachim (Jehoiachin), as twice testified exactly in the chronicle (see n. 95), is 463 years, then subtraction of H' should yield I'. If one assumes the author or scribe worked as he went for subtotals like these, then 463−124 yields 339: CCCXXXVIIII instead of our text's CCCLXXIIII. That is, an X turned into an L and the V fell out. (The same figure results, of course, if one follows the alternate version of H', adding in 21 for Samuel and then subtracting it out again to produce I': 463+21−124−21.)

J', seventy years of exile, is impeccable; just as elsewhere ($641^{19-20}/129^{180-181}$), the chronicle considers the seventy years to have begun after Joachim.[99]

---

[98] Mommsen (above, n. 86 [1892]), p. 87.

[99] Although $640^{2-3}/127^{137}$ seems to begin them after Zedekiah — for whose reign, however, it gives no data.

Mommsen put a question mark next to K', "et deserta fuit iudea et templum eorum annos DCCX,"[100] and I too have no idea what this period is or what its length should be.

If one now puts together a new list of A'−J' (omitting K'), the following is obtained:

	From Adam to Noah	2242
A'	From Abraham to Isaac	— (superfluous)
B'	From Noah to Abraham	1170
C'	From Abraham to Jacob in Egypt	180
D'	In Egypt	430
E'	In desert	40
F'	Joshua rules	32
G'	Book of Judges	390
H'	United Monarchy	122 or 143
I'	Kingdom of Judah	339
J'	Exile until Cyrus' second year	70
	From Creation to Cyrus	5015 or 5036 years

This sum is 99 or 120 years more than the figure our text (A) in fact gives: 4916. I would assume, therefore, that the text which our author was summing looked very much like this one, except that an I was added and a C lost, or else a C and two X's were lost, somewhere along the way, whether in copying or in calculating. Things like that happen all the time, in this text as elsewhere (see notes 94−95). It would be foolhardy to claim confidence that things happened just the way suggested here. All we hope to have shown is just how easy it is for something like this to have happened - and, therefore, just how unnecessary it is to assume that dating Cyrus to a.M. 4916 instead of a.M. 4841, as usual in this document, indicates the use of another source. 4916 is at fact quite at home in this text, just as much as 4841 (see n. 93), whether as a simple corruption of the latter, as we first suggested, or as a corrupted result of calculations based on the data scattered through the text. This bolsters our argument that there is no reason to suppose that the closing section, which includes the reference to Agrippa II, comes from a source other than that which underlies the rest of the document. Nor is there any reason to expect that this last section might supply anything new about the date of Agrippa II's death. Indeed, as we saw, it probably says nothing at all about Agrippa's death, referring instead only to the beginning of his reign.

---

[100] Mommsen (above, n. 86 [1892]), p. 87.

List of First Publications

Introduction: On the Jewish Background of Christianity

First published in this volume.

Temple and Desert: On Religion and State in Second Temple Period Judaea

First published in Hebrew in *Priesthood and Monarchy* (Proceedings of the 1983 Convention of the Israel Historical Society, edd. I. Gafni and G. Motzkin; Jerusalem 1987), pp. 61–78. English version appears here by permission of the Historical Society of Israel, Jerusalem.

On Pharisaic Opposition to the Hasmonean Monarchy

First published in Hebrew in *Nation and History,* I (ed. M. Stern; Jersualem 1983), pp. 39–50. English version appears here by permission of the Historical Society of Israel, Jerusalem.

"Kingdom of Priests" — a Pharisaic Slogan?

First published in Hebrew in *Zion* 45 (1979/80), pp. 96–117. English version appears here by permission of the Historical Society of Israel, Jerusalem.

"The Contemners of Judges and Men"

First published in Hebrew in *Leshonenu* 47 (1982/83), pp. 18–24. English version appears here by permission of the Academy of the Hebrew Language, Jerusalem.

"Scribes and Pharisees, Hypocrites:" Who are the "Scribes" in the New Testament?

First published in Hebrew *Zion* 50 (1984/85 = *Zion Jubilee Volume* L [1935–1985]), pp. 121–132. English version appears here by permission of the Historical Society of Israel, Jerusalem.

On Sacrifice by Gentiles in the Temple of Jerusalem

First published in this volume.

Residents and Exiles, Jerusalemites and Judaeans (Acts 7:4; 2:5,14):
On Stephen, Pentecost and the Structure of Acts

First published in this volume.

On Christian Study of the Zealots

First published in this volume; a Hebrew version is forthcoming in *The Masada Myth* (ed. D. Bitan; to be published by Keter).

On Barnabas and Bar-Kokhba

First published in Hebrew in *Zion* 46 (1980/81), pp. 339–345. English version appears here by permission of the Historical Society of Israel, Jerusalem.

Joseph ben Illem and the Date of Herod's Death

Parallel publication in Hebrew in *Eretz-Israel in the Tannaitic Period: Shmuel Safrai Jubilee Volume* (edd. I. Gafni and M. Stern; forthcoming). English version appears here by permission of Yad Izhak ben-Zvi, Jerusalem.

"Caesarea" and its "Isactium": Epigraphy, Numismatics and Herodian Chronology

First published in Hebrew in *Cathedra* 51 (April 1989), pp. 21–34. English version appears here by permission of Yad Izhak ben-Zvi, Jerusalem.

Pontius Pilate's Appointment to Office and the Chronology of Josephus' *Antiquities,* Books 18–20

First published in Hebrew in *Zion* 48 (1982/83), pp. 325–345. English version appears here by permission of the Historical Society of Israel, Jerusalem.

Pontius Pilate's Suspension from Office: Chronology and Sources

First published in Hebrew in *Tarbiz* 51 (1981/82), pp. 383–398. English version appears here by permission of Magnes Press, Jerusalem.

Ishmael ben Phiabi and the Chronology of Provincia Judaea

First published in Hebrew in *Tarbiz* 52 (1982/83), pp. 177–200. English version appears here by permission of Magnes Press, Jerusalem.

Texts, Coins, Fashions and Dates: Josephus' *Vita* and Agrippa II's Death

First published in this volume.

Ancient Sources*

---

* Includes, in the main, passages cited in text or *discussed* in the notes.

Test. Levi

8:1ff.	61
8:17	93
13:1−2	97

Test. Moses

6:1	47

Wisd. Sol.

2:24	19
5:15	19

Qumran

1QH

4:30−38	22
11:17	23
12:16−17	37

1QM

1:3	37
2	37
7:13, 15	93

1QS

3−4	20
3:13	20, 98
5	20
5:9	22
8:1−10	37
8:13−16	37
9	20
9:3−7	37
9:9−11	22
9:19−20	37
9:21−23	36
11:21	20

1QSa

1:23−25	94

1Q21	61

4QFlorilegium

1:5	37

4QpNahum	47, 101

4QpPsalm[a]

1−10, iii:9−12	87

4QTestimonia	22

11QMelchizedek	47

11QTemple

58:3−4	86
64:6−13	81−88

Damascus Document

5:8−10	21

Philo

De migr. Abr.

9−11	17
32−35	17
89−93	17, 21, 25

De Virtutibus

54	46

Leg. ad Caium

107	214
179	216
202	42
206	214, 216
231−232	214−215
261−329	215
296−297	110−111
296	215
299−305	215
300	215
305	171
356	215

Josephus

Vita

1−6	61
1	247
3−5	241
5	202, 241
11−12	241

12	13, 265	2.270	230
13	241	2.284	225, 245
30ff.	271−272	2.409−417	111−115
31	271	2.564	140
40−41	270−272	2.567	37
43	271	2.651	140
174−177	270	3.11	37
177	271	3.352	61
186	271	3.443	169
336−367	252, 269, 270	4.262	108, 109
342−343	270−271	4.275	109
359−360	243, 246, 250, 253, 270	4.640	163
361−364	248	5.73	37
410	270	5.459	35
414−429	247, 262	6.285	34
424−425	32	6.300−305	219
430	247, 262	6.351	35
		7	32, 266
C.Ap		7.23	169
		7.437ff.	30−32
1.36	212		
2.48	109		
		Ant.	
BJ		1.80−81	174
		3.75ff.	61
1.58	34	3.318−319	108
1.70	39, 52	3.320	220, 221, 237, 238
1.343, 351	178	4.15, 23	61
1.370−371	179−180	4.214	94
1.386	180	8.116−117	103, 108
1.613	172	8.227−228	61
1.648−2.9	162	11.87	108
2	32	11.336	109
2.10ff.	157	13.171−173	12, 39
2.118	33	13.242−243	109
2.119	36	13.288	265
2.140	36	13.292−295	48
2.152−153	31, 36	13.298	265
2.155−156	13	13.301	39, 52−53
2.169−177	202	13.318	12
2.169−174	215	14.41	46
2.200	158	14.465	178
2.221−223	224−225	14.487−490	176−178
2.223−246	235	15.9	177
2.223	233, 234	15.121	180
2.224	235	15.354	181
2.232	226	15.403−409	205−217
2.243	223	16.14	109
2.244	226	16.136	171
2.245−247	231−234	16.137−138	174
2.259−263	31	16.163	47
2.264	33	16.187	61
2.266	42		

Rabbinic Literature

Modern Authors

Migliario, E. 244, 253, 254
Mildenberg, L. 147, 151
Milik, J.T. 20, 61
Miller, S.S. 55, 162, 164
Milligan, G. 119
Mionnet, T.E. 172
Moehring, H.R. 262–264
Momigliano, A. 40, 253, 265
Mommsen, T. 185, 258, 260, 275–282
Moran, W.L. 57
Moretti, L. 169, 173, 175
Morin, J.–A. 140
Morris, J. 214
Motzo, [R.] B. 253, 270
Moule, C.F.D. 133
Moulton, H. 119
Müller, C. 248, 276
Münzer, F. 253
Munck, J. 133
Munk, S. 219
Murphy-O'Connor, J. 2, 24

Naber, S.A. 181
Neusner, J. 49, 64, 70, 74, 90, 121, 191
Niebuhr, B.G. 257
Niese, B. 171, 181, 250, 251, 258, 276
Nikiprowetzky, V. 17, 41
Nodet, E. 38, 191
Nöldeke, T. 174
Noldius, C. 246
Norden, E. 186

Oded, B. 118
O'Dell, J. 45
Oesterreicher, B. 184
Ogg, G. 183
Olmstead, A.T. 91
Oost, S. I. 228–230, 232
Oppenheimer, A. 147
Oppolzer, T. Ritter von 158, 164, 165
Orlinsky, H.M. 127
Orrieux, C. 39–41, 45, 49
Orth, W. 195
Otto, W. 158, 161, 179, 180, 186, 205–206,
213, 217, 222, 264

Pagi, A. 255
Pani, M. 190
Parker, R.A. 157, 164, 165, 175, 203, 205
Patin, C. 246
Pellerin, J. 172, 255
Pelletier, A. 102, 226, 263

Pesch, R. 95, 121, 127
Petersen, L. 244
Petuchowski, J.J. 75, 76
Pfeiffer, R.H. 93
Pharr, C. 187
Pines, S. 187
Plassart, A. 227
Plümacher, E. 118
Pococke, R. 168
Pohle, L. 131
Posnanski, A. 245
Preisigke, F. 92
Prigent, P. 148, 151, 152
Prinz, J. 73

Qedar, S. 190
Qimron, E. 21, 86, 87, 116

Rabello, A.M. 103, 108, 147
Rabin, C. 47, 125
Rad, G. von 97
Rajak, T. 31–32, 35, 121, 125, 244, 263,
270
Rappaport, U. 40, 175, 178, 261, 273
Reese, T.J. 131
Reicke, B. 120
Reimarus, H.S. 138
Reinach, T. 118, 256
Reinhold, M. 122
Reuther, R. 133
Reynolds, J. 195
Reznick, L. 151
Rhoads, D.M. 140–142, 219
Ricciotti, G. 226
Richard, E. 118, 120, 122
Richards, G.C. 252, 262
Richardson, P. 147, 152
Richter, O. F. von 168
Riddle, D.W. 99
Rieks, R. 175
Riess, F. 159, 161
Ringel, J. 168, 169, 171
Ritschl, A. 65
Ritter, B. 97
Rivkin, E. 88
Robert, L. 168
Röslin, H. 161
Rofé, A. 46
Rokeah, D. 4, 65, 147, 153
Roloff, J. 127
Rosenberg, A. 251, 259, 276
Rosenzweig, F. 79

Names and Subjects

Wissenschaftliche Untersuchungen zum Neuen Testament

Alphabetical Index
of the First and the Second Series

Kleinknecht, Karl Th.: Der leidende Gerechtfertigte. 1984, [2]1988. *Volume II/13.*
Klinghardt, Matthias: Gesetz und Volk Gottes. 1988. *Volume II/32.*
Köhler, Wolf-Dietrich: Rezeption des Matthäusevangeliums in der Zeit vor Irenäus. 1987. *Volume II/24.*
Kuhn, Karl G.: Achtzehngebet und Vaterunser und der Reim. 1950. *Volume 1.*
Lampe, Peter: Die stadtrömischen Christen in den ersten beiden Jahrhunderten. 1987, [2]1989. *Volume II/18.*
Maier, Gerhard: Mensch und freier Wille. 1971. *Volume 12.*
– Die Johannesoffenbarung und die Kirche. 1981. *Volume 25.*
Marshall, Peter: Enmity in Corinth: Social Conventions in Paul's Relations with the Corinthians. 1987. *Volume II/23.*
Meade, David G.: Pseudonymity and Canon. 1986. *Volume 39.*
Mengel, Berthold: Studien zum Philipperbrief. 1982. *Volume II/8.*
Merkel, Helmut: Die Widersprüche zwischen den Evangelien. 1971. *Volume 13.*
Merklein, Helmut: Studien zu Jesus und Paulus. 1987. *Volume 43.*
Metzler, Karin: Der griechische Begriff des Verzeihens. 1991. *Volume II/44.*
Niebuhr, Karl-Wilhelm: Gesetz und Paränese. 1987. *Volume II/28.*
– Heidenapostel aus Israel. 1992. *Volume 62.*
Nissen, Andreas: Gott und der Nächste im antiken Judentum. 1974. *Volume 15.*
Okure, Teresa: The Johannine Approach to Mission. 1988. *Volume II/31.*
Pilhofer, Peter: Presbyteron Kreitton. 1990. *Volume II/39.*
Probst, Hermann: Paulus und der Brief. 1991. *Volume II/45.*
Räisänen, Heikki: Paul and the Law. 1983, [2]1987. *Volume 29.*
Rehkopf, Friedrich: Die lukanische Sonderquelle. 1959. *Volume 5.*
Reinmuth, Eckhardt: see *Holtz.*
Reiser, Marius: Syntax und Stil des Markusevangeliums. 1984. *Volume II/11.*
Richards, E. Randolph: The Secretary in the Letters of Paul. 1991. *Volume II/42.*
Riesner, Rainer: Jesus als Lehrer. 1981, [3]1988. *Volume II/7.*
Rissi, Mathias: Die Theologie des Hebräerbriefs. 1987. *Volume 41.*
Röhser, Günter: Metaphorik und Personifikation der Sünde. 1987. *Volume II/25.*
Rüger, Hans Peter: Die Weisheitsschrift aus der Kairoer Geniza. 1991. *Volume 53.*
Sänger, Dieter: Antikes Judentum und die Mysterien. 1980. *Volume II/5.*
Sandnes, Karl Olav: Paul – One of the Prophets? 1991. *Volume II/43.*
Sato, Migaku: Q und Prophetie. 1988. *Volume II/29.*
Schimanowski, Gottfried: Weisheit und Messias. 1985. *Volume II/17.*
Schlichting, Günter: Ein jüdisches Leben Jesu. 1982. *Volume 24.*
Schnabel, Eckhard J.: Law and Wisdom from Ben Sira to Paul. 1985. *Volume II/16.*
Schutter, William L.: Hermeneutic and Composition in I Peter. 1989. *Volume II/30.*
Schwartz, Daniel R.: Studies in the Jewish Background of Christianity. 1992. *Volume 60.*
Schwemer, A. M.: see *Hengel.*
Scott, James M.: Adoption as Sons of God. 1992. *Volume II/48.*
Siegert, Folker: Drei hellenistisch-jüdische Predigten. Part 1. 1980. *Volume 20.* – Part 2. 1992. *Volume 61.*
– Nag-Hammadi-Register. 1982. *Volume 26.*
– Argumentation bei Paulus. 1985. *Volume 34.*
– Philon von Alexandrien. 1988. *Volume 46.*
Simon, Marcel: Le christianisme antique et son contexte religieux I/II. 1981. *Volume 23.*
Snodgrass, Klyne: The Parable of the Wicked Tenants. 1983. *Volume 27.*
Speyer, Wolfgang: Frühes Christentum im antiken Strahlungsfeld. 1989. *Volume 50.*
Stadelmann, Helge: Ben Sira als Schriftgelehrter. 1980. *Volume II/6.*
Strobel, August: Die Studie der Wahrheit. 1980. *Volume 21.*
Stuhlmacher, Peter (Ed.): Das Evangelium und die Evangelien. 1983. *Volume 28.*
Tajra, Harry W.: The Trial of St. Paul. 1989. *Volume II/35.*
Theißen, Gerd: Studien zur Soziologie des Urchristentums. 1979, [3]1989. *Volume 19.*
Thornton, Claus-Jürgen: Der Zeuge des Zeugen. 1991. *Volume 56.*
Wedderburn, A. J. M.: Baptism and Resurrection. 1987. *Volume 44.*
Wegner, Uwe: Der Hauptmann von Kafarnaum. 1985. *Volume II/14.*
Wilson, Walter T.: Love without Pretense. 1991. *Volume II/46.*
Wolff, Christian: see *Holtz.*
Zimmermann, Alfred E.: Die urchristlichen Lehrer. 1984, [2]1988. *Volume II/12.*